COHORT ANALYSIS IN SOCIAL RESEARCH

SOCIAL SCIENCE RESEARCH COUNCIL

COMMITTEE ON THE METHODOLOGY
OF LONGITUDINAL RESEARCH

Members, 1979 –1980

Burton H. Singer, Chairman
Columbia University

Gregory Markus
University of Michigan

Gary Chamberlain
University of Wisconsin

Carl Morris
University of Texas

James S. Coleman
University of Chicago

John R. Nesselroade
Pennsylvania State University

James J. Heckman
University of Chicago

Seymour Spilerman
Columbia University

Douglas A. Hibbs, Jr.
Harvard University

Nancy Brandon Tuma
Stanford University

Paul Holland
Educational Testing Service

Halliman H. Winsborough
University of Wisconsin

Staff: Peter B. Read

COHORT ANALYSIS IN SOCIAL RESEARCH

Beyond the Identification Problem

Edited by
William M. Mason · Stephen E. Fienberg

With 44 Figures

Springer-Verlag
New York Berlin Heidelberg Tokyo

William M. Mason
The Population Studies Center
University of Michigan
Ann Arbor, Michigan 48104
USA

Stephen E. Fienberg
Department of Statistics
Carnegie-Mellon University
Pittsburgh, Pennsylvania 15213
USA

Library of Congress Cataloging in Publication Data
Main entry under title:
Cohort analysis in social research.
  Bibliography: p.
  1. Cohort analysis—Addresses, essays, lectures.
I. Mason, William, M.   II. Fienberg, Stephen E.
HB849.47.C63   1985   300'.72   84-10581

© 1985 by Springer-Verlag New York Inc.
All rights reserved. No part of this book may be translated or reproduced in any form
without written permission from Springer-Verlag, 175 Fifth Avenue, New York, New
York 10010, U.S.A.
The use of general descriptive names, trade names, trademarks, etc., in this publication,
even if the former are not especially identified, is not to be taken as a sign that such
names, as understood by the Trade Marks and Merchandise Marks Act, may accordingly
be used freely by anyone.

Printed and bound by R.R. Donnelley and Sons, Harrisonburg, Virginia.
Printed in the United States of America.

9 8 7 6 5 4 3 2 1

ISBN 0-387-96053-8 Springer-Verlag New York Berlin Heidelberg Tokyo
ISBN 3-540-96053-8 Springer-Verlag Berlin Heidelberg New York Tokyo

PREFACE

The existence of the present volume can be traced to methodological concerns about cohort analysis, all of which were evident throughout most of the social sciences by the late 1970s. For some social scientists, they became part of a broader discussion concerning the need for new analytical techniques for research based on longitudinal data. In 1976, the Social Science Research Council (SSRC), with funds from the National Institute of Education, established a Committee on the Methodology of Longitudinal Research. (The scholars who comprised this committee are listed at the front of this volume.) As part of the efforts of this Committee, an interdisciplinary conference on cohort analysis was held in the summer of 1979, in Snowmass, Colorado. Much of the work presented here stems from that conference, the purpose of which was to promote the development of general methodological tools for the study of social change.

The conference included five major presentations by (1) William Mason and Herbert Smith, (2) Karl Jöreskog and Dag Sörbom, (3) Gregory Markus, (4) John Hobcraft, Jane Menken and Samuel Preston, and (5) Stephen Fienberg and William Mason. The formal presentations were each followed by extensive discussion, which involved as participants: Paul Baltes, William Butz, Philip Converse, Otis Dudley Duncan, David Freedman, William Meredith, John Nesselroade, Daniel Price, Thomas Pullum, Peter Read, Matilda White Riley, Norman Ryder, Warren Sanderson, Warner Schaie, Burton Singer, Nancy Tuma, Harrison White, and Halliman Winsborough.

All of the formal papers subsequently underwent major revisions to reflect the conference discussions, and two of the discussants' comments, those of Duncan and Freedman, were developed into formal papers. This volume presents these seven papers, as well as Ryder's classic exposition and two additional papers, one by Robert Johnson and one by James Heckman and Richard Robb that address issues not already covered in the conference presentations. This set of papers thus represents a substantial updating of material presented in the original conference. In particular, the identification problem in its simplest form is a point of departure for most of the chapters. Indeed, most of these contributions offer researchers assistance with a variety of problems in cohort analysis that do not relate directly to the identification problem.

The appearance of these papers as a published volume is the result of a major collaborative effort involving substantial contributions from Burton Singer, Peter Read and Herbert Smith, as well as those of the editors. We are pleased to acknowledge here the persistence, commitment and hard work of these three colleagues. The volume itself was produced using computing and typesetting facilities at Carnegie-Mellon University. Diana Bajzek was an invaluable aid in preparing the copy for typesetting, and for the generous lending of her expertise and guidance to this project we are most grateful. Barbara Krest prepared the computerized text for the entire manuscript, while Margie Krest prepared the mathematics and the tables, supervised the proofreading, and was responsible for the final aspects of photo-typesetting. Without all of their outstanding efforts and assistance we would have been unable to complete the volume.

William M. Mason
Stephen E. Fienberg

CONTENTS

1. INTRODUCTION: BEYOND THE IDENTIFICATION PROBLEM

William M. Mason

Stephen E. Fienberg[†]

The term "cohort" was in common use during Roman antiquity, when it referred to a division within a legion. Since then, cohort has come to refer to considerably more, and in fact the original meaning of the word has been lost in everyday colloquy. The use of cohorts to refer to groups or aggregates defined by point of entry into a social system has long been present in the social sciences, but cohort *analysis* as a focus in its own right has fluctuated in its visibility, due, perhaps, to swings of interest in the study of social change.

In recent history, it may not be accidental that Norman Ryder's (1965) seminal contribution to the subject of cohort analysis, "The Cohort as a Concept in the Study of Social Change," was written at a time when the ferment of social change was again perceptible in the United States. More than any other previous publication, this article suggested the potential for insight that is available from a cohort perspective—not merely in demography, Ryder's own discipline—but in the social and behavioral sciences more generally. Ryder's article, therefore, is an appropriate starting point in any consideration of the recent history of cohort analysis. Although Ryder succeeded in specifying the conceptual relevance of cohorts to an extraordinary range of substantive issues, he did not address the technical and methodological questions that inevitably surround empirical research. Many important questions about the conduct of cohort analysis remained unanswered in his discussion. For social scientists working with data that would sustain a cohort-oriented approach, methodological guidance was needed as well

[†] William M. Mason is affiliated with the Department of Sociology and the Population Studies Center, The University of Michigan, and Stephen E. Fienberg is affiliated with the Departments of Statistics and Social Sciences, Carnegie-Mellon University.

as conceptual clarification.

The fundamental question in cohort analysis is that of determining whether the phenomenon under examination is cohort-based, or whether some other conceptualization—age-based, for example—is more appropriate. This question received early attention in epidemiology, in the study of tuberculosis. Andvord (1930) suggested the value of a cohort perspective in the analysis of tuberculosis mortality, and Frost (1939) went further, attempting to show through graphical display that apparent changes in the age-distribution of tuberculosis mortality could be more easily interpreted as a decline in tuberculosis mortality over cohorts than as changes in the age-specific mortality regime over time.

Even a superficial examination of the "either-or" question leads to the conclusion that "both" might also be acceptable. That is, there is, *in general*, no logical reason for ruling out the possibility that both cohort and age may be relevant to the study of some phenomenon. Furthermore, it is but a short step to conclude that not only might aging- and origin-related processes (i.e., age and cohort) be relevant to the matter at hand, but also that instantaneous processes (i.e., period) might also be pertinent. Indeed, the instantaneous processes might dominate. For example, recent work by Kahn and Mason (1982) suggests that political alienation, as measured in sample surveys, varies primarily as a function of time, and much less so as a function of either age or cohort. Once this point is accepted, however, the problem of distinguishing the effects of age from those of period and cohort can become difficult.

In much of cohort analysis, data have typically been available, or have been constructed, in the form of a measure of central tendency conditional on age, separately for different years, or more generally for different times of observation and measurement. Analysts have rarely gone beyond this form of data array, to conceptualize and measure the phenomena and events that might be held to underlie the effects of ages, periods or cohorts. Rather, they have asked, much as is typically done in an analysis of variance setup, whether there are row differences, column differences, or diagonal differences, in the measure of central tendency for the dependent variable. Although it is possible to determine the presence of row, column and diagonal "effects," their interpretation can not be treated as a naive generalization of row and column effects in the typical analysis of variance model. The reason is that there is an identification problem, due to the linear dependency of age, period and cohort. In particular, there is an exact equality

$$C = P - A$$

where C denotes time of system entry, P denotes system time, and A denotes duration in the system. Because of this equality, it is not possible to separate the effects of cohorts, ages and periods in a generalized linear model of the form

$$Y = f(C, P, A)$$

without some kind of restriction on the function f. Once an appropriate restriction has been chosen, it becomes possible to estimate and interpret the coefficients of age, period and cohort in the generalized linear model.

The linear dependency, $C = P - A$, has come to be characterized as creating an identification problem for f. The identification problem, and technically correct ways to deal with it (e.g., imposing linear restrictions on the coefficients of f), have been independently discovered a number of times (e.g., Greenberg *et al.*, 1950; Sacher, 1960; Hall, 1971) in different substantive areas. Mason *et al.* (1973), who also rediscovered the identification problem, noted its existence in a variety of contexts and suggested that, with the aid of prior reasoning in support of one or more linear restrictions, it is possible to carry out analyses that distinguish between, and assess the effects of, age, period and cohort on a response variable.

The work of Mason *et al.* (1973) and also Fienberg and Mason (1978) seemed to suggest, perhaps for the first time, a general methodology for cohort analysis when all three of age, period and cohort were potentially of interest. Although nothing fundamentally new was offered, the abstraction of the identification problem and its solution from highly focussed specific analyses drew attention to the *methodology* of cohort analysis. One consequence of this was that where previously articles had been written presenting data from one perspective (e.g., cohort), only to be followed by others arguing for a different perspective (e.g., age), research was now being conducted using a three-way perspective in which the goal was to determine *through data exploration* whether the process under study was some combination of age, period and cohort phenomena.

A number of dissatisfactions grew out of this, among them the following. First, the view was advanced that because of the equality $C =$

$P - A$, it is fundamentally meaningless to attempt to estimate separate effects for C, P and A, even if it is technically possible to do so with the aid of constraints in the estimation procedure (Goldstein, 1979). The basis of this view was that since any of age, period or cohort can be viewed as a form of interaction between the other two markers, it is impossible for all three to vary independently. Hence, age-period-cohort (APC) analysis is logically impossible.

A second reaction to the growth of interest in APC analysis was that the specification is too simple. In particular, the ANOVA-type model which includes only additive components for ages, periods and cohorts is regarded by some (Glenn, 1976) as omitting potentially meaningful interactions (e.g., between cohort and age). This view is exactly the opposite of the first one.

A third view was that APC specifications are doomed to failure because the introduction of constraints on f necessarily results in biased estimates of the effects of age, period and cohort.

A fourth reaction was that even if constraints on f are technically possible, they are practically inadmissible in the sense that the chances of making a theoretically correct restriction, *and knowing that you have done so*, are vanishingly small.

Finally, and perhaps most importantly, as the body of technical and substantive literature using APC analysis accumulated, it came to be perceived that the promise of cohort analysis held out by Ryder's (1965) article was not being fulfilled. No major theoretical insights or empirical findings seemed to be surfacing, despite the continued interest in APC analysis.

The existence of the present volume can be traced to these methodological concerns about cohort analysis, all of which were evident throughout most of the social sciences by the late 1970s. For some social scientists, they became part of a broader discussion concerning the need for new analytical techniques for research based on longitudinal data. In 1976, the Social Science Research Council established a Committee on the Methodology of Longitudinal Research. As part of the efforts of this Committee, an interdisciplinary conference on cohort analysis was held in the summer of 1979, in Snowmass, Colorado. Much of the work presented here stems from that conference, the purpose of which was to promote the development of general methodological tools for the study of social change.

The conference consisted of five formal presentations, each followed by extensive discussion.` All of the formal papers subsequently underwent major revisions to reflect the conference discussions, and two of the discussants' comments were developed into formal papers. This volume presents these seven papers, two additional ones addressing issues not already covered in the conference presentations, as well as Ryder's classic paper. The APC identification problem in its simplest form is a point of departure for most of the chapters. Indeed, most of these contributions offer researchers assistance with a variety of problems in cohort analysis that do not relate directly to the identification problem. At the same time, each paper bears on the dissatisfactions with APC analysis that were noted earlier in this introduction.

Ryder's paper is included here to remind readers of the lodestone for cohort conceptualization and to refresh our appreciation of the potential contribution of cohort analysis in social research. The paper ranges over diverse substantive areas, in each one suggesting hypotheses about the impact of cohort membership and the mechanisms by which cohort differentials are produced. The paper stands as an exceptionally valuable statement on the promise of a cohort perspective. One of its most distinctive features is its Durkheimian stance on the usefulness of conceptualizing processes involving cohorts as macro phenomena which can not be understood by mere psychological reduction. In addition, the paper has great stimulus value because of its choice of examples, which typically involve social processes or events of substantial magnitudes.

Fienberg and Mason discuss the purpose of APC analysis, and how this is related to statistical inference; the need for a multilevel specification; how the form in which the data are available affects aggregation bias; interactions in the APC model; and common fallacies in criticisms of APC specifications.

Hobcraft, Menken and Preston provide a sweeping review of cohort analysis in demography. They discuss different mechanisms by which cohort and age differences emerge, and organize specific applications with respect to the nature of the endogenous variable used—e.g., fertility and mortality. In their exposition, these authors touch on virtually all of the criticisms levelled against APC analysis.

Heckman and Robb discuss cohort analysis from an economic perspective. Among the most important subjects dealt with are the problem of multiple clocks, i.e., more than one linear identity among the conditioning variables; the question of higher-order interactions in APC models, and a latent variable approach. The paper in general stresses the need to move beyond the accounting framework through the use of proxy variables.

Mason and Smith, in their analysis of tuberculosis mortality, illustrate the kind of substantive reasoning that APC analysis requires. This work also demonstrates the use of interactions in APC analysis, and a way of making the transition from the accounting framework to variables that come closer to measuring the phenomena of interest.

Johnson starts with a reason for resolving the identification problem in a particular way, and adds placement in time and space to the Coale-Trussell model for age-specific fertility structures. The effort is particularly valuable on this last count, since much formal work in demography is stated without reference to cohort differences.

Markus presents a modelling effort that entirely bypasses the use of the accounting framework. In its place he uses a lag specification on the endogenous variable which proves useful in understanding voting behavior.

In the spirit of Ryder's original paper on cohort analysis, Duncan examines the effects of age and cohort as well as sex, color, education and income on a response interpretable as a measure of conformity. One of his emphases is on possible age-period and cohort-period interactions. Because of the limited amount of data available and the irregular spacing of the surveys he uses, Duncan looks at parallel analyses treating age and cohort as the independent variables instead of adopting the full-blown APC methodology. In the process he explores the idea of education-induced cohort effects and their interaction with age.

The Jöreskog and Sörbom contribution extends the "Jöreskog approach" to modelling with latent variables to include true longitudinal data for cohorts. For the case of multiple indicators of a latent continuous response variable, Jöreskog and Sörbom provide a solution to the treatment of longitudinal data in cohort analysis, and illustrate the approach using data on personality development.

The paper by Freedman deals only indirectly with cohort analysis. Instead, it provides a critique of the careless use of regression-like models in the social sciences, and points to the need to take seriously the basic assumptions that underlie statistical models. Freedman then adapts his critique to a discussion of the Jöreskog and Sörbom paper, and these authors respond in turn.

Fienberg, in a Comment on Freedman, provides a rebuttal to the suggestion that social scientists should look to the natural sciences for examples of how to do good research, noting that Freedman's natural science examples possess the same kinds of flaws that Freedman identifies in the quantitative work of social scientists. In a final response, Freedman attempts to recapitulate the points of agreement and disagreement between his views and Fienberg's.

It is fair to ask what rewards await the reader of this diverse collection of papers. The answer is straightforward: resolutions of many of the issues in the debate about cohort analysis that were present in the late 1970s, and valuable insights into a number of other problems that arise in the conduct of cohort analysis. Some of the papers explicitly address technical difficulties, and we believe that they put to rest the most overt of these difficulties. In other instances, new technical problems, far removed from the artificial issues that previously occupied the debating arena, have emerged. Apart from the articulation of technical issues, the volume also provides empirical studies that bear scrutiny as examples of substantive research based on a cohort perspective.

REFERENCES

Andvord, K.F. (1921). Is tuberculosis to be regarded from the aetiological standpoint as an acute disease of childhood? *Tubercle* **3**, 97–116.

Fienberg, S.E. and Mason, W.M. (1978). Identification and estimation of age-period-cohort models in the analysis of discrete archival data, in K. F. Schuessler (ed.), *Sociological Methodology 1979*. San Francisco: Jossey-Bass, pp. 1–65.

Frost, W.H. (1939). The age selection of mortality from tuberculosis in successive decades. *American Journal of Hygiene* **30**, 91–96.

Glenn, N.D. (1976). Cohort analysts' futile quest: Statistical attempts to separate age, period and cohort effects. *American Sociological Review* **41**, 900–904.

Goldstein, H. (1979). Age, period and cohort effects—a confounded confusion, in G. Kanji (ed.), *Bulletin in Applied Statistics*. Sheffield City Polytechnic, Sheffield: United Kingdom, pp. 19–24.

Greenberg, B.G., Wright, J.J. and Sheps, C.G. (1950). A technique for analyzing some factors affecting the incidence of syphilis. *Journal of the American Statistical Association* **25**, 373–399.

Hall, R.E. (1971). The measurement of quality change from vintage price data, in Z. Griliches (ed.), *Price Indexes and Quality Changes.* Cambridge, Mass.: Harvard University Press, pp. 240–271.

Kahn, J. and Mason, W.M. (1982). A test of Easterlin's Explanation of Political Alienation. Population Studies Center of The University of Michigan. Ann Arbor, Michigan.

Mason K.O., Mason, W.M., Winsborough, H.H. and Poole, W.K. (1973). Some methodological issues in cohort analysis of archival data. *American Sociological Review* **38**, 242–258.

Ryder, N.B. (1965). The cohort as a concept in the study of social change. *American Sociological Review* **30**, 843–861.

Sacher, G.A. (1960). Analysis of life tables with secular terms, in B.L. Strehler, J.D. Ebert, H.B. Glass and N.W. Shock (eds.), *The Biology of Aging.* Washington, D.C.: The American Institute of Biological Sciences, pp. 253–257.

2. THE COHORT AS A CONCEPT IN THE STUDY OF SOCIAL CHANGE*

Norman B. Ryder[†]

Society persists despite the mortality of its individual members, through processes of demographic metabolism and particularly the annual infusion of birth cohorts. These may pose a threat to stability but they also provide the opportunity for societal transformation. Each birth cohort acquires coherence and continuity from the distinctive development of its constituents and from its own persistent macroanalytic features. Successive cohorts are differentiated by the changing content of formal education, by peer-group socialization, and by idiosyncratic historical experience. Young adults are prominent in war, revolution, immigration, urbanization and technological change. Since cohorts are used to achieve structural transformation and since they manifest its consequences in characteristic ways, it is proposed that research be designed to capitalize on the congruence of social change and cohort identification.

1. SOCIAL CHANGE AND DEMOGRAPHIC METABOLISM

This essay presents a demographic approach to the study of social change. The particular meaning here given to change is structural transformation rather than the network of actions and interactions predicated in the routine operation of the institutional structure. Discussion is restricted to the variations in social organization that are reflected in measurements on individuals, summarized in aggregate distributions of performances and

* Revision of a paper read at the annual meeting of the American Sociological Association, August, 1959. Reprinted from *American Sociological Review*, **30**, (1965), 843–861.

† Office of Population Research, Princeton University.

characteristics. Changes in an individual throughout his life are distinguishable from changes in the population of which he is a component. The biological ineluctability of the individual life cycle carries no necessary implication for transformation of the population. Every society has pretensions to an immortality beyond the reach of its members. The lives and deaths of individuals are, from the societal standpoint, a massive process of personnel replacement, which may be called "demographic metabolism." This essay is concerned with interdependencies between social change and population process, including in the latter both demographic metabolism and the life cycles of individuals considered in the aggregate.

Society is a functioning collectivity of organic components. It persists as if independent of its membership, continually receiving raw material by fertility and discharging depleted resources by mortality. To survive, it must meet the challenge to persistence implicit in this continual change of membership, and especially the incessant "invasion of barbarians." Every individual arrives on the social scene literally without sociopsychological configuration. As a requisite for effective performance, the society seeks and promotes a minimal degree of stability and predictability, and frequently succeeds. The agencies of socialization and social control are designed to give the new member a shape appropriate to the societal design.

Perhaps stability is a more likely institutional goal than innovation because it is simpler and safer, at least in the short run, but any fixed set of solutions to problems posed by a threatening environment becomes a liability whenever such problems change. The capacity for societal transformation has an indispensable ally in the process of demographic metabolism. Mortality and fertility make flexibility possible just as they make stability problematic. The continual emergence of new participants in the social process and the continual withdrawal of their predecessors compensate the society for limited individual flexibility. For every species the inevitability of death impels the development of reproduction and thus variation and evolution; the same holds for societies. The society whose members were immortal would resemble a stagnant pond.[1] Of

---

[1] Lemuel Gulliver reported that the Luggnaggians solved the problem with their Struldbruggs by desocializing them at 80. Comte hypothesized that progress is maximized by a length of life neither too ephemeral nor too protracted (Martineau, n.d., pp. 152–153).

course death is no more an unmixed blessing to the society than it is an unmixed curse to the individual. Metabolism may make change likely, or at least possible, but it does not guarantee that the change will be beneficial. As a minimum, mortality permits perennial reappraisal of institutionalized formulae.

The aggregate by which the society counterbalances attrition is the birth cohort, those persons born in the same time interval and aging together. Each new cohort makes fresh contact with the contemporary social heritage and carries the impress of the encounter through life. This confrontation has been called the intersection of the innovative and the conservative forces in history (MacIver, 1963, pp. 110–111). The members of any cohort are entitled to participate in only one slice of life—their unique location in the stream of history. Because it embodies a temporally specific version of the heritage, each cohort is differentiated from all others, despite the minimization of variability by symbolically perpetuated institutions and by hierarchically graduated structures of authority.

To assert that the cause of social change is demographic replacement would be tantamount to explaining a variable by a constant, yet each fresh cohort is a possible intermediary in the transformation process, a vehicle for introducing new postures. The new cohorts provide the opportunity for social change to occur. They do not cause change; they permit it. If change does occur, it differentiates cohorts from one another, and the comparison of their careers becomes a way to study change. The minimal basis for expecting interdependency between intercohort differentiation and social change is that change has variant import for persons of unlike age, and that the consequences of change persist in the subsequent behavior of these individuals and thus of their cohorts.

For the most part, the literature on the cohort approach is divisible into two almost antipodal categories. On the one hand, the cohort concept, under the label "generation," has long been used by historians of the arts—in rebellion against the Procrustean frame of chronological sections favored by conventional historians—as well as by political journalists and other humanistic interpreters of the passing scene (see e.g., Petersen, 1930; Peyre, 1948; Renouard, 1953; and in sociology, Mannheim, 1952, pp. 276–322). The other field of application has been the work of demographers, particularly the recent redirection of the study of fertility time series away from the period-by-period format toward an appraisal of temporal variations from cohort to cohort (Ryder, 1956). Although written by a demographer, the present essay is concerned not with the many contributions to technical demography which utilize the cohort concept, but rather with the sociological arguments underlying it, and the conceptualization of social change it suggests.

2. THE COHORT FROM A MACROANALYTIC STANDPOINT

A cohort may be defined as the aggregate of individuals (within some population definition) who experienced the same event within the same time interval. In almost all cohort research to date the defining event has been birth, but this is only a special case of the more general approach. Cohort data are ordinarily assembled sequentially from observations of the time of occurrence of the behavior being studied, and the interval since occurrence of the cohort-defining event. For the birth cohort this interval is age. If t is the time of occurrence and a is the age at that time, then the observations for age a, time t, apply (approximately) to the cohort born in year $t-a$, as do observations for age $a-1$, time $t-1$, and so forth.

The cohort record is not merely a summation of a set of individual histories. Each cohort has a distinctive composition and character reflecting the circumstances of its unique origination and history. The lifetime data for one cohort may be analyzed and compared with those for other cohorts by all the procedures developed for a population in temporal cross-section. The movement of the cohort, within the politico-spatial boundaries defining the society, is a flow of person-years from time of birth to the death of the last survivor. This differs from a synthetic cross-section because time and age change *pari passu* for any cohort. A cohort has an age distribution of its person-years of exposure, provided by its successive sizes age by age. The age distribution varies from cohort to cohort because of mortality and migration. Thus a cohort experiences demographic transformation in ways that have no meaning at the individual level of analysis, because its composition is modified not only by status changes of the components, but also by selective changes of membership.

The most evident manifestation of intercohort differences is variation, and particularly abrupt fluctuation, in cohort size, attributable to changes in the numbers of births from year to year or, less commonly, from brief heavy migration or mortality the impact of which is limited to a narrow age span. A cohort's size relative to the sizes of its neighbors is a persistent and compelling feature of its lifetime environment. As the new cohort reaches each major juncture in the life cycle, the society has the problem of assimilating it. Any extraordinary size deviation is likely to leave an imprint on the cohort as well as on the society. In the United States today the cohorts entering adulthood are much larger than their predecessors. In consequence, they were raised in crowded housing, crammed together in schools, and are now threatening to be a glut on the labor market. Perhaps they will have to delay marriage, because of too few jobs or homes, and have fewer children. It is not entirely coincidental that the American cohorts whose fertility levels appear to be the highest in this century were those with the smallest numbers.

Size is only one characteristic by which the cohort aggregate is differentiated from its temporal neighbors. Many statistical facets of cohort composition, broadly influential as independent variables, differ at age zero from one cohort to the next, and remain approximately unchanged throughout the cohort's history. Consider the various inherited items like race, mother tongue and birthplace. The cohort is not homogeneous in such characteristics, but the distribution of its heterogeneity tends to be fixed throughout its life in a shape which may differ from those of preceding and succeeding cohorts. Other birth and childhood characteristics are differentiating: for example, family structure by age, sex and generation determines the relative frequency of only children, younger and older children of like or unlike sex, and younger or older parents. Intercohort variability in these characteristics may derive from fertility, mortality or migration, to the extent that these are selective for the characteristic concerned and variable through time. Differential migration is the most striking influence in the short run, but differential natural replacement is generally more important in the long run.

Cohort differentiation is not confined to characteristics fixed at birth. Other status changes tend to be highly localized by age, relatively universal in occurrence, and influential in the rest of life (Neugarten *et al.*, 1965). Age is not only a general rubric for the consequences, rewards and penalties of experience; it is an important basis for role allocation in every society (Levy, 1952, p. 307). Age ascription is the cross-sectional counterpart of cohort differentiation. Similarities of experience within and differentiation of experience between age groups are observable in every culture. Similar functioning is imposed by society on those sharing an age at a particular time. Any legislation that is age-specific, either *de jure*, or, by virtue of its content, *de facto*, differentiates cohorts. Such norms give a distinctive age pattern to the life cycle of each cohort. If age-specific norms, or the context within which they are being applied, change through time, cohort experiences will be differentiated.

Thus marriage has a high probability of occurring within a narrow age span and is responsive to the exigencies of the moment. The members of a cohort are influenced in the age at which they marry, the persons they choose to marry and even their eventual likelihood of marriage by the particular set of circumstances prevailing at the time they reach marriage age. The outcome is not so individualistic as the romantic love ethos might suggest. The state of the marriage market is an aggregate phenomenon: the probability of marriage depends not only on an individual's personal characteristics, but also on the comparative characteristics of all others of the same sex, and also on the availability of those of the opposite sex who meet the approximate criteria of nubility. Underlying this is the propitiousness of the period for marriage, the relevance of which for cohort delineation depends directly on the age variance of marriage for the cohort. The same is true of any major event in personal history which is concentrated by age.

The time of completing education is also highly age-specific in its location and influential both in personal futures and in societal change. The intimate relation of education to social change is properly emphasized in programs of social and economic development. It is "the modern world's cutting edge." Changes through time in the proportions completing various stages of education are familiar trends in modern life which provide an indelible differentiation of cohort character and behavior (Parsons, 1959). The differentiation encompasses not only mere duration but also the quality of teaching, the nature of instructional materials and the content of the curriculum (Foote, 1958).

The consequences of distinctive educational preparation prevail in the cohort's occupational flow-chart. The experience of the cohort with employment and labor force status begins with the character of the employment market at its time of entry.[2] The cohort is distinctively marked by the career stage it occupies when prosperity or depression, and peace or war, impinge on it. The occupational structure of the cohort is not crystallized upon entry into the labor force, but the configuration imposed on individual economic histories has a high sequential dependence through time (Jaffe and Carleton, 1954). One explanation advanced for the baby boom is that the cohorts responsible had an unprecedented educational advantage when they sought their first jobs (Easterlin, 1961). Projections of labor force participation rates for women have been successfully designed on a cohort basis, because of the observed continuity of differences between cohorts (Durand, 1948).

The attractive simplicity of birth cohort membership as signified by age cannot conceal the ways in which this identification is cross-cut and attenuated by differentiation with respect to education, occupation, marital status, parity status, and so forth. Every birth cohort is heterogeneous. To some extent all cohorts respond to any given period-specific stimulus. Rarely are changes so localized in either age or time that their burden falls exclusively on the shoulders of one cohort. Intercohort analysis is profitably supplemented with cross-classification by relevant compositional variables (Evan, 1959). The meaning of sharing a common historical location is modified and adumbrated by these other identifying characteristics (Ralea, 1962). Different subsets of the cohort have different time patterns of development. Youth of manual and nonmanual origins differ in length of educational preparation and age at marriage. The various members of a cohort follow differently paced occupational lines. This may be especially true of intellectual histories. The differing tempi of careers in literature, music and mathematics yield different productivity modes by age, and therefore responsiveness to different historical circumstances, despite membership in the same birth cohort (Berger, 1960).

As a minimum, the cohort is a structural category with the same kind of analytic utility as a variable like social class (Lipset *et al.*, 1954). Such

---

[2] Bracker (1954) noted that the graduates of American universities of the class of 1929 were united by the distinction of being educated for prosperity and then vaulted into depression.

structural categories have explanatory power because they are surrogate indices for the common experiences of many persons in each category. Conceptually the cohort resembles most closely the ethnic group: membership is determined at birth, and often has considerable capacity to explain variance, but need not imply that the category is an organized group.

Two research suggestions may be advanced. In the first place, age should be so interpreted in every statistical table as to exploit its dual significance—as a point in the cohort life cycle and as a temporal location. Age is customarily used in statistical analyses merely in the former role, if not as a cross-sectional nuisance to be controlled by procedures like standardization. This implicitly static orientation ignores an important source of variation and inhibits the progress of temporal analysis. In the second place, age-cum-cohort should be used not only as a cross-classification to explain the internal variations of other groups, but as a group-defining variable in its own right, in terms of which distributions by other variables may be compared through time. In this way, research results may be compared in cumulated fashion, linking the outputs of the various studies using the same cohort identifications, just as has been done with other quasi-group categorizations. Each such study can enhance the significance of others for the same cohort. Comparison of such composite cohort biographies would yield the most direct and efficient measurement of the consequences of social change.

The proposed orientation to temporal differentiation of cohorts emphasizes the context prevailing at the time members of the cohort experience critical transitions. The approach can be generalized beyond the birth cohort to cohorts identified by common time of occurrence of any significant and enduring event in life history. Cohorts may be defined in terms of the year in which they completed their schooling, the year they married, the year in which they migrated to the city, or the year in which they entered the labor force full-time.[3] Each of these events is important in identifying the kinds of situation to which persons respond differently, and establishing a status to which future experiences are oriented. The research implication of this viewpoint is that more effort

---

[3] As an exotic example, Hyman Enzer has recently completed a study of the cohort of all 118 American authors whose first novels came out in 1958 (see Dempsey, 1963).

should be devoted to collecting items of dated information, to identify not only statuses but times of entry into them. Birth date serves as a surrogate for cohort identification by date of occurrence of other relevant events. It is a satisfactory approximation to the extent that variance in the age at which the event in question occurs is small. Thus the cohort approach may be generalized to consider any class of event in terms of the experience of successive cohorts defined by time of initial exposure to the risk of occurrence of that event.

The strategic focus for research on social change is the context under which each cohort is launched on its own path. The prototype is the cohort of persons entering the labor force each year. The annual meeting of prospective employers and employees produces an occupational distribution which manifests and foretells social change. The process requires macroanalysis because the possibility of an individual finding a particular job, or of an employer securing a needed talent, is a function of the entire set of comparative characteristics of all participants in the market. The educational system has prepared the new labor force entrants for this confrontation. Although the stimulus for innovation is most likely to come from the employers, the feasibility of new directions depends in part on how well they have been anticipated by the educational system. Indeed the conditions determining labor supply go all the way back to the composition of the relevant cohorts at birth. The implicit link between reproduction in one year, and characteristics of the labor market some two decades later, is an important channel for transmission of disturbances through time.

Out of the confrontation of the cohort of any year and the societal structures into which it seeks entry, a shape is forged which influences the directions in which the structures will change. More generally, the proximate indication of direction of change is the movement of personnel from one status to another, as the result of quasi-market activity in one or another role sphere. The market metaphor extends into the consideration of differential rewards, and thus of changing role evaluations, cognate with the Davis-Moore (1945) theory of social differentiation. The importance for social change of the kind of selectivity exercised in forming the cohort is largely obscured in this essay by exclusive attention to the birth cohort, which is more random in composition than any other cohort type. The study of the formation of cohorts defined in terms of specific role markets promises to provide a focused view of the processes that transform the different parts of the social system.

3. THE IMPACT OF HISTORICAL CHANGE
ON COHORTS

The preceding section emphasized several stages in the cohort life cycle at which major transitions occur, and proposed that the temporal context of these transitions would differentiate cohorts. The same point can be made from the opposite direction, by observing types of major change, and the extent to which participation in them is age-specific and therefore cohort-differentiating.   All those alive at the same time are contemporaries but they respond and contribute to social history in different ways unless they are also coevals. In particular, the potential for change is concentrated in the cohorts of young adults who are old enough to participate directly in the movements impelled by change, but not old enough to have become committed to an occupation, a residence, a family of procreation or a way of life. Furthermore the fact of change facilitates their development of other orientations than those of their parents and their community.

The most dramatic instance is war. Participation in war is limited in age, and the extent of war is limited in time. The Great War weakened a whole cohort in Europe to the extent that normal succession of personnel in roles, including positions of power, was disturbed. Sometimes the old retained power too long; sometimes the young seized power too soon.[4] The most obvious effect of war is the mortalilty and morbidity of the participants, but war transforms non-combatants as well. Several novels have utilized the theme of the peculiar poignancy of those who were old enough to comprehend the war but not old enough to participate in it (Gläser, 1928; Brittain, 1949; Hughes, 1963). The intellectual development of Mannheim, who brought the cohort concept into

---

[4] An extensive bibliography is given in Neumann (1942).

sociology, can be partly explained by the historical location of his cohort.[5] Teenagers in France can now meet easily with German youth groups because they are free of war memories.[6] German youths moving into the labor force are reported to be repudiating the labor discipline of their elders, whom they identify with the Nazi era.[7] The cohort consequences of war extend into the intellectual realm. Following the decimation of some French cohorts in the Great War, a split developed between those following the traditional path in mathematics, and those concerned with creating a new vocabulary. The latter produced the bible of modern mathematics, the *Elements of Bourbaki* (Félix, 1961).

Anyone reading the newspapers of the past decade needs no reminder of the prominence of uncommitted cohorts in the task forces of nationalistic or revolutionary political movements. The persons most active in the Protestant Reformation and in the Revolutions of England, France and America were youthful (Sorokin, 1947, p. 193). The contemporary "Children's Crusade" is too recent to have been investigated carefully, but there are some suggestive analyses of the position of youth in revolutionary change.[8] In his discussion of China, Levy (1949, pp. 297 *et seq.*) places primary emphasis on the role of the "ch'ing-nien" in societal transformation: this term for young adults has been retained by the aging leaders of the Communist movement. Irene Taeuber (1964) has advocated a research program for China based on the fact that the Communists have now been in power 15 years; change is imminent as these new cohorts are ushered in. Eisenstadt (1956, pp. 98 *et seq.*) has documented the experience of youth movements in Israel and in prewar Germany. Both of these were rebellions against elders and their ideas, viewing youth alone as pure enough to accomplish the task of

[5] John Kecscemeti, the preface to Mannheim (1952). In turn, Mannheim ascribes growing interest in the cohort problem to political discontinuities in the late 19th century.

[6] A movie opened in Paris in 1963, called: "Hitler? Never Heard of Him".

[7] Wagner (1956) has discussed the significance for the German labor movement of the absorption of cohorts who grew up under National Socialism.

[8] For example, *U.S. News and World Report*, June 6, 1960; *Look*, January 3, 1961. These accounts are more impressive for the frequency than for the detail of instances reported. Somewhat more helpful is Baldwin (1960).

re-creating society.[9] Perhaps the affiliation of youth with the revolutionary phase of a charismatic movement is linked with the appeal for them of techniques of violence (Gerth, 1940). Rintala (1958) has suggested that people who undergo disruptive historical experiences during their formative years may be unusually vulnerable to totalitarian appeals. Young people who are students, or unemployed, in the big cities of developing nations, are likely to be available for demonstrations and have large places in which to congregate.

A popular but unsupportable argument is that the emergence of a new cohort somehow guarantees progress. Mentré (1920) reports approvingly Comte's opinion to this effect; Mannheim (1952, p. 297) reports disapprovingly Cournot's like opinion. The entry of fresh cohorts into the political stream represents a potentiality for change, but without specification of its content or direction. The prominent role played by youth in the totalitarian movements of this century has been widely noted (Heberle, 1951, Ch. 6). A new cohort provides a market for radical ideas and a source of followers, and they are more likely than their elders to criticize the existing order.[10] Replacement of much older by much younger leaders, as Eisenhower by Kennedy, may have a profound symbolic impact. The direction of change may be to the left or to the right, toward democracy or toward totalitarianism, but whatever the trend, it is most manifest in youth.

Whether new cohorts are more or less crucial to the implementation of a revolution, they are clearly differentiated by its occurrence (Hinshaw, 1944, p. 69). The case of the Soviet Union is well documented by Bauer *et al.* (1960). Stalin created a generation of modern technicians to supplant the old Bolsheviks, because the latter's skills in the dialectic and in conspiratorial politics did not suit the age of machine tools and modern armies. Now the decision system is passing into the hands of cohorts brought up under socialism (Rostow, 1960, pp. 134–135). Journalists have recently begun to draw the line between those brought up under

---

[9] Many accounts of the Negro civil rights movement in the United States have contained the assertion that Negro youth provide the initiative for protest, in impatience with the gradualism of their elders.

[10] This may not be so if youth is directly affected by the change, as with school desegregation (Hyman and Sheatsley, 1964).

Stalin and those whose impressionable years coincided with de-Stalinization (Johnson, 1963). Although these latest cohorts are not yet in position of political power, they are beginning to have some influence, particularly through cultural activities.

The adaptive transformation of revolutionary movements has frequently been discussed from a structuralist standpoint (Parsons, 1951, p. 507). The audacity and independence required to overthrow a regime are not the skills requisite for administering a stable government in the sequel. The lions and the foxes must change places. If this comparative statics model is reconsidered in processual terms, it is clear that cohort differentiation will result. Rostow (1960) has suggested naming the process the "Buddenbrooks dynamics." If change occurs, those who are brought up in the new world will differ from those who initiated the change. In consequence, more change will occur, but interest is transferred from wrecking a hated system to the task of constructive continuity. Gradually death claims both winners and losers of the old struggle. Support for the new system becomes broad and stable. Thus the cohort succession serves as cause and effect in the phases of revolutionary transformation.

An experiential chasm between cohorts also occurs when immigration or colonization produces an intersection of two cultures. The European immigrant arriving in the New World identified himself with an ethnic group resembling the culture in which he was raised. His children went to American schools, chose American playmates, and often escaped from the subculture (Herberg, 1960, pp. 28–31). The parents' inadequacy as a basis for orientation toward the new society reinforced the children's resort to peer groups. Similarly, the impact of western culture on primitive peoples is likely to yield disruption of family life, changing mutual evaluation of the generations, and ideological identification of youth with resistance. Kwame Nkrumah recently remarked on the appearance in Ghana of a new cohort without firsthand knowledge of colonial rule and without the habit of obsequiousness to the European. Mannoni (1956) has provided an absorbing account of the structural complexities in a population containing two generations of colonists and two generations of natives.

Traumatic episodes like war and revolution may become the foci of crystallization of the mentality of a cohort. The dramatic impact may mark indelibly the "naive eyes and virgin senses" of the cohort in the vanguard and change them into an entelechy with an explicit mission, a virtual community of thought and action. Yet such vivid experiences are unnecessary to the argument. Cohorts can also be pulled apart gradually by the slow grind of evolutionary change. The nucleus and epitome of social change, as determinant and consequence, is the city. Urbanization is the outstanding manifestation of the world transformation of the past few centuries. Cities have been populated largely by the continual infusion of new cohorts. Rural-urban migration is highly selective of younger persons; changes requiring population transfer will be undertaken only by the more flexible and less burdened members of the society (Bogue, 1961). The young move away from the community that would envelop them in the traditional mold and into a new way of life. America may be less tradition-bound than Europe because fewer young couples establish homes in the same place as their parents.

The principal motor of contemporary social change is technological innovation. It pervades the other substructures of society and forces them into accommodation. The modern society institutionalizes this innovation and accepts it as self-justifying. To the child of such a society, technological change makes the past irrelevant. Its impact on the population is highly differential by age, and is felt most by those who are about to make their lifelong choices. Technological evolution is accomplished less by retraining older cohorts than by recruiting the new one, and the age of an industry tends to be correlated with the age of its workers. Accessions to the labor force flow most strongly into the new and growing industries; separations from the labor force are predominantly out of declining industries (Hawley, 1950, p. 25; Clark and Dunne, 1955).[11] The distinctive age composition of the industrial structure is nowhere more evident than in the rapid industrialization of a previously traditional economy. In effect, it is accomplished not so much by educating the population as a whole as by introducing each new cohort in turn to the modern way of life. In traditional society, age is a valid surrogate for relevant experience, but when the industrial revolution occurs, age comes to signify historical location and degree of disfranchisement by change, rather than the due prerogatives of seniority.

---

[11] On December 1, 1963, a federal arbitration board authorized American railroads to eliminate most of their firemen, by attrition.

4. INDIVIDUAL DEVELOPMENT AND THE FAMILY

Implicit in the foregoing account of the interdependency of social change and cohort differentiation is the assumption that an individual's history is highly stable or at least continuous. If a person's future were molded irrevocably by his earliest experiences, there would be a strong case for assembling data for aggregates of individuals on a cohort-by-cohort basis. The model dominating the literature on human development presents life as a movement from amorphous plasticity through mature competence toward terminal rigidity (Child, 1954; Anderson, 1957; Welford, 1958; Birren, 1959). The preparatory phase, during which individuals are susceptible to influence, is distinguished from the participatory phase, during which their predetermined destiny is unfolded. The central sociopsychological postulate in the spirit of Freud is that the core of personality is laid down at the beginning of life; what may look like changes later are merely minor variants on the established theme. The popularity of this assertion is as indubitable as its irrefutability. Discussion in this vein confuses ineluctable species characteristics and culturally variable designs, and fails to cope with the phenomenon of societal change.

In the conventional development model, the very young organism is presented as fluid, polymorphous, multipotential and perverse, susceptible to suggestion and rudimentary of will. Each interaction between organism and environment modifies the shape the organism takes into the next encounter. The earlier a situation imposes itself, the more likely it is to add an enduring element, partly because early learning is general enough to escape outright contradiction in subsequent particular experience. Gradually capacities are shaped and strengthened by use, with increasing self-regulation and independence of fluctuations. New experience is assimilated on the stratum of first impressions in a way that preserves self-consistency. The self-perception of persistence is ratified by others' recognition.

Thus the organism acquires an adult's efficiency at the price of a child's versatility. New ideas compete on unequal terms with old ones, because the latter have a place in the structure and have been used to direct behavior. Systematization and ritualization of response frees energy for higher-level integration. When a new situation accords with previous experience learning may be rapid, but not when it competes with established responses. The products of earlier education become debris that chokes off later growth. In due course the adult organism rigidifies and deteriorates into senility.

Any model of individual development which postulates early crystallization is embarrassing to the person explaining rapid social change. If personality is viewed as a quasi-hereditary phenomenon, the possibilities of change are reduced, following the biological analogy, to evolution through natural selection—a very slow process—and to mutation. Hagen (1962) finds himself in this box in his attempt to construct a theory of social change concordant with his belief that persons cannot move in later life from psychological stances established in childhood. Hagen's mutation-like proposal is that parents who encounter status frustration cannot change themselves, but their children may perceive the source of parental anxiety and avoid it by retreating. Their children, in turn, by a similar unconscious perception, may become innovators. The tempo of transformation is thus constrained to a generational rhythm.

The complexity of this construction is a direct consequence of two articles of faith: that social change cannot occur without personality change, and that personality change cannot occur once childhood is past. The present writer would propose that the social system rather than the personality system belongs at the center of any model of societal transformation. In this view personality is considered a by-product, at the individual level, of socialization procedures designed to achieve various objectives at the societal level. Socialization is a process of committing an individual to a term of service in a group, by progressively confining his behavioral potentialities within an acceptable range and by preparing him for the types of role he will be expected to play (Sewell, 1963). Far from being monopolized by the parents, socialization is a continuous process throughout life, shared in by every group of which a person may become a member. Even if the family-fostered self were immune to modification, the society could still retain the necessary degrees of freedom by altering the criteria for selection, from among different personality types, to fill the various roles.

Important to the present argument are two propositions: first, that social change implies a transformation of the relative contributions to socialization made by the various possible agencies of socialization; second, that this transformation identifies the cohort as a social reality, reflecting and implementing the social change to which it owes its existence. The principal socialization agency in every society is the family. It is an omnipresent authoritarian component of the child's environment, a primary group satisfying virtually the entire range of needs and furnishing the context within which the concept of self relative to others first arises. Family socialization is adequate to the extent that the structure of relationships portrayed and utilized in family life resembles that of the society into which the young adult must move. When a society breaks out of a static familistic mold, the family no longer suffices for the tasks of socialization.

Most writing about what is here called a cohort employs instead the term "generation," signifying all those within a broad (characteristically unspecified) age span during a particular epoch, and implicitly those with common characteristics because of common experiences. It is also used in synchronic structural analysis concerning relations between persons of markedly differing age, such as institutionalized deference (Cain, 1964). For the sake of conceptual clarity, "generation" should be used solely in its original and unambiguous meaning as the temporal unit of kinship structure, and the first two ideas should be signified by the terms "cohort" and "relative age status" respectively. "Generation" may be a fitting general temporal referent in societies where the dominant mode of role allocation is ascription on the basis of kinship. In such a context cohort identity is often trivial because the bulk of temporal variation coincides with the life cycle, as reproduced in annual cross-section. But societies undergoing cultural revolution must generally break the grip of the family on the individual. In so doing they diminish the social significance of "generation," in both its kinship and relative age connotations, and produce the kind of social milieu in which the cohort is the most appropriate unit of temporal analysis.

A prominent theme in discussions of modern society is intergenerational conflict. Although some of this is probably intrinsic to the family life cycle, current analyses emphasize the exacerbation of the tendency by social change, through intercohort differentiation (Davis, 1940; Elkin and Westley, 1955). As an Arab proverb has it, "Men resemble the times more than they do their fathers." Role differentiation that gives the old power over the young is justified when age is correlated strongly and positively with control of cultural content, but the correlation may even become negative during rapid social change because age differences in one direction signify cohort differences in the opposite direction. This is a familiar literary theme, as in Turgenev's *Fathers and Sons*. For reviews of the literature, see: Mentré (1920), Sorokin (1941, pp. 504 *et seq.*), and Renouard (1953).

Many writers have used the succession of cohorts as the foundation for theories of sociocultural dynamics. This approach has been aptly labelled "generationism," because the writers mistakenly transfer from the generation to the cohort a set of inappropriate associations. Some generationists maintain that there is a periodicity to sociocultural change caused by the biological fact of the succession of generations at thirty-year (father-son) intervals.[12] There is no such periodicity. Other generationists develop a conflict theory of change, pitched on the opposition between the younger and the older "generations" in society, as in the family. But a society reproduces itself continuously. The age gap between father and son disappears in the population at large, through the comprehensive overlapping of life cycles. The fact that social change produces intercohort differentiation and thus contributes to inter-generational conflict cannot justify a theory that social change is produced by that conflict. Generationists have leaped from inaccurate demographic observation to inaccurate social conclusion without supplying any intervening causality. All these works suggest arithmetical mysticism, and the worst of them, as Troeltsch said, are *"reine Kabbala."*

---

[12] The Spanish philosopher, Ortega y Gasset, and his disciple, Julian Marias, assert that modern history is punctuated by 15-year caesurae, beginning with 1626, the year Descartes turned 30 (Renouard, 1953).

5. CHANGING AGENCIES OF CHILD SOCIALIZATION

With the advent of modern society, changes in the agencies of socialization establish a context favorable to the identification of cohorts. The individual mobility and achievement-based status required of a modern occupational structure seem much more harmonious with the conjugal family than with the traditional web of kinship obligations (Goode, 1962, Ch. 1). Revolutionary regimes may adopt specific policies to reduce the importance of the family as an agency of socialization and as a bulwark of the old stratification system. Consider, for example, the Soviet emphasis on early education of the child away from home, the Chinese attempt to shift the locus of authority away from the older generation, and the Israeli use of the kibbutz to communalize child care and restrict parent-child interaction to the affectional realm. Such attempts to place collective identification above family solidarity may not have been completely successful (Talmon-Garber, 1959), but they are consistent with reorientations throughout the modernizing world. The potentially perpetual consanguineal unit is being supplanted by a conjugal family with a limited lifetime, and the institutional scope of family affairs is narrowing.

In particular, the reallocation of responsibility for child socialization away from the family and toward the school on the formal level and the peer group on the informal level gives analytic form to the cohort, just as specific historical changes give it analytic content. Parental capacity to prepare the child for his adult roles depends on the simplicity and stability of life. In a society of specialization and change parents are inadequate models for children and the specialized agency of formal education must be created. The school develops a commitment to the implementation of societal values, teaches the skills needed to perform adult tasks, and contributes to manpower allocation. As the content of education evolves, it differentiates the knowledge of parent and child, and equips successive cohorts with a progressively enlarged culture. To the extent that school instruction differs from what is learned at home, it provokes independent thought. The radical potentiality of education is clearest in the university, which has the function of discovering as well as transmitting knowledge.

By substituting teachers for parents, society symbolizes the difference in historical location between child and parent, and attenuates the bonds between them. Education expands in a modern society to encompass almost all members of each cohort and for a progressively longer age span, not only up into early adulthood but also down into the "formative" period cherished by personality theorists. The long time during which individuals are embedded in the lockstep age-hierarchized school system gives the cohort an ample opportunity to identify itself as a historical entity. The school is a cohort creator.

Socialization in every society is the function not only of institutionalized authorities but also of coevals. An increase in such "self-socialization" is to be expected during social change, because this makes the experiences of the peer group (the cohort) unique, and develops similarities within and differences between cohorts. One of the themes in *The Lonely Crowd* (Riesman, Denney, and Glazer, 1950) is the replacement of the inner-directed type, whose standards are his parents', by the other-directed type, whose standards are his contemporaries'. The congruence with the present position is obvious.

The peer group is a subset of one's cohort. It consists of people of the same age with whom one has attitude-forming relationships, or, to use an old-fashioned but etymologically apt term, one's cronies (Pitts, 1960). It is oriented to its members' needs and interests rather than to the pursuit of goals defined by external authority. Perhaps when a collectivity rather than an individual is being socialized, it develops a sense of cohort solidarity and alters the outcome of socialization. Although providing nonadult approval, it need not be deviant, and may even give strong support to the conventional moral code (Reiss, 1960).

Peer groups are functional in modern society (Eisenstadt, 1956, 1963). If the principles regulating family life harmonize with those of other institutional spheres, an individual can attain full membership in the society through behavior learned in the family. But modern society is regulated by criteria which contradict those appropriate to kinship. For the individual this poses the problem of transition from one universe of discourse to the other; for the society it poses the problem of developing bases of extra-familial solidarity. The solution is the peer group, which has the primary group characteristics of the family and the achievement orientation of the society.

It is tempting to treat the peer group phenomenon as signaling the creation of a sense of solidarity if not reality as a social group, and thus derive support for the view that a cohort is more than a mere category in statistical tables. Solidarity is encouraged by idealized self-definitions in reaction to ill-specified rights and responsibilities of the status, by sharing anxieties concerning imminent and hazardous transitions, and by explicit associations that encourage the development of attitudes unsanctioned by family or community. The age (and cohort) variance of membership in voluntary associations is smaller in youth than later, because small age differences mean more during development. The mass media aim specifically labelled appeals at these ages. Vocabularies specific to the age and time are invented to serve as communications channels and boundary-maintaining mechanisms.

In an epoch of change, each person is dominated by his birth date. He derives his philosophy from his historical world, the subculture of his cohort. The community of date equips each cohort with its own expanse of time, its own style and its own truth. The ideas, sentiments and values of members of the same cohort converge; their actions become quasi-organized. As social change creates divergence in the experience of successive cohorts, it may transform them from locations into actualities (Mannheim, 1952). It is possible for most of a society's youth to develop an ideological direction (though probably under adult leadership) but the burden of proof is on those who insist that the cohort acquires the organized characteristics of some kind of temporal community. This may be a fruitful hypothesis in the study of small groups of coevals in artistic or political movements but it scarcely applies to more than a small minority of the cohort in a mass society. Commonality is likely but not community.[13]

Age-homogeneous groupings of children and adolescents are common to all societies. Mostly they remain undeveloped because kinship groups form the basic units of task performance. In some cases the cohort—known to anthropologists as an "age grade"—may function continuously throughout life. In the Hamitic culture of East Africa, for example, the age grade is a system of compulsory association enduring from puberty on, with permanent privileges and obligations. The system

---

[13] "Belonging to a generation is one of the lowest forms of solidarity." In Rosenberg's (1959, pp. 241–258) opinion, generation identifications are concocted by journalists out of trivial or ephemeral data.

cuts across family lines, gives the individual interests in tribal concerns, and may be used for governmental or religious functions (Driberg, 1958). This is very different from the history of a modern adolescent peer group. The features that make it attractive to its members are liabilities for its persistence (cf. Matza, 1964). The peer group has fluid boundaries, with individual members drifting into and out of association. Its numbers are ordinarily small and its functions vague and diffuse. It may provide recruits for radical movements, but it is just as likely to veer toward frivolity or criminality. Its dilemma is that it is terminated by the arrival of adulthood. The peer group has little time to develop effective strength. It faces the common difficulties of any group composed mostly of transients. The members are dispersed by the growth of heterosexual interests, by the formation of families of procreation, and by movement into the labor force and out of the conveniently age-homogeneous arrangements of school.

The peer-group phenomenon provides insufficient support for a cohort approach to social change but it does exemplify the tendency toward cohort identification within the time structure of a changing population. The peer group is a symptom of the strain imposed on modern youth by its location at the fulcrum of change. The schedule of development includes a psychosocial moratorium between preparation and participation (Erikson 1950, 1963). This is when the youth first gets a chance to temper with reality the rigid precepts implanted in childhood. Lessons too sophisticated for children can now be learned. There are many answers for the questions of the age, from various and often contradictory sources. The imprecision of youth's role definition encourages receptivity to new ideas. Movement out of the equilibrated orientation provided by family and school and into a cognitively unstructured realm leaves them doubtful and uncertain but sometimes creative (Lewin, 1939). The new cohort of young adults lives in a phase of the life cycle when dramatic transitions are occurring in rapid succession. Perhaps the pace of personal change increases sensitivity to the possibilities of social change.

6. SOURCES OF INDIVIDUAL STABILITY IN ADULT LIFE

The cohort approach to social analysis derives strong support from the continuity of individual life, from a time-specific and thus historically located initiation. A person's past affects his present, and his present affects his future. Persistence is enhanced by the tendency to structure inputs, so that each will disturb as little as possible the previous cognitive, normative or even esthetic design, and, in the extreme, to reject dissonant items. Although individuals differ in the ingenuity with which they may retain disparate elements or achieve reformulation, the feasibility of extensive transformation is obviously quite limited. Individuals seek coherence, and manifest continuity to the extent that they achieve it. An individual's life is an organic entity, and the successive events that constitute it are not random but patterned.

The initial contribution to the design of a lifetime is made at conception, when the individual is provided not only with a fixed genetic constitution but also, under ordinary circumstances, with the two parents to whom society will assign responsibility for his early socialization. Furthermore, every society seizes upon the circumstances of birth as modes of allocating status, limiting the degrees of freedom for the person's path through life. Virtually every subsequent occurrence will depend on the societal plan for utilizing characteristics present at birth: sex, race, kinship, birthplace and so forth. Perhaps the most important influence of status ascription on the future of an individual in a modern society is its effect on access to different amounts and kinds of formal education.

Beyond the age of noncommitment, the new adult begins a process of involvement in the various spheres of life, in which his actions and those of others progressively reduce the degrees of freedom left to him in the societal scheme (Becker, 1960). Facing various decisions among alternative roles open to him, an individual generally makes choices somewhat congruent with his value-orientations—unless he is to be credited with pure perversity. Within each role, once allocated, he forms a growing commitment to a line of activity. Each contract between group and individual contains a relatively determinate description of role requirements, and the contract is strengthened by stabilized interactions between the individual and occupants of interdependent roles. The temporal commitment is perhaps most relevant to the present argument. Thus a company's interest is served by bureaucratic arrangements, such as pensions and seniority rules, which penalize movement out of the system. On the job, the older employee becomes adjusted to his work, gravitating toward tasks that are congenial to him, and learning enough about them to exploit their advantages and minimize their liabilities. His psychological stake in his niche includes a modification of aspirations in consonance with his true abilities and the demands of the system for them. It should be clear that though this example is occupational, similar principles operate in every group of which a person becomes a member.

The apparent rigidity of an older worker in the face of a demand to adapt to a new procedure may flow simply from the circumstance that something valuable is being taken away from him (Tannenbaum, 1961). The difficulties of learning new skills are more formidable for one who has acquired and utilized traditional work practices (Mead, 1953). This may also hold for the domestic technology of contraception (see Hill *et al.* , 1959). Career continuity is bolstered by investing time and money in a particular kind of vocational preparation. Continuous obsolescence of the individual is a feature of contemporary industrial society. It is to be expected that the old hands will resist innovation; otherwise they may be displaced before they are ready to retire. Resistance may be successful for a while, because the oldest workers are most likely to occupy positions of authority. The term "vested interests" suggests capitalistic profits threatened by change, but it applies equally to the skilled worker standing guard over his way of doing things. Perhaps this is especially true for higher levels of technical skill, where workers are less interchangeable, and the individual and the industry commensurately less flexible (Moore, 1946, p. 60).

Around his job, the individual establishes a network of spatial arrangements linking places where he lives, shops, plays and visits. An older man with a family feels obliged to remain in a situation from which a younger unencumbered person would readily move. The assumption of the parental role makes a person an agent of the society as a teacher of its new members, and the private attitude to which a man once felt himself entitled as a youth must now be subordinated to the more conventional public postures expected of the father (Pressey and Kuhlen, 1957, pp. 494

et seq.). "Nothing makes a younger generation settle down faster than a still younger generation showing up." Children are powerful instruments in making conformists of parents. They terminate definitively the brief period of "horizontal" freedom between the vertical structure of the family of orientation and the vertical structure of the family of procreation.

In a modern society, most adult roles are located in hierarchized structures. Factories, churches, labor unions and political parties distribute income, prestige and power along an approximately age-graded continuum. Memberships in such structures decrease the probability of individual transformation. In the majority of occupations a steadily upward progression of status occurs throughout most of the age span. Seniority can be viewed as commitment to particular modes of solving particular problems. The personnel of organizations tend to fall into Old Guard and Young Turk positions, emulating generations within a family. Young men must wait a long time for positions of power and responsibility, and may never arrive if they display ideas and attitudes deviating from those of their seniors (Berger, 1960). Conformity to such vertical structures, and acceptance of the rewards and duties defined by superiors, implies resistance to change. To advance in a particular economic order requires support of that order. Success reinforces the way in which success has been achieved; failure is resisted from whatever position of accrued power has been attained. Social change creates continuing conflict between the rewards of seniority and the penalties of membership in older cohorts.

Students of political affiliation have been concerned with the ages at which people's experiences have most influence on their political behavior.[14] The hypothesis that youths acquire a structure of political attitudes from parents and peers, which persists unless disturbed by dissonant events, seems to be contradicted by the conservatism of older voters. Some of the tendency for older Americans to vote Republican may be explained by theories of aging, and by association with preferred statuses accompanying age, but a residual remains to be explained by intercohort differentiation (Crittenden, 1962). Perhaps the stereotype of the older

---

[14] For summaries of the literature, see Lipset et al. (1954), and Hyman (1959).

person as a dogmatic conservative fits a person whose education dates back to a time when attitudes now regarded as conservative were more common. Yet persistence and continuity in the political as in the occupational sphere seem to grow with commitment to adult affairs, as exposure to alternatives is reduced, and penalties of change increase (Hinshaw, 1944, p. 69).

As life takes on a steadier tempo, routinization predominates. Routines are barriers to change because they limit confrontation with the unexpected and the disturbing. Older people learn to exercise greater control over a narrower environment, and avoid risks of venturing into unstructured situations. The feasibility of personal transformation is probably limited more by restricted membership than by physiological aging. A persistent research problem is the difficulty of distinguishing between characteristics which are indeed intrinsic to aging, and those which merely appear to be so because of the cohort contribution to the age vector in times of change. Social change ordinarily touches older persons less closely. They lead a more restricted social life, they read less, they attend fewer movies, and their friends, books and movies are more carefully chosen to conform to their biases. Their residences and their friendships become more stable. The longer a person persists in an established mode of conduct, the less likely its comprehensive redefinition, especially if he invests it with normative content. Aging involves disengagement and withdrawal, a restriction on the quantity and intensity of interaction with others, and an approach toward self-centered and idiosyncratic behavior. Consistency through time is achieved by developing a vested interest in forms to which past behavior has again and again been oriented. To change the basic conceptions by which one has learned to assess the propriety of situations would be to make a caricature of one's life.

In later years, the cohort identity is blurred. Age becomes progressively less precise as an index of a person's social characteristics. Individuals experience what Cain (1964) calls asynchronization—they possess different "ages" in the various institutional spheres. People vary physiologically, and also in the extent to which they continue to learn. Adjacent cohorts tend to permeate one another as the pattern of life chances works itself out. Definitions of age become predominantly social rather than biological categories; they change with time, and with the groups one joins and leaves. The intrinsic aging process may be variously accelerated or retarded by many different institutional arrangements.

The research recommendation implicit in the preceding discussion of the sources of continuity in individual lives is longitudinal analysis. The category includes case histories, repeated interviews with the same respondents (of which panel studies are a special case), analyses of diaries and dated letters, and, on a larger scale, continuous work histories or morbidity histories, for insurance purposes.[15] The *raison d'être* of the longitudinal approach is the organization of personal data in temporal sequence, to determine the causal potentiality of otherwise isolated acts. This procedure has dominated behavioral inquiry, particularly under psychoanalytic influence, has become standard operating procedure in social psychology, and has been described as "the perfect type of sociological material" (Blumer, 1939; Thomas and Znaniecki, 1919, p. 6).

The data produced by such inquiries are disjunctive with most statistical analyses of aggregates in two ways. First, the intensive detail of longitudinal analyses proliferates hypotheses but ordinarily lacks that broad evidential basis requisite to generalized verification which is a principal virtue of census tabulations, for instance. In this sense life histories and statistical analyses are complementary approaches (Volkart, 1951, p. 24). But their potential complementarity is prejudiced by the second disjuncture—between the time axes of the two procedures. The life history has been called the long-section and the statistical the cross-section view of culture. The typical emphasis of the latter on simultaneity between corresponding events from different lives implies over-valuation of the existing situation—"the sociological error par excellence" (Dollard, 1935). Aggregate analysis destroys individual sequences, and diverts attention from process. By implying that the past is irrelevant, cross-sectional analysis inhibits dynamic inquiry and fosters the illusion of immutable structure (Evan, 1959).

This outcome can be avoided by using the cohort approach. The cohort record, as macro-biography, is the aggregate analogue of the individual life history. It provides the necessary temporal isomorphism for linking small-scale intensive longitudinal analyses with extensive surveys of the society at a point of time. It has the time dimension of the former and the comforting statistical reliability of the latter. In a similar vein, Ortega has rejected both the collectivist and the individualist

---

[15] For a summary of the technical problems, see Goldfarb (1960).

interpretations of historical reality, in favor of an orientation based on the cohort—"the dynamic compromise between mass and individual—the most important conception in history" (Ortega y Gasset, 1933, pp. 13–15).

7. SOURCES OF FLEXIBILITY: INDIVIDUAL AND GROUP

The predominant theme of literature on socialization and development is early crystallization. Perhaps this is because students of child development are most concerned with the personality, the control of primary drives, and the internalization of general value orientations, and not with the learning of specific norms and skills to be demanded of the adult. Clearly childhood socialization cannot prepare a person for all the roles of his later years. Indeed, parents effectively inhibit many types of learning by selectively sheltering their children from and exposing them to the world outside the home. Many types of economic, political and social participation are effectively limited to later life, e.g., the problem of support for older parents is not ordinarily encountered by the "child" until he approaches middle age. Socialization continues throughout the whole of life. Specific socialization occurs every time a person occupies a role in a new group, for every group has and is an agency for socialization and social control (Brim, 1964, pp. 1–5). Although the codes of new groups the individual joins are often limited in content, they may tend to contradict the general precepts of earlier training. That there is considerable flexibility is evident from the experience of social and cultural mobility. For all the resistance of the culturally conditioned personality, individuals do move between cultures, subcultures and classes.

Socialization need not mean rigidification. Normative postures are often acquired imperfectly, incompletely and tentatively. Perhaps it is simpler to indoctrinate entrants with a set of immutable recipes for action in prescribed situations, but room is almost always left for interpretation. The situations to be encountered cannot all be anticipated, and the appropriate prescriptions for them may require improvisation. Experience can strain the sacred formula to the point of forcing reconstruction. The intellectual convenience of the assumption that development ceases once adulthood is attained must be sacrificed in the face of the annoying complexity of reality (Strauss, 1959). Behavior can be modified by increasing rewards for innovation, expanding tolerance of some kinds of deviation, and softening penalties for movement. Indoctrination can be designed to encourage experimentation rather than unreflective obedience, and place primary emphasis on adherence to broad principles. Of particular importance are institutionalized procedures that provide legitimate modes of modification, such as debate in political negotiation and disciplined doubt in scientific inquiry. Such procedures impose a burden of doubt and strain on individual participants, but do leave room for social change through individual change.

Although the difficulty of teaching an old dog new tricks may be inherent, it is also possible that this is a myth given approximate reality by training programs based on it. The feasibility of adult change is probably contingent in large part on the character of early training, and on the opportunities provided for retraining. Perhaps older workers are less adaptable because the earlier cohorts of which they are members received a limited general education. Potential obsolescence may in the future be reduced by more general training, so that people will still be able to acquire in their later years the new capacities and skills needed for continuing employment. It is not outside the bounds of speculation to look toward the day when accelerating change will make economic an extension of education throughout the entire life span, as a continual adjunct to the work week, or as a routine sabbatical renovation.

Yet the flexibility of the social system and its components need not rely on the imperfect tentativeness of socialization procedures, nor on the prospects of retraining the individual. Every group has some control over its own demographic metabolism, and over the content of socialization. The society achieves pattern and direction partly through general selection mechanisms. Change can be mediated through modifications of role allocation as well as through flexible socialization. The system of role allocation can be manipulated to achieve stability and continuity for the group and for the individual, and permit the continuing transformation required by a dynamic society.

Like individuals, organizations (including the total society) have characteristics that influence their degrees of freedom with respect to change. In particular, the different system levels vary in the feasibility of transformation by substituting rather than by modifying components. In biology, the capacity for change is greater at the organismic than at the cellular level. The life of a cell is short relative to that of its encompassing organism. In turn, the organism must die but the species persists and changes, through reproduction and selection. Each higher level has greater modifiability through time, based on the feasibility of metabolism of lower-level components. The analogy of society and organism was always somewhat unfortunate, for reasons unnecessary to rehearse, and also because it may have obscured the more fruitful analogy between society and species. The society is a looser and less sharply defined system than the organism because its constituents possess the possibility of independent mobility in space. In turn, the society is a more flexible system than the species, because it has greater possibility of independent mobility in time. It can control not only the physical replacement of members, like the species, but also the replacement of norms through cultural transmission. In a sense, the society has two types of membership: biological, consisting of human organisms, and cultural, consisting of social norms. The replacement of each is of course interdependent with the replacement of the other.

Now the processes of normative replacement and personnel replacement occur at all levels of social organization. The study of the demographic metabolism of specific groups is a relatively uncharted area of great importance to the student of social change. The individual differs from the organization because he is attached to a mortal body, and lacks the capacity for freedom with respect to time which is within the grasp of the organization. Organizations, like individuals, may acquire structural rigidities, but they can modify their course by replacing individuals as well as by transforming them, through their hiring and firing policies. The scope of possibilities for transforming the character and direction of an organization obviously includes succession in crucial leadership roles and the changing criteria for advancement as different talents become more or less valued (Gusfield, 1957).

Indeed, in some respects the subsystems of a society may be even more flexible in this regard than the society itself. They have more scope for applying conditions for remaining and more ways of recruiting new individuals. Enfranchisement and disfranchisement are much more discriminating in their selectivity than natural processes (Simmel, 1956). A society does have some control over the character of its membership, to the extent that differential fertility and mortality are subject to social arrangement, and to the extent that the population is changed by migration, but it is at least common for a society to accept a contractual obligation to all those born within its boundaries (an obligation it has in a sense inherited from its predecessor, the family). But it is perhaps most meaningful from the standpoint of the transmutability of the total society to consider the extent to which its components are groups and organizations rather than individuals. Organizations persist if and because they are successful. New organizations are continually born and old ones die. The replacement of individuals within an organization is paralleled by the replacement of organizations within a society. Once again the opportunities for research are abundant.

8. CONCLUSION

The case for the cohort as a temporal unit in the analysis of social change rests on a set of primitive notions: persons of age a in time t are those who were age $a-1$ in time $t-1$; transformations of the social world modify people of different ages in different ways; the effects of these transformations are persistent. In this way a cohort meaning is implanted in the age-time specification. Two broad orientations for theory and research flow from this position: first, the study of intra-cohort temporal development throughout the life cycle; second, the study of comparative cohort careers, i.e., inter-cohort temporal differentiation in the various parameters that may be used to characterize these aggregate histories.

The purpose of this essay is to direct the attention of sociologists toward the study of time series of parameters for successive cohorts of various types, in contradistinction to conventional period-by-period analyses. There has been a considerable growth of cohort research in recent years, but the predominant emphasis is still on comparative cross-sectional inquiry. Admittedly the new approach shares the vices as well as the virtues of all studies with an extended time dimension. It is cumbersome, inefficient and laborious; data collection is very time-consuming; and the implicit incomparability accumulates as the group changes its composition, and as the data collectors change their definitions (Kessen, 1960). Yet such difficulties are not so much those of the method itself as meaningful reflections of the research investment necessary to study a long-lived species experiencing structural transformation.

Measurement techniques should be designed to provide data that correspond with the theoretical formulations of the phenomena under examination. In the present essay, the purpose has been to present a frame of reference within which theories can be constructed and empirical inquiry prosecuted. Considering the modest results so far achieved in dynamic analysis, sociologists would be well-advised to exploit the congruence of social change and cohort differentiation.

REFERENCES

Anderson, J.E. (1957). Dynamics of development: System in process, in D.B. Harris (ed.), *The Concept of Development.* Minneapolis: University of Minnesota Press, pp. 25–46.

Baldwin, H. (1960). Turkey's new soldiers. *New York Times,* (June 5).

Bauer, R.A., Inkeles, A., and Kluckhohn, C. (1960). *How the Soviet System Works.* New York: Vintage Books.

Becker, H.S. (1960). Notes on the concept of commitment. *American Journal of Sociology* **66**, 32–40.

Berger, B.M. (1960). How long is a generation? *British Journal of Sociology* **11**, 557–568.

Birren, J.E. (1959). Principles of research on aging, in J.E. Birren (ed.), *Handbook of Aging and the Individual.* Chicago: University of Chicago Press, pp. 3–42.

Blumer, H. (1939). *Critiques of Research in the Social Sciences I: An Appraisal of Thomas and Znaniecki's "The Polish Peasant in Europe and America".* New York: Social Science Research Council, Bulletin 44.

Bogue, D.J. (1961). Techniques and hypotheses for the study of differential migration: Some notes from an experiment with U.S. data. *International Population Conference* **Vol. I**, New York, 405–412.

Bracker, M. (1954). There's no class like the class of '29. *New York Times Magazine,* (May 23), p. 14 *et seq.*

Brim, O.G., Jr. (1964). Socialization through the life cycle. *Social Science Research Council Items* **18** (March).

Brittain, V. (1949). *Born 1925*. London: Macmillan.

Cain, L.D., Jr. (1964). Life course and social structure, in R.E.L. Faris (ed.), *Handbook of Modern Sociology*. Chicago: Rand McNally, pp. 272–309.

Child, I.L. (1954). Socialization, in G. Lindzey (ed.), *Handbook of Social Psychology*. Cambridge, Mass.: Addison-Wesley, **Vol. II**, pp. 655–692.

Clark, F.L.G. and Dunne, A. (1955). *Ageing in Industry*. London: Nuffield Foundation.

Crittenden, J. (1962). Aging and party affiliation. *Public Opinion Quarterly* **26**, 648–657.

Davis, K. (1940). The sociology of parent-youth conflict. *American Sociological Review* **5**, 523–535.

Davis, K. and Moore, W.E. (1945). Some principles of stratification. *American Sociological Review* **10**, 242–247.

Dempsey, D. (1963). First novelists, last words. *Saturday Review* **66**, (October 12), 34.

Dollard, J. (1935). *Criteria for the Life History*. New Haven: Yale University Press.

Driberg, J.H. (1958). Age grades. *Encyclopaedia Britannica* **Vol. I**, 344–345.

Durand, J.D. (1948). *The Labor Force in the United States, 1890–1960*. New York: Social Science Research Council.

Easterlin, R.A. (1961). The American baby boom in historical perspective. *American Economic Review* **51**, 869–911.

Eisenstadt, S.N. (1956). *From Generation to Generation*. Glencoe, Ill.: The Free Press.

Eisenstadt, S.N. (1963). Archetypal patterns of youth, in E.H. Erikson (ed.), *Youth: Change and Challenge*. New York: Basic Books, pp. 24–42.

Elkin, F. and Westley, W.A. (1955). The myth of adolescent culture. *American Sociological Review* **20**, 680–684.

Erikson, E.H. (1950). *Childhood and Society*. New York: W.W. Norton.

Erikson, E.H. (1963). Youth: Fidelity and diversity, in E.H. Erikson (ed.), *Youth: Change and Challenge*. New York: Basic Books, pp. 1–23.

Evan, W.M. (1959). Cohort analysis of survey data: A procedure for studying long-term opinion change. *Public Opinion Quarterly* **23**, 63–72.

Félix, L. (1961). *The Modern Aspect of Mathematics*. New York: Science Editions.

Foote, N.N. (1958). Anachronism and synchronism in sociology. *Sociometry* **21**, 17–29.

Gerth, H.H. (1940). The Nazi party: Its leadership and composition. *American Journal of Sociology* **45**, 530–571.

Gläser, E. (1928). *Jahrgang 1902*. Berlin: Gustav Kiepenheuer.

Goldfarb, N. (1960). *An Introduction to Longitudinal Statistical Analysis*. Glencoe, Ill.: The Free Press.

Goode, W.J. (1962). *World Revolution and Family Patterns*. Glencoe, Ill.: The Free Press.

Gusfield, J.R. (1957). The problem of generations in an organizational structure. *Social Forces* **35** (May), 323–330.

Hagen, E.E. (1962). *On the Theory of Social Change*. Homewood, Ill.: The Dorsey Press.

Hawley, A.H. (1950). *Human Ecology*. New York: Ronald.

Heberle, R. (1951). *Social Movements*. New York: Appleton-Century-Crofts.

Herberg, W. (1960). *Protestant, Catholic, Jew* (rev. ed.). New York: Doubleday.

Hill, R., Stycos, J.M., and Back, K.W. (1959). *The Family and Population Control*. Chapel Hill: University of North Carolina Press.

Hinshaw, R.P. (1944). The relationship of information and opinion to age. Ph.D. dissertation, Princeton University.

Hughes, R. (1963). *The Fox in the Attic*. New York: Signet.

Hyman, H. (1959). *Political Socialization*. Glencoe, Ill.: The Free Press.

Hyman, H.H. and Sheatsley, P.B. (1964). Attitudes toward desegregation. *Scientific American* **211**, 16–23.

Jaffe, A.J. and Carleton, R.O. (1954). *Occupational Mobility in the United States 1930–1960*. New York: Columbia University Press.

Johnson, P. (1963). The new men of the Soviet sixties. *Reporter* **28** (May 9), 16–21.

Kessen, W. (1960). Research design in the study of developmental problems, in P.H. Mussen (ed.), *Handbook of Research Methods in Child Development*. New York: John Wiley, pp. 36–70.

Levy, M.J., Jr. (1949). *The Family Revolution in Modern China*. Cambridge, Mass.: Harvard University Press.

Levy, M.J., Jr. (1952). *The Structure of Society*. Princeton, N.J.: Princeton University Press.

Lewin, K. (1939). Field theory and experiment in social psychology: Concepts and methods. *American Journal of Sociology* **44**, 868–896.

Lipset, S.M., Lazarsfeld, P.G., Barton, A.H., and Linz, J. (1954). The psychology of voting: An analysis of political behavior, in G. Lindzey (ed.), *Handbook of Social Psychology.* Cambridge, Mass.: Addison-Wesley, **Vol. II**, pp. 1124–1175.

MacIver, R.M. (1963). *The Challenge of the Passing Years.* New York: Pocket Books.

Mannheim, K. (1952). The problem of generations, in *Essays on the Sociology of Knowledge.* New York: Oxford University Press, pp. 276–322.

Mannoni, D.O. (1956). *Prospero and Caliban.* London: Methuen.

Martineau, H. (n.d.). *The Positive Philosophy of Auguste Comte.* **Vol. II.** London: Trübner.

Matza, D. (1964). Position and behavior patterns of youth, in R.E.L. Faris (ed.), *Handbook of Modern Sociology.* Chicago: Rand McNally, pp. 191–216.

Mead, M. (1953). *Cultural Patterns and Technical Change.* Paris: UNESCO.

Mentré, F. (1920). *Les Générations Sociales.* Paris: Editions Bossard.

Moore, W.E. (1946). *Industrial Relations and the Social Order.* New York: Macmillan.

Neugarten, B.L., Moore, J.W., and Lowe, J.C. (1965). Age norms, age constraints and adult socialization. *American Journal of Sociology* **70**, 710–717.

Neumann, S. (1942). *Permanent Revolution.* New York: Harper.

Ortega y Gasset, J. (1933). *The Modern Theme.* New York: W.W. Norton.

Parsons, T. (1951). *The Social System.* Glencoe, Ill.: The Free Press.

Parsons, T. (1959). The school class as a social system: Some of its functions in American society. *Harvard Educational Review* **20**, 297–318.

Petersen, J. (1930). *Die Literarischen Generationen.* Berlin: Junker and Dunnhaupt.

Peyre, H. (1948). *Les Générations Littéraires.* Paris: Bowin.

Pitts, J. (1960). The family and peer groups, in N.W. Bell and E.F. Vogel (eds.), *A Modern Introduction to the Family.* Glencoe, Ill.: The Free Press, pp. 266–286.

Pressey, S.L. and Kuhlen, R.G. (1957). *Psychological Development Through the Life Span.* New York: Harper.

Ralea, M. (1962). Le problème des générations et la jeunesse d'aujourd'hui. Rencontres Internationales de Genève, *La vie et le temps.* Neuchâtel: Baconniere, pp. 59–73.

Reiss, A.J., Jr. (1960). Sex offenses; the marginal status of the adolescent. *Law and Contemporary Problems*, 309–333.

Renouard, Y. (1953). La notion de génération en histoire. *Revue Historique* **209**, 1–23.

Riesman, D., Denney, R., and Glazer, N. (1950). *The Lonely Crowd*. New Haven: Yale University Press.

Rintala, M. (1958). The problem of generations in Finnish Communism. *American Slavic and East European Review* **17**, 190–202.

Rosenberg, H. (1959). *The Tradition of the New*. New York: Horizon Press.

Rostow, W.W. (1960). *The Stages of Economic Growth*. New York: Cambridge University Press.

Ryder, N.B. (1956). La mesure des variations de la fécondité au cours du temps. *Population* **11**, 29–46.

Sewell, W.H. (1963). Some recent developments in socialization theory and research. *Annals* **349**, 163–181.

Simmel, G. (1956). The persistence of social groups, in E.F. Borgatta and H.J. Meyer (eds.), *Sociological Theory*. New York: A.A. Knopf, pp. 334–358.

Sorokin, P.A. (1941). *Social and Cultural Dynamics* **Vol. IV**. New York: American Book Company.

Sorokin, P.A. (1947). *Society, Culture and Personality*. New York: Harper.

Strauss, A.L. (1959). *Mirrors and Masks*. Glencoe, Ill.: The Free Press.

Taeuber, I.B. (1964). China's population: An approach to research. *Social Science Research Council Items* **18**, 13–19.

Talmon-Garber, Y. (1959). Social structure and family size. *Human Relations* **12**, 121–146.

Tannenbaum, A.S. (1961). Adaptability of older workers to technological change. *Institute for Social Research Newsletter*, October.

Thomas, W.I. and Znaniecki, F. (1919). *The Polish Peasant in Europe and America, Vol. III, Life Record of an Immigrant*. Boston: Gorham.

Volkart, E.H. (1951). *Social Behavior and Personality*. New York: Social Science Research Council.

Wagner, H.R. (1956). A new generation of German labor. *Social Research* **23**, 151–170.

Welford, A.T. (1958). *Ageing and Human Skill*. New York: Oxford University Press.

3. SPECIFICATION AND IMPLEMENTATION OF AGE, PERIOD AND COHORT MODELS*

Stephen E. Fienberg

William M. Mason[†]

1. INTRODUCTION

For the past 80 years or more, social scientists have attempted to analyze cross-time data, using as explanatory variables age and time (or phenomena that are time-specific). When such data are analyzed in aggregate forms, age and time are typically grouped and polytomized. More recently, some investigators have adopted an analytic focus in which cohort membership, as defined by the period and age at which an individual observation can first enter an age-by-period data array, is held to be more important than age or period for substantive understanding. This focus has led to age-cohort and period-cohort models, as distinguished from age-period models.

This paper is concerned with models for situations in which all three of age, period and cohort are potentially relevant for the study of a substantive phenomenon. Relevance can be manifest for a number of reasons. First, the process under examination may be thought to depend on all three of age, period and cohort; in this case theory requires

* We are indebted to Michael Meyer for helpful discussions on degrees of freedom and interactions, and to Carol Crawford for wordprocessing. Preparation of this paper was supported in part by Grant SES 80-08573 from the National Science Foundation to the University of Minnesota; Office of Naval Research Contract N00014-80-C-0637 at Carnegie-Mellon University; National Science Foundation grants SOC 78-17407 and SES 81-12192 to the University of Michigan; National Institute of Child Health and Human Development Grant 1R01 HD 15730-01 to the University of Michigan.

† Stephen E. Fienberg is affiliated with the Departments of Statistics and Social Sciences, Carnegie-Mellon University, and William M. Mason is affiliated with the Department of Sociology and the Population Studies Center, The University of Michigan.

formulation of a model in which outcomes are determined jointly by age, period and cohort. Mason and Smith (1984, this volume) provide an example of the relevance of the full age-period-cohort specification. Second, the process studied may be thought by some investigators to depend on any one or two of age, period and cohort but not all three, and by other investigators to depend on a different proper subset. Here the age-period-cohort (APC) specification may also be appropriate so long as competing reduced models (in the sense of Fienberg and Mason, 1978) are compatible.[1] Third, a single investigator may have in mind a specific reduced specification, but would want to fit the full APC model for baseline comparisons. The education example in Fienberg and Mason (1978) illustrates this case. Fourth, the APC model can serve as the starting point for more complicated modelling efforts involving the addition of specific interaction terms. We explore this latter approach in some detail.

There is, in a sense, a possible double parsimony associated with APC models. They can involve fewer parameters than, say, an age and cohort plus interactions model. There can also be an epistemological parsimony associated with such models since they require alternative conceptualization rather than extensions to handle ad hoc interactions, as might be the case with two-variable perspectives. Adding parameters to capture pieces of interaction between, say, age and period not reflected in the additive interaction terms (i.e., "main effects") for cohort is not precluded. Mason and Smith (this volume) illustrate such an approach in dealing with anomalous results in the fit of APC models to tuberculosis mortality rates.

We further narrow our focus in this paper by an emphasis on *accounting* specifications, using as our accounting categories age, period, and cohort. As with their "green-eyeshade" counterparts, these models do not explain so much as they provide categories with which to seek

---

[1] If the competing specifications are compatible, then an evaluation is possible using an age-period-cohort parameterization. If the alternatives are incompatible, then their formal evaluation is carried out using procedures developed for the evaluation of nonnested models (Cox, 1961; Atkinson, 1970; Quandt, 1974). Since theoretical reasoning surrounding the use of age, period and cohort in models of social processes has thus far typically not been so precise as to produce many instances of competing nonnested reduced models, it appears that the class of applications we direct our attention to contains the majority of cohort analyses.

explanation. For accounting models to have value, the parameterizations of the general framework must be linked to phenomena presumed to underlie the accounting categories. This is a conceptual linkage minimally, and maximally an empirical linkage as well. If measurement of the underlying phenomena is possible, the accounting categories can be dispensed with. But if the accounting categories are superfluous, then the variety of problems we touch on in this paper are generally, though not always, of considerably less interest. For example, the identification problem created by the linear dependency of age, period and cohort is irrelevant if underlying empirical measures are available for any one of age, period or cohort (e.g., a business cycle measure for period, or cohort size for cohort membership). On the other hand, the design issues we touch on are pertinent regardless of the wealth of information that may be available for measurement purposes.

Accounting models have long been objects of attention, largely because of the conundrum posed by the identification problem. This problem is solved and relatively well understood by now (Fienberg and Mason, 1978). In our view it is appropriate to shift attention to other problems that arise in cohort analysis, and this we do in the present paper.

Using our earlier paper as a point of departure, this essay focusses on a number of points that have been considered problematic. We begin in Section 2 with a discussion that relates modelling efforts to historical and universal processes. Of interest here are arguments over the relevance of statistical inference. We also discuss the relevance of the group or macro level perspective afforded by an APC model, and provide a framework in which to understand the complications introduced by data aggregation. Section 3 reviews the various data structures that have been accompanied by cohort based models, and Section 4 reviews the technical details of the APC accounting framework. To the APC description of Fienberg and Mason (1978) we add a continuous-time polynomial representation, and we conclude that the identification problem in APC models is inescapable—no matter which representation we choose to work with.

Fienberg and Mason (1978) adopt the rather dogmatic view that age-period, age-cohort, and cohort-period effects are virtually inestimable when added to the basic APC model. This is true only in a narrow sense, and Section 5 presents extensions of the APC model which allow for restricted interactions. In most of the extensions the estimability of the interaction terms hinges primarily on dimensionality, and not identification and specification arguments.

2. ON DEFINING THE PROBLEM

2.1. Scope

The planning of cohort studies, and discussions of various approaches and study designs, can be aided by a framework for thinking about (a) the purposes of the analysis, (b) the nature of the data batch, and (c) the relevance and role of the distinction between micro and macro levels of analysis. The remarks we offer here are not limited in their relevance to APC analysis, and are not new, although their elaboration in this context may be unusual. They are, moreover, equally applicable to APC models in their simplest form, more complex models, reduced models, and models in which some or all of the accounting dimensions are replaced by more direct measures of the substantive phenomena presumed to underlie the dimensions.

To begin with, we distinguish between different potential analytic goals. The polar extremes often invoked are (i) the use of cohort analysis to organize historical material surrounding a particular era, place and set of events, and (ii) the use of cohort analysis to abstract from historical context to some more general universe. An example of the former might be Ryder's (1965, reprinted in this volume) mention of the rise of the Bourbaki group in French academic mathematics as a consequence of the mortality induced by World War I. The example is highly time and place specific, and cohorts are invoked to clarify the composition of the innovating group known as Bourbaki. No particular model is specified by Ryder, but one could envision coding mathematicians by date of birth (or date of degree), age (or time since degree), and choice of subject matter. The resultant data structure could be analyzed from the standpoint of an APC specification or some other, more complex, formulation. The researcher could use the results to describe accomplishments in a particular era, but it might also be justifiable to interpret them as indicating something more universal—perhaps the function of wars as instrumentalities for increasing or inducing creativity. The researcher's intent as to generalizability is rarely clear from specific analyses.

Lack of clarity regarding the broader goals of the analysis engenders confusion about the usefulness of the results. On one hand, to those most concerned with historical specificity, the abstraction imposed by a statistical model looks like neglect of substantive information about the setting in which the data are embedded. On the other hand, to those most interested in generalizability, some sacrifice of historical detail is essential: It is inherently difficult to accommodate historical richness in statistical models, and it is undesirable to attempt to do so to any considerable degree. To complicate matters, there remains the further problem of deciding whether the model employed is reasonable, given the supposition that modelling of the substantive phenomenon is in principle meaningful. Determining whether a model is reasonable is not always separable from the question of abstraction or focus. For example, whether to include interactions above and beyond the "additive" components of an APC specification might hinge on the analyst's sense that the goal is to generalize rather than to fit certain obtrusive facets of the data.

In thinking about the focus of the modelling effort, it is helpful to consider the nature of the data batch. Are the data fruitfully thought of as essentially all that are conceivably available for analysis (as might be the case, for example, in working with census data), or can the data be thought of as a sample? Thinking about the nature of the data batch in conjunction with the focus of analysis suggests the following classification:

	Data Batch	
	All	Sample
Historical, Descriptive Emphasis	(1)	(2)
Universal, Processual Emphasis	(3)	(4)

Cell (3) is empty: By definition, if your interest is in generalizing from the data you can not have it all. Even if you were working from perfect census data, your batch would be a sample in time. The remaining cells are nonempty, and the problem of determining how to treat a given study must be addressed in these instances. Whether a study belongs in cell

(1), (2), or (4) seems to depend on how one wishes to think about the discrepancies between observed data and fitted values.

In general, we are concerned with modelling efforts in which expressions such as

$$Y = \text{fit} + \text{residual}$$

are employed.   Expressions of this kind depend on some prior conceptualization of the phenomenon under study.   Whether they are informative depends on abstract evaluation of the conceptualization, but also on realized values of the fitted terms and residuals.   The residuals, or discrepancies between the observed response variable and the numerical values fostered by the modelling process, can have any of the following sources:

  (i) Sampling accidents (discrepancy between sample and finite population *or* super-population).

 (ii) Stochastic fluctuation for individuals or groups (this can be present even if there are no sampling errors).   The system is subject to shocks which may or may not be treated as "random."

(iii) Curve fitting errors: If the model is wrong the "predictions" are likely to be wrong.

Now, what is the linkage between cases (1), (2), (4) and the classification of ways to think about residuals?   First, if you think of residuals as arising solely from specification errors, then you can only be concerned with historical description, and you have to think that you have all of the data relevant to the problem.   Second, if you think of the residuals as due to sampling accidents, then you clearly can not think of the data batch as consisting of all the data, but you could have either a historical or a more abstractive interest.   That is, thinking of your data as a sample does not force a decision as to emphasis, but it does require consideration regarding whether inference is to a finite population or to a super-population (Hartley and Sielken, 1975).   Third, if you think of the residuals as reflecting stochastic fluctuation but not sampling accidents, then you are again thinking in terms of historical, noninferential analyses. You are saying you have all the data and the right model.   Your model does not capture every nuance of historical reality, but you do not intend it to—that would contradict the parsimony sought by modelling.

Clearly there is no logical ordering here.   You could start by saying that you were interested in historical description and that you thought you had all the data. From this you would be drawn to thinking of residuals as indicating either stochastic fluctuation of no interest to you, or indicating curve fitting errors.

Given that one conceives of the data batch as some kind of sample, it is by no means obvious that a plausible super-population will come to mind, and it is certainly not the case that standard errors will be readily computable. Thus, taking the stance that inference is desirable is far removed from being able to carry out the inference. When it is not possible to carry out the inference, what can be the role of statistical modelling?

When the basis of inference is unclear it seems helpful to think of the results of statistical modelling as providing windows. What we gain is a view of the world from a particular location. Shifting our view by applying another model amounts to looking at the data through a different window. We have experience in the interpretation of statistical models when there is a reasonably good mesh between data and assumptions. The panoply of numerical information from statistical models tells us what the world would look like if the assumptions were met. We may decide that the view is a helpful one, or that it is so implausible that the "as if" perspective can not be maintained: The data depart too much from the underlying assumptions of the statistical model employed.

2.2. Levels of Analysis

Historically, the conceptual attractiveness of cohorts as analytic differentia has been that they refer to sets of individuals with shared experiences. The question is sometimes raised whether APC models describe individual behavior, group behavior or a combination of the two. This question is rooted not so much in a concern for when a set of individuals can be said to form a group, but rather owes its currency to a tendency on the part of some discussants to link the level of aggregation in a data set to a conceptual unit of analysis. There is, for example, a suggestive power to "grouped data," as in averages or other summary measures, conditional on age and period.

If the unit of analysis is at issue, then the nature of explanation compatible with APC models is no less so. In this subsection we suggest that cohort analysis of any kind is inherently multi-level. The statement of this position forms one answer to the question of the appropriate unit of analysis. A second answer is attendant upon the multi-level conception: Given a perspective on the desired conceptual units of analysis, it becomes possible to assess the impact of data aggregation. In the next subsection we show that common forms of data aggregation can lead to biased estimates of effects in APC models, or expanded models.

To the extent that there is anything distinctive about APC models or cohort analysis more generally, with respect to the conceptual units of analysis, it is that the notion of cohorts when used in the social sciences frequently carries with it the tacit assumption that the object of study is not context free. Given this assumption, adequate APC models can not simply reflect formulations of behavior at a single level of aggregation or analysis, and must instead be sustained by a broader multi-level perspective.

Within a multi-level perspective (Mason, 1980) group or macro level phenomena can have an impact on individual or micro level phenomena.[2] To test theoretical understanding of group phenomena it is necessary to specify how the macro variables are translated into micro impacts. Doing so requires a theoretical conception of how specific macro variables might affect certain micro variables, and it requires also that the linkages between levels actually be measured. Thus, for a macro phenomenon to have an impact on the endogenous variable, its force must be realizable through variables measured at the micro level. This is an ultimate test of a macro theory. When we estimate APC models, we are unlikely to be able to develop such tests, given data restrictions. APC specifications are incomplete because of this, but then so are the alternatives. The acid test described here is a goal rarely attained, but its pursuit will promote clarity in conceptualization and explanation.

The goal of articulating linkages across levels of organization is not reductionist, and it is not unusual. It is precisely this linkage which remains to be determined before the scientific case against cigarette

---

[2] It is also the case that micro phenomena can have an impact at the macro level. The demonstration of this requires temporal data. Mason (1980) focusses on situations in which the only available data are cross-sectional, and does not treat causation from the micro to the macro level. The Easterlin (1961) argument for the generation of population waves (see also Smith, 1980) hypothesizes a micro process for boom and bust fluctuations in fertility which goes well beyond the purely mechanical.

smoking can be closed (Brown, 1978; U.S. Department of Health, Education and Welfare, 1979).   In quantitative statistical analyses, attention to a total logical structure including cross-level linkages requires the specification of variables which measure how relevant macro phenomena are translated into micro experiences.   Cohort size, for example, is one of the most commonly cited "mechanisms" by which cohorts are differentiated.   This variable has been hypothesized to be responsible for variation in a remarkable array of phenomena, including employment rates, wage rates, fertility, divorce, crime, and political alienation (Easterlin, 1978).   A full statement of any cohort model which attributes the impact of cohort membership to cohort size must, in our view, include specification of the mechanisms which lead to the hypothesized consequences and designate variables presumed to be indicators of the mechanisms involved.

The multi-level perspective we advocate is generally applicable across the entire spectrum of cohort models, not just to APC specifications.   To summarize this discussion, we are proposing the following: (a) When used, the accounting categories (age, period and cohort) must be well justified.   This means that the analyst must be able to conceptualize how the accounting categories might be replaced with substantive variables, and that upon doing so the resulting specification must retain plausibility. (b) The interpretations intended by the use of the substantive variables must be, in principle, verifiable.   That is, it should be possible to state the intervening steps between the macro level and the micro level, even if data are unavailable to verify the interpretation in full detail.   (c) When possible, the verification should be attempted.

2.3. Data Aggregation

A parallel is sometimes drawn between the degree of aggregation in a data set and the conceptual unit of analysis, so that, for example, the use of aggregated data is held to necessitate a conceptual analytic focus with similarly aggregated units of analysis.   There is no such ready connection between the conceptual units of analysis and the degree of aggregation in the data.   Nonetheless, once conceptual units of analysis have been selected, the relevance of data aggregation can be studied.   This is no less true for models in other contexts, but we shall consider the implications of the form of the data for APC and related models since questions about aggregation seem especially persistent for them.

The potential deleterious effects of aggregation that most concern us are those of coefficient bias. We consider the impact of data aggregation on coefficient bias with the aid of a general equation which links a response variable to age, period, and cohort in discrete form, and to micro level explanatory (M_r) variables, macro level global explanatory (G_s) variables, and macro level aggregate explanatory variables $(\overline{M}_r)$ constructed from micro variables. A global variable is not decomposable into a corresponding micro level variable, whereas an aggregate variable is (Lazarsfeld and Menzel, 1961). The equation is considerably more general than would be needed were we to restrict our attention solely to APC specifications. This is appropriate, since in many applications it is possible to move beyond the simplest case of APC modelling to include other variables or to substitute for one of the accounting dimensions. In the equation, g is an operator over the row space of Y, and f is an operator over the column space of the predictors, that is, it defines the functional form relating $g(Y)$ to the predictors. Consider

$$g(Y_{ijkl}) = f(A_i, P_j, C_k, M_{ijklr}, G_s, \overline{M}_r), \tag{1}$$

where

$i = 1,...,I$ denotes age;

$j = 1,...,J$ denotes period;

$k = i + j - 1 = 1,...,K$ denotes cohort;

$l = 1,...,n_{ij}$ denotes micro observations within age-period combinations;

$r = 1,...,R$ denotes (micro) M-variables, that is, variables for which values can vary over l within age-period combinations;

$s = 1,...,S$ denotes (global) G-variables (which cannot vary over l within age-period combinations);

$\overline{M}_r =$ the aggregation of the rth micro variable (so that $\overline{M}_r$ does not vary over l within age-period combinations).

We use equation (1) to catalog a variety of possibilities with respect to data aggregation. The basic question we consider is: Under what conditions, defined by combinations of assumptions about g and f, will coefficient estimates be biased, relative to a baseline or fundamental specification? This fundamental specification is one in which g is the identity transformation. That is, we suppose the comparisons are best made with the situation in which the analyst has all of the possible relevant information.

To generate the catalog we allow g to be either linear or nonlinear, and cross these possibilities with the parallel dichotomy for f. We then use the resulting four combinations to consider bias in the coefficients of the predictors of equation (1).

If g is a linear operator, we might think of the following standard situations in which the analyst has available

$$\overline{Y}_{ijk+}, \quad n_{ij}, \quad \text{and/or} \quad \hat{\sigma}^2_{Y_l}|_{ij}$$

for the ij combinations. This includes the standard case of a dichotomous response variable, since in that instance $\overline{Y}_{ijk+}$ is a proportion, and the conditional binary counts are recoverable from the information given. The generalization to a polytomous response variable is straightforward. If g is a nonlinear operator, we might think of the ij conditional medians. Saying that f is linear is to indicate that f is linear in the parameters, but not necessarily in the predictor variables. If f is nonlinear, then f is nonlinear in the parameters. An operator h may or may not exist which would linearize the relationship. Table 1 summarizes the outcome of our consideration of aggregation bias relative to the case in which all of the micro data are available. It has been arrived at by application of elementary ideas concerning aggregation and the analysis of covariance.

The results summarized in Table 1 suggest that even under the simplest form of aggregation, in which both g and f are linear operators, some, but not all, effects have or can have unbiased estimators. We will first review the results for g linear, and then take up the case in which g is nonlinear. To begin with, suppose we consider just the age, period and cohort coefficients. If the only available response variable is represented as a set of ij conditional means, and if the n_{ij} or estimated conditional variances are available, *and* if f is linear, then it is possible to obtain unbiased estimates of the age, period and cohort effects (case (i)). On the other hand, suppose g defines conditional averages, and f defines an

Table 1. The Effects of Data Aggregation on
Coefficient Bias, for APC and More General Models

	f is linear	f is nonlinear
	g is linear	
A, P and *C* coefficients	(i) unbiased	(ii) biased unless Y is discrete with recoverable ij counts
M coefficients	(iii) biased unless g operates within distinct combinations of values of M-variables	(iv) biased unless g operates within distinct combinations of values of M-variables and Y is discrete with recoverable ij counts
G coefficients	(v) unbiased if the G-variables vary between ij categories but not within	(vi) biased unless Y is discrete with recoverable ij counts
$\overline{M}$ coefficients	(vii) biased unless $\overline{M}$ is a valid proxy of a G-variable	(viii) biased unless $\overline{M}$ is a valid proxy of a G-variable and Y is discrete with recoverable ij counts
	g is nonlinear	
A, P and *C* coefficients	(ix) biased	(x) see (ii)
M coefficients	(xi) biased	(xii) see (iv)
G coefficients	(xiii) biased	(xiv) see (vi)
$\overline{M}$ coefficients	(xv) biased	(xvi) see (viii)

Note: This table assumes that if Y is discrete, then the functional form of choice (f) is nonlinear.

exponential function (case (ii)). Then the effects will in general be biased, since the mean of a set of logarithms is not equal to (or a simple function of) the logarithm of a mean. The exception to this result occurs when the response variable is inherently discrete. In that case we presume sufficient information exists to resolve the conditional means (proportions), say, back into the dichotomous or polytomous counts. In this instance it is possible to obtain unbiased estimates for the age, period and cohort effects.

To say that it is possible to obtain unbiased estimates does not imply that they are automatic. In case (i), application of ordinary least squares when the response variable is treated as a set of cell means will provide biased coefficient estimates. Weighted least squares, using the n_{ij} or $\hat{\sigma}^2_{Y_l}|ij$, will yield unbiased estimates. Likewise, if the response variable is inherently discrete, it is not enough to know this and then to regress conditional proportions on age, period and cohort. This will lead to biased coefficients for more than one reason. Rather, one would usually want to recover the dichotomous or polytomous counts within ij-combinations, so that the full information available from the data could be used (case (ii)).

Next consider the coefficients of the micro (M) variables, assuming to begin with that f is linear. If the operation of g is such that the Y_{ijkl} cannot be related to the M_{ijklr}, then the estimator for the effects of the M-variables will be biased (case (iii)). Suppose that we have available the $\overline{Y}_{ijk+}$ and the underlying response variable is not discrete. Then the estimable relationship between the $\overline{Y}_{ijk+}$ and M_{ijklr} amounts to a relationship between means (i.e., between $\overline{Y}_{ijk+}$ and $\overline{M}_{ijk+r}$), and the regression line through the means is not necessarily the same as the regression line through the micro data. An exception occurs if the operation of g is such that the Y_{ijkl} can be related to the M_{ijklr}. This will happen when the operation of g is conditional on the distinct combinations of values of the M-variables. Suppose, for example, that race and sex are the M-variables. Then if the response variable consists of $\overline{Y}_{ijk+}$ conditional on the race-sex combinations, all micro information is preserved. If f is nonlinear, the only condition under which the M effects are unbiased occurs when Y is discrete with recoverable dichotomous or polytomous counts, and the underlying recoverable tabulation is $Y \times A \times P \times M_1 ... \times M_r ... \times M_R$ (case (iv)).

Estimating the G coefficients is relatively unproblematic, if g and f are linear operators. Under these conditions (case (v)), the effects will be unbiased if the level of aggregation is such that it is natural for values of the G-variables to vary across ij categories, but not within them. Given this degree of aggregation, the space spanned by the G-variables is a subset of the space spanned by the age, period and cohort accounting categories. If f is nonlinear (case (vi)) this result is no longer correct, unless the response variable is discrete and the ij-conditional dichotomous or polytomous counts are recoverable. This is, of course, a common situation, as when the data consist of percentages and base n's, conditional on age and period, and it also makes sense to define global variables as varying over age-period categories.

The coefficients of the $\overline{M}$-variables (variables which are linear aggregations of micro variables) will be unbiased if both g and f are linear, *provided* that the $\overline{M}$-variables are valid proxies of unmeasured G-variables. If the $\overline{M}$-variables are included only because the M_{ijklr} are unavailable, however, the coefficients of the $\overline{M}$-variables will be biased (case (vii)). The same conclusion holds if f is nonlinear (case (viii)) with the additional stipulation that Y must be discrete, with recoverable ij-conditional dichotomous or polytomous counts. Thus, the conclusions we reach concerning $\overline{M}$-variables are identical to those for G-variables provided that the $\overline{M}$-variables are valid substitutes for the G-variables. The $\overline{M}$-variables would generally not be so regarded if they were included only because the M_{ijklr} were unavailable. If this were the reason for inclusion, then the conclusions of cases (iii) and (iv) would apply.

Finally, we consider the possibility that g is nonlinear. When this condition holds, then all coefficients will generally be biased. Exceptions to this conclusion occur when Y is discrete with recoverable counts as specified for cases (x), (xii), (xiv) and (xvi). These exactly parallel cases (ii), (iv), (vi) and (viii), respectively. As an example, suppose that the analyst is given ij-conditional logits and the $\{n_{ij}\}$. Then it is possible to recover the ij-conditional binary counts, and thus possible to obtain unbiased estimates of the age, period and cohort effects in a logit model.

The preceding exercise shows that there are forms of data aggregation which entail biased estimation of effects. There are also forms of data aggregation which permit unbiased estimation, and, depending on the nature of the response variable, amount to nothing more than compact representation of the data with no loss of information. It is a simple error, commonly made, to assume that because the data are in tabular form the data have been aggregated. This need not be the case. Adopting a multilevel perspective, as we have done here, permits the recognition that having full information rests on knowing the Y_{ijkl} and the M_{ijklr} (if relevant). Given a decision as to the meaning of full information, it is possible to assess the impact of data aggregation on coefficient bias. The degree of aggregation poses a complication which is separate from the choice of units of analysis.

3. DATA STRUCTURES

When social and demographic researchers write about cohorts and cohort analysis, they typically have in mind a particular form of data array, and a design for collecting the relevant information. In this section, we discuss the six major data structures used in cohort analyses, and related aspects of design and data collection. We begin with the simplest structure and build toward the more complex, noting as we pass which structures link naturally to cross-sectional data collection, and which to longitudinal data collection. Some structures are compatible with both longitudinal data collection and repeated cross-sections, and we so note. To make the diagrams of the data structures comparable across types we adopt the convention of letting periods or time vary horizontally, and cohorts and age vary vertically.

3.1. Single Cross-Section Studies

If we collect data by means of a single cross-sectional survey, then we can structure them by age groupings as in Figure 1 to represent a single *synthetic cohort.*

This structure is most useful when it can be assumed that cohort and period effects are *known*, or known to be nonexistent. When this is true, cohort differences in a single cross-section can be treated as age differences, or at least can be manipulated to reflect age differences. Using this approach for two or more cross-sections substantially separated in time leads to multiple synthetic cohorts. These have been used in demographic settings.

Of course, we could approach a single cross-section somewhat

Figure 1. Synthetic Cohort from a Single Cross-Section

Period

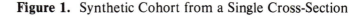

Age
(Cohort)

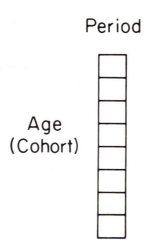

differently, assuming that age and period effects were known, or known to be nonexistent. Then the age differences could be treated or manipulated to reflect cohort differences.

One problem with the single cross-section study is that the kind of prior knowledge indicated above is usually not available. Hence applications are based on approximations to this particular ideal. A second problem, and a serious one, is that engendered by selectivity. Suppose that we are interested in cohort fertility and choose to examine only the fertility of women no longer in the childbearing age range—and that our data come from a single cross-section. Then we immediately run into the problem of differential mortality by cohort, and this creates selectively different samples by cohort. A different example encounters selectivity at the opposite end of the age distribution. Mare (1979) examines probabilities of continuing to a next level of education on a cohort by cohort basis, using the *Occupational Changes in a Generation II* data (Featherman and Hauser, 1975). For data of this kind, the selectivity encountered is that the younger the cohort, the less likely individuals are to have completed their education. Hence, comparisons between cohorts that are insensitive to this problem are likely to be biased.

3.2. Studies of a Single Cohort Followed Over Time

As the name of this data structure suggests, it is longitudinal in form. In this instance there are multiple time points for a single cohort, as in Figure 2, as opposed to multiple cohorts observed at a single point in time.

Figure 2. A Single Cohort

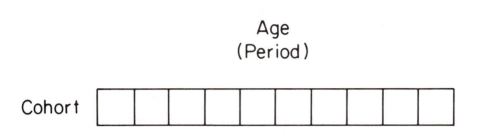

This design is especially useful for analyzing a developmental process, and requires assumptions parallel to those for a synthetic cohort—in this case that period and cohort effects are known or known to be nonexistent. Clearly, the analyst might wish to be able to follow more than one cohort, but matters of cost are always relevant. One example of such a study is that of Wolfgang, Figlio and Sellin (1972), which follows the criminal careers of all males born in 1945, residing in Philadelphia from age ten to age eighteen. In fact, recently Wolfgang and his collaborators have followed up the original study with a second cohort of males born in 1958 (Wolfgang, 1982).

3.3. Multiple Cross-Section Studies

This data structure is based on independent replicated cross-sectional surveys, or an aggregate cross-sectional population data. The resulting data are typically displayed in the form of a rectangular age by period table as in Figure 3, but as Fienberg and Mason (1978) note, they can also be displayed in a parallelogram-shaped age by cohort or period by cohort table.

If age groups and period have the same spacing, then subsamples in

Figure 3. Age by Period Display of
Repeated Cross-Sectional Surveys

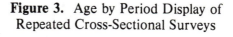

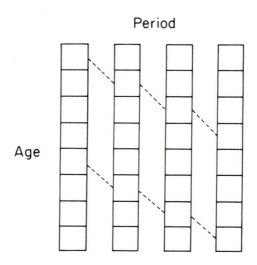

the same cohort can be linked across surveys (periods) as indicated by
the broken lines in Figure 3.   This is consequently the first design
discussed thus far admitting the possibility of calculating age effects
adjusted for period and cohort differences; and cohort effects adjusted for
period and age differences.   Indeed, this is the first design we have
considered which does not require us to assume that some of the
potential effects are known to be nil.

    There are abundant examples of this form of data, analyzed from a
cohort perspective (e.g., Greenberg, Wright, and Sheps, 1950; Carr-Hill,
Hope and Stern, 1972; Farkas, 1977; Pullum, 1977, 1980; Fienberg and
Mason, 1978; and Mason and Smith (1985, this volume)).

    The design is not without difficulties.   First, there is an identification
problem, assuming that we use an APC accounting framework.   This
problem arises from the dependency between age, period and cohort.   Its
solution depends on prior knowledge, reasoning about the process under
scrutiny, or theory more generally.   In many examples, there is no
coherent body of substantive reasoning which underlies the partitioning.
Hence, the accounting framework is not used optimally and the success of
the identifying restriction employed is left in doubt.

A second problem arises in the estimation or calculation of effects depending on the design of the data structure, *given* that the data are multiple cross-sections. In particular, the data are inherently unbalanced. Although the data array is rectangular with respect to age and period, it is not rectangular with respect to cohort membership. Moreover, if the data structure were in some way augmented to make cohort membership balanced, the design would become unbalanced with respect to age and period. There is no solution to the problem, and it is a serious one, since it can influence the calculated effects to such an extent as to make them virtually useless.

A third problem is that data arrayed in the form of repeated cross-sections give stocks and not flows. That is, there is no information about cross-time linkages within individuals. An exception to this problem can occur if the response variable is irreversible and discrete. If the response is whether an individual "survives" from one period to the next, then we can determine cross-time linkages. The reason is straightforward. If we envision a cross-tabulation of "alive" vs. "dead" at time t against "alive" vs. "dead" at time $t+1$ then one of the cells must be zero—"dead" at time t and "alive" at time $t+1$. This fact, together with our knowledge of the univariate distributions at each point in time, suffices to determine all cell frequencies in the four-fold table. This knowledge is of little use to us, however, if we seek to extend the problem by replacing the accounting categories with underlying variables and *these* variables are reversible. This is especially troublesome when we are dealing with population data that are in principle longitudinal but have been aggregated in a cross-sectional manner, thus destroying the cross-time links.

3.4. Retrospective Multiple-Cohort Studies Based on a Single Cross-Sectional Survey

This design locates individuals on the basis of a single cross-sectional survey, and elicits retrospective longitudinal data from them. Thus we get direct information from multiple cohorts for past periods. One way to structure such data is in the form of an upper-triangular period by cohort array, as in Figure 4. Here common age groups across cohorts can be linked by moving from upper left to lower right, provided that the period and cohort groupings are of the same size or length. Our information on the multiple cohorts then ends with the period of the cross-sectional survey, and there is full age-specific data for only the oldest cohort.

Figure 4. Retrospective Multiple-Cohort Study from Single Cross-Sectional Survey

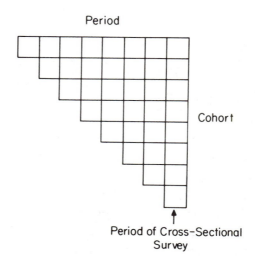

Birth histories ascertained from a single cross-section of marriage-age women constitute a prime example of the application of this type of data structure. The World Fertility Survey, for example, collected this kind of information (International Statistical Institute, 1975).

The new feature the retrospective design presents is that there is complete preservation of the individual longitudinal records. Although this is a great asset, it is also a problem, since we must now deal with the dependence of data across time. Other problems created by this design include:

(a) Memory decay.

(b) Telescoping.

(c) Selective reporting (particularly if the collection of data is official—of course in some societies the official status of a survey may mean to the respondent that the survey will brook no opposition).

(d) Hidden attrition—this problem is of course present for any cross-section of cohorts. We are dealing only with censoring of whatever the process may be. Or we may simply be dealing with survivors. Moreover, if we fashion a longitudinal APC accounting model there is still a linear dependency among age, period, and cohort with which we must deal.

3.5. Prospective Multiple Cohort Studies

We find these studies in psychology (Nesselroade and Baltes, 1974) and medicine, when there is a developmental process which is held potentially to vary with cohort. We begin with a cross-sectional sample, and group the individuals into cohorts. The key to this design is that we track all cohorts from a specified initial time period, with subsequent follow-ups at regular intervals. We do *not* add new cohorts. The data have a lower-triangular cohort by period structure, as seen in Figure 5, which is an inverted image of Figure 4.

Figure 5. Perspective Multiple-Cohort Design

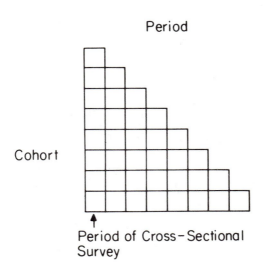

Data of this kind need not be longitudinal. In general, however, we would expect the data to be collected in panels or waves, thus permitting the study of "flows" as well as "stocks." This particular design is really nothing more than what is typically called a *panel design* or *panel study*. The emphasis we are placing on the design is unusual, however, since panel designs are usually implemented not because the investigators wish to study cohort processes, but because they are interested in "flows" as well as "stocks," i.e., because they are interested in "turnover."

One problem with this design is actual mortality (again the survivor problem), which will affect the older cohorts more strongly than it will the younger cohorts (except perhaps during a war period). A second problem is that this design is subject to panel attrition apart from differential mortality. Whether this attrition is related to cohort membership is unclear, but in general we would expect it to be. Finally, there is a design imbalance, so that the effects of age, period and cohort in an accounting model have the usual dependency problems associated with estimated parameters in unbalanced models. The linear dependence or identification problem also remains.

3.6. Staggered Prospective Multiple Cohort Studies

This design is similar to the preceding one except that each cohort is initiated at the same age, with subsequent follow-ups at regular intervals, as illustrated in Figure 6.

Figure 6. Staggered Prospective Multiple-Cohort Study

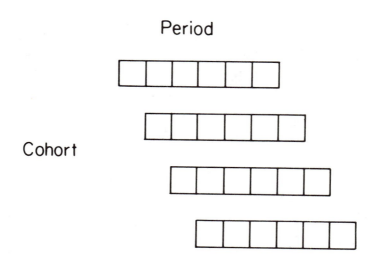

The advantage of this longitudinal design relative to the previous one is that all cohorts are observed the same number of times. Unfortunately this means that periods are unbalanced, and if their effects matter this design will not be optimal. The design suffers from the potential effects of panel attrition but not the effects of differential cohort mortality, unless something major happens to the environment (such as war or the discovery of the fountain of youth). The major disadvantage of this design is its cost in both time and money. As a consequence there are few good examples to point to. What is typically required is a major government data collection effort such as that associated with the National Assessment of Educational Progress sponsored by the U.S. Department of Education. Those data have thus far not been examined from the APC perspective, however.

4. APC ACCOUNTING MODELS

As used by a wide variety of investigators, the APC model is typically applied to a data array in the form of a cross-classification of age by period, or cohort by period or cohort by age. The same APC parameterization can be applied interchangeably to each of these three arrays—each containing the same information. For specificity we assume here the multiple cross-section design of Section 3.3, and deal with an age by period or $I \times J$ array, where the spacing of the I age categories is equal to the inter-period differences. Thus the $K = I+J-1$ diagonals of the array correspond to birth cohorts.

The basic APC model focusses on some parameter associated with a response variable, Y, e.g.,

$$\theta = E(Y), \tag{2}$$

where E denotes the expectation operator and Y is treated as a continuous random variable, or

$$\theta = \log(p/(1 - p)), \tag{3}$$

where $p = \Pr(Y = 1)$ if Y is a dichotomous random variable. The model then expresses θ as a linear function of age, period, and cohort effects (α's for ages, π's for periods, γ's for cohorts), i.e.,

$$\theta_{ijk} = f(\alpha_i, \pi_j, \gamma_k) = \mu + \alpha_i + \pi_j + \gamma_k, \tag{4}$$

subject to the restrictions

$$\sum_{i=1}^{I} \alpha_i = \sum_{j=1}^{J} \pi_j = \sum_{k=1}^{K} \gamma_k = 0, \tag{5}$$

with $K = I+J-1$. The k-subscript, which indexes cohorts, is of course redundant but we include it here in the specification to remind us of the symmetry of age, period, and cohort in the model. The linear restrictions in (5) represent an arbitrary choice on our part, and any other of the standard ANOVA-like conventions, such as setting the effects of the first levels of the variables equal to zero, would suffice. When the APC model was first introduced, investigators realized that the model could not be made more complex by the introduction of *unrestricted* interaction terms of the form $(\alpha\gamma)_{ik}$ given the terms already present in (4). Yet much of the discussion in the cohort literature focusses qualitatively on just such interactions, e.g., cohort-specific age effects. It is possible to introduce restricted forms of interaction, and we do so in Section 5.

To complete the specification of the APC model of expressions (4) and (5) we need to do something about the linear components of the effects. Since

$$\text{Cohort} = \text{Period} - \text{Age},$$

the *linear* component of any one set of *effects* is either the sum or the difference of the linear *components* of the other two sets of effects. This is known as the APC "identification problem." Given the specification of (4) and (5), the nonlinear components of the effects of age, period and cohort are identifiable—even if the linear components are not.

When the specification of expression (4), developed here for use with multiple cross-sections, is used for longitudinal studies, the same identification problems remain. That is, panel data and multiple cross-sections are equally informative about the parameters of the APC accounting model. But since panel data allow the modelling of flows as well as stocks, investigators working with such data should be able to develop a richer class of models than the APC accounting models discussed here.

It has been suggested that the crudeness of the age and cohort classification scheme used in the multiple cross-section $I \times J$ array leads to the APC identification problem (Winsborough, 1976). There are two ways to think about this suggestion. First, we can think of one of the classifications in the data array being made more refined while leaving the other classification as is. For example, we might envision use of a finer age gradient, while keeping the period gradient constant and less refined. Fienberg and Mason (1978) consider this case, and point out that not only does the original identification problem remain, but an additional one is also created. If it is supposed that the period classification is made more refined, doing nothing to the age classification, it is possible that the original identification problem is solved, but this can only be due to a loss in ability to track individuals through time correctly. Thus, either the identification problem is not solved, or it is solved at the expense of creating an even bigger problem.

A second way to use the suggestion is to think in terms of continuous age, period, and cohort measurements. We do this below. Of course, cohort membership defined as an instantaneous event runs counter to the typical social science use of the term. We entertain this definition only to explore the implication of continuity.

Reformulating expression (4) in terms of continuous age (A), period (P), and cohort (C) gives

$$\theta_{APC} = f(A, P, C), \tag{6}$$

where

$$C = P - A, \tag{7}$$

and f is taken as a polynomial in A, P, and C. Thus, for example, the second-order or "response surface" APC model becomes

$$\theta_{APC} = \beta_0 + \beta_1 A + \beta_2 P + \beta_3 C + \beta_{11} A^2 + \beta_{12} AP$$
$$+ \beta_{22} P^2 + \beta_{12} AC + \beta_{23} PC + \beta_{33} C^2. \tag{8}$$

Here the β's are regression-like effect parameters.

Does this reformulation solve the identification problem? The answer is no, because the basic linear identification problem, associated with expression (7), remains. Indeed, we now must ask if the second-order effects are identifiable. Using expression (7) we have

$$C^2 = P^2 + A^2 - 2AP, \tag{9}$$

$$CP = P^2 - AP, \tag{10}$$

$$CA = AP - A^2. \tag{11}$$

Thus, only three of the six second-order coefficients can be identified, and if we choose to resolve this identification problem by focussing on the effects of A^2, P^2, and C^2 we can not pick up interaction effects at the second-order level (see Heckman and Robb, 1985, this volume).

Alternatively, eliminating the squared terms will allow estimation of the second-order interactions, but the two alternatives are equivalent. Thus, the choice between

$$\theta_{APC} = \beta_0 + \beta_1 A + \beta_2 P + \beta_3 C + \beta_{11} A^2 + \beta_{22} P^2 + \beta_{33} C^2 \qquad (12)$$

and

$$\theta_{APC} = \beta_0 + \beta_1 A + \beta_2 P + \beta_3 C + \beta_{12} AP + \beta_{13} AC + \beta_{23} PC \qquad (13)$$

must depend on information external to the analysis.

There is a related point here, which has more, perhaps, to do with parsimony than it does with questions of identification. Suppose we use the following model

$$\theta_{APC} = \beta_0 + \beta_1 A + \beta_2 P + \beta_3 C + \beta_{11} A^2 + \beta_{22} P^2 + \beta_{33} C^2. \qquad (14)$$

This model reflects an initial choice to give precedence to C^2, P^2 and A^2 over AP, AC and CP. Use of the model does not necessarily mean that we think the linear by linear interactions are unimportant, but could as well reflect our triage system for the identification problem. With a bit of luck, we might discover upon estimation that the coefficients for $-C^2$, P^2 and A^2 were essentially equal. Then expression (9) shows that we could replace (14) by

$$\theta_{APC} = \beta_0 + \beta_1 A + \beta_2 P + \beta_3 C + \beta_{12} AP, \qquad (15)$$

which has a linear by linear interaction term. Model (15) is simpler than model (14), has been arrived at from a consideration of parsimony, and shifts the interpretation from a purely "additive" to an interactive one by recasting the meaning of nonlinearity in this instance. Here, as elsewhere, the more parsimonious representation is helpful to the extent that results obtained with it are interpretable. We point out the potential for translation from (14) to (15) because even here, where we place so much stress on the use of external information to make decisions concerning identifying restrictions, it is still worthwhile to bear in mind the possible gains in clarity that an explicit concern for parsimony can yield.

When we choose θ_{APC} to be an mth-order polynomial in A, P, and C, at the mth-level there are

$$\binom{m + 2}{m} = \frac{(m + 2)(m + 1)}{2}$$

regression coefficients, of which $m+1$ are estimable. Only three of these are powers: A^m, P^m and C^m. For this reason $m-2$ mth-order interaction terms will be estimable as well (for $m > 2$). Thus, while the polynomial approach does not eliminate the identification problem, it does suggest a way to get at higher-order interactions. We discuss this approach further in Section 5.

Finally, continuing with the polynomial approach, when θ_{APC} is the *sum* of an $(I-1)$th-order polynomial in A, a $(J-1)$th-order polynomial in P, and a $(K-1)$th-order polynomial in C, i.e.,

$$\theta_{APC} = f_A(A) + f_P(P) + f_C(C), \tag{16}$$

we can use expression (16) interchangeably with expression (4) in analyzing the usual multiple cross-section data array (Winsborough, 1976).

5. EXTENDING THE APC MODEL
TO INCLUDE INTERACTIONS

An implicit message in Ryder's (1965, and reprinted in this volume) distinguished paper, and an explicit message in Glenn's (1976) discussion, is that for many, perhaps most, problems it is desirable to include age-cohort or other interactions. Fienberg and Mason (1978) touch on this matter and conclude that inclusion of such interactions will require even more identifying restrictions (see also the discussion in Section 4). Although virtually all of the APC modelling to date has assumed that the inclusion of interaction terms is not possible, and our earlier paper (Fienberg and Mason, 1978) suggests the same, it *is possible* to extend the basic APC model to include interactions.

To understand why such a possibility exists, we continue considering an $I \times J$, age by period array. Were we to fit an additive age-period model there would be $(I-1)(J-1)$ degrees of freedom (d.f.) for assessing the fit of the model. As noted by Fienberg and Mason (1978), the inclusion of a set of cohort effects in this kind of model is a way to get a simple and parsimonious description of age by period interactions. For the APC model of expression (4) there are an additional $I+J-2$ cohort parameters (taking into account the linear constraint in (5)), and one unidentifiable linear effect, leaving

$$(I - 1)(J - 1) - (I + J - 2) - 1 = (I - 2)(J - 2)$$

d.f. for assessing fit.[3] Clearly, then, there must be room for modelling age by period interaction effects over and above the effects captured by cohorts. Similarly, if we view period effects as simple and parsimonious descriptions of age by cohort interaction effects, then the $(I-2)(J-2)$ residual d.f. must leave room for the modelling of additional age by cohort effects over and above the effects captured by period.

To date we have conceived of four different strategies for extending the APC model to include additional interaction effects. Three of these are suggested in part by the polynomial version of the APC model discussed in Section 4, while the fourth is in the spirit of the examination of residuals for a small number of outliers.

5.1. Polynomial Models

Recall from Section 4 that for continuous age, period, and cohort variables our model takes the form of expression (6) subject to the restriction of expression (7). In addition, imposing the linear restriction embodied in expression (16), there are three second-order polynomial terms (A^2, P^2, and C^2), and we have noted that their inclusion prevents us from including in an identifiable way the other three second-order terms (AP, AC, and PC).

In general, for the mth-order model there are $m+1$ identifiable terms at the mth level, and the model in expression (16) uses only three of these. Thus, at the mth-order there are potentially $m-2$ d.f. available for modelling interaction terms (see the related discussion in Heckman and Robb, 1984, this volume; an earlier version of their paper stimulated the preparation of this section).

Suppose we wish to model age by cohort interactions. At the mth-order there are $m-1$ such terms:

$$AC^{m-1}, A^2C^{m-2}, ... , A^{m-1}C.$$

---

[3] For the basic APC model we require that $\min(I,J) \geqslant 3$ for there to be residual d.f. with which to assess the fit of the model.

Since

$$(A + C)^m = P^m,$$

only $m-2$ of these will be identifiable, and it is in a sense arbitrary which we think of ourselves as excluding. For the present discussion, we adopt the convention that the coefficient of $A^{m-1}C$ equals zero.[4] Thus, *we can use up* the residual $m-2$ d.f. at the mth level by adding in all age by cohort interaction terms at that level, subject to an identifying restriction.

To adopt this approach in practice we could proceed hierarchically, first adding in age by cohort terms of the third order, then the terms of the fourth order, etc. Thus we would replace (16) by

$$\theta_{APC} = f_A(A) + f_P(P) + f_C(C) + f_m(A,C), \tag{17}$$

where $f_m(A,C)$ is a polynomial which includes all age by cohort interaction terms up to the m-th order. For $m = 3$ this model uses $m-2 = 1$ extra d.f., and thus $I \geq 4$ is required for there to be any residual d.f. for assessing the fit of the model, and for a third-order interaction model to have meaning. Similarly, for $m = 4$ the model uses 3 extra d.f. and we require that $I \geq 5$, and $J \geq 4$ if $I = 5$, to assess the fit of the model.

A second approach to fitting such polynomial interaction terms for age by cohort is to single out those interaction terms that involve a linear component of age, i.e.,

$$AC^2, AC^3, \ldots, AC^{K-1}.$$

Thus, instead of (17) we employ

$$\theta_{APC} = f_A(A) + f_P(P) + f_C(C) + \beta_{133}AC^2$$
$$+ \beta_{1333}AC^3 + \ldots + \beta_{13\ldots3}AC^{K-1}. \tag{18}$$

This model uses up the extra d.f. at the third-order level, and one extra d.f. at each order up to $K-1$. The d.f. associated with (18) are

---

[4] This is arbitrary, and similar to fixing $\beta_3 = 0$ in equation (8) to resolve the linear identification problem. Clearly, the resulting parameter estimates make sense only if this identification choice is grounded in substance. On the other hand, our estimates of the θ's will be the same no matter which convention we adopt to deal with this new identification problem at the mth order, and we can use an arbitrary convention to get an indication of the importance of the mth-order age by cohort interaction terms.

$$(I - 2)(J - 2) - (I + J - 3) = (I - 3)(J - 3) - 2,$$

and we require that $\min(I,J) \geq 4$.

To the model of expression (18) we might also add a set of age by period interaction terms that involve a linear component of age:

$$\beta_{122}AP^2 + \beta_{1222}AP^3 + \ldots + \beta_{12\ldots2}AP^{J-1} . \tag{19}$$

This would use up an extra $J-2$ d.f., leaving

$$(I - 4)(J - 3) - 3$$

d.f. for assessing goodness-of-fit. To do this requires $I \geq 5$ and $J \geq 4$. In order to be successful in this approach, leaving enough d.f. to assess the fit of our model, we need a relatively large data array.

5.2. Polynomial Models with Induced Metrics

One way to take advantage of the models introduced in the preceding subsection without using too many d.f. is to use a metric or set of numerical scores for one of the accounting dimensions. Suppose for example that, on the basis of prior or external information, the score v_i is assigned to the ith category of age. Then we can replace $f_A(A)$ in (16) by αv_i for the ith category of age, and use

$$\beta_{13}v_iC + \beta_{133}v_iC^2 + \beta_{1333}v_iC^3 + \ldots + \beta_{13\ldots3}v_iC^{K-1} \tag{20}$$

and

$$\beta_{122}v_iP^2 + \beta_{1222}v_iP^3 + \ldots + \beta_{12\ldots2}v_iP^{J-1} \tag{21}$$

for the age by cohort and age by period interaction components. This model is in the spirit of that given by expression (18) with (19) added to the right-hand side. It finesses the linear identification problem by inducing a nonlinear metric on age, and gains us $I-2$ d.f. By dropping the quadratic term in age, however, we have open 1 d.f. at the second order, and thus we have added the term $\beta_{13}v_iC$ to the front end of expression (20) and used an extra d.f. The d.f. for assessing goodness-of-fit have therefore increased by $I-3$, to

$$(I - 4)(J - 3) - 3 + (I - 3) = (I - 4)(J - 2) - 2.$$

The critical feature of such an approach is that external information must be used to develop the induced metric.

Johnson (1985) employs the approach just outlined in an analysis of age-specific marital fertility schedules. His induced metric for age rests heavily on the "assumption that marital fertility has a regular age pattern in all human populations," and he derives a set of $\{v_i\}$ based on the work of Coale and Trussell (1974). We give Johnson's values for $\{v_i\}$ in Table 2, together with his data, which consist of counts of the observed number of births (b_{ijk}) and the total number of expected births under natural fertility (n_{ijk}) for $I = 12$ two-year age groups and $J = 4$ two-year periods.

Johnson assumes that the $\{b_{ijk}\}$ are realized values of independent Poisson random variables with means $\{m_{ijk}\}$. He models

$$\theta_{ijk} = \log (m_{ijk}/n_{ijk}), \tag{22}$$

where the specification for the $\{\theta_{ijk}\}$ is as described above. If we take the $\{n_{ijk}\}$ as fixed (known) positive scale factors, then expression (22) can be written as a loglinear model for the $\{m_{ijk}\}$:

$$\log m_{ijk} = \log n_{ijk} + \theta_{ijk}, \tag{23}$$

where the $\{n_{ijk}\}$ are used as "offsets" or initial values in an iterative maximum likelihood calculation (Haberman, 1978, pp. 124–133).

Since $I = 12$ and $J = 4$ for the data in Table 2, the final model (equation (19)) of the preceding subsection has only 5 d.f., whereas the model just described with added interaction terms given by expressions (20) and (21) has 14 d.f. This model fits the data well ($G^2 = 17.3$ with 14 d.f.), as does the basic APC model of expression (14), with $f_A(A)$ replaced by αv_i for the ith category of age ($G^2 = 33.1$ with 29 d.f.). Comparing likelihood ratio statistics we find

$$\Delta G^2 = 33.1 - 17.3 = 15.8$$

with 15 d.f., and thus have a basis for settling on the original APC specification as modified by the induced metric on age. In fact, the age-cohort model (with no period effects) fits the data extremely well.

5.3. Tukey 1 d.f. Models and Their Generalizations

The approaches for the inclusion of interactions described up to this point are based on 1 d.f. interaction components added to the basic APC model, and depend on interactions defined explicitly by nonlinear combinations of age, period or cohort. It is also possible to define 1 d.f. interactions which structure *main effects*. Models whose interaction

Table 2. Induced Metric for Age Categories, and Age by Period
Display of Observed and Expected Births under Natural
Fertility (in parentheses) from Davao, Philippines
Sample Surveys as Given by Johnson (1985)

Age Group	Age Metric (v_j)	Period			
		1971–72	1973–74	1975–76	1977–78
20–21	−0.02	269 (301)	261 (288)	151 (202)	79 (100)
22–23	−0.08	405 (471)	329 (383)	218 (286)	157 (178)
24–25	−0.13	411 (490)	389 (514)	282 (330)	167 (236)
26–27	−0.28	342 (430)	302 (466)	312 (406)	161 (236)
28–29	−0.41	328 (462)	261 (397)	186 (334)	171 (283)
30–31	−0.56	305 (452)	217 (405)	133 (276)	120 (223)
32–33	−0.72	254 (435)	214 (385)	145 (287)	91 (184)
34–35	−0.86	224 (383)	180 (376)	113 (264)	66 (186)
36–37	−1.00	163 (271)	142 (311)	124 (252)	52 (173)
38–39	−1.14	104 (228)	98 (297)	78 (195)	59 (159)
40–41	−1.28	80 (171)	75 (158)	36 (111)	31 (103)
42–43	−1.42	40 (100)	32 (98)	23 (74)	17 (51)

components amount to a structuring of main effects have their origins in a test for interaction devised by Tukey (1949) for two-way ANOVA without replicates.

Within the APC framework, a natural analogue to the Tukey 1 d.f. model might be, for example, one which structures interactions between age and cohort in terms of the age and cohort main effects, in the following way:

$$\theta_{ijk} = \mu + \alpha_i + \pi_j + \gamma_k + \delta\alpha_i\gamma_k. \tag{24}$$

This model introduces a single new parameter, δ, for interactions between age and cohort, and thus has $(I-2)(J-2)-1$ d.f.

Expression (24) can be thought of as arising from latent constructs for age and cohort. Suppose there are unmeasured variables $U(A)$ and $U(C)$ associated with age and cohort effects, respectively. Further suppose that $U(A) \neq A$ and $U(C) \neq C$ (otherwise there is no point to this formulation), where A and C are given their usual scoring in sequential (A) and calendar (C) time. If we actually had measurements on $U(A)$ and $U(C)$ we could fit

$$\theta_{ijk} = \mu + \eta U(A) + \xi U(C) + \pi_j + \lambda U(A) U(C). \tag{25}$$

This would amount to an instance of the polynomial approach with an induced metric, discussed earlier. Substituting α_i's for $\eta U(A)$ and γ_k's for $\xi U(C)$ in (25) yields

$$\theta_{ijk} = \mu + \alpha_i + \pi_j + \gamma_k + \frac{\lambda(\alpha_i\gamma_k)}{\eta\xi}. \tag{26}$$

Thus we recover model (26) if we set

$$\delta = \frac{\lambda}{\eta\xi},$$

and δ differs from λ only by arbitrary scale factors for $U(A)$ and $U(C)$. Thus δ can be interpreted as the linear effect of the multiplicative term involving the two unmeasured age and cohort constructs.

The notion of cohort trajectories provides another way of understanding the model given by expression (24). Following a suggestion by O.D. Duncan, suppose we look at the quantities

$$\omega_{ijk} = \theta_{ijk} - \theta_{i-1,j-1,k} \tag{27}$$

for $2 \leq i \leq I$ for the kth cohort. These quantities describe the successive first-differences or the trajectory for this cohort. Under the basic APC model of expression (4), we get

$$\omega_{ijk} = (\alpha_i - \alpha_{i-1}) + (\pi_j - \pi_{j-1})$$

$$= \Delta\alpha_i + \Delta\pi_j, \tag{28}$$

where the Δ's denote first-differences. For this simplest case, the description of trajectory is independent of cohort, as it must be given the "additive" nature of the model. When we substitute in (27) for the model given by expression (24), however, we get

$$\omega_{ijk} = \Delta\alpha_i + \Delta\pi_j + \delta(\Delta\alpha_i)\gamma_k. \tag{29}$$

In (29) the effects of cohort on trajectory enter into the model for the $\{\omega_{ijk}\}$ explicitly in the form of a reduced-parameter version of the interaction between age and cohort. That is, the contribution of age to the trajectory of each cohort differs in a constrained way across cohorts.

On first encounter the Tukey 1 d.f. approach may appear artificial, perhaps because of the rationale we have offered in terms of a linkage between main effects and unmeasured constructs. This is probably a consequence of unfamiliarity. Although we would not claim the universal applicability of the Tukey 1 d.f. approach, the linkage between main effect and unmeasured variable may be just what the analyst wants in situations where use of an APC model is contemplated. In these cases, the analyst typically does not have available measures of the variables presumed to underlie age, period or cohort differences. In addition, variables which are merely linear transformations of scaled A, P or C provide little analytic leverage. But the analyst may well have an unmeasured process in mind which is reflected in a hypothesized pattern of main effects. Thus, there are undoubtedly situations in which the extension of the Tukey 1 d.f. approach to the APC modelling context may be quite suitable.

We could go further than the 1 d.f. interaction model of expression (24), by assuming a multiplicative age by cohort interaction where the age and cohort parameters in the interaction are different from those in the basic model, i.e.,

$$\theta_{ijk} = \mu + \alpha_i + \pi_j + \gamma_k + \phi_i\psi_k. \tag{30}$$

In this instance we use the data to induce metrics on the ordered age and cohort categories, in order to allow the variables so scaled to interact multiplicatively. This approach uses up $2I+J-4$ extra d.f. (not just 1 d.f.) and the model thus has $(I-3)(J-4)-12$ d.f. Fitting such a model requires a truly large data array. For example, we could not apply the model to the data of Table 2, even if we had an additional period.

For counted data where θ_{ijk} represents the log expected value as in expression (23) or the log-odds or logit as in expression (3), Chuang (1980) describes a modification of the Newton-Raphson procedure that can be used to estimate parameter values for these models.[5]

5.4. Using Dummy Variables to Adjust for Outliers

In assessing the fit of the APC model to a set of data we want to look at not only summary measures but also standardized residuals, say of the form

$$r_{ijk} = \frac{Y_{ijk} - \hat{\theta}_{ijk}}{\text{estimated S.E. } (Y_{ijk} - \hat{\theta}_{ijk})} \qquad (31)$$

In some cases, a poor fit of the APC model will be reflected by large standardized residuals (either positive or negative) for several cells. In others, one or two residuals will stand out.

Suppose the residual for cell (i,j) is very large, and thus is thought of as an "outlier." Then we could set that cell aside and fit the APC model to the remaining ones. This is equivalent to using up 1 d.f. for a dummy variable associated with cell (i,j), and is yet another way to introduce interaction into the basic model.

The dummy variable approach for outliers can be used to deal with more than one discrepant cell either by introducing a dummy variable for each outlier, by using a single dummy variable for several outliers whose residuals from the APC model are of similar size or by using other criteria for grouping cells. Mason and Smith (1985) use external information to define an indicator variable, closely related to a dummy, whose inclusion substantially improves the fit of their model in an analysis of tuberculosis mortality. The outliers in this instance reflect the government's shifting of

---

[5] For extensions, generalization and discussions of the Tukey 1 d.f. model in conventional ANOVA see Johnson and Graybill (1972), Mandel (1969, 1971), and Cook (1975).

healthy civilian men into the armed forces during World War II while screening tubercular cases from entry into the military, which led to artifactual increases in tuberculosis mortality for younger men in the civilian population during the 1940s. Mason and Smith deal with this phenomenon by constructing an age-period interaction term which is one outside the affected age-period groups, and otherwise takes on values reflecting the decrease in the civilian population base for each affected age group during World War II. Thus, these authors use a single degree of freedom to draw into the model a "nuisance" phenomenon which cuts across several outlier cells. The justification for a procedure such as this is enhanced by *a priori* substantive understanding of the problem, as usual.

In assessing the fit of the basic APC model we have noted previously that the fitted values $\{\hat{\theta}_{ijk}\}$ remain the same no matter how we choose to resolve the linear identification problem, provided that we do not resort to over-identification. The standardized residuals are likewise unaffected by the resolution of the identification problem. Indeed, no linear restriction whatsoever is required to obtain fitted values and residuals (Fienberg and Mason, 1978, p. 18).

6. DISCUSSION

We have ranged from broad gauged discussion of perspectives to the narrowly statistical. What have we accomplished?

To begin with, we have attempted to provide a framework in which to think about the various purposes to which APC modelling and quantitative cohort analysis in general can be put. Our conclusion is that quantitative cohort analysis can be used for a variety of purposes, including the extremes of descriptions embedded in historical settings and inferences about social mechanisms thought to exert their forces indefinitely.

Second, we have suggested that although cohorts are often thought of as groups, a cohort perspective ideally involves two or more levels of conceptualization to flesh out the framework. An empirical realization of a multilayered framework is difficult to achieve, but remains a worthy goal for the conceptual clarity it can promote.

Third, we have shown that, given a multilevel framework in which connections are established between macro forces and individual actors, it is possible to assess the impact of data aggregation in terms of coefficient bias. In general, the commonly intuited connotation of "grouped" data is misleading. There is not necessarily a direct mapping between the conceptual units of analysis and the refinement inherent in a particular degree of data aggregation. At best aggregation amounts to a compact data storage and presentation device, at worst to a roadblock which can not be bypassed.

Fourth, different kinds of data structures can be used for different cohort analytic approaches. We have reviewed and characterized these structures.

Fifth, we have shown that the identification problem in APC models is not due to crudeness of measurement. It remains even when measurement of age, period and cohort is infinitely refined in calendar and sequential time.

Lastly, we have described four ways to extend APC models to include interactions beyond those represented by one of the accounting dimensions, given the presence of the other two.

We were led to formulate a view on the scope of quantitative cohort analysis because few cohort analysts make their own stance clear in the course of their research. This omission can only add to the difficulties in rendering judgments as to the appropriateness and adequacy of the model chosen. Critics of cohort analyses rarely have clear ideas of the intellectual needs which motivate their assessments, and can hardly be expected to supply goals left unstated in the work they examine. We hope that our views on scope and purpose will be found workable by others, or revised until they become helpful, so that empirical quantitative cohort analytic studies can be both carried out and evaluated productively.

We introduced the idea of multilevel analysis into the discussion for two reasons. First, it is well known that a goodly supply of data, when combined with access to a computer, creates an almost irresistible urge to carry out statistical manipulations. Many such urges have been satisfied by fitting APC models. Doubtless every statistical technique or approach receives its share of this kind of devotion. We have attempted to point to a minimum requirement for a conceptual framework to be used in association with an APC model, or, for that matter, any quantitative cohort model. The specification of a multilevel model is a formidable requirement; if followed it should offset the ease with which APC specifications can be identified, and it should lead to worthwhile substantive contributions. Koopmans' (1949) discussion of the need for substantive theory in connection with identifying restrictions in simultaneous equations models is equally applicable in the cohort, and specifically APC, modelling context.

A second reason for introducing the idea of multi-level analysis into the discussion of APC modelling is that there has been for some time confusion about the conceptual units of analysis in cohort studies, and the problem has been exacerbated by an awareness of data aggregation. We have exploited a two-level conception of variables, as well as a classification of types of explanatory variables, to trace the implications of data aggregation. The results are too detailed to recapitulate here, but we hope that a study of them will at least banish the mistaken association often made between "grouped" data and "group" models.

There were two reasons for discussing identification in "additive" APC models yet again. First, we wanted to show that an argument sometimes advanced in defense of APC specifications—that the identification "problem" would go away if only we had infinitely refined measurement of age, period and cohort, is just not correct. APC modelling must therefore be defended on other grounds. Second, it turned out that the line of attack used on the continuous variable representation of age, period and cohort was a suggestive one for the study of interactions above and beyond the "main effects" of age, period and cohort.

Finally, we presented the material on additional interactions in APC models because of the demand for the extension of the APC framework to deal with phenomena whose conceptualization may require more than "main effects" for age, period and cohort. The availability of a variety of approaches to interaction in the APC accounting framework disarms a major criticism, and could materially enhance the framework's usefulness.

Apart from the omission of interactions there have been a number of criticisms of APC modelling, and it may be useful to review them in light of the foregoing discussion.

One objection to APC specifications holds that the need to make an identifying restriction is evidence of the impossibility of the task. According to this view, age, period and cohort effects can not be separated because one of the accounting dimensions is a constrained interaction of the other two. As is well known, the variable which "carries" the interaction in a generalized linear model expression can not vary independently of its constituents. Thus, according to the argument, it makes no sense to construct a model in which age, period and cohort are thought to play separate explanatory roles, because no single dimension can vary by itself.

This view seems to assume that the user of an APC specification has no substantive hypotheses or theoretical model concerning the relevance or salience of cohort membership. It is literally true that cohort membership can not vary independently of age and period. In fact, the generalization of this point holds for interactions of any sort in any analysis of variance problem. One way of dealing with interaction, suited to many problems, is to view the response variable as a nonadditive combination of the explanatory variables. Another way to deal with interaction is to try to conceptualize the phenomenon in terms of other variables. This alternative can hardly be said to be inferior to the former approach. It is identical to the approach with which APC specifications allow and are consistent. Following this approach, one begins with conceptualization and attempts to move toward explicit measurement, in order to test understanding of the interaction. This is always a goal in APC specifications, if not always an attainable one. Insofar as the analyst does not reify the accounting categories, that is, does not make the mistake of thinking that each of the accounting dimensions is indistinguishable from its theoretical meaning for a specific substantive phenomenon, there is no logical impediment to APC modelling. It is true that some empirical analysts have failed to specify their substantive framework, but such errors should not be confused with the properties of the accounting framework itself.

A second objection to APC specifications holds that the "additive" APC model requires the analyst to *believe* that cohort contrasts, say, are constant over ages and periods. This is incorrect. There is a difference between attempting to work with an approximation of something more complex, and believing that the reality is actually the approximation. Nothing in the additive APC framework prevents the analyst from supposing that along the diagonals of an age by period array the interaction (i.e., cohort) coefficients vary. Rather, it suffices to suppose that whatever the within cohort variability, the differences between cohorts are meaningful. This is again a common stance in analysis of variance. Rare is the data set—and much cherished for classroom illustrations—which exhibits perfect additivity. As long as the departures from additivity satisfy certain conditions (e.g., not "too" large, and no pattern to them), we are usually satisfied with the approximation provided by the additive model in the typical $r \times c$ case. Likewise, when we work with an interaction model for a multiway problem, we often choose to ignore certain higher-order interactions. This is the same point all over again: We are working with an approximation.

A third objection to APC specifications, touched on above, contends not only that they are inherently additive, but also that additive APC specifications are generally uninteresting, or at most of interest in particular substantive areas (e.g., demography). Regrettably, we have in the past contributed to the view that APC models are inherently additive, but have taken the opportunity here to clarify the possibilities and provide new results which show that it is not necessary to restrict one's attention to purely additive APC models. Whether additive APC specifications are of limited use, or of use in certain fields but not in others, is of course separate from the presumed unavailability of interactions in the accounting framework. The claims of limitation are certainly untested empirically. Moreover, given the depth of substantive reasoning we espouse for the application of the accounting framework, we do not soon expect to see a compelling disquisition showing that additive APC specifications are generally less helpful than interactive ones, or that certain substantive areas are better suited than others to additivity. The connections between theory and research seem too complex to validate such conclusions.

A fourth objection to APC specifications is that they are atheoretical and should be eschewed in favor of models which replace the accounting dimensions with measured variables. The charge that APC specifications are atheoretical is incorrect, as we have already discussed. Particular analyses may be atheoretical, but that is not a function of the framework. Moreover, the use of measured variables is hardly a guarantee of the presence of theory. This objection is also unreasonable in its insistence on the use of measured variables when there are clearly so many instances where measures of any sort are seemingly impossible to find. Nevertheless, as we have said before, the use of measured variables is an important goal for any research involving quantitative cohort analysis.

The use of available information is always appropriate as an objective.

We have tried to clear away the underbrush of misconceptions which has surrounded the use of APC specifications. For those who would use them we urge attention to the caution that considerable substantive reasoning must be brought to bear *prior* to data analysis. For those who would argue that the accounting framework is inherently meaningless, we have tried to show that the arguments we are aware of are invalid. APC specifications can not be applied willy-nilly, but they can be used to adjudicate between compatible reduced models, to estimate full specifications when there is justification, and particularly when indicators of the substantive phenomena which underlie the accounting dimensions are lacking. Any quantitative cohort analysis is a form of time-series analysis. As such, the development and estimation of a cohort model requires sensitivity and delicacy; this has been underlined for us by the empirical work of Mason and Smith (this volume). The APC accounting framework is not something one needs to be "for" or "against." It is, rather, a framework that can be used when alternatives are unavailable or less appealing.

REFERENCES

Atkinson, A.C. (1970). A method for discriminating between models. *Journal of the Royal Statistical Society, Series B* **32**, 323–353.

Brown, B.W., Jr. (1978). Statistics, scientific method and smoking, in J.M. Tanur *et al. Statistics: A Guide to the Unknown*, Second Edition. San Francisco: Holden-Day, pp. 59–70.

Carr-Hill, R.A., Hope, K., and Stern, N. (1972). Delinquent generations revisited. *Quality and Quantity* **6**, 327–352.

Chuang, J-L. C. (1980). Analysis of categorical data with ordered categories. Ph.D. Dissertation. Minneapolis-St. Paul: School of Statistics, University of Minnesota.

Coale, A.J. and Trussell, T.J. (1974). Model fertility schedules: Variations in the age structure of childbearing in human populations. *Population Index* **40**, 185–257.

Cook, R.D. (1975). Analysis of interactions. Unpublished manuscript, Minneapolis-St. Paul: School of Statistics, University of Minnesota.

Cox, D.R. (1961). Tests of separate families of hypotheses, in Vol. 1 of
    J. Neyman (ed.), *Fourth Berkeley Symposium on Mathematical Statistics
    and Probability*. Berkeley, California: University of California Press,
    pp. 105–123.

Easterlin, R. (1961). The American baby boom in historical perspective.
    American Economic Review **51**, 869–911.

Easterlin, R. (1978). What will 1984 be like? Socioeconomic implications
    of recent twists in age structure. *Demography* **15**, 397–432.

Farkas, G. (1977). Cohort, age and period effects upon the employment
    of white females: Evidence for 1957–1968. *Demography* **14**, 843–861.

Featherman, D.L. and Hauser, R.M. (1975). Design for a replicate study
    of social mobility in the United States, in K. C. Land and S. Spilerman
    (eds.), *Social Indicator Models*. New York: Russell Sage Foundation,
    pp. 219–251.

Fienberg, S.E. and Mason, W.M. (1978). Identification and estimation of
    age-period-cohort models in the analysis of discrete archival data, in
    K. F. Schuessler (ed.), *Sociological Methodology 1979*. San Francisco:
    Jossey-Bass, pp. 1–67.

Glenn, N.D. (1976). Cohort analysts' futile quest: Statistical attempts to
    separate age, period and cohort effects. *American Sociological Review*
    41, 900–904.

Greenberg, B.G., Wright, J.J., and Sheps, C.G. (1950). A technique for
    analyzing some factors affecting the incidence of syphilis. *Journal of
    the American Statistical Association* **251**, 373–399.

Haberman, S.J. (1978). *Analysis of Qualitative Data. Vol. 1: Introductory
    Topics*. New York: Academic Press.

Hartley, H.O., Sielken, R.L. (1975). A "super-population viewpoint" for
    finite population sampling. *Biometrics* **31**, 411–422.

Heckman, J. and Robb, R. (1985). Using longitudinal data to estimate
    age, period and cohort effects in earnings equations. This volume.

International Statistical Institute (1975). *The World Fertility Survey: The
    First Three Years, January 1972–January 1975*. The Hague-Voorburg,
    Netherlands: International Statistical Institute.

Johnson, E.E. and Graybill, F.A. (1972). Analysis of a two-way model
    with interaction and no replication. *Journal of the American Statistical
    Association* **67**, 862–868.

Johnson, R.A. (1985). Analysis of age, period and cohort effects in
    marital fertility. This volume.

Koopmans, T.C. (1949). Identification problems in economic model
    construction. *Econometrica* **17**, 125–144.

Lazarsfeld, P.F. and Menzel, H. (1961). On the relation between individual and collective properties, in A. Etzioni (ed.), *Complex Organizations*. New York: Holt, Rinehart and Winston, pp. 422–440.

Mandel, J. (1969). The partitioning of interaction in analysis of variance. *Journal of Research of the National Bureau of Standards, B* **73B**, 4, 309–328.

Mandel, J. (1971). A new analysis of variance model for non-additive data. *Technometrics* **13**, 1–18.

Mare, R.D. (1979). Social background composition and educational growth. *Demography* **16**, 55–71.

Mason, W.M. (1980). Some statistics and methodology of multi-level analysis. Ann Arbor: Population Studies Center of the University of Michigan.

Mason, W.M. and Smith, H.L. (1985). Age-period-cohort analysis and the study of deaths from pulmonary tuberculosis. This volume.

Nesselroade, J.R. and Baltes, P.B. (1974). *Adolescent Personality Development and Historical Change*: 1970–1972. Monographs of the Society for Research in Child Development, **39** (1, Serial No. 154).

Pullum, T.W. (1977). Parameterizing age, period and cohort effects: An application to U.S. delinquency rates, 1964–1973, in K. F. Schuessler (ed.), *Sociological Methodology 1978*. San Francisco: Jossey-Bass, pp. 116–140.

Pullum, T.W. (1980). Separating age, period and cohort effects in white U.S. fertility, 1920–1970. *Social Science Research* **9**, 225–244.

Quandt, R.E. (1974). A comparison of methods for testing nonnested hypotheses. *Review of Economics and Statistics* **41**, 92–99.

Ryder, N.B. (1965). The cohort as a concept in the study of social change. *American Sociological Review* **30**, 843–861. Reprinted in this volume.

Smith, D.P. (1981). A reconsideration of Easterlin cycles. *Population Studies* **35**, 247–264.

Tukey, J. (1949). One degree of freedom for non-additivity. *Biometrics* **5**, 232–242.

United States Department of Health, Education and Welfare (1979). *Smoking and Health: A Report of the Surgeon General*. Washington, D.C.: Government Printing Office.

Winsborough, H.H. (1976). Discussion of "Identification and estimation of age, period and cohort effects in the analysis of discrete archival data" by S.E. Fienberg and Wm. M. Mason. *Proceedings of the Social Statistics Section*. Pt. 1. Washington, D.C.: American Statistical

Association, pp. 138–139.

Wolfgang, M. (1982). Delinquency and birth cohort: II. Paper presented at the annual meeting of the American Association for the Advancement of Science, Washington, D.C.

Wolfgang, M.E., Figlio, M., and Sellin, T. (1972). *Delinquency in a Birth Cohort.* Chicago: University of Chicago Press.

4. AGE, PERIOD, AND COHORT EFFECTS IN DEMOGRAPHY: A REVIEW*

John Hobcraft

Jane Menken

Samuel Preston[†]

1. AGE, PERIOD, AND COHORT SOURCES OF VARIATION IN DEMOGRAPHY

Narrowly defined, demography deals with the measurement of vital events (birth, death, and marriage) and migration, studies the factors that influence the rate at which those events occur, and, to a lesser extent, investigates the consequences of the patterns of these events. In this paper, we adopt this narrow definition of the field and consider only the first three events so that by limiting the scope of our review, we can examine these selected topics in detail.

In one way or another, demography has concerned itself with the measurement of age, period, and cohort effects for well over a century. The first social information to become available in time series with age detail was the number of deaths and births, information that dates back to the eighteenth century in Sweden and to the nineteenth century in most countries of Western Europe. These early statistics established with absolute clarity that vital rates varied enormously with age, and one of

* We would like to acknowledge valuable discussions with Walter Gilks, who has considerably clairifed our ideas on the subject. Work on this paper was supported in part by grant number HR 5739 from the Social Science Research Council of the United Kingdom and grant number 5-R01-11720 from the U.S. National Institutes of Health. This paper is reprinted from *Population Index* **48**(1), 4–43 (Spring 1982).

† John Hobcraft is affiliated with the London School of Economics, London, England, Jane Menken is affiliated with the Office of Population Research, Princeton University, and Samuel Preston is affiliated with the Population Studies Center, University of Pennsylvania.

the earliest analytic problems was how to "control" this variation in order to elucidate differences in rates between populations or over time. The early solutions to this problem were to develop summary measures that were independent of age composition—life expectancy, gross reproduction rate, and net reproduction rate—or to "standardize" rates by artificially imposing one population's age structure on another population. Comparisons based on these measures contain assumptions, almost always implicit, about the age, period, and cohort effects that underlie the observed data.

These simple algebraic techniques are still central in demographic curricula, and the measures have acquired a significance beyond their original purpose. These well-entrenched measures created a useful common lexicon for demography. However, they were developed before the era of high-speed computers and sophisticated multivariate techniques, and in a sense their currency may have made demographers less receptive than some other social scientists to newer developments.

Another reason for the demographer's somewhat different perspective is that many of the standard measures can be calculated from either period age-specific or cohort age-specific information. In the past, period-based calculations led demographers to conclusions and predictions that later experience proved wrong. As a result, the relationship of a period-specific measure to the remaining life experience of cohorts active in that period has become as compelling a question for demographers as is the delineation of age, period, and cohort effects.

The phrase "age, period, and cohort effects" is probably an unfortunate one. Ages, periods, and cohorts do not have either direct or indirect effects on demographic or social phenomena. Age is a surrogate—probably a very good one in most applications—for aging or more generally for physiological states, amount of exposure to certain social influences, or exposure to social norms. However, it is clear that individuals age physiologically and socially at different rates.[1] To understand the sources of variation in vital rates, it is more satisfactory wherever possible to measure the underlying variables for which age is a proxy. Indicators of period and cohort are much further removed from

---

[1] An interesting discussion of the many influences reflected in the age variable in studies of fertility may be found in Rindfuss and Bumpass (1978).

variables that presumably influence vital processes. "Period" is a poor proxy for some set of contemporaneous influences, and "cohort" is an equally poor proxy for influences in the past. Measured "effects" of periods and cohorts are thus measures of our ignorance: in particular, of whether the factors about which we are ignorant are more or less randomly distributed along chronologically measurable dimensions. When these factors can themselves be directly measured, there is no reason to probe for period or cohort effects. When the factors cannot be identified explicitly, it would seem that analysts probing for age, period, and cohort effects are, more precisely, partitioning observed variation to ages, periods, and cohorts.

Demographers' efforts to examine age, period, and cohort sources of variation have frequently taken the form of postulating mathematical models of age variation in vital events. The influence of periods and cohorts, where measured at all, is registered by allowing one or more parameters in the model to vary in intensity from period to period or cohort to cohort. There are three sound reasons for preoccupation with age models. First, because age is closely related to physiological state, biological models and reasoning can be used to provide predictions or theories of the way that age should be related to vital events. The biological theories, though of course inexact, nevertheless provide a firmer and more precise basis for prediction than do the primarily social theories that would relate to period or cohort. Second and more important, age is quite simply the most important source of variation in vital rates. At present, death rates vary among countries of the world by at most a factor of eight, and birth rates by at most a factor of five. On the other hand, death rates are more than one hundred times higher in the United States at ages 70–74 than at ages 10–14.[2] Proportionate age variation in fertility rates is even greater since many ages have zero rates. A third reason for emphasis on age models is that age data are subject to great error in most of the world, so that models of age variation, fitted to reported age data, can be used to "discipline" and correct reported figures.

---

[2] Figures for 1966 show death rates at ages 70–74 of 35.0/1,000 for females and 61.8/1,000 for males, compared with 0.31/1,000 and 0.5/1,000 at ages 10–14 (Keyfitz and Flieger, 1968).

Thus, no one would dispute the importance of age as an influence on demographic processes. Period effects also are evident from casual inspection of time series on fertility, mortality, marriage, and divorce. All (or many) ages tend to have similar patterns of rise and fall in vital rates from period to period, and the fact that the fluctuations often correspond to changes in social conditions that are expected to influence rates (e.g., wartime, changes in health technology, and economic recession) helps to confirm the importance of these influences even to the most skeptical observer. The real question about the applicability of age-period-cohort analysis to demography relates to the substantive importance of cohort influences. Do age patterns, for individuals who have the timing of an event (such as their birth or marriage) in common, respond only to period influences, so that the experience of a cohort can be described completely by age effects and the effects of the periods its members live through, or do they respond to additional, cohort influences as well? And, if so, how does the cohort influence manifest itself?

A related question is whether or not period effects are age-specific. If they are, the experience of a cohort is largely determined by those period influences that coincide with ages of greater or lesser susceptibility.

Demographers also have another, largely pragmatic and non-theoretical reason for considering period and cohort effects, which is their need for forecasting future trends in vital rates. If, especially over the short term, either period or cohort effects predominate, then one avenue for providing projections is to model the observed trend in these effects and continue it into the future.

Before considering in detail empirical examples attempting to identify the importance of cohort influences in demography, it is useful to review various theories of these influences that have structured the applications.

2. COHORT THEORIES IN DEMOGRAPHY

2.1. The Conventional Linear Model

Much of the relevant demographic work is based on the usual assumption that, either in the original or a transformed scale, the dependent variable is a linear function of age, period, and cohort effects; only the resolution of the problem of overidentification varies. The linear model is appropriate when a cohort has some unique susceptibility to the phenomenon in question, a susceptibility that is established by the time of initial observation and that manifests itself as a constant through the periods and ages of observation. The model appears in the classic work of Greenberg, Wright, and Sheps (1950) on syphilis and is also implicit in some of the earliest work on generation approaches to the projection of mortality (see especially Derrick, 1927, and Kermack, McKendrick, and McKinlay, 1934a,b). The model can be written as

$$f(r_{apc}) = W + W_a + W_p + W_c, \qquad (1)$$

where r_{apc} is the age-period-cohort specific rate, $f(\ )$ is a simple transformation (e.g., linear, logarithm, or logit), W is an overall constant, and W_a, W_p, and W_c are the effects for age group a, period p, and cohort c, respectively. The logit transformation is usually selected for demographic applications since it is the natural one to adopt for rates. The problems of estimating the parameters of this model are hardly unique to demographic studies and are treated elsewhere (e.g., Fienberg and Mason, 1978). One approach to these problems is suggested in the Appendix.

Here we note only that it is possible and sensible to view a constant-effect cohort model as fitting a particular model to the set of two-way interactions in the age-period dimensions. This can be visualized as follows for a 4 × 4 table where the age and period effects are indicated along the margins and the cohort effects appear as constants along the diagonals in the body of the table. Thus, if e_{ij} is an element of the table of residuals, $e_{ij} = c_k$ for i,j such that $k = j - i + 4$. The c_k are fitted to the residuals on the transformed scale under the age and period model.

2.2. Cohort-Inversion Models

An alternative model is conceptually far more common in demographic work, although rarely formally estimated. The basic and intuitively reasonable idea behind what will be referred to as cohort-inversion models is that cohorts experiencing particularly hard or good times early in life will respond inversely later in life. There are at least three types of cohort-inversion models. The first derives from an assumption that the

$$
\begin{array}{c|cccc}
 & P_1 & P_2 & P_3 & P_4 \\
\hline
a_1 & c_4 & c_5 & c_6 & c_7 \\
a_2 & c_3 & c_4 & c_5 & c_6 \\
a_3 & c_2 & c_3 & c_4 & c_5 \\
a_4 & c_1 & c_2 & c_3 & c_4 \\
\end{array}
$$

cohort is not homogeneous with respect to the occurrence of the marker event.

1. *Heterogeneous Susceptibility.* For mortality, this type of model corresponds to the theory of "impaired lives," which can be summarized as follows: a cohort is viewed as starting life with a distribution of susceptibility to mortality among its members; unfavorable health conditions early in life will eliminate the more susceptible and thus reduce cohort mortality later in life. This hypothesis was recently invoked in attempts to "explain" the slowdown or reversal of continued mortality decline in the 40 to 70 age range in many Western countries, by suggesting that the substantial mortality reductions that had occurred in childhood had led to the survival into adulthood of many more susceptible people, who succumbed more rapidly to the increased risks in later life. The resumption of substantial mortality declines in the United States and elsewhere has cast doubts upon the validity of these explanations, although the thesis is clearly a tenable one deserving further scrutiny (Vaupel, Manton, and Stallard, 1979). A similar hypothesis is plausible for divorce, with vulnerable marriages being weeded out from a cohort more rapidly when conditions are unfavorable in early marriage or when divorce is more socially acceptable (Preston and McDonald, 1979). Such a theory could be extended to migration from place of birth, where the more mobile in a cohort perhaps respond more readily to period-induced changes in underlying propensities to migrate. The transition from birth order i to birth order $i+1$ could be subject to the impaired-lives phenomenon through underlying differences in fecundity, fertility

control, and motivations, which are subject to period influences leading to a cohort-inversion phenomenon. In each case, for nonrenewable cohort processes, heterogeneity of response within the cohort may lead to the cohort-inversion phenomenon.

2. *Fixed and Changing Target Models.* A second type of cohort-inversion model has most often been suggested in fertility analyses. It is argued that individual cohorts of women have in mind some completed fertility target and that the timing of the achievement of this target is affected by period influences. For example, adverse conditions early in reproductive life that cause postponement of births may lead to an increase, or "catch-up" phenomenon, later in the childbearing period. Such theories have been used to account for the substantial rises in period total fertility after each world war and even for the rises in England and Wales during the years 1942 and 1943. Hajnal (1950a,b) explicitly set out to discover whether postponement was sufficient (although not necessary) to have brought about the rises in England and Wales and concluded that it was for 1942–1943 but that it could not entirely account for the peak in 1947.

Among the most consistent proponents of this cohort-target theory of fertility has been Ryder (1973, 1978). He proposes (1978) that, "couples are conceptualized as having both quantitative and temporal intentions with respect to childbearing. They intend a particular number of births and at a particular tempo... ." In a long series of articles (e.g., 1963, 1964, 1965a, 1965b, 1969, 1971, 1973, 1980), Ryder has argued that it is essential (or at least advisable) to analyze fertility for cohorts, especially if determinants are being studied, and that both the quantum and timing of fertility have to be interpreted as cohort variables, with timing often being distorted by period phenomena. Ryder (1953) and Lee (1977) have gone some way toward formalizing this type of model, including, in the latter, an elaboration of the impact of a constant target.

However, Westoff and Ryder (1977) conclude that the target intentions are not immutable. In their study, many women changed their reported intentions about family size over a five-year period. One interpretation "would be that the respondents failed to anticipate the extent to which times would be unpropitious for childbearing, that they made the understandable but frequently invalid assumption that the future would resemble the present—the same kind of forecasting error that demographers have often made. Perhaps the answers to questions about intentions are implicitly conditional: 'This is how I think I will behave if things stay the way they are now, but, if they don't I may change my mind.'" Recently, both Lee (1980) and Butz and Ward (1979) have moved toward formalization of this third type of cohort-inversion model, which incorporates the idea of changing targets. In their models, which will be reviewed more fully later in this paper, all couples are trying to attain a particular desired completed family size at each point in time, but this target changes from period to period.

Because models of this type are not usually treated within the general linear model framework, it seems useful to do so here.

For a renewable event, such as fertility, the ultimate or target total fertility for a particular cohort can be denoted by F_w^c, where w is the highest age considered, and the births achieved by age a by F_a^c. For a nonrenewable event (e.g., first marriage), the target can be defined as the proportion who will ever have the event, denoted by $1 - l_w^c$ (using life table notation with $l_0^c = 1$). The proportion of the cohort who have had the event by age a is denoted by $1 - l_a^c$. Models can be formed either in terms of the number of events remaining per person, E_a^c, given by $F_w^c - F_a^c$ or $l_a^c - l_w^c$, or the proportion remaining, R_a^c, given by $(F_w^c - F_a^c)/F_w^c$ or $(l_a^c - l_w^c)/(1 - l_w^c)$.

Then the extension of the linear model (1) to include fixed targets introduces an inventory-control mechanism of a sort, i.e.,

$$f'(r_{apc}) = v + v_a + v_p + v_c\, g'(E_a^c)$$

or   (2)

$$f''(r_{apc}) = u + u_a + u_p + u_c\, g''(R_a^c),$$

where f' and f'' are transformations of the rates and g' and g'' are transformations of the measure of distance from the target. The logit transformation, defined only for proportions, is not appropriate for g' but has certain advantages over a linear or logarithmic transformation for the other functions. Both the logarithmic and the logit formulations eliminate the possibility of estimating negative rates but would still be subject to the usual normalization constraints.

Since models of this type have received attention only rather recently, it is not surprising that a number of problems remain to be resolved. First, it should be noted that the value of F_w^c or l_w^c in (2) is regarded as known, so that some estimate is required if incomplete cohorts are not to be excluded from the analysis. Second, if it is assumed that the target fertility for a cohort is equal to its observed completed fertility, there are fitting problems. An alternative, less awkward formulation would allow fertility to fall short of or overshoot the target due to period-specific influences and would treat both F_w^c and I_w^c as unknown. Another problem is encountered if the early part of a cohort's experience is not observed. For example, if birth registration begins when cohort c is aged a, none of its fertility prior to age a can be observed. The detection of a cohort-inversion phenomenon then becomes difficult, if not impossible.

The specification of a cohort-inversion model with period-specific targets is a straightforward extension of (2) but introduces problems with some possible formulations that cannot handle achieved cohort fertility greater than the period taget. It is clearly only a first approximation for such models to assume homogeneity of the population with respect to targets, so that one direction for future work is the introduction of heterogeneity.

Several competing models have been suggested to attempt to capture the so-called cohort-inversion model. Because the theoretical underpinnings seem plausible, empirical tests of these alternatives and others not proposed here against real data are being carried out (e.g., Gilks and Hobcraft, 1980) for a few cases, and more tests would be valuable.

2.3. Continuously-Accumulating Cohort Effects

Cohort effects occur whenever the past history of individuals exerts an influence on their current behavior in a way that is not fully captured by an age variable. If only events that occur prior to the initial observation influence cohort behavior, then the linear model is appropriate. However, cohorts are continuously exposed to influences that affect their biological susceptibilities and social propensities. Obvious examples are wars and epidemics that may break out in the middle of a cohort's life and leave an imprint on all subsequent behavior. If these disturbances affect all cohorts then alive in similar fashion, they can best be treated in the form of lagged period effects. But if, as seems more likely, their imprint is differentiated by age and becomes embodied in cohorts differentially, then a more complex form of cohort analysis is required.

This is the version of cohort theory promoted by Ryder (1965a, reprinted in this volume) in his classic paper.

> The case for the cohort as a temporal unit in the analysis of societal change rests on a set of primitive notions: persons of age a in time t are those who were age $a - 1$ in time $t - 1$; transformations of the social world modify people of different ages in different ways; *the effects of these transformations are persistent* [Our italics]. In this way a cohort meaning is implanted in the age-time specification. Two broad orientations for theory and research flow from this position: first, the study of intra-cohort development throughout the life cycle; second, the study of comparative cohort careers, i.e., intercohort temporal differentiation in the various parameters that may be used to characterize these aggregate histories.

Few examples have appeared in which cohort behavior at a specified point in life is explicitly treated as a function of lagged effects of earlier period-age interactions, the persistent transformations described by Ryder. However, we would be remiss not to recognize this potentially important approach to cohort analysis, even though the procedures for investigation are undeveloped. In fact, there is some question whether or not such a model is analytically, as contrasted with conceptually, feasible.

3. AGE MODELS IN DEMOGRAPHY

As already mentioned in the introduction, demographic models have been concerned primarily with age variation of rates either for time periods or for cohorts but very rarely with explicit consideration of an age-period-cohort framework. However, these models, which have fewer free parameters than the number of age effects to be estimated in a full age-period-cohort model, can be used to remove the identification problem and thus allow estimation of the period and cohort parameters without constraints other than normalization.

3.1. Empirical Models

Many of the age models in mortality analysis are formed by using vectors of age-specific rates for a particular period in various countries and estimating statistical relations among the rates in order to represent normal changes in age-specific rates as mortality levels change. Other models have estimated the relationship of the rates to some summary measure (e.g., expectation of life at age 10). The earliest example of such models was the Breslau life table of Halley in 1693 (see Smith and Keyfitz, 1977), which was subsequently used for the calculation of annuities (see also Pearson, 1978). Model life tables in use today are based on period mortality data from a wide range of countries and have summarized age variations through regression models on the infant mortality rate (United Nations, 1955, 1956; Gabriel and Ronen, 1958), on expectation of life at age 10 (Coale and Demeny, 1966), or on various other measures (Ledermann, 1969). Principal components models have also been employed (Ledermann and Breas, 1959; Le Bras, 1979; Hogan and McNeil, 1979).

Most population specialists appear to believe that cohort mortality effects are sufficiently minor that they need not be incorporated into models of mortality relations. It is certainly true that their incorporation would be quite difficult and perhaps not worth the cost. But there are indications that some exploration along these lines is desirable. For example, Figures 1 and 2 plot historic female death rates at ages 55–59 for Sweden and for Scotland against, respectively, cohort and period estimates of life expectancy. It is clear that relations between death rates and the cohort measures are far more regular than those involving period measures. There is less scatter about the cohort relationship, particularly for Sweden, and more impressively, Swedish and Scottish relations appear to be quite similar when plotted on a cohort basis but are quite different for periods. Early Swedish and Scottish data were placed in different families of model life tables by Coale and Demeny (1966), but it may not have been necessary to draw this distinction had cohort data been used. That the basic cohort relation is quite different from the period relation is evident from the sharper slope of the cluster of points in Figure 1. It also appears that use of cohort data helps to normalize relations between male and female age-specific mortality and hence may provide a firmer foundation for model construction that relates mortality of the sexes.

In part, period rates are employed in the development of age models of mortality because they are so much more readily available than cohort data. However, there is now a great deal of information awaiting application of sound age-period-cohort analysis (see Case *et al.*, 1962; Vallin, 1973; Netherlands, Centraal Bureau voor de Statistiek, 1975; Bolander, 1970; and U.S. National Center for Health Statistics, 1972).

Figure 1. Relationship between Expectation of Life for Cohorts
and Mortality Rate for Women Aged 55–60:
Sweden and Scotland

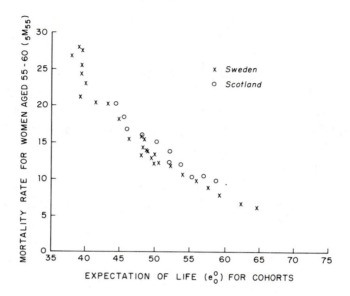

Figure 2. Relationship between Expectation of Life for Periods
and Mortality Rate for Women Aged 55–60:
Sweden and Scotland

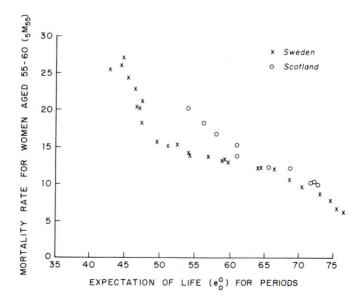

The evidence is that there is still much to be learned from these data.

In the same empirical tradition, Henry (1961) described an age pattern of fertility in the absence of deliberate control that he called "natural fertility" and that is thought to give an indication of the variation with age of fecundity or capacity to bear children.

3.2. Mathematical Models

Another major tradition in modeling age patterns of demographic phenomena involves more explicit mathematical models fitted to age-specific data. Often, the form of these curves is derived from some theoretical basis. The curve-fitting approach could be regarded as starting with Cardano in 1570 and De Moivre in 1725 and perhaps including the famous life table of Graunt in 1662 (see Smith and Keyfitz, 1977; Pearson, 1978). The earliest laws of mortality that gained wide acceptance were due to Gompertz in 1825 and Makeham in 1867 (see Smith and Keyfitz, 1977). In many different forms, this descriptive tradition persists to the present day in actuarial work (cf. Benjamin and Haycocks, 1970, Chapter 14). Other mortality models do have a quasi-theoretical basis (cf. Beard, 1971; Strehler, 1962; Brillinger, 1961). Hernes (1972) proposed a mathematical model of marriage with a theoretical basis for cohorts.

In fertility studies, there have been many attempts to fit various mathematical curves, without a behavioral or theoretical interpretation, to age-specific data. Functions employed include polynomials, beta distributions, Hadwiger functions, Wicksell or gamma distributions and log-normal distributions, and Gompertz curves fitted to cumulated fertility (see Duchêne and Gillet-de Stefano, 1974, for a useful review and comparison of all but the Gompertz, for which see Farid, 1973, and Brass, 1974b).

3.3. Relational Models

A recent and promising approach to modeling age patterns of demographic rates combines the empirical and mathematical procedures. Age patterns present in a particular population or cohort are viewed as a simple statistical transformation of a "standard" age pattern that is empirically specified. The analyst must then solve for the parameters that best transform the standard into the observed set of rates in the population or cohort. This procedure has the advantage that it incorporates regularities in age patterns that can only be replicated mathematically by many-parameter models; also, the parameters of the transformation usually have a straightforward substantive interpretation. The procedure also provides more flexibility to age patterns than is normally contained in the empirical models, since these are usually one-parameter models of how age patterns change as levels change.

The first demographic application of relational models was by William Brass (1971, 1974a). He took as a standard one of the U.N. model life tables and demonstrated empirically that many observed life tables could be reproduced closely by a two-parameter transformation of the logit of the survivorship function in that standard. Later work has increased the number of parameters (Zaba, 1979) and has synthesized Brass's model into a principal components framework (Le Bras, 1979; Hogan and McNeil, 1979).

In a similar vein, Coale (1971; Coale and Trussell, 1974) extracted a single standard from Henry's age patterns of natural fertility and proposed a two-parameter transformation of that standard in order to model observed age curves of marital fertility. One parameter is interpretable as the level of natural fertility, and the other is related to the extent of anti-natal practices. Brass (1974b) demonstrated how the Gompertz mathematical model of fertility could be converted to relational form. Coale has also developed a relational model of nuptiality in which a Swedish "standard" is adopted and three interpretable parameters are employed (Coale, 1971; Coale and McNeil, 1972; Ewbank, 1974). This model differs from the others cited in that one of the three parameters transforms the age scale itself. Rogers, Raquillet, and Castro (1978) propose a model of the age pattern of migration that derives from the work of Coale and associates on marriage and fertility.

Relational models have considerable promise for age-period-cohort analysis. For example, the parameters that transform the standard to produce an observed matrix of age-period rates can be assumed to be linear functions of corresponding parameters in periods and cohorts. In this fashion, the identification problem is readily solved. However, several of the models are based on transformations of cumulative functions (survivorship, proportion ever marrying). In these cases, first differences of the standards would have to be employed, which may result in more complex expressions.

One problem in all of these models is that cohort effects are not explicitly controlled in the models that are used to describe normal period-age variation in mortality. If such effects are important, then the model age patterns developed will depend on the distribution of cohort effects in the populations yielding information for the standard. If the distribution is similar to that in a particular population being compared with the standard, no cohort effects may appear even though they are present. If the distributions differ between the standard and the actual population, age or cohort disturbances may appear even when they are absent. There is, therefore, some doubt about the use of these models to overcome identification problems in estimating age-period-cohort models. However, these doubts are probably less serious than those raised by the commonly used procedures for fitting such models, which often involve point fitting or use of moments and only rarely use more efficient procedures such as least squares or maximum likelihood.

At this stage it is useful to consider demographic work that has attempted to identify, sometimes loosely, period and cohort effects. The statistical methods used to identify these effects are, in many cases, inadequate by modern standards. Our purpose here is not to criticize or even review the procedures in detail, but to consider the range of problems examined and the models proposed for them. In so doing, it is convenient to group the studies according to the phenomenon they examine.

4. MORTALITY

Apparently the first reorganization of a time series of age-specific mortality rates in such a way as to distinguish the set of rates pertaining to persons born in the same year or period was that of Derrick (1927), who argued that cohorts provided a more consistent basis for projecting mortality than did period rates. This conclusion was based on a graphical examination of the logarithms of age-specific death rates for England and Wales from 1841 to 1925, omitting the experience of World War I, which indicated that the ratio of mortality for one cohort to that of another cohort was approximately constant for all ages above 10. This is essentially a log-linear model with age and cohort effects, which can be written $\log(r_{apc}) = w + w_a + w_c$. Presumably the modern analyst would infer from the dropping of the experience of World War I that a proper model should also include period effects. Although Derrick's fitting procedures and methods of analysis would not meet modern standards, his graphical procedures correspond closely with modern approaches to displaying the presence or absence of interactions (e.g., Duncan and McRae, 1979, p. 75).

Convincing demonstration of the power of a cohort approach to data was left to three Scottish actuaries. Kermack, McKendrick, and McKinlay (1934a,b) computed the ratio of English death rates in 10-year age intervals in the decades from 1851–1860 to 1921–1930 to age-specific rates for 1841–1850. They then noted "a general tendency for numbers of approximately the same magnitude to be arranged diagonally in the Tables ... it is now to be noted that a diagonal line in the diagram represents the course of a group of people all born in a particular year" (p. 698). They reached similar but somewhat less convincing conclusions for Scotland using 1855–1864 as a base period and for Sweden using 1750–1759 rates as a base. The authors were aware that the apparent regularity could be a fortuitous result of a series of independent conditions affecting successively older ages (i.e., age-period interaction) but considered this combination of events to be very unlikely. Instead, they argued that the health of a cohort was principally determined by environmental conditions encountered in its first 15 years of life.

A second remarkable feature of the study was the authors' observation that death rates at ages 0–4 did not show the earliest improvement but improved only when the cohort changes reached well into the ages of maternity. They argued that early childhood mortality was closely linked to the health and physique of mothers. The mechanisms that they postulated have received ample verification only in the past decade, largely on the basis of individual-level studies in developing countries. The combination of infection and diarrheal disease in early years of life has been shown to have a very important and enduring effect on indices of growth and development; furthermore, mothers who are unusually small tend to have lower birth weight babies who are at much higher risk of death (Mata, 1977). Preston and van de Walle (1978) pursued an identical approach for the analysis of nineteenth-century data for three urban departments of France and found very similar results. Relative mortality levels tended to be arrayed diagonally rather than vertically, and infant improvements awaited maternal improvements. It was also found that the initiation of mortality improvements in a department tended to coincide with improvements in water supply and sewage disposal.

It should be noted that both studies were successful in demonstrating cohort effects only because mortality data were available before the process of mortality decline had begun.[3] In this case, early periods and cohorts maintained very similar age patterns of mortality, and it was reasonable to choose an early period age pattern as standard. If data had been available only after the decline had reached all cohorts and subsequent mortality levels had been measured relative to an already-deformed standard, then periods and cohorts alike could have shown a steady pace of mortality change. Distinguishing period and cohort effects would then have required more sophisticated statistical procedures and would have been crucially dependent on the choice of standard, whether represented explicitly by a mathematical law or implicitly by a functional form chosen for estimation purposes.

Only one year after Kermack, McKendrick, and McKinlay's article, a more elaborate examination of period and cohort effects appeared. Cramér and Wold (1935) fitted Makeham curves to both period and generation mortality experience for Sweden.[4] Their primary interest was in forecasting mortality rates. They did not consider the question of whether the period or cohort curves fit the observed mortality rates better. Instead, they went on to model the individual parameter values over time and to compare goodness of fit statistics for the period parameter values with those for cohorts. For example, they fitted logistic curves to values of $\log b_3$ for successive cohorts and, separately, to values of $\log b_3$ calculated for successive periods. They concluded that there was little or no difference in fit between the cohort and period approaches.

Cramér and Wold made a substantial contribution to another aspect of

---

[3] The studies were also dependent, though less critically so, on the assumption that mortality change would appear in the form of equi-proportionate declines in death rates at all ages. The index numbers of relative mortality levels would not have tended to cluster diagonally were this assumption seriously violated. Nevertheless, the fact that mortality declines were initiated in a cohort-specific rather than period-specific way would still have been clearly registered in the data even if proportionality had not pertained.

[4] The Makeham curve uses three parameters to describe age-specific mortality rates, m_a, as $m_a = b_1 + b_2 b_3^a$.

the age-period-cohort problem by demonstrating, in an appendix, that it is impossible to define a general Makeham *surface* for mortality rates in both the period and cohort dimensions. This problem of the interrelationship of generation and period mortality recently received attention from Cox and Scott (1977) and is closely related to recent work on bivariate exponential distributions in the analysis of competing risks (see David and Moeschberger, 1978, Chapter 4).

The relevance of cohort analysis to public health issues was first publicized in a posthumous paper on tuberculosis by Frost (1939), although the idea goes back to Andvord (1921, 1930), who believed that infection rates in childhood largely determined cohort experience. Frost's demonstration was principally graphical. He showed that age-specific death rates from tuberculosis in Massachusetts between 1880 and 1930 appeared to be more regular (similar from set to set) for cohorts than for periods. In particular, the highest age-specific rate for cohorts always occurred at ages 20–29, while for periods there was more variability. This variability was not particularly convincing support for cohort effects, however, since the period peak for males rose by only 30 years of age in the 60-year period reviewed, rather than in a one-to-one correspondence; furthermore, the period peak was constant for females at ages 10–29 throughout the period of observation.[5] The notion that tuberculosis was more responsive to influences early in the life of a cohort than to current conditions gained credibility because of the potentially long latency of the disease. But Frost's main statistical contribution seems to have been the demonstration that age patterns of mortality from tuberculosis look quite different for cohorts than for periods. Disentangling cohort from period effects in his data would be quite difficult because the period data begin well after the time when declines in mortality from tuberculosis had begun. There is no clearly appropriate standard to use for distinguishing between the effects; all periods and cohorts experience successively reduced mortality in his tables.

Frost's brief demonstration was usefully followed up by Springett (1950), among others, who examined tuberculosis experience in other geographic areas and concluded that "one assumption will explain most of

---

[5] From data for ages 5–59 in Table 1 of Frost (1939).

the observed results, viz. that the relative age distribution of mortality is constant in cohorts rather than in years" (p. 392). However, he also demonstrated that the age pattern of tuberculosis mortality, whether studied by cohort or period, showed considerable variation. It tended to be broad and flat in densely populated urban regions and among males and to be sharply peaked in sparsely populated regions and among females. These differences have not been explained convincingly; they clearly caution against using rigid mathematical "laws" of age variation in tuberculosis.

Sacher (1957, 1960, 1977) fitted a just-identified log-linear age-period-cohort model to tuberculosis data from Connecticut. His results were obtained by assuming that there was no cohort trend for six decades, an assumption that is perhaps unwise and opens his analysis to serious questions. Unfortunately the sources of his data are also not clearly specified.

Mason and Smith (1985, this volume) examine these and other data on tuberculosis from a modern age-period-cohort modelling perspective in this volume.

The pioneering application of sound statistical procedures to age-period-cohort analysis of morbidity and mortality was by Greenberg, Wright, and Sheps (1950). The authors specified the first properly identified age-period-cohort model, adopting a parameterization of age effects through a beta distribution. All three types of effect were found to be statistically significant using an analysis of variance framework and F-tests, rather than today's more usual chi-square tests. Barrett's studies of cancer of the cervix, heart, and bladder (1973, 1978a,b) employed similar approaches to identify the models.

Another disease that has received considerable attention from a cohort perspective is lung cancer. Case (1956a) pointed out that cohort mortality from lung cancer invariably rose with age in England and Wales, whereas period rates formed an inverted U-shape, with a peak around age 60–65. Again the demonstration was graphical, and again the importance of cohort effects rested on the plausibility of biological mechanisms rather than on statistical tests. Indeed, the period rates were no less regular in appearance than cohort rates. But almost all other forms of cancer mortality rise with age. The most obvious explanation of lung cancer's peculiarity, which was supported by additional evidence then available, was that successively younger cohorts were smoking cigarettes more heavily, thus achieving higher death rates at each successive age than older cohorts. In a second paper, Case (1956b) displayed graphs of cohort mortality from cancer at 21 different sites for England and Wales using data for 1911-1954. It is interesting to note that the graph for uterine cancer, another site frequently thought to display cohort effects related to childbearing patterns, is nearly the reverse of that for lung cancer. For uterine cancer, cohort age patterns tend to peak around age 65 to 70, while period patterns trend sharply upwards with age (see p. 186). There are some reasons to expect uterine cancer mortality to decline with age, so that once again the cohort rates may be providing a truer picture of physiological processes. But the point is simply that, without introducing such external information (or reasoning), it would not be possible to distinguish effectively between cohort and period effects. A purely statistical test that gave dominance to cohort effects in lung cancer would surely award it to period effects in uterine cancer.

Beard (1963) specified a full age-period-cohort log-linear model for death rates due to cancer of the lung and was probably the first author to make the linear identification constraint explicit for such a model. His fitting procedure seems to make use of quadratic contrasts, which are properly defined for each dimension. Two assumptions on linear scaling are then adopted. First, the cohort effects are chosen to approximate the proportion of smokers in the population, which they do reasonably well except for the extreme cohorts, although the fit is not presented for each cohort individually. It is then claimed that the period effects should approximate the average cigarette consumption some 10 to 15 years earlier, and again the fit of the reparameterized model to available data is moderately good. This approach of making the arbitrary linear constraint take a value that allows one of the effects to be assimilated to some external reference distribution seems eminently sensible, although it cannot be used to suggest causation, as Beard acknowledges. (A similar tactic might profitably be used in fertility models by making the structure of the age effects correspond as closely as possible to natural fertility).

Thus, in mortality analyses, it seems clear that in many cases cohort effects are biologically plausible and have been demonstrated in a variety of ways that may not be statistically rigorous but are nevertheless convincing.

5. NUPTIALITY AND DIVORCE

Very few simultaneous analyses of period and cohort effects on marriage patterns exist. Ewbank (1974) approached the problem by first estimating a five-parameter age curve for data on the single-year Swedish cohorts (male and female) of 1872–1929. In a second stage, he examined the residuals for what he refers to as "partial period effects." A similar strategy was used by Goldman (1980) to examine anomalies in male mortality in the Far East by analyzing residuals in period data from the model age patterns for cohort effects and by Vasantkumar (1979) to study mortality among black male Americans.

Another analysis of recent Swedish marriage data (for cohorts up to 1959) focused much more on estimation of trends in period and cohort effects so that the nuptiality pattern could be projected for recent cohorts. Thurston (1977) employed the "constant effects" log-linear model. To identify her model, Thurston assumed that the age pattern was constant over time and chose to match a Coale two-parameter nuptiality model (for those who ever marry) as closely as possible. The effects extracted for periods and cohorts provide an illuminating illustration of the problems of projecting trends under conditions of rapid change.

No explicit models of age-period-cohort effects on divorce have come to our attention. Wunsch (1979) and Preston and McDonald (1979) come to opposite conclusions about the relative regularity of period and cohort effects in their studies, respectively, of recent trends in Europe and of U.S. trends over the century from the late 1860s to the late 1960s. The need for further empirical work on divorce is clear.

6. FERTILITY

There has been relatively little analytic work explicitly directed at the separation of age, period, and cohort effects in fertility. Several authors argue that the greater stability of cohort completed fertility over time compared with period total fertility is an indication of a tendency for real groups of women to even out their experience so as to achieve notional reproductive targets or norms. This tendency corresponds with the cohort-inversion viewpoint elaborated earlier and has been used to argue that population projections should be based upon cohort cumulative fertility (cf. Akers, 1965). The U.S. Bureau of the Census (cf. 1977) now prepares its projections from cohort fertility information. However, the critical question of whether the future volume of fertility for cohorts of reproductive age can best be estimated from period or cohort data has not yet been answered satisfactorily.

To demonstrate the existence of cohort effects requires either explicit age-period-cohort models or at least a demonstration that cohort completed fertility is different from a weighted average of period total fertilities (weighted by a constant age pattern of fertility). This point first seems to have been made by Ryder (1953) in an unpublished paper and by Lee (1974a) and first examined statistically by Brass (1974b).

Ryder (1953) analyzed Swedish age-specific fertility rates for 200 years, divided into 40 quinquennial periods, between 1751 and 1950 for quinquennial groups of women aged 15–49. He noted that the period total fertility rate (TFR) was more variable than the cohort TFR, with "long stretches during which the two series remain apart, despite the fact that the components of both are derived from the same table of age-specific fertility." He suggested that the cohort series would tend to be smoother than the period series because the cohort TFR is drawn from seven successive periods and is thus a type of moving average. The cohort TFR for the women who are 15–19 in period j is given by

$$\text{Cohort TFR} = 5 \sum_{a=1}^{7} r_{a,j+a-1} \, , \tag{3}$$

where r_{ap} is the fertility of women in age group a in period p. There are, however, other measures that are averages taken over seven periods and seven ages, in fact $7!-1$ or 5,039 of them. If we consider the 7×7 matrix $\{r_{ap}\}$ for the first seven periods, a total fertility rate averaged over the seven periods can be defined so that one value is selected from each row and each column of $\{r_{ap}\}$. Ryder singled out the trohoc (or reversed cohort) for special attention. The trohoc TFR starting in period j is given by

$$\text{Cohort TFR} = 5 \sum_{a=1}^{7} r_{a,j+7-a} \, . \tag{4}$$

In terms of the models discussed thus far, it is obvious that if an additive model (with no cohort effect) is appropriate, i.e., if

$$r_{ap} = W + W_a + W_p \, , \tag{5}$$

then so long as the $\{r_{ap}\}$ are selected so that all seven age effects and seven period effects go into the sum, the 5,040 definitions of the moving average should have the same expected value and all time series should exhibit the same variability.

Ryder calculated a complex index of variability. Its definition need not concern us here; however, the relative values are of interest:

Index of Variation

	Index of Variation
period TFR	7,488
cohort TFR	223
trohoc TFR	233
average of 5,040 permutations	770

Clearly, the moving averages across periods are less variable than the period TFR. The cohort TFR, while showing considerably less than average variation, differs little from the trohoc. Ryder pointed out that both of these averages were heavily weighted by fertility in adjacent time periods for the adjacent age groups with the highest fertility rates, so that the age-weighting scheme is quite similar. Thus, the similarity of cohort and trohoc variability provides little evidence of a powerful cohort effect or a cohort-inversion phenomenon.

The analysis of U.S. fertility using additive models has led different authors to opposite conclusions about the existence or importance of cohort effects. A number of these studies have employed the cohort fertility tables for single years of age and single-year periods issued recently by the U.S. National Center for Health Statistics (Heuser, 1976).

Pullum (1980) modeled data for U.S. white females for the period 1917–1973 from this source using a logit-linear approach. He considered four models, three with each possible pair of age, period, or cohort main effects, and the fourth with all three main effects. Two indicators of fit were provided, the first a chi-squared statistic and the second an index of dissimilarity, which can be interpreted as the minimum proportion of cases that would have to be shifted for perfect agreement between the model and the table. As he did not have the exposures to risk available, all calculations were based on a nominal thousand woman-years per cell.

The models were fitted to 11-year runs of the data, although 21-year runs were employed in some cases. In general the fits were remarkably good, although longer periods were not considered "because of the evidence of increasing interactions between age and period which cannot be described as cohort effects." Pullum measured the impact of adding a cohort effect to an age-period model by the difference in the chi-squared statistics for the age-period and the age-period-cohort model divided by the difference in their respective degrees of freedom; the impact of adding period effects to an age-cohort model was measured in similar fashion. Adding the period dimension had greater impact per degree of freedom (and often absolutely) than adding the cohort dimension, although inclusion of both sometimes led to noticeable further improvement. To check whether formulation of a true set of complete cohort rates changed the outcome, Pullum assembled the 22 complete birth cohorts and again tried the various models. Again, period was a more successful explanatory variable than cohort. His conclusion was that, for 11- or even 21-year periods, a simple main-effects age-period model was quite adequate and preferable to an age-cohort one. Both this negative finding and the fact that real cohorts of women bear children for 30-year periods suggest that constant-effect cohort analysis of fertility in developed countries may not be promising; most cohort fertility theories (as opposed to models), of course, do not postulate constant-effects.

Pullum also suggested that such models could usefully be applied to order-specific fertility rates. Isaac *et al.* (1979) undertook the analysis of birth probabilities by race, age, order, and year using data from the Heuser (1976) volume updated through 1976. Parameters were estimated for three models: an additive model including age, period, and cohort effects and two multiplicative (log-linear) models positing age and period effects and including or omitting the cohort dimension. Each birth order (0–4) was analyzed separately by race using ordinary least squares regression procedures. No mention is made of how the overidentification problem was handled. The authors found that the multiplicative models in general explained more variance and argued that the cohort effects could be eliminated "with little or no empirical loss" because addition of the cohort dimension to an age-period model hardly increased the explanatory power.

Sanderson (1976) calculated his own set of age- and order-specific birth probabilities beginning with the cohort of women born in 1900 and continuing through calendar year 1966. His investigation was directed toward an examination of the Easterlin hypothesis (cf. 1973, 1978) regarding cohort fertility. He also assumed a log-linear model and estimated age, period, and cohort effects for each order using an unconventional and dubious method that arbitrarily apportioned any trend in the birth probabilities equally to the current year and cohort components. His period effect plots closely resemble those prepared by Isaacs *et al.* In general, Sanderson found cyclical variation in the cohort components, especially for the lower birth orders. The amplitude was greatest for the first and second births, and the cyclical movements were not necessarily in phase with one another.

Page (1977) also concluded that an adequate description of fertility rates can be achieved without introducing cohort effects into her model. This work is of special interest for substantive and methodological reasons. Page was able to model both the age and duration effects, reaching conclusions that offer considerable insight into patterns of changing fertility. However, Gilks (1979) later examined the same data and models, adjusting the data to allow for changes in defintions over time and using somewhat different estimation procedures. This led him to qualify some of the original conclusions. Because these studies clearly illustrate the lack of agreement on estimation procedures for such analyses, a rather detailed discussion is offered here.

Page took period fertility rates by age and marriage duration for Sweden, England and Wales, and Australia. For each period (and separately by country), she fitted models with age and duration main effects, adopting various "robust" or "resistant" fitting procedures of the type proposed by Tukey (1977). The model used is, effectively,

$$\log(r_{apd}) = u_p + u_{ap} + u_{dp} + e_{apd} \tag{6}$$

which is a version of the model

$$\log(r_{apd}) = w + w_p + w_a + w_{ap} + w_d + w_{pd} + e'_{apd} \tag{7}$$

with no marginal constraints on the period dimension. Models (6) and (7) can be reparameterized one to another, but care is required in interpreting the estimates. The fitting procedure uses data and model-determined weights. Although the Tukey-type procedures are intuitively attractive, since each model changes weights for a given cell, model discrimination on statistical criteria is virtually impossible. Page in fact adopted a method of assessing overall goodness-of-fit that gives all non-zero cells equal weights, ignoring those used in the fitting procedure itself. She then calculated the proportion of variance in the rates accounted for by the model. By this criterion, the fits are very good indeed.

Page then examined the structure of the effects. She found that the age effects, $\{u_{ap}\}$, were approximately constant over time and corresponded closely in shape to the age pattern of natural fertility (Henry, 1961). There was some age-period interaction, in that the slope of the age effects became greater for more recent periods.

Page went on to study the structure of the duration effects, $\{u_{dp}\}$. They showed a marked change over time, moving from a concave to a more linear pattern, indicating interactions. Page suggested that the interaction might be at least partly due to year of marriage effects. She therefore normalized the duration effects for each time period so that the effect was zero for duration two and then combined the new terms, $\{u'_{pd}\}$, for marriage cohorts rather than time periods. These normalized (within marriage cohort) effects declined fairly linearly for each cohort above duration two, although with differing slopes for each cohort. Since fertility at duration zero was always substantially higher than the values implied by the straight line, Page adopted an ad hoc adjustment of adding 0.3 to the predicted value at this duration so that the model became

$$\log(r_{apd}) = u'_p + u'_a + (d-2)u'_{(p-d)} + 0.3b, \qquad (8)$$

where u'_p is the redefined period effect, u'_a is the natural fertility set of age effects, $u'_{(p-d)}$ is now a marriage cohort effect, and b is one when duration is zero and zero otherwise. This is a considerable simplification of the earlier model and still appears to fit the Swedish experience tolerably well. Similar results were reported for England and Wales.

It is worth quoting Page's concluding remarks (1977, pp. 103-4):

> Demographers have become increasingly accustomed to thinking of fertility in terms of cohort experience; in this framework, period effects tend to be viewed as contributing irregularities to cohort patterns. Here, by twisting the data kaleidoscope a different way, we have focused on the existence of period regularities. Our data show that, at any given time, all birth and marriage cohorts react, in some sense, as a single unit to whatever factors determine the general level of fertility at that time ...

It is as if each cohort were characterized by a latent exponential decline in its fertility as it passes through marriage, interrupted only by period effects to which all cohorts respond by proportionately the same amount.

Gilks (1979) both adjusted the data for England and Wales and used different procedures for estimating the parameters of similar models. For example, he tested goodness-of-fit by using the weighted sum of squares of the residuals of the fitted models, with weights defined by a biweight function over all the residuals. He found the age patterns more variable over time and less like the pattern of natural fertility. The respecified (within marriage cohort) duration effects were approximately linear for later cohorts, although generally slightly convex. Perhaps most importantly, with his methods of analysis, England and Wales showed considerable effects of World War II on fertility patterns and levels that did not show up in the original analysis. During this period the duration effects (normalized and reconsidered for marriage cohorts) became quite nonlinear. Gilks also found severe problems with the rearrangement of durational effects for periods into ones for marriage cohorts and concluded that these data require models that include marriage cohort effects explicitly, with the usual caveats about confounding of linear parts of main effects.

Both Page and Gilks noted considerable patterning of their residuals in each period table. Particularly poor fits are seen at the early durations, mainly because much of the fertility shortly after marriage results from premarital conceptions. For young ages at marriage, this excess fertility in the first eight months of marriage clearly causes consequential waves in the fertility rates by duration, through the removal of a high proportion from exposure to risk for the next year or so.

Thus, despite methodological and substantive disagreements, both of these investigators suggest that fertility responds not only to age and period effects, but to marriage duration, marriage cohort, and age at marriage. Their work indicates that models considerably more complex than those specified thus far may be required for adequate analysis of fertility. In the remaining studies in this review, complexity is introduced either by specifying nonlinear cohort effects or by adding additional variables.

Lee (1974b, 1977, 1980) has moved work on age, period, and cohort effects closer to theories of fertility. In the first paper (1974b), he examined several possible models of homeostatic fertility control, including a period and a cohort formulation. In the former case, age-specific fertility rates were a function of the size of the labor force; in the latter, they depended only on the relevant cohort size. The implications of each of these models for the autocorrelation function of fertility (the correlation of the birth rate at time t with that at time $t - m$, for values of m in years) were examined. Lee found that when fertility responded either to relative cohort size or period labor force size, there would be fluctuations in fertility of about 40 years, rather than the generational-length fluctuations expected when relatively constant age-specific rates were applied to an irregular initial age distribution. Fluctuations consistent with controlled fertility were not observed for preindustrial European populations; however, U.S. fertility exhibited cycles similar to those predicted by the cohort or period control models. Lee concluded that the latter model was more plausible since the estimated elasticity in the TFR estimated for the cohort model was very close to -1, which would dampen any disturbance and lead to a prediction of a constant number of births regardless of cohort size.

As Lee correctly acknowledged, cycles that are compatible with control may be induced by factors not considered in his model. Nevertheless, his work is suggestive that control mechanisms operate primarily through period effects if at all. At least he is able to demonstrate nonexistence of a high degree of control operating through cohorts. All these conclusions require further qualification since simple (and linear) models were posited for the control process.

Lee (1977) went on to develop a stock-adjustment or cohort-inversion model by distinguishing between terminators (who desire no more children) and non-terminators, although he presumed that both groups always have the same achieved fertility. This assumption seems unlikely to be true and makes his model indistinguishable in many respects from one that ignores the distinction. Even so, his model is more attractive conceptually for this distinction. In its simplest form and ignoring a nine-month or one-year lag, Lee's model can be written as

$$r_{apc} = b_a(T_p - F_a^c), \qquad (9)$$

where F_a^c is the cumulated fertility of the cohort c that is age a in period p, and b_a can be interpreted as the rate of adjustment at age a or the proportion of desired additional births achieved in each year and is further defined as the "ratio of the fertility rate of those wanting additional births to the number of additional births wanted by those wanting more."[6] T_p is the total fertility desired. It may change over time and is approximated by desired (or expected) completed fertility as measured by questions on reproductive intentions. In this paper, Lee also used a rearranged version of equation (9) to estimate T_p.

He found that if, for a particular marriage cohort, the target is constant over time and b_a is constant over age, the model implies that marital fertility declines exponentially with age. Interestingly, this model therefore corresponds closely to Page's (1977) parameterization of marriage cohort contributions to fertility rates. Lee also presented some evidence that b_a increases slightly with age and suggested a linear change, which leads to a model of the form used by Jain and Hermalin (1971) for fertility within a cohort.

A somewhat different view on the subject of period and cohort influences on fertility was taken by Ryder (1980) in a recent paper in which he attempted to decompose period total fertility rates into components attributable to changes in the quantum and tempo (or volume and timing) of cohort fertility. Employing the Heuser (1976) data updated through 1975, Ryder first projected completed fertility for birth cohorts through 1950, on the assumption that age-parity-specific birth rates remain fixed at their 1975 level. He then calculated an *index of distributional distortion*, defined, for a given period, as the sum over cohorts of the proportion of its total fertility that each cohort experiences in that period. Regardless of level of cohort fertility, the index would equal unity if each cohort had the same age distribution (or tempo) of fertility. This index was proposed as a period-specific measure of change in cohort tempo that can have both long-term and short-term components. Ryder related the long-term changes to alterations in the cohort mean age of childbearing. After adjusting for this type of change, he treated the residuals as short-term deviations. For the United States, the three major fluctuations were associated with wars—World Wars I and II and the Vietnam War.

---

[6] However, this interpretation is only sensible if all women are perceived as wanting additional births, and thus it implies a homogeneity of both achieved and desired fertility or at least of desired additional fertility. As mentioned previously, this homogeneity assumption is implicit in the cohort-inversion models proposed so far but could be reduced or overcome by introducing parity into the models.

Ryder also defined a period-specific measure of changes in the quantum of cohort fertility as the period total fertility rate divided by the index of distributional distortion. The trends in these measures led him to conclude that changes in quantum of cohort fertility explain most of the variation in period rates during the time period 1922–1936; changes in tempo (i.e., the index of distributional distortion) have been dominant since then. Most of the baby boom, according to this analysis, would have occurred without any changes in quantum of cohort fertility and depended scarcely at all on numbers of unwanted children.

Butz and Ward (1979) independently partitioned the period TFR into exactly the same two components. Their timing index is Ryder's index of distributional distortion (or tempo of fertility), and their average completed fertility is Ryder's measure of change in the quantum of cohort fertility. Their calculations differ only in the method of estimating completed fertility for cohorts still of reproductive age.

The main thrust of the Butz and Ward paper is the development of a new theory about why these indices change. The authors hypothesize that the timing index depends on the way in which couples make decisions about when to have their next child and that a couple makes the decision by gauging the pace of its current births not against actual completed fertility but against the "completed fertility it expects at the time the birth decision is made." They describe the timing index based on known completed fertility as an *ex post* timing index and one based on the completed fertility expected at time *t* as the *ex ante* timing index for time *t*.

Their *ex ante* measures were derived from two quite different procedures for estimating expected completed fertility. The first depends on an economic model in which fertility for the next year is determined by fertility in the current year, current age of the woman, and predictions for the next year of women's employment and wages and husbands' income. Values of male income and female wages and employment ratios were projected independently and entered into the model to yield estimates of fertility rates used to calculate the *ex ante* timing index. The second version of the *ex ante* timing index is based on expectations data collected by the Current Population Surveys. The levels and movements of both indices are quite similar. Butz and Ward, like Ryder, concluded that for recent time periods "most of the year-to-year change in period fertility rates is due purely to the altered timing of births." They also suggested that, to a great extent, current fertility is determined by the couple's assessment of its total expected fertility and its projected economic situation.

Lee (1980) extended the analysis of the model proposed in his 1977 paper (and given in equation (9)). He assumed that T_p, the desired completed family size in period p, was the same for all cohorts and examined the implications of time trends in T_p for period total fertility. He found that if T_p is increasing, then the period total fertility rate will be higher than T_p because the rate of childbearing must increase at every age to compensate for lower fertility at the younger ages. Similarly, if T_p is declining, the period total fertility rate will be lower than T_p since couples will have attained a higher proportion of T_p by any given age.

If target fertility fluctuates, then the period TFR rate will fluctuate also, but its turning points may precede those of T_p. The counter-intuitive reason for this finding is that the period TFR depends upon the gap between current cumulated fertility and target fertility, which is the additional desired fertility. As the rate of increase in T_p slows, this gap narrows, so that the period TFR begins to fall when the rise in T_p begins to slow down. From this theoretical framework, it also can be predicted that the fertility of older women will fluctuate proportionately most, that of young women least.[7]

This simplified model does not preclude negative fertility in terms of declining desired completed fertility, as Lee acknowledges. Nor does it fit real data especially well. His model can be rearranged to give

$$F_a^c = T_p - r_{apc}/b \, ,$$

where a is here used to represent duration of marriage. It is clear that a linear regression of this form does not fit 1974 data for England and Wales at all well. For practical fitting purposes, alternative approaches through log-linear or logit relations seem more sensible. Despite these criticisms, the Lee model is an extremely useful abstraction for understanding the theory of fertility.

Lee also has begun to develop models in which negative fertility is precluded. He finds that irreversibility of fertility causes an asymmetric response to rising and falling levels of target fertility that cannot be

---

[7] For a fuller discussion see the reference to Yule (1906) in Appendix A.

ignored without producing large errors in estimates of final cohort fertility.

Models that incorporate factors other than age, period, and cohort are considerably more difficult to apply. Suppose one was interested in modeling the behavior of the fertility rate r_{apcdmy}, where the subscripts represent, respectively, age, period, cohort, marriage duration, age at marriage, and year of marriage. Solution of the identification problem in a linear model is obviously much more demanding than in the simple age-period-cohort case. Just as age and period uniquely identify cohort membership, so do age at marriage and duration of marriage uniquely identify the marriage cohort. Furthermore, certain sets of three of the six indices are sufficient to identify the remaining three. For example, age, period, and year of marriage identify not only cohort but also duration of marriage and age at marriage. There are substantial difficulties in fitting models of this type, although one approach is outlined in Appendix B. Furthermore, the analyst must address several new practical problems: for example, how to deal with marital disruption (perhaps by eliminating all non-marital rates even though they would contribute to age, period, and cohort rates, or by defining duration as pertaining to years since most recent marriage); and how to handle the many zero cells that will emerge in the high duration-low age categories. Presumably because of the complexity of these problems, there has not been, to our knowledge, any attempt to estimate the full-blown model.

Brass (1974b) used two models that included some of these effects to examine possible differences between a weighted average of period total fertilities and actual completed cohort fertility. The first, which is implicitly given in his paper, was, in the notation used here, essentially a log-linear model of period and duration main effects for each age at marriage group:

$$\log(r_{pdm}) = u + u_p + u_d + u_m + u_{pd} + u_{dm} (+e_{pdm}), \qquad (10)$$

where all six linear effects are implicitly included in the model and u_{dm} incorporates all the age main effects. Addition over the duration of marriage diagonals gave expected values of cohort completed fertility. Brass's second model was a hybrid one and not very clearly specified. For each age at marriage group, a log-linear model like (10), with period and duration main effects, was fitted. The residuals on the natural scale (constrained to sum to zero) were then modeled by fitting straight lines.

If the expected value under model (10) is denoted by r'_{pdm}, this seems to imply that

$$r_{pdm}/r'_{pdm} = y_{dm} + z_{dm}p + e'_{pdm},$$ (11)

with $\Sigma_p(y_{dm} + z_{dm}p) = 0$ for all d, m. This adaptation was intended to allow for changes in the durational pattern of fertility over time and must pick up some of the duration-period interaction. Given the mixed form of the model, it is hard to say how much of the part of the interaction so fitted would correspond to marriage cohort effects, however defined.

Brass concluded from this second model that:

> The notable feature of the comparisons is the broad general agreement between the series of observed and expected rates, although the individual differences are considerable relative to the range of variation. ...There is no indication of a cohort effect of the kind which would arise from 'making-up' or 'making-down' of births. The cohorts which were married in early 1940's and experienced the low war-time fertilities ended up with rather fewer children than the averaging of time-periods would give; those subject to the higher early 1930's rates at the beginning of marriage exceeded the expectations. These deviations would suggest the possibility that the time-period fertility level early in marriage might persist for a cohort rather than the reverse. But, on average, the women married in 1945–48 when fertility was high ended with families in good agreement with the model levels and those from the low initial rate cohorts of 1951–55 needed to exceed them. The overwhelming impression is that the cohort completed family sizes reveal no significant feature which distinguishes them from time averages.

A few comments are in order. The standard error of the actual completed fertility of cohorts married in 1931–1951 is, at 0.0549, noticeably less than the standard error predicted under either model (0.0714 for the first and 0.0679 for the second), suggesting greater cohort stability than expected. In addition, Brass's detailed results (such as he presents) show some evidence of a cohort-inversion effect. In particular, the war cohorts, which experienced lower fertility initially, show signs of overcompensation during the immediate postwar period but subsequently have lower than expected rates. This finding is consistent with the view that some women who had delayed childbearing would not make up postponed births either through infecundity or because they substituted other activities for childbearing (cf. Rindfuss and Bumpass, 1978). The cohort-inversion models proposed earlier in this paper (with the possible exception of the period-target model) may not be capable of capturing this type of effect. Brass's interpretation may be correct, but there is at least a prima facie case for more careful model specification and a suggestion that a cohort effect may exist. Again the problems of model specification and estimation need to be solved before conclusive results can be obtained.

Gilks and Hobcraft (1980) have begun investigating explicit models containing (some or all of) age, period, cohort, duration, age at marriage, and year of marriage effects employing data for England and Wales. They have concluded from their preliminary analyses that cohort-inversion formulations fit the data no better than conventional fixed-effects age-period-cohort models and that better fitting models can be found that only incorporate age and period effects, at least for the period 1938–1975. Their work with the more elaborate data set, which adds the age at marriage, duration of marriage, and time of marriage dimensions, is still in progress. It has proved somewhat inconclusive thus far, owing to substantial difficulties encountered in finding a model capable of capturing the range of variability in patterns for this period.

Their work again illustrates our conclusion from this review that nearly the same data sets, analyzed on the basis of differing theoretical considerations about the nature of cohort reactions, yield quite different results from those achieved by statistical models that are not derived from consideration of the underlying phenomenon being studied.

7. SUMMARY

We have reviewed the state of the art of age-period-cohort analysis for demographic dependent variables. Major examples of such analyses have appeared both in mortality and fertility studies. In the area of mortality, the conventional approach to such analysis appears to be well suited to a wide range of applications and often yields plausible and useful results. There are several reasons for its suitability. First, early childhood experience (for subsequent periods) does seem quite important in many major disease and death processes, so that cohorts are legitimately viewed as acquiring early on a certain fixed susceptibility. Second, data sometimes stretch back far enough that stationary "standards" of age patterns can be developed empirically and applied to later experience.

Third, logarithmic or logistic transformations do seem to linearize comparisons of age schedules or mortality quite effectively, so that standard statistical procedures are appropriate. Nevertheless, there are many instances when application of age-period-cohort analysis is anything but routine and where external constraints are required, typically in the form of theoretically based and mathematically expressed age patterns of mortality, in order to distinguish effectively between period and cohort effects. A set of models of age patterns of mortality that are based on cohort as well as period experience could be constructed and might find useful application.

The conventional approach is much less suitable for the analysis of fertility, except perhaps in natural fertility populations where physiological mechanisms play a dominant role. Once goal-directed behavior is introduced, it is important to base any empirical examination on theories or assumptions about how such goals are formulated and pursued. Only if one is prepared to accept the assumption that all of the pertinent goals and strategies are formulated before the initiation of childbearing and remain unaffected by subsequent events would conventional analysis suffice. This assumption is untenable for modern developed populations, and the forms of analysis appropriate to age-period-cohort investigations of fertility will have to develop hand in hand with the theories of reproductive behavior.

APPENDIX A: YULE'S MODEL

Yule, in a remarkable paper in 1906, introduced what was effectively a cohort-inversion model for marriage. He observed that wars in France, Prussia, and Denmark had led to substantial postponement of marriages with subsequent "catching-up" afterwards. The swings in vital rates induced by wars and pestilence were documented at least as early as Sussmilch (1761), and Malthus (1978) argued that these were induced by period changes in trade, missing the concept of postponement. Yule, following Hooker (1898), went on to argue that:

> Those who postpone marriages in one year only survive to marry, or possibly marry, in the next; the divergence of the marriage rate in any one year from normal depends, therefore, not on the postponements

caused by unfavourable factors in that year alone, but *on the difference between the postponements of that year and the postponements of the year before.* If the postponements are increasing from one year to the next, the marriage-rate will be below normal, but not necessarily falling; the marriage-rate will only fall if the volume of postponements is increasing at an increasing rate, i.e. if the unfavourable factors are *accelerating.* But applying this idea to the case of oscillations, we see that the marriage-rate ought to attain its maximum not when the favourable factors are at a maximum and the unfavourable at a minimum or shortly after, but when the favourable factors are increasing and the unfavourable decreasing most rapidly.

Yule gave evidence that no such phenomenon appeared to occur for marriage in more normal times, with cycles in marriage frequency in England and Wales having the same periodicity and phase as other indices. He also suggested that the postponement argument was even less applicable to the analysis of birth rates in normal times and that wars had a lesser effect on births than marriages. His work constitutes an important precursor of the recent research on period targets for fertility and is more subtle than most recent arguments within a "cohort-inversion" framework.

APPENDIX B: AN APPROACH TO HIERARCHICAL FITTING OF LINEAR OR POLYNOMIAL AGE-PERIOD-COHORT MODELS

Recent work (e.g., Fienberg and Mason, 1978) on age-period-cohort models has focused heavily on the identification problems when a linear model for the rates (or for a transformation such as logarithm or logit) is proposed. In addition to the usual analysis of variance type constraints on the sums of the age, period, and cohort effects, there is the additional problem caused by the confounding of linear effects in each of the three variables. In many ways the simplest approach to this problem seems to be to work with the modified model (for the expected value)

$$f(r_{apc}) = W + (b_1 - t_1)a + (b_2 + t_1)p + (b_3 - t_1)c + {}_2R_{A-1}(a)$$
$$+ {}_2R_{P-1}(p) + {}_2R_{C-1}(c), \qquad (A.1)$$

where $_2R_{A-1}(a)$ denotes a polynomial in a with terms included for all powers of a between 2 and $A-1$, with A denoting the number of age groups included in the analysis; $_2R_{P-1}(p)$ and $_2R_{C-1}(c)$ are defined similarly; and t_1 is an arbitrary constant, which can always be set equal to one of b_1, b_2, or b_3 to remove one of the linear terms and identify the model. Following the spirit of Goodman's notation (cf. Bishop, Fienberg, and Holland, 1975) for fitting contingency tables through marginal configurations, it is possible to define L_A as the linear part due to age and $_2R_{A-1}$ as the remaining part due to the polynomial defined above. Then the conventional age-effects model, denoted by S_A, is equivalent to $[L_A, _2R_{A-1}]$, and $[S_A, S_P]$ is equivalent to $[L_A, _2R_{A-1}, L_P, _2R_{P-1}, L_C]$, since a model consisting of any two of the linear effects actually includes all three.   This formulation makes the problem clear and allows hierarchical fitting of models. Provided the confounding of linear effects is recognized and no attempt is made to attach meaning to the linear effect parameters, the results are interpretable. Following the concept of marginality expounded by Nelder (1977), it seems reasonable to restrict such hierarchical fitting to those cases where the relevant linear term is always included before the corresponding polynomial, as the polynomial terms are defined relative to the linear and grand mean term. Consideration would then be restricted to two or three types of hierarchy, namely,

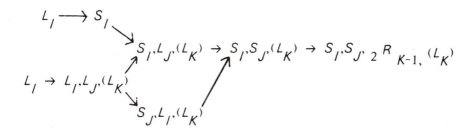

where I can be any one of A, P, or C; J one of the remaining two; and K the final one, giving six possible ways of achieving each of the hierarchies above. (The term L_K is bracketed to indicate its redundancy and non-explicit fitting—an approach that is similar to the fitting of a two-way margin implying fitting on the one-way margins in normal hierarchical models for contingency tables.)   The hierarchy could be completed by inclusion of the saturated model S_{IJ} where S_{IJ} is used to denote a model that has the IJ interaction present in addition to the I and J effects, and model selection can be carried out on the usual criteria using chi-squared statistics as the basis of choice (cf. Fienberg, 1980).

The problems become even more complex when other factors are added to the models (see the related discussion by Heckman and Robb, 1985, this volume). For example, a model for fertility rates may be proposed in which

$$f(r_{apcdmy}) = W + W_a + W_p + W_c + W_d + W_m + W_y + ..., \tag{A.2}$$

where the subscripts represent the usual age, period, and cohort influences and, additionally, duration of marriage, and year of marriage, respectively. There are now three separate linear identification problems, which can be highlighted as before by breaking up the model into linear and remaining polynomial terms:

$$\begin{aligned} f(r_{apcdmy}) = \; & w + (b_1 + t_1 - t_2)a + (b_2 + t_2 + t_3)p \\ & + (b_3 - t_1 - t_3)c + (b_4 - t_1)d + (b_5 - t_2)m + (b_6 - t_3)m \\ & + {}_2R_{A-1}(a) + {}_2R_{P-1}(p) + {}_2R_{C-1}(c) + {}_2R_{D-1}(d) \\ & + {}_2R_{M-1}(m) + {}_2R_{Y-1}(y) ..., \end{aligned} \tag{A.3}$$

where b_1 to b_6 are the linear effects and t_1, t_2, and t_3 are arbitrary constants that can always be used to force up to three of the effects to zero. It is a simple matter to go on to elaborate hierarchies of models as was done earlier for the simpler case.

Perhaps more interesting is to consider how all these effects might be discovered informally in a conventional log- or logit-linear model framework. For the simple age-period-cohort case it suffices to examine either the pattern of residuals after fitting a two main-effect model or the pattern of interaction terms from the saturated model. Consistent positive or negative values along each of the diagonals defining the third dimension would indicate the value of trying a constant-effect age-period-cohort model; regular tendencies for a string of positive (or negative) values to be followed by a string of negative (or positive) values along each cohort diagonal would suggest a cohort-inversion approach, although care is required due to the non-normalization across cohorts. In this more complex situation it is simpler to examine parameter estimates from a model specifying three two-way interactions than to study the residuals from a three main-effect model for each of the three possible two-way margins (note that the three variables have to be chosen to span the entire table space.) There are two reasons for this: there will be substantially fewer values to examine and, more importantly, the parameter estimates are controlled for covariation across the other two-way margins, whereas the residuals would not be so controlled and would be harder to interpret. A simpler approach to examination of residuals might be to fit the model with two of the two-way margins and display residuals for the third two-way combination: this would control for covariation but would still require examination of more values. An alternative approach is to launch into a full six-effect model from the outset, but in view of the triple identification problem this requires care, although ultimately such models need testing.

REFERENCES

Akers, D.S. (1965). Cohort fertility versus parity progression as methods of projecting births. *Demography* **2**, 414–428.

Andvord, K.F. (1921). Is tuberculosis to be regarded from the aetiological standpoint as an acute disease of childhood? *Tubercle* **3**, 97–116.

Andvord, K.F. (1930). Hvad kan vi laere ved å folge tuberkulosens gang fra generasjon til generasjon? [What can we learn by studying tuberculosis by generations?] *Norsk Magasin for Laegevidenskapen* **91**, 642–660.

Barrett, J.C. (1973). Age, time and cohort factors in mortality from cancer of the cervix. *Journal of Hygiene* **71**, 253–259.

Barrett, J.C. (1978a). A method of mortality analysis: Application to breast cancer. *Revue d'Epiémiologie et de Santé Publique* **26**, 419–425.

Barrett, J.C. (1978b). The redundant factor method and bladder cancer mortality. *Epidemiology and Community Health Medicine* **32**, 314–316.

Beard, R.E. (1963). Discussion of "Actuarial methods of mortality analysis" by B. Benjamin, pp. 38–54. *Proceedings of the Royal Society of London, Series B* **159**, 56–64.

Beard, R.E. (1971). Some aspects of theories of mortality, cause of death analysis, forecasting and stochastic processes, in W. Brass (ed.), *Biological Aspects of Demography.* London: Taylor and Francis, pp. 57–68.

Benjamin, B. and Haycocks, H.W. (1970). *The Analysis of Mortality and Other Actuarial Statistics.* Cambridge, England: Cambridge University Press.

Bishop, Y.M.M., Fienberg, S.E., and Holland, P.W. (1975). *Discrete Multivariate Analysis: Theory and Practice.* Cambridge, Mass.: MIT Press.

Bolander, A.-M. (1970). A study of cohort mortality in the past hundred years, in *Kohortdödligheten i Sverige: Tre Studier över Dödlighetstrenderna Förr, Nu och i Framtiden* [Cohort Mortality of Sweden: Three Studies Describing Past, Present, and Future Trends in Mortality]. Statistiska Meddelanden, Be **3**. Stockholm: Statistiska Centralbyrån, pp. 5–51.

Brass, W. (1969). A generation method for projecting death rates, in F. Bechhofer (ed.), *Population Growth and the Brain Drain.* Edinburgh: Edinburgh University Press, pp. 75–91.

Brass, W. (1971). On the scale of mortality, in W. Brass (ed.), *Biological Aspects of Demography.* London: Taylor and Francis, pp. 69–110.

Brass, W. (1974a). Mortality models and their uses in demography. *Transactions of the Faculty of Actuaries* **33**, 123–142.

Brass, W. (1974b). Perspectives in population prediction: Illustrated by the statistics of England and Wales (with discussion). *Journal of the Royal Statistical Society, Series A* **137**, 532–583.

Brillinger, D.R. (1961). A justification of some common laws of mortality. *Transactions of the Society of Actuaries* **13**, 116–119.

Butz, W.P. and Ward, M.P. (1979). Will U.S. fertility remain low? A new economic interpretation. *Population and Development Review* **5**, 663–688.

Case, R.A.M. (1956a). Cohort analysis of mortality rates as an historical or narrative technique. *British Journal of Preventive and Social Medicine* **10**, 159–171.

Case, R.A.M. (1956b). Cohort analysis of cancer mortality in England and Wales, 1911–1954, by site and sex. *British Journal of Preventive and Social Medicine* **10**, 172–199.

Case, R.A.M. *et al.* (1962). *Serial Abridged Life Tables, England and Wales,* 1841–1960. London: Chester Beatty Research Institute.

Coale, A.J. and Demeny, P. (1966). *Regional Model Life Tables and Stable Populations.* Princeton, N.J.: Princeton University Press.

Coale, A.J. (1971). Age patterns of marriage. *Population Studies* **25**, 193–214.

Coale, A.J. and McNeil, D.R. (1972). The distribution by age of the frequency of first marriage in a female cohort. *Journal of the American Statistical Association* **67**, 743–749.

Coale, A.J. and Trussell, T.J. (1974). Model fertility schedules: Variations in the age structure of childbearing in human populations. *Population Index* **40**, 185–258.

Cox, P.R. and Scott, W.F. (1977). International studies in generation mortality (with discussion). *Journal of the Institute of Actuaries* **104**, Part 3, 297–333.

Cramér H. and Wold, H. (1935). Mortality variations in Sweden: A study in graduation and forecasting. *Skandinavisk Aktuarietidskrift* **11**, 161–241.

David, H.A. and Moeschberger, M.L. (1978). *The Theory of Competing Risks.* London: Griffin.

Derrick, V.P.A. (1927). Observations on (1) errors of age in the population statistics of England and Wales, and (2) the changes in mortality indicated by the national records. *Journal of the Institute of Actuaries* **58**, 117–146.

Duchêne, J. and Gillet-de Stefano, S. (1974). Ajustement analytique des courbes de fécondité générale [Analytic adjustment of general fertility curves]. *Population et Famille* No. 32, 53–93.

Duncan, O.D. and McRae, J.A. (1979). Multiway contingency analysis with a scaled response or factor, in K.F. Schuessler (ed.), *Sociological Methodology, 1979.* San Francisco: Jossey-Bass, pp. 68–85.

Easterlin, R.A. (1973). Relative economic status and the American fertility swing, in E.B. Sheldon (ed.), *Family Economic Behavior: Problems and Prospects.* Philadelphia: J.B. Lippincott, pp. 170–223.

Easterlin, R.A. (1978). What will 1984 be like? Socioeconomic implications of recent twists in age structure. *Demography* **15**, 397–432.

Ewbank, D. (1974). An Examination of Several Applications of the Standard Pattern of Age at First Marriage. Unpublished Ph.D. dissertation, Princeton University.

Farid, S.M. (1973). On the pattern of cohort fertility. *Population Studies* **27**, 159–168.

Fienberg, S.E. and Mason, W.M. (1978). Identification and estimation of age-period-cohort models in the analysis of discrete archival data, in K.F. Schuessler (ed.), *Sociological Methodology, 1979*. San Francisco: Jossey-Bass, pp. 1–65.

Fienberg, S.E. (1980). *The Analysis of Cross-classified Categorical Data, 2nd edition.* Cambridge, Mass.: MIT Press.

Frost, W.H. (1939). The age selection of mortality from tuberculosis in successive decades. *American Journal of Hygiene* **30**, 91–96.

Gabriel, K.R. and Ronen, I. (1958). Estimates of mortality from infant mortality rates. *Population Studies* **12**, 164–169.

Gilks, W.R. (1979). The Examination of a Model of Marital Fertility Depending on Both Age and Duration of Marriage. Unpublished M.Sc. dissertation, University of Southampton.

Gilks, W.R. and Hobcraft, J. (1980). Personal communication.

Goldman, N. (1980). Far Eastern patterns of mortality. *Population Studies* **34**, 5–19.

Greenberg, B.G., Wright, J.J. and Sheps, C.G. (1950). A technique for analysing some factors affecting the incidence of syphilis. *Journal of the American Statistical Association* **45**, 373–399.

Hajnal, J. (1950a). Births, marriages and reproductivity, England and Wales, 1938–47, in *Papers of the Royal Commission on Population, Volume II: Reports and Selected Papers of the Statistics Committee.* London: H.M. Stationery Office, pp. 303–422.

Hajnal, J. (1950b). The analysis of birth statistics, 1939–1943, in *Papers of the Royal Commission on Population, Volume II: Reports and Selected Papers of the Statistics Committee.* London: H.M. Stationery Office, pp. 134–177.

Heckman, J. and Robb, R. (1985). Using longitudinal data to estimate age, period and cohort effects in earnings equations. This volume.

Henry, L. (1961). Some data on natural fertility. *Eugenics Quarterly* **8**, 81–91.

Hernes, G. (1972). The process of entry into first marriage. *American Sociological Review* **37**, 173–182.

Heuser, R.L. (1976). *Fertility Tables for Birth Cohorts by Color: United States, 1917–1973,* DHEW Publication No. (HRA) 76–1152. Rockville, MD: U.S. National Center for Health Statistics.

Hogan, H.R. and McNeil, D.R. (1979). On fitting statistical relations to age-specific mortality data. Unpublished paper, Princeton University.

Hooker, R.H. (1898). Is the birth rate still falling? *Transactions of the Manchester Statistical Society*, 101–126.

Isaac, L., Cutright, P., Jackson, E., and Kelly, W.R. (1979). Period effects on race and parity-specific birth probabilities of American women, 1917–1976: A new measure of fertility. Unpublished paper, Florida State University.

Jain, A.K. and Hermalin, A.I. (1971). Fecundity models for estimating fertility over the reproductive period, in *International Population Conference/Congrès International de la Population, London, 1969, Vol. 1*. Liège: International Union for the Scientific Study of Population.

Kermack, W.O., McKendrick, A.G., and McKinlay, P.L. (1934a). Death rates in Great Britain and Sweden: Some general regularities and their significance. *Lancet* **1**, 698–703.

Kermack, W.O., McKendrick, A.G., and McKinlay, P.L. (1934b). Death rates in Great Britain and Sweden: Expression of specific mortality rates as products of two factors, and some consequences thereof. *Journal of Hygiene* **34**, 433–457.

Keyfitz, N. and Flieger, W. (1968). *World Population: An Analysis of Vital Data*. Chicago: University of Chicago Press.

Le Bras, H. (1979). (Translated by J. Hobcraft.) Model Life Tables. Unpublished manuscript, United Nations.

Ledermann, S. and Brass, J. (1959). Les dimensions de la mortalité [The dimensions of mortality]. *Population* **14**, 637–682.

Ledermann, S. (1969). *Nouvelles Tables-Types de Mortalité* [New Model Life Tables], Institut National d'Etudes Démographiques, Travaux et Documents, Cahier No. 53. Paris: Presses Universitaires de France.

Lee, R.D. (1974a). Forecasting births in post-transition populations: Stochastic renewal with serially correlated fertility. *Journal of the American Statistical Association* **69**, 607–617.

Lee, R.D. (1974b). The formal dynamics of controlled populations and the echo, the boom and the bust. *Demography* **11**, 563–585.

Lee, R.D. (1977). Target fertility, contraception, and aggregate rates: Toward a formal synthesis. *Demography* **14**, 455–479.

Lee, R.D. (1980). Aiming at a moving target: Period fertility and changing reproductive goals. *Population Studies* **34**, 205–226.

Malthus, T.R. (1798). *First Essay on Population*. Reprinted by MacMillan, London, 1966.

Mason, Wm.M. and Smith, H.L. (1985). Age-period-cohort analysis and the study of deaths from pulmonary tuberculosis. This volume.

Mata, L. (1978). *The Children of Santa Maria Cauqué: A Prospective Field Study of Health and Growth.* Cambridge, Mass.: MIT Press.

Nelder, J.A. (1977). A reformulation of linear models (with discussion). *Journal of the Royal Statistical Society, Series B* **26**, 86–102.

Netherlands, Centraal Bureau voor de Statistiek (1975). *Generatie-Sterftetafels voor Nederland: Afgeleid uit Waarnemingen over de Periode 1871–1973* [Generation Life Tables for the Netherlands: Derived from Observations in the Period 1871–1973]. The Hague: Staatsuitgeverij.

Page, H.J. (1977). Patterns underlying fertility schedules: A decomposition by both age and marriage duration. *Population Studies* **31**, 85–106.

Pearson, K. (1978). *The History of Statistics in the 17th and 18th Centuries against the Changing Background of Intellectual, Scientific and Religious Thought; Lectures by K. Pearson given at University College London during the Academic Sessions, 1921–1933,* edited by E.S. Pearson. London: Griffin.

Preston, S.H. and van de Walle, E. (1978). Urban French mortality in the nineteenth century. *Population Studies* **32**, 275–297.

Preston, S.H. and McDonald, J. (1979). The incidence of divorce within cohorts of American marriages contracted since the Civil War. *Demography* **16**, 1–25.

Pullum, T.W. (1980). Separating age, period, and cohort effects in white U.S. fertility, 1920–1970. *Social Science Research* **9**, 225–244.

Rindfuss, R.R. and Bumpass, L.L. (1978). Age and the sociology of fertility: How old is too old? in K.E. Taeuber, L.L. Bumpass, and J.A. Sweet (eds.), *Social Demography.* New York/London: Academic Press, pp. 43–56.

Rogers, A., Raquillet, R., and Castro, L.J. (1978). Model migration schedules and their applications. *Environment and Planning A* **10**, 475–502.

Ryder, N.B. (1953). The measurement of temporal variations in age-specific fertility. Unpublished paper.

Ryder, N.B. (1963). The translation model of demographic change, in *Emerging Techniques in Population Research.* New York: Milbank Memorial Fund, pp. 65–81.

Ryder, N.B. (1964). The process of demographic translation. *Demography* **1**, 74–82.

Ryder, N.B. (1965a). The cohort as a concept in the study of social change. *American Sociological Review* **30**, 843–861. Reprinted in this volume.

Ryder, N.B. (1965b). The measurement of fertility patterns, in M.C. Sheps and J.C. Ridley (eds.), *Public Health and Population Change: Current Research Issues.* Pittsburgh: University of Pittsburgh Press, pp. 287–306.

Ryder, N.B. and Westoff, C.F. (1967). The trend of expected parity in the United States: 1955, 1960, 1965. *Population Index* **33**(2), 153–168. (Also Chapter III of *Reproduction in the United States, 1965,* by N.B. Ryder and C.F. Westoff. Princeton, NJ: Princeton University Press, 1971.)

Ryder, N.B. (1969). The emergence of a modern fertility pattern: United States, 1917–1966, S.J. Behrmann, L. Corsa, and R. Freedman (eds.), *Fertility and Family Planning: A World View.* Ann Arbor, Mich.: University of Michigan Press, pp. 99–123.

Ryder, N.B. (1971). Notes on fertility measurement. *Milbank Memorial Fund Quarterly* **49**(4, Part 2), 109–127.

Ryder, N.B. (1973). A critique of the National Fertility Study. *Demography* **10**, 495–506.

Ryder, N.B. (1978). A model of fertility by planning status. *Demography* **15**, 433–458.

Ryder, N.B. (1980). Components of temporal variations in American fertility, in R.W. Hiorns (ed.), *Demographic Patterns in Developed Societies.* London: Taylor and Francis, pp. 11–54.

Sacher, G.A. (1957). Discussion, in *Mammalian Aspects of Basic Mechanisms of Radiobiology.* NAS-NRC Publication No. 513, Report No. 21. Washington, D.C.: National Academy of Sciences, pp. 121–125 and 137–142.

Sacher, G.A. (1960). Analysis of life tables with secular terms, in B.S. Strehler (ed.), *Biology of Aging.* Washington, D.C.: American Institute of Biological Sciences, pp. 253–257.

Sacher, G.A. (1977). Life table modification and life prolongation, in C.E. Finch and L. Hayflick (eds.), *Handbook of the Biology of Aging.* New York: Van Nostrand Reinhold, pp. 532–638.

Sanderson, W. (1976). Towards an economic analysis of the baby boom: A test of the Easterlin hypothesis. Unpublished paper, Stanford University.

Scotland, General Register Office. Various vital statistics reports. Edinburgh: General Register Office.

Smith, D.P. and Keyfitz, N. (1977). *Mathematical Demography: Selected*

Papers. Biomathematics Vol. 6. Berlin/New York: Springer-Verlag.

Springett, V.H. (1950). A comparative study of tuberculosis mortality rates. *Journal of Hygiene* **48**, 361–395.

Strehler, B.L. (1962). *Time, Cells and Aging.* London/New York: Academic Press.

Süssmilch, J.P. (1761). *Die Göttliche Ordnung* [The Divine Order], 2nd ed. Berlin.

Thurston, R. (1977). An analysis of recent Swedish nuptiality. Unpublished paper, Princeton University.

Tukey, J.W. (1977). *Exploratory Data Analysis.* Reading, Mass.: Addison-Wesley.

U.N. Department of Economic and Social Affairs (1956). *Manuals on Methods of Estimating Population, Manual III: Methods for Population Projections by Sex and Age.* Population Studies, No. 25. New York: United Nations.

U.N. Department of Social Affairs. Population Branch (1955). *Age and Sex Patterns of Mortality: Model Life-Tables for Under-Developed Countries.* Population Studies, No. 22. New York: United Nations.

U.S. Bureau of the Census (1977). *Projections of the Population of the United States: 1977 to 2050.* Current Population Reports, Series P-25: Population Estimates and Projections, No. 704. Washington, D.C.: Government Printing Office.

U.S. National Center for Health Statistics (1972). *Cohort Mortality and Survivorship: United States Death-Registration States, 1900–1968.* Vital and Health Statistics, Series 3: Analytical Studies, No. 16. Rockville, MD: U.S. National Center for Health Statistics.

Vallin, J. (1973). *La Mortalité par Génération en France, depuis 1899* [Cohort mortality in France since 1899]. Institut National d'Etudes Démographiques, Travaux et Documents, Cahier No. 63. Paris: Presses Universitaires de France.

Vasantkumar, N.J.C. (1979). Age Patterns of Mortality of American Blacks, 1940 to 1970. Unpublished Ph.D. dissertation, Princeton University.

Vaupel, J.W., Manton, K.G., and Stallard, E. (1979). The impact of heterogeneity in individual frailty on the dynamics of mortality. *Demography* **16**, 439–454.

Westoff, C.F. and Ryder, N.B. (1977). The predictive validity of reproductive intentions. *Demography* **14**, 431–453.

Wunsch, G. (1979). Effect of changes in nuptiality on natality in Western Europe. Paper presented at the IUSSP Seminar on Nuptiality and

Fertility, January 1979, Bruges.

Yule, G.U. (1906). On the changes in the marriage and birth rates in England and Wales during the past half century. *Journal of the Royal Statistical Society* **69**, 88–147.

5. USING LONGITUDINAL DATA TO ESTIMATE AGE, PERIOD AND COHORT EFFECTS IN EARNINGS EQUATIONS*

James Heckman

Richard Robb[1]

The literature on the determinants of earnings suggests an earnings function for individual i which depends on age a_i, year t, "vintage" or "cohort" c_i, schooling level s_i, and experience e_i. Adopting a linear function to facilitate exposition we may write

$$Y_i(t, a_i, c_i, e_i, s_i) = \alpha_0 + \alpha_1 a_i + \alpha_2 t + \alpha_3 e_i + \alpha_4 s_i + \alpha_5 c_i, \qquad (1)$$

where e_i is experience, usually defined for males as age minus schooling, $(e_i = a_i - s_i)$,[1] and Y_i may be any monotone transformation of earnings.

Each variable in equation (1) has some argument supporting its inclusion in the equation. Age (a_i) may be a direct determinant of earnings through maturation or other physiological effects. It may also be a signal used by employers to estimate productivity. Year effects (t) may arise from disembodied technical progress that affects all workers or else through other general labor market variables that determine individual earnings. Work experience (e_i) is interpreted as a proxy for "human capital acquisition" (see Mincer, 1974) or other activities that raise the perceived productivity of workers as a function of their work experience.

* This research was supported by NSF Grant SES-8107963, NIH Grant NIH-1-R01-H016846-01 and a Guggenheim Fellowship awarded in 1978–1979. The first draft of this paper was read at an SSRC Conference at Mr. Kisco, New York, October, 1978. We have benefited from discussions with Tom MaCurdy. A later draft was presented at an LSE Conference on The Analysis of Panel Data on Income in June, 1982.

[1] The authors are affiliated with the Department of Economics, University of Chicago, and the National Opinion Research Center.

[1] This measure is less adequate for females. See Mincer and Polachek (1974) for measures of work experience for females that recognize the intermittent nature of lifetime female labor supply.

Schooling (s_i) is known to increase earnings (but the precise reason for this is not yet known). The cohort variable (c_i) is a stand in for variety of plausible cohort specific phenomena. Easterlin (1978) and Welch (1979) suggest that workers born into a large cohort carry an economic disadvantage throughout their careers (and conversely for those born into small cohorts). Easterlin (1961) suggests that workers of one cohort have different labor market expectations and therefore may pursue different careers and family plans (e.g., workers reared in the Depression may be pessimistic or risk averse while workers reared in the 1950s may be overly optimistic). A variety of other cohort specific phenomena might be suggested. These arguments taken together justify the list of variables used in equation (1) but not necessarily the functional form of the equation.[2]

It is obviously not possible to estimate all of the coefficients of equation (1) without further restrictions because of the definitional interdependencies among the variables. That is,

$$e_i = a_i - s_i,$$

$$t = a_i + c_i.$$

Direct estimation of (1) by least squares is impossible because of multicollinearity among the variables.

One can substitute for c_i and a_i to reach a commonly utilized specification of the earnings function:

$$Y_i(t,e_i,s_i) = [\alpha_0 + (\alpha_2 + \alpha_5)t] + [\alpha_1 + \alpha_3 - \alpha_5]e_i$$
$$+ [\alpha_1 + \alpha_4 - \alpha_5]s_i. \tag{2}$$

In a cross section, the year effect $[(\alpha_2 + \alpha_5)t]$ is impounded in the intercept term. Clearly one can estimate the *difference* between the effect of experience (α_3) and the effect of schooling (α_4) in a cross section. But holding schooling constant, an extra year of experience is also an extra year of age as well as reduction in the person's (birth) cohort by one year.

---

[2] We consider more general functional forms in the next section.

A similar difficulty arises in estimating the schooling coefficient holding experience constant.

The way we have defined them, age, period, and cohort variables and experience, age and schooling variables obey exact linear relationships among each other. This suggests that equation (1) makes no sense. An analyst cannot claim that the variables on the right hand side of (1) can be independently varied. Equation (1) is not identified.

The justification for (1) that implicitly appears in the literature is that most or all of the variables on the right hand side of (1) are proxy variables for underlying unobserved variables that are not themselves linearly dependent. Thus age (a_i) is a proxy for physiological variables and screening measures used by employers. The year effect (t) is a proxy for macroeconomic or market variables that in principle can be measured. The experience variable (e_i) is a proxy for training and other variables that raise perceived productivity that in principle can be measured. Schooling (s_i) is only a proxy for ability or productivity (or both) and the cohort variable (c_i) is a crude proxy for a variety of causal variables.

This argument suggests that equation (1) is only a crude approximation of what we are really interested in. The approximation is so crude that it creates a problem of its own. The correct formulation of (1) is as an errors in variables model (see, e.g., Aigner *et al.* (1984) for a survey of such models). Equations like (1) should not be taken too literally and at a minimum one should look for better proxies for the underlying unobserved variables.

This paper considers the general issue of whether or not longitudinal data can be used to estimate equation (1) or its errors in variables analogue. We conclude that the age-period-cohort problem as currently formulated is ill posed. On the issue of errors in variables, we do not have much to say beyond pointing to the existing econometric literature that indicates how access to longitudinal data affords the analyst additional instrumental variables in estimating an errors in variables model. But this point is worth making because this approach is not currently used in age-period-cohort analysis.

We make the following additional points. (1) Contrary to Fienberg and Mason (1978), the linear dependencies in the definitions of variables of equation (1) affect identification of interaction and higher order terms (Fienberg and Mason, 1985, correct this mistake in their paper in this volume). (2) Convenient "normalizations" in fact are often interpreted as if they have content. They may lead to erroneous interpretations of the data. (3) Additional information must be used to break the identification problem.

1. THE IDENTIFICATION PROBLEM

The central issue considered here is whether or not longitudinal data (repeated observations over time on the same individuals) can be used to identify further parameters of equation (1) above and beyond the estimable combinations of parameters in equation (2) that can be identified from a cross section. It is by now well known (e.g., Cagan, 1965) that such data do not solve the identification problem. The "year effect"—previously impounded in the intercept in equation (2) operates in the course of a panel, unless the economic environment is stationary.

Suppose that the year effect can be ignored $(\alpha_2 = 0)$. In this case, longitudinal data can be used to estimate some of the parameters of the model. For example, two successive post school observations on the same cohort permit estimation of $(\alpha_1 + \alpha_3)$, an age plus experience effect. Then, clearly the effect of cohort, α_5, can be estimated from the cross section (see equation (2) and the discussion surrounding it). Hence $\alpha_1 + \alpha_4$ can be estimated. Note that panel data and a time series of cross sections of unrelated individuals are equally informative on these parameters. Note further that as long as $\alpha_1 \neq 0$ all of the parameters of the model cannot be uniquely estimated.

The problem is that it is often plausible that $\alpha_2 \neq 0$. Suppose that we falsely assume that $\alpha_2 = 0$. Two successive (annual) observations on the same cohort provide an estimate of age plus experience plus year effects $(\alpha_1 + \alpha_2 + \alpha_3)$. Assuming the year effect (α_2) is positive, $\alpha_1 + \alpha_3$ would be overestimated. In a cross section, earlier cohorts have both higher ages and experience levels. Thus for early cohorts, too large a component of earnings would be attributed to age plus experience. Too little would be attributed to the cohort effect. Hence the estimate of α_5, the cohort effect, would be downward biased.

Our discussion of identifiability also applies if each variable on the right hand side of (1) is measured as a categorical variable. Thus define the vectors of dummy variables $\mathbf{A}$, $\mathbf{T}$, $\mathbf{E}$, $\mathbf{S}$ and C to correspond to each of the continuous variables a, t, e, s, and c. $\mathbf{A}$ is a vector such that for a person age a, the ath element is 1 and all the remaining elements are zero. Each of the other vectors is defined correspondingly. Defining coefficient vectors D_j appropriately, and normalizing the first element in each vector to zero to avoid trivial linear dependencies associated with using dummy variables (see, e.g., Goldberger, 1968), we reach

$$Y_i(A_i, T, E_i, S_i, C_i) = D_0 + D_1 A_i + D_2 T + D_3 E_i + D_4 S_i + D_5 C_i. \quad (3)$$

Corresponding to the condition $e_i = a_i - s_i$ in equation (1) is the condition for equation (3) that for an observation with the eth element of E_i nonzero, the jth element of A_i is nonzero if and only if the $(e-j)$th element of A_i is nonzero. (Since it makes no sense to have negative values of schooling, experience or age, it is necessary to require that $e \geq j$). Corresponding to the condition that $t_i = a_i + c_i$ in equation (1) is the requirement for equation (3) that for an observation with element t of T equal to one, the jth element of A_i is nonzero ($j \leq t$) if and only if the $(t-j)$th element of C_i is nonzero. Thus there are induced linear dependencies among the vectors of categorical variables and the D_i are not identified without further restrictions.

The remarks concerning identifiability made for the models with linear variables and with dummy variables carry over with full force to models with higher order interactions. Linear dependencies that arise from accounting identities become nonlinear identities. This point is not noted in the literature (see, e.g., Fienberg and Mason, 1978, p. 23). To illustrate this point consider the simple linear model of equation (1) and suppose $\alpha_2 = \alpha_5 = 0$. Thus, there is one restriction: $a_i = e_i + s_i$. Suppose that we are interested in exploring second order interaction terms as well. Thus to the model of equation (1), we add six terms for all the quadratic interactions and six parameters.

$$E_i(t, a_i, c_i, s_i) = \alpha_0 + \alpha_1 a_i + \alpha_3 e_i + \alpha_4 s_i + \beta_1 a_i^2 + \beta_2 e_i^2 + \beta_3 s_i^2$$
$$+ \beta_4 a_i e_i + \beta_5 a_i s_i + \beta_6 e_i s_i.$$

The identity $a_i = e_i + s_i$ implies the following three restrictions on the model:

$$a_i^2 = e_i^2 + 2e_is_i + s_i^2,$$

$$a_ie_i = e_i^2 + e_is_i,$$

$$a_is_i = e_is_i + s_i^2.$$

Clearly all three terms on the left-hand side of the equations must be substituted out to avoid exact linear dependencies in the model. Thus, from the six coefficients which arise when quadratic interaction terms are introduced, only three *combinations* of coefficients can be estimated. In a model with cubic terms, of the ten coefficients associated with the cubic terms, only four distinct combinations of coefficients can be estimated.

More generally, in a model with interaction terms of order k with j variables[3] and one linear restriction among the variables of the $\binom{j+k-1}{k}$ coefficients only $\binom{j+k-2}{k}$ *combinations* of the coefficients associated with terms of order k can be identified. Further, in a model with interaction terms of order k with j variables and l linearly independent restrictions on the $\binom{j+k-1}{k}$ coefficients, only $\binom{j+k-l-1}{k}$ *combinations* of the coefficients can be identified.[4] These propositions can easily be verified by elementary combinatorial algebra.[5]

2. THE DANGER OF TAKING A NORMALIZATION TOO LITERALLY

One approach to "solving" the age-period-cohort identification problem is to ignore one of the three effects. The danger in taking this approach

---

[3] An interaction term of order k is the product of k elementary variables. Thus $a_1^3a_2^4a_3^2$ is an interaction of order 9.

[4] Clearly $j + k - l - 1 > 0$ for the proposition to be meaningful.

[5] See, e.g., Feller (1968), Chapter 2, for one presentation of the relevant combinatorial calculations.

arises in confusing a normalization for a substantive interpretation. Studies by Weiss and Lillard (1978) and Johnson and Stafford (1974) provide an interesting illustration of this point. Both use NSF panel data on the earnings of scientists. Both find that for mathematicians and physicists the disparity in real wages between recent Ph.D. entrants and individuals with more professional experience increased during the 1960s. This is in contrast to the situation in economics and sociology where there is no evidence of increasing disparity between social scientists in the two experience classes.

Johnson and Stafford explain this result in terms of "year-experience interaction" in the labor market for scientists. Supplies of fresh Ph.D.'s were enlarged by federal subsidies just as demand for scientific personnel fell off. Due to a presumed rigidity in salary structures for tenured professors, much of the needed wage adjustment fell on young workers. A similar phenomenon was not at work in the market for social scientists where the demand for fresh Ph.D.'s held steady or even expanded.

The following modification of earnings equation (1) captures the Johnson-Stafford argument. Assume that there is no age effect and permit interaction terms between e and c, e and t and c and t but assume no interaction between s and the other variables. Then

$$Y(e,c,t,s) = \phi_0 + \phi_1 e + \phi_2 c + \phi_3 t + \phi_4 ec + \phi_5 et + \phi_6 ct + \phi_7 s$$
$$+ \phi_8 e^2 + \phi_9 c^2 + \phi_{10} t^2 + \phi_{11} s^2 . \tag{4}$$

The Johnson-Stafford story suggests that for scientists $\phi_5 > 0$, i.e., that in later years the contrast in earnings between experienced and inexperienced workers widens.

Weiss and Lillard claim that later cohorts have a higher growth rate of earnings due to "embodied technical change." They argue that $\phi_4 > 0$. They offer evidence on this point from an empirical model that "normalizes" year effects to zero.

Using the definitions given above equation (2), $t = e + c + s$. Substitute into (4) to reach an equation similar to one utilized by Weiss and Lillard:

$$Y(e,c,s) = \phi_0 + (\phi_1 + \phi_3)e + (\phi_2 + \phi_3)c$$

$$+ (\phi_3 + \phi_7)s + (\phi_4 + \phi_5 + \phi_6 + 2\phi_{10})ec + (\phi_5 + 2\phi_{10})es$$

$$+ (\phi_6 + 2\phi_{10})cs + (\phi_5 + \phi_8 + \phi_{10})e^2 + (\phi_6 + \phi_9 + \phi_{10})c^2$$

$$+ (\phi_{10} + \phi_{11})s^2.$$

Evidence of a positive coefficient on the ec variable is clearly consistent with $\phi_4 = 0$, $\phi_5 > 0$ and $\phi_6 + \phi_5 + 2\phi_{10} > 0$. Thus the Weiss-Lillard evidence for their story is entirely consistent with the Johnson-Stafford story.

As there was no apparent "experience-cohort" interaction for social scientists, the Johnson-Stafford story appears to be the more plausible one for scientists because it is unlikely that embodiment of knowledge effects would be more pronounced for scientists than for social scientists.

This discussion illustrates two points: (1) The danger of taking a normalization too seriously, and (2) the value of additional information (e.g., the data on the market for social scientists) to resolve the identification problem.

3. SOLVING THE IDENTIFICATION PROBLEM WITH BETTER INFORMATION

The identification problem discussed in this paper arises because of dependencies among proxy variables. By assumption the underlying variables are not definitionally dependent. By improving the quality of the proxy variables it may be possible to secure identification of the effects of the unobserved variables and to avoid the collinearity that arises from using crude proxies.

The age-period-cohort effect identification problem arises because analysts want something for nothing: a general statistical decomposition of data without specific subject matter motivation underlying the decomposition. In a sense it is a blessing for social science that a purely statistical approach to the problem is bound to fail. We are forced to use our training as social scientists to improve on the crude age-period-cohort effect proxies (and the age, experience and schooling proxies).

One approach to this problem assumes that specific measured variables proxy the underlying unobserved variables. Thus in the context of an earnings equation, it is plausible to replace the year effect with variables indicating the state of the national and local labor market. Moreover, the concept of "cohort" can be refined. It is plausible that a cohort consists of a sequence of adjacent years (e.g., Depression or 1950s youth, etc.).[6]

If some individuals experience "breaks" in labor market experience so that $a_i \neq e_i + s_i$, and if the time spent in such breaks has no effect on earnings, it is possible to estimate separate age, experience and schooling effects in the earnings equation. The assumption that there is no parameter in the earnings function that is associated with time not at work is controversial. There are models such as those presented by Mincer and Polachek (1974) that give plausible reasons why time out of the labor force should result in skill atrophy.[7]

Other work by Lazear (1976) and Hanuschek and Quigley (1978) uses longitudinal data in an effort to break the exact linear dependence between age and experience. They measure experience by hours worked (see also Mincer (1978) who suggests an alternative to the Hanuschek-Quigley specification). It is important to note, however that human capital theory implies no simple or even montonic relationship between past hours of work and past investment, so that the value of this proxy is doubtful.[8]

---

[6] Cagan (1965) and Hall (1971) define vintage or cohort to be the same for an annual succession of vehicles based on comparable engineering specifications. Fienberg and Mason (1978) use a similar approach in their model of educational attainment.

[7] Even if there is no coefficient associated with time out of the labor force, age, experience and schooling are likely to be highly correlated so that estimates of these effects, if achieved, would not be expected to be very precise.

[8] Moreover, this "solution" creates the additional problem that work experience measures are not exogenous in an earnings equation.

4. A LATENT VARIABLE APPROACH

The approaches outlined in section 3 go only part way toward solving the problem. They achieve estimates of the "true" model only by assuming that some proxy is perfect. In fact, a better way to formulate the original problem is to write the earnings equation as a latent variable model.

To focus on essential ideas consider only age, period and cohort effects in a linear model. Earnings are assumed to be a function of a physiological variable at age a, P_a, a macro-variable at time t, M_t, and a cohort variable, E_c. Thus

$$Y(a,c,t) = P_a + E_c + M_t. \tag{5}$$

By assumption P_a, E_c and M_t are unobserved linearly independent variables. They may be decomposed into functions of observed and unobserved variables.

$$P_a = \phi_a(x_a ; \theta_a) + u_a, \tag{6a}$$

$$E_c = \phi_c(x_c ; \theta_c) + u_c, \tag{6b}$$

$$M_t = \phi_t(x_t ; \theta_t) + u_t. \tag{6c}$$

The x_j, $j = a,c,t$ are observed exogenous variables. $E(u_j|x_j) = 0$. The x_j functional forms of ϕ_j are assumed known but the θ_j are unknown parameters. The covariance matrix for the u_j is unrestricted. Thus define $u = (u_a, u_c, u_t)$ and $\theta = (\theta_a, \theta_c, \theta_t)$, and

$$E(u'u) = \Sigma.$$

Inserting equations (6) into (5) results in a reduced form estimating equation for y in terms of the x variables. Standard identification criteria apply. If the ϕ functions are all linear, in order to be able to estimate θ no linear dependencies among the x variables are permitted. Access to panel data and/or repeated observations over time enables us to estimate the components of variance arising from u_a, u_c, and u_t.[9,10]

Proxies may also be available for P_a, E_c and M_t. The associated

---

[9] The estimation problem is very similar to one considered by Nerlove (1967).

[10] Johnson and Hebein (1974) break the age-period-cohort effect identification problem by assuming that one of the components is an unobservable random component.

vectors of proxies are denoted respectively P_a^*, E_c^* and M_t^*. We assume that

$$P_a^* = b_a P_a + V_a, \tag{7a}$$

$$E_c^* = b_c E_c + V_c, \tag{7b}$$

$$M_t^* = b_t M_t + V_t, \tag{7c}$$

where V_i are suitably dimensioned mean zero vectors and the b_i are suitably dimensioned vectors. Intercepts could be added to these equations but this generality is foregone here to simplify the exposition. If the covariance matrices associated with V are diagonal we have the classical factor structure model provided that V is uncorrelated with P_a, E_c and M_t.

The conventional approach to age-period-cohort analysis assumes that a, c and t are perfect proxies for P_a, E_c, and M_t, respectively, except that the appropriate scaling elements (the b's) are unknown. Equivalently, these approaches assume that a, c, t are the sole determinants of P_a, E_c and M_t and that all of the ϕ functions are linear. The approaches surveyed in section 3 assume either that a richer (linearly independent) set of perfect proxies is available or that a richer set of x variables is available. The conventional approach makes overly strong assumptions and is wasteful of potential information. If we are prepared to be more specific about what our models mean and what we are trying to estimate, other proxies are available. Moreover, once we begin to take a position on what it is we seek to estimate we are usually able to produce x variables that plausibly determine P_a, E_c and M_t, so that the θ parameters can be estimated. With suitable covariance restrictions, equations (5)–(7) define a multiple-cause-multiple-indicator (MIMIC) model of the sort first analyzed by Jöreskog and Goldberger (1975) and extended in the econometric literature (see the survey by Aigner *et al.*, 1984).

There are a variety of plausible error structures for the u_j. For simplicity, we ignore covariance among different components of u. The most plausible error structure makes u_t identical across all observations at a common point in time but assumes u_t is serially correlated. There are two plausible specifications for u_c. The first assumes that u_c is common to all members of a cohort but lets u_c be serially correlated across cohorts. The second specification assumes that u_c is an independent draw from a common distribution for each member of the cohort. The second specification assumes that u_c is an individual specific effect. Neither specification of u_c precludes the other.

Given the physiological interpretation placed on P_a and the known population variability in the aging process, it is plausible that u_a is a person specific component that varies across age for the same person. It is plausible that once the main effect of age is removed, the u_a components are uncorrelated across people but they may be correlated over age for the same person.

Panel data are required to identify the variance components of the person specific components u_a and u_c (under the second specification). A time series of cross sections suffices to identify the components of variances of u_a and u_c (under the first specification). A general analysis of identification in this model requires taking a position on the order of the time series process for each element of u as well as taking greater care in specifying the cross covariance terms in greater detail than has been done here. Such analysis is, by now, entirely conventional in econometrics. (See, e.g., Aigner et al., 1984).

From the vantage point of the general MIMIC model presented in this section it should be clear that the linear dependency problem that motivates much research on the problem of estimating age, period and cohort effects is really the least significant aspect of the problem of estimating equation (5). The real problem is finding more and better proxies, better explanatory variables and sharper behavioral models that eliminate the vacuity inherent in context free statistical accounting schemes.

REFERENCES

Aigner, D. et al. (1984). Latent variables in econometrics, in Z. Griliches and M. Intrilligator (eds.), Handbook of Econometrics. North Holland, forthcoming.

Cagan, P. (1965). Measuring quality changes and the purchasing power of money: An explanatory study of automobiles. National Banking Review 3, 217–236. Reprinted in Z. Griliches (ed.), Price Indexes and Quality Change. Cambridge, Mass.: Harvard University Press, 1971.

Easterlin, R. (1961). The American baby boom in historical perspective. *American Economic Review* **51**, 869–911.

Easterlin, R. (1978). What will 1984 be like? Socioeconomic implications of recent twists in the age structure. *Demography* **15**, 397–432.

Feller, W. (1968). *An Introduction to Probability Theory and Its Application.* New York: Wiley.

Fienberg, S.E. and Mason, W.M. (1978). Identification and estimation of age-period-cohort models in the analysis of discrete archival data, in K.F. Schuessler (ed.), *Sociological Methodology 1979.* San Francisco: Jossey-Bass, pp. 1–67.

Fienberg, S.E. and Mason, W.M. (1985). Specification and implementation of age, period and cohort models. This volume.

Goldberger, A.S. (1968). *Topics in Regression Analysis.* London: MacMillan.

Hall, R.E. (1971). The measurement of quality change from vintage price data, in Z. Griliches (ed.), *Price Indices and Quality Change.* Cambridge, Mass.: Harvard University Press.

Hanuschek, E. and Quigley, J. (1978). Implicit investment profiles and intertemporal adjustments in relative wages. *American Economic Review* **68**, 67–79.

Johnson, T. and Hebein, F. (1974). Investment in human capital and growth in personal income 1956–1966. *American Economic Review* **64** (4), 604–613.

Johnson, G. and Stafford, F. (1974). Lifetime earnings in a professional labor market: Academic economists. *Journal of Political Economy* **82**, 549–570.

Jöreskog, K. and Goldberger, A. (1975). Estimation of a model with multiple indicators and multiple causes of a single latent variable. *Journal of the American Statistical Association* **70**, 631–639.

Lazear, E. (1976). Age, experience and wage growth. *American Economic Review* **66** (4), 548–580.

Mincer, J. (1974). *Schooling, Experience and Earnings.* New York: Columbia University Press.

Mincer, J. (1978). Comments on the Hanuschek-Quigley paper. Unpublished mimeo, Columbia University.

Mincer, J. and Polachek, S. (1974). Family investments in human capital: Earnings of women. *Journal of Political Economy* **82**, March/April, S.76–S.109.

Nerlove, M. (1967). Distributed lags and unobserved components of economic time series, in W. Fellner (ed.), *Ten Economic Essays in the*

Tradition of Irving Fisher. New York: Wiley, pp. 120–169.

Weiss, Y. and Lillard, L. (1978). Experience, vintage and time effects in the growth of earnings: American scientists, 1960–1970. *Journal of Political Economy* **86** (3), 427–447.

Welch, F. (1979). The effects of cohort size on earnings: The baby boom baby's financial bust. *Journal of Political Economy* **87** (5), 565–599.

6. AGE-PERIOD-COHORT ANALYSIS AND THE STUDY OF DEATHS FROM PULMONARY TUBERCULOSIS*

William M. Mason

Herbert L. Smith[t]

Our purpose is both substantive and methodological. Substantively, we crystallize the results of prior research and expectations into an extended rationale for the application of the age-period-cohort accounting framework to the problem of understanding historical variability in the rate of tuberculosis mortality. This framework is then used to analyze a ninety year data series of tuberculosis mortality rates for the state of Massachusetts and a similar forty year series for the United States. The age-period-cohort accounting framework yields age effects with an expected pattern not well understood, period effects consistent with the advent of successful chemotherapeutic regimes after World War II, and steadily declining cohort effects whose interpretation has yet to be verified. In an attempt to pin down a possible interpretation, we show that cohort nativity composition affects the trend of cohort mortality in the Massachusetts series, and both level and trend in the United States series. Our findings consolidate the results and anticipations of past research on TB mortality based in part on two-effect models and graphic display of rates, and to some extent clarify various proposed interpretations of the historical trend; they leave open the ultimate

* We thank Carol Carter for invaluable help in obtaining the source data for Massachusetts, Albert Anderson and Jonathan Sell for programming assistance, Carol Crawford for typing, and David Freedman, Warren Sanderson and the other conference participants for their thoughtful comments on the first draft. We are especially indebted to Stephen Fienberg for statistical advice, Halliman Winsborough for encouragement and comments, and Otis Dudley Duncan, whose skeptical reaction to an earlier draft ultimately led us to discover a major error which this draft corrects.

[t] The authors' names are listed in alphabetical order; this is truly joint work. William M. Mason is affiliated with the Department of Sociology and the Population Studies Center, The University of Michigan, and Herbert L. Smith is affiliated with the Department of Sociology, Indiana University.

question of why tuberculosis mortality declined in the industrializing countries. Methodologically, we show that the age-period-cohort accounting framework is helpful in organizing otherwise disparate theoretical and empirical material. Its usefulness appears to depend, however, on strong priors about the patterns in the coefficients as well as specific historical knowledge. Data analysis with unarticulated expectations and meager knowledge may be a recipe for error. A conventional exploratory stance, which works well for models of the additive analysis of variance type, is less suited to the age-period-cohort context, because of the need for identifying restrictions engendered by the inherent interaction among the three accounting categories.

1. INTRODUCTION

In the United States, United Kingdom, Australia and Scandinavia tuberculosis (TB) is no longer a leading cause of death. For these countries TB death rates have fallen steadily since the beginning of the twentieth century and, where records for earlier times exist, it is known that TB death rates have fallen steadily since at least the mid-nineteenth century.[1] This decline in TB mortality predates effective medical treatment of the disease in any of its manifestations, and even the acceptance of the germ theory of disease (Dubos and Dubos, 1952).

The demonstration in 1940 that the application of sulfonamides to guinea-pigs arrested the progress of tuberculosis led within a few years to the modern era of effective treatment of the disease (Toman, 1979). It is thought by some (Comstock, 1975) that prior to the existence of modern medication, physical segregation of active cases of tuberculosis from the rest of the population was helpful in the aggregate—if not to the individuals affected. As for the factors initiating and sustaining the secular decline prior to effective public health measures, few explanations

---

[1] We believe this characterization to hold for the industrialized countries more generally, but our sampling of the literature has been limited to English language articles concerning data obtained from a relatively limited number of countries. It is clear that there is currently a negative association cross-nationally between tuberculosis mortality or morbidity and level of economic development (Lowell, 1976).

have been offered, none substantiated. Moreover, no general framework has been put forward with which to evaluate the contribution of modern chemotherapy and prophylaxis, much less that of other factors, to the virtual disappearance of TB mortality in the technically developed countries.[2]

Writing more than two decades ago, Grigg (1958, p. 151) asked: "Could there be a relationship between the stalemate in the advancement of knowledge in tuberculology and the absence of original working hypotheses in this field?" Our sampling of the voluminous research literature in this area suggests that, contrary to Grigg's view, there has been for some time a rich array of evidence and hypotheses concerning the epidemiology of tuberculosis. What has been missing is a framework in which to assemble the evidence. Even with it, a full, detailed, and, above all, convincing historical model of fluctuations in TB mortality over the past century may be unattainable. If so, this would be merely a reflection of inadequate records and data rather than any lack of hypotheses.

In this paper we consider the usefulness of an age-period-cohort accounting framework for articulating some of the basic evidence concerning TB mortality, and apply it to a ninety year data series for Massachusetts and a forty year series for the United States. The dim prospects for explaining the secular trend in TB mortality might suggest that what we have to say is best left unwritten. Short of the major accomplishment such explanation would represent, our work has value in the following respects. First, the framework and estimates we present should aid further attempts to explain secular variation in tuberculosis. Second, the accounting framework we employ structures the data in such a way that consideration of the impact of modern chemotherapy on TB mortality is necessarily part of the specification. Third, this framework may prove helpful in epidemiologic research yet to be carried out on TB mortality in developing countries, and useful for the study of other diseases. Fourth, the study of TB mortality is also revealing for

---

[2] TB continues to exist in the developed countries, although it is now almost entirely manifest as morbidity. Recent misuse of antituberculin drugs in less developed countries has resulted in the development of some highly treatment-resistant forms of the bacillus, and contributed to a rise in the incidence of the disease in the developed countries as a result of population migration.

methodological reasons, as we are able to elucidate previously unarticulated facets of the accounting framework employed here.

2. AGE, PERIOD AND COHORT EFFECTS
IN TUBERCULOSIS MORTALITY

Comstock (1975) describes the process by which individuals contract TB as consisting of two stages. The first concerns exposure to the disease; the second concerns the chance of its development following invasion by the tubercle bacillus. Although communicable, TB is not acutely contagious: Invasion of a host by the tubercle bacillus depends on the chance of coming into contact with an infectious case (Edwards and Palmer, 1969), the infectiousness of the case (Chapman and Dyerly, 1964), the duration of exposure (Comstock *et al.*, 1974), and the treatment status of the case—at least since the advent of efficacious medication (Kamat *et al.*, 1966). In the second of Comstock's (1975) stages, the essential questions are whether, for how long, and under what conditions the host can resist the disease. Lancaster (1978, pp. 25–26) writes that "there is usually a state of balance between host and bacillus, under which the lesions can be healed; but conditions of privation, over-crowding as in barracks or occupation, overwork, malnutrition, diabetes, psychosis and pregnancy are known to influence the balance unfavorably and the symptoms of the disease may become manifest." For recent populations it matters crucially whether the host is treated with medication available since the late 1940s.

We assign some of the factors associated with exposure to risk of infection, as well as some of those associated with the development of the disease given infection, to the categories of an age-period-cohort framework. This provides a substantive basis for an age-period-cohort parameterization and potentially gives meaning to each of the three dimensions (age, period and cohort), which in turn enables the refinement of hypotheses concerning variability in TB mortality. Given a substantively justified age-period-cohort parameterization we then examine the two data series mentioned earlier. The task of linking a relatively full array of socioeconomic and other factors to age, period and cohort is well beyond our present means and will probably remain so indefinitely.   The current exercise nevertheless helps to clarify the potential matchup between causal factors and age, period and cohort.

2.1. Cohort and Age

The attractiveness of the cohort as the analytic unit by which to characterize changes in TB mortality stems from the work of Andvord (1930) and Frost (1939), who showed that apparent changes in the pattern of cross-sectional age-specific rates could be viewed as translations of declining TB mortality across cohorts with a relatively constant pattern to the within-cohort age-specific rates.   Instead of trying to understand why TB was increasingly becoming a fatal disease of the aged, attention could focus on why successive cohorts had decreasing TB mortality rates.[3] It is also relevant that infection by the bacillus is thought to have been quite prevalent when TB mortality was high (Pope and Gordon, 1955), that infection apparently occurred early in life, and that the disease had (and has) a highly variable incubation period, tending to the lengthy. It would be a step toward closure to link these aspects of the disease to cohort differentiation.   The lengthiness of incubation lessens the attractiveness of periods as basic markers because period changes (exclusive of effective medication) in the chance of contracting the

---

[3] Although widely cited in epidemiological research, epidemiological methodology textbooks (e.g., McMahon et al., 1960; Susser, 1973) and elsewhere (e.g., Ryder, 1968), this point has not been fully understood by some (e.g., Pope and Gordon, 1955; Lowell, 1976) although other contributors have made good use of it (e.g., Spicer, 1954; Hinman et al., 1976; Hemminki and Paakkulainen, 1976; Stevens and Lee, 1978).   In a sweeping and detailed review article which reproduces Frost's (1939) data, Pope and Gordon (1955, pp. 329–330) also present charts of age-specific TB mortality by year, accompanied by the comment that, "No longer is tuberculosis primarily a disease of young adult life in the United States, but rather a disease of middle life, and in men of old age. While the causes of this change in age-distribution are still not clear, from the epidemiological viewpoint it is believed to reflect the adjustment of man to the disease."   And in an authoritative compendium Lowell (1976, p. 3) writes, "Experience has shown that in several countries after the initial epidemic stage has passed, the natural trend of tuberculosis is one of decline. Tuberculosis death rates tend to concentrate in the older age groups, and fewer deaths occur in young children. *Similarly, new cases tend to shift to older age groups*" (emphasis ours). Frost (1939) explained that assertions such as these required age-specific cohort rates as evidence.   Pope and Gordon (1955) were referring to cross-sectional data. Lowell's claim is advanced without data or citations, but in an earlier work, Lowell (1969, pp. 72–73) makes a similar claim based on age-specific period rates. The persistence of this methodological error is an indication that a dominant accounting framework has yet to emerge in the study of temporal variability in TB.

disease are not likely to be seen immediately. So slow is the incubation that individuals of not too advanced age in older cohorts may die of something else instead of TB induced by a perturbation at some specific point in time. Moreover, if TB colonies were suddenly established and all individuals known to be suffering from the disease occupied them as of a particular point in time, TB would still continue to appear in the noninstitutionalized population because of the slow incubation of the disease, and it would still be differentiable by cohort.

Early exposure to TB also suggests a reliance on the cohort as the primary analytic category since available evidence (Andvord, 1930; Frost, 1939; Springett, 1950) indicates that, until the advent of effective chemotherapy, successive cohorts moved through life *as though* they had different probabilities of dying by tuberculosis assigned at birth. If this perception is correct, the central question is: What caused changes in these probabilities? McKeown (1976) offers a one-factor explanation of the decline in TB mortality, but refers in his discussion to gross period, not cohort mortality. Since gross period rates amount to moving averages of cohort rates, his explanation can be construed as applying to cohort differentials in TB mortality.

McKeown (1976) argues that improved nutrition preceded and in fact caused the decline in TB mortality in England and Wales, and suggests that this thesis is valid for other populations as well. There is some fairly direct short-term and cross-sectional evidence suggesting a relationship between nutrition—specifically, the consumption of meat and dairy products—and tuberculosis (Pope and Gordon, 1955). By what process would nutritional improvement differentiate cohorts? We consider the force of a single improvement, maintained thereafter, and then the consequence of steady improvement in diet.

Suppose that to begin with there were no cohort differentials in TB mortality. The occurrence of a rapid transition beyond a threshold level of nutrition would improve the resistance of all cohorts present at the time of the change. Older cohorts would benefit less from the change than younger cohorts since they would already have had more opportunity to experience TB morbidity and mortality. Future cohorts would benefit even more, for two reasons. First, they would begin life with the higher nutritional level, thereby receiving its maximum benefit through resistance. Second, the curtailment of the disease in older cohorts would reduce exposure to the risk of infection.

The simplest step function for nutritional improvement amounts to a single application of an exogenous pressure on tuberculosis, followed thereafter by an endogenously created decline in exposure due to the new and increased, but still constant, resistance to the disease given exposure. A continually improving diet adds to this process an exogenous pressure via steady improvement in the resistance to TB and thus accelerates the decline in exposure. By either scenario younger and future cohorts fare better than older ones. We shall return to the problem of understanding cohort differences in our discussion of the within-cohort age pattern of TB mortality, since interpretation of cohort and age variability is intrinsically linked.

Within cohorts there is age variability in TB mortality rates. Description of this variability must distinguish between recent years, for which TB has become a rare cause of death in the developed countries, and earlier years, when TB was falling from its position as a leading cause of death in these countries. It is the earlier years that concern us. For them the age pattern of mortality within cohorts was: high during infancy, low in childhood, high again at early adulthood, and declining thereafter (Comstock *et al.*, 1974). This pattern characterizes deaths due to TB of all types combined. Pulmonary tuberculosis was, however, most prevalent, and accounted for the bulk of all TB mortality after infancy. It therefore determined the mortality peak at early adulthood. In further discussion of age differentials we shall ignore infant mortality, which presents special problems of its own.

Specification of within-cohort age-specific TB mortality depends on the time frame and type of TB; there is also evidence to suggest that it depends on population density and sex (Springett, 1950). Although descriptively revealing, empirical research has yet to deal with the meaning of age differences and the internal variability of these differences within populations. It may be that no single representation of the meaning of age is responsible for this diversity. Age may have multiple meanings even in reference to a particular kind of TB, in particular kinds of areas, for a specific sex. This problem of multiplicity has been noted for the study of other phenomena (Hagenaars and Cobben, 1978).

The following discussion refers to age variability without consideration of factors which internally differentiate populations. We will suggest a single interpretation of the age-patterning historically apparent in TB mortality. Given this interpretation it is possible to view population density and sex as covariates with age in the determination of TB mortality.

If the pattern to be apprehended is a set of stacked cohort-specific age trajectories, the problem is to understand the existence and form of the age distribution and the separation of the cohort trace lines from each other. The remarkably consistent age pattern within cohorts may reflect a distribution function of the incubation time of the disease. This would account for the existence, but not the form of the age pattern. Functional forms often resist explanation.

Understanding the separation of the cohort trace lines from each other is again the problem of explaining the decline in TB mortality by cohort. The interpretation of the age pattern and the cohort differences thus merges. The hypothesis that the age trajectory is the manifestation of an incubation distribution function for those exposed to the bacillus is consistent with a general account of the layering of the within-cohort age-specific trajectories. Each cohort is subject to a regime of probabilities for exposure to the tubercle bacillus, to infection of the host given exposure (hereafter we combine exposure and infection since the two are virtually impossible to distinguish in archival data), contraction of the disease given infection, and death given contraction of the disease. Specifically, let $g(x)$ designate a distribution function of the proportion dying of TB at duration x, for all those contracting the disease. This function varies not with age, but with time since exposure. Assume the function is constant across cohorts (until the era of effective medication). Now suppose that each cohort has a (possibly) different lifetime probability of infection by the bacillus, but that its cumulative distribution of infection by age has the same functional form across cohorts. If $F(u)$ is the cumulative infection distribution for a cohort, its associated density function is $f(u) = F'(u)$. Finally, assume that each cohort has an age-invariant probability of contracting the disease given invasion of the host by the bacillus. For a given cohort, let this probability be c. Then, for a cohort, the proportion dying at age a is given by

$$q(a) = c \int_0^a g(x) f(a - x) dx , \qquad (1)$$

or in discrete notation,

$$q_a = c \sum_{x=0}^{a} g_x f_{a-x} \qquad (2)$$

This formulation will produce the same age-specific mortality pattern for each cohort while allowing differential cohort mortality; that is, it will reproduce a stack of within-cohort age-specific mortality curves all having the same shape.[4]

On logical grounds alone, if $g(x)$ is constant across cohorts, $F(u)$ or c must be free to vary, otherwise there can be no variation in cohort TB mortality. The nutrition thesis is consistent with variation in both $F(u)$ and c. Moreover, infection by the bacillus and contraction of the disease given the presence of infection are known to have varied by cohort. The constant c could be replaced by an age-specific function which would enrich the formulation but make it less tractable. Without c or an associated age-specific function the nutrition thesis, and the resistance argument more generally, is eliminated; cohort differences become solely a consequence of differential infection. Improved resistance can not directly reduce infection by the bacillus. It can, however, thwart development of the disease given infection of the host by the bacillus, and through this mechanism indirectly reduce the chance of infection. Hence a resistance component must be explicit in the model.

Since the age pattern of TB mortality varies with the type of TB and with population density among other things, it seems appropriate to allow for the possibility that $g(x)$ varies across disease types and that $F(u)$ and c vary across disease types, sociodemographic conditions, and cohorts. Thus, the diversity noted earlier could be accounted for with a single understanding of the meaning of the age pattern. Problems remain. For example, the interpretation is incomplete since the forms of $g(x)$ and $F(u)$ are unspecified. Our purpose in offering an admittedly incomplete formulation is to spur others to re-examine the meaning of age variability in TB mortality. Formal models developed for the prevalence of TB in modern times (with medication present) may provide leads (Bailey, 1975, pp. 302–309), as may the formal models of demography (Coale, 1972; Henry, 1976; Keyfitz, 1977) or disease (Chiang, 1980, pp. 300–332), especially if enlightened by knowledge of the biochemistry of the disease.

It is doubtful whether data for the historical period in question will ever be available in detail sufficient to unravel the meaning of age variability in TB mortality. Still, if age differences continue to be

---

[4] The essential notion employed in expressions (1) and (2) is that of a convolution of two distributions (Coale, 1977, p. 140; Chiang, 1980).

discussed they must be dealt with, if only by plausible speculation. The incorporation of the age pattern into the cohort perspective offered here crystallizes the difficulty inherent in modelling with archival data. There are at least two kinds of information ($F(u)$ and c) required for each cohort, but the accounting framework defines no more than one parameter per cohort, in the form of contrasts subject to a normalization. These contrasts, moreover, reflect an unidentifiable mixture of $F(u)$ and c.

2.2. Period

TB mortality varies over time. Gross period variability is not, however, what we seek to interpret. Rather, cohorts assume primacy as the units through which the decline in mortality occurred. In this view, period variability is understood in terms of effects which cut across all cohorts existing at specific points in time. Period effects are assumed to have constant impact across ages and cohorts. They can indicate changes as fundamental as the development and implementation of an effective new medical technology, or the impact of phenomena such as changes in disease classification or war.

There has been significant chemotherapeutic innovation in the treatment of tuberculosis since World War II. The most important drugs are Streptomycin, p-amino-salicylate and Isoniazid, which were introduced from the mid-1940s through the early 1950s, and Ethambutol and Rifampin, which were introduced during the early 1960s. Clearly the first wave of medication did not eliminate TB mortality, otherwise there would have been no need for Ethambutol and Rifampin. Nor did the second wave; even in the most developed countries there is still some mortality due to TB.

Did modern chemotherapy and prophylaxis accelerate the decline in TB mortality? Although the clinical evidence of the effectiveness of modern drug regimens is indisputable, placement of this impact in a historical context requires a different framework, namely a population model which includes ages, periods and cohorts as accounting categories. We would expect the effects of the medical revolution to be detectable as period effects in an age-period-cohort accounting framework. The drugs are presumably administered to those in need regardless of age; their effect is swift; their elimination would rapidly be shown to be deleterious for the population as a whole.

With pervasive distribution, and over a long enough span of time, the availability of the modern drugs to a population modifies the classic bimodal distribution of TB mortality within cohorts and renders less relevant the long and variable incubation period of the disease. Under these conditions, for those born after the chemotherapeutic innovations were incorporated into the public health system, birth cohort is no longer salient—whenever the disease appears it can be treated successfully. Indeed, even when a person is judged susceptible to the disease, its development can be held in check indefinitely. In this respect, the medical revolution in the treatment of tuberculosis differs from improvements in nutrition. Even if the nutritional level increased steadily, its presumed effect was apparently such as not to eliminate or greatly alter the age-specific pattern of TB mortality within cohorts. It is thus plausible to match a trend in nutrition to cohorts, and successful medical innovation to periods. When the disease becomes a very minor cause of death, as it has in the United States, and there is no longer substantial cohort differentiation in TB mortality, it continues to be helpful to view the medical innovation as matched with periods.

3. METHODOLOGIES FOR DESCRIPTION OF TUBERCULOSIS MORTALITY

Researchers into the epidemiology of tuberculosis have, at least implicitly, recognized three sources of variation in mortality rates: age, period and cohort. In practice, however, the analytic procedures employed have generally treated TB mortality as a function of two of these sources of variation, characterizing the third residually if at all. We next consider these two-effect models, and then describe the three-effect accounting framework.

3.1. Two-Effect Models

The "generation method" of Kermack et al. (1934) appears to be the central building block for past models of TB mortality. This method involves creating ratios within cohorts of the mortality rates of neighboring age groups. These ratios are then averaged across all cohorts for each specific age. The result is a set of age-specific multipliers which may be applied to the baseline rate of a given cohort in order to yield that cohort's mortality at all ages. Spicer (1954) used this technique in conjunction with

$$M(t, \theta) = Ae^{-k(t-\theta)}f(\theta), \tag{3}$$

where the mortality rate M at age θ in year t is a function of θ and $t - \theta$, with constants A and k. Since year minus age $(t - \theta)$ uniquely determines a cohort, the term $Ae^{-k(t-\theta)}$ can be interpreted as the baseline rate for cohorts. It declines exponentially. The discrete function $f(\theta)$ is the set of computed age-specific multipliers. Hinman et $al.$ (1976) assigned greater weight to more recent cohorts when determining their set of age-specific multipliers. Stevens and Lee (1978) opted for an "age-specific cohort slope"

$$k_i = \frac{\log y_i - \log y_{i-5}}{\log i - \log(i-5)}, \tag{4}$$

where y_i is the death rate at age i (for five-year age groups). This, they noted, has the virtue of incorporating the size of the age interval into the basic Kermack ratio. They projected future mortality rates from these slopes (k_i), keeping an eye out for cases in which $k_{ia} \neq k_{ib}$ (where k_i is the same age-specific slope across cohorts a and b). Such occurrences are deviations from the generation effect model, and indicate expected rates which may vary substantially from observed rates.

These models have appeal in varying degrees. They are classically demographic, and they are descriptive or "exploratory" in the contemporary sense (Tukey, 1977). They also have in common the treatment of some function of mortality as a linear combination of age and cohort. Period phenomena are captured only as residuals. This is unsatisfactory if the desire is to account for period phenomena—and recent literature has veered toward this goal (Hemminki and Paakkulainen, 1976; Stevens and Lee, 1978). First, the omission of a dimension that should be present—in this case, period—can result in biased estimates of the effects of the included dimensions. The net age and cohort patterns of TB mortality are likely to be biased if period also affects TB mortality. Second, if period phenomena are believed relevant, then examining the discrepancy between observed and fitted values to determine the period effects obscures reasoning about identification. For example, upon taking logarithms, expression (3) becomes log-additive, with a linear term $(-k(t - \theta))$ and a polynomial $(f(\theta))$ on the right hand side. If the residuals are ransacked for period effects, the analyst will be shadow boxing with an under-identified model. Finally, note that Spicer (1954) assumes the baseline mortality rate (which is at the root of the "generation effect" approach) declines exponentially. Hinman *et al.* (1976) assume that it approaches a constant. Restrictions of this kind should be unnecessary within a cohort perspective.

3.2. Age-Period-Cohort Models

Age-period-cohort accounting models have been used in the social sciences (e.g., Cagan, 1971; Hall, 1971; Carr-Hill *et al.*, 1972), in epidemiology (Greenberg *et al.*, 1950; Barrett, 1973; 1978a; 1978b; 1980), and specifically in the analysis of TB mortality (Sacher, 1957; 1960; 1977). Models of this kind are useful when the dependent variable is thought to be a function of age, period and cohort, as has been suggested here. The need for all three categories of effect can arise from separately conceived, but compatible, one- or two-factor theories, as well as from a single coherent view embracing all three dimensions. Although age-period-cohort accounting models can incorporate constraints such as those employed by Spicer (1954) and Hinman *et al.* (1976), they need not, and in our use do not. Mason *et al.* (1973) and Fienberg and Mason (1978) provide further, detailed, discussions of age-period-cohort models. We use such models in our analyses of TB mortality, and turn next to a sketch of the approach we take, concluding this section with a review of Sacher's (1957; 1960; 1977) use of the accounting framework.

For the substantive phenomenon at hand, the response variable is mortality due to tuberculosis. We shall treat it as dichotomous: For each age-period combination there are counts of people who die of tuberculosis and those who do not. These counts are used to form odds of dying versus not dying (of TB) which can then be logged and estimated using minimum logit chi-square or maximum likelihood methods applied to models of the following kind:

$$\Omega_{ij} = \kappa + \beta_i + \gamma_j + \delta_k \tag{5}$$

$$(i=1,...,I;\ j=1,...,J;\ k=1,...,K)$$

$$\Sigma_i\beta_i = \Sigma_j\gamma_j = \Sigma_k\delta_k = 0,$$

where Ω_{ij} is the log-odds of dying of tuberculosis at age i in period j, the β_i are age contrasts, the γ_j are period contrasts, the δ_k are cohort contrasts, and κ is a constant.

Linear trends in the effects of age, period and cohort are inestimable (under-identified) without the use of a linear restriction on the contrasts. Equality constraints are among the simplest and are, perhaps, most readily justified. From other research on the epidemiology of tuberculosis we know there are cases in which mortality is little affected by moving from time t to time $t+1$, or from age a to age $a+1$. Since the choice of the constraint can alter the parameter estimates of the model (but not necessarily the fit) a sound reason for establishing such a constraint is essential. We discuss our identifying restrictions in the context of our data analyses.

As initially formulated, the model we work with is additive in the logarithmic scale, but multiplicative and therefore interactive in the odds. It is not at the outset interactive in the sense of including terms jointly in age and period, age and cohort, cohort and period, or higher order combinations in addition to age, period and cohort. The omission of higher order terms of this kind has been criticized on generalized substantive grounds by Glenn (1976). Although an additive age-period-cohort formulation seems appropriate to us, especially for the years before the chemotherapeutic revolution, the United States data series contain a historical accident having little to do fundamentally with tuberculosis, but affecting TB mortality rates nevertheless. We deal with this problem by including an age-period interaction term. It turns out to be possible to estimate a variety of interactions within the age-period-cohort accounting framework (Chuang, 1980; Fienberg and Mason, 1985, in this volume).

The only previous application of the age-period-cohort accounting framework to tuberculosis mortality is due to Sacher (1957; 1960; 1977).[5] Sacher was interested in showing how period-specific life tables could distort the actual mortality pattern of a population under conditions of secular change in the environment. For this purpose he fastened on data for Massachusetts reported by Frost (1939).[6] Age effects were interpreted as the population's true physiological relationship with the disease. Secular change came in two forms: epoch of birth and epoch of death or, in our terms, cohort and period. Cohort effects included factors operating at the time of birth that related to the presence of the disease and the likelihood of infection. Change in nutrition was cited as an example. Factors operating at the time of death—period effects—included changes in the efficacy of medical treatments and changes in tuberculosis diagnosis and classification. In the earliest version of his analysis Sacher included risk of infection as a factor operating at the time of death (1957, p. 122), but later (1977) appears to have dropped it as an explicand.

Sacher solved the identification problem by assuming that there were no differences in cohort effects for people born in the cohorts of 1815 through 1865 (Sacher, 1960). His results were as follows. Mortality declined following birth to a low at ages 5–9, then rose to a peak at around 25 and a plateau thereafter. Period effects declined monotonically for all the years under observation (1880–1940). Cohort effects were essentially fixed through the birth cohort of 1895, then began to drop precipitously.

Sacher's work has a number of questionable aspects, the most important being his choice of identifying restrictions.[7] His decision to equate contrasts for the early cohorts was motivated at one point by the belief that the restriction is consistent with internal evidence "that

[5] Most of the work presented in this paper was completed before we learned of Sacher's research. We are indebted to John Hobcraft for bringing it to our attention.

[6] Sacher (1960, p. 256) cites Frost (1939) as the source of his data, but this can not be correct since Sacher's series extends to 1940. In a later publication Sacher (1977, pp. 602–603) cites Merrell (1947) as the source for data from Connecticut. It is probable that the data source for all of Sacher's work on TB mortality was Merrell (1947), who updated Frost's data for Massachusetts through 1940. Our reading of Sacher's three publications on tuberculosis suggests that all are based on the same set of data and the same analysis.

[7] Also, it is not entirely clear why Sacher's effects for the cohorts of 1815–1865 are unique and nonzero, what happened to the single-cell cohorts of 1805 and 1935, or how age effects for the five-year age groups 0–4 and 5–9 were estimated.

conditions were stationary during the first half of the nineteenth century"
(Sacher, 1960, pp. 256–257), at another by the assertion that there were
no changes in the nutritional status of the population for these cohorts
(1957, p. 124). Neither justification is persuasive. Frost's (1939) data
show cohort differences for the early years, and Sacher does not adduce
evidence for the idea that nutrition was constant from 1815 to 1865 but
increased thereafter.

By constraining the early cohort contrasts to be equal Sacher obtains
results inconsistent with his interpretation of the meaning of these effects
and with the work of others. The secular decline in period effects is
mystifying; there are no claims that death-averting TB treatments existed
or were improving over this interval. Sacher (1977) concludes that the
pattern of net age effects he obtains represents the true physiological
relationship between the disease and its host. In fact the pattern is that of
an averaging of age-specific mortality rates across periods. Sacher claims
to have purged the age effects of environmental change when actually he
has assumed no environmental change over much of this period because
of his choice of identifying restrictions.

Despite these problems, Sacher's work is singular, particularly in its
early (1957) careful identification of three distinct sources of variability in
TB mortality. Although the analyses that follow differ in their results,
they are similar in both method and motivation.

4. DATA

No single extant data series is ideal for the historical study of tuberculosis
mortality, and progress in understanding its decline depends on piecing
together results from different data sets. In the following sections two
series provide the data for application of the age-period-cohort accounting
framework to pulmonary tuberculosis mortality. The first pertains to
Massachusetts males, for whom TB mortality has been recorded in ten-
year age groups every decennium from 1880 forward (we stop with 1970).
The second pertains to United States white males, with TB mortality in
five-year age groupings every quinquennium from 1935 forward (we stop
with 1975). The two series are complementary, the Massachusetts data
apparently providing the earliest coverage of any state, the United States

data providing the greatest detail in recent years. Together they appear to provide reasonable coverage for age-period-cohort analysis of TB mortality for men in the United States.[8] We expect the results from each data set to strengthen interpretations based on the other, especially those concerning medical advances, whose effects should have appeared at the same time in both Massachusetts and the United States as a whole. The remainder of this section compares the two data sets to illustrate some of their outward similarities and differences and discusses details specific to each.[9]

4.1. Comparison of Massachusetts and United States Data

To facilitate comparison of the Massachusetts and United States data, Figure 1 overlays U.S. period rates for white males on Massachusetts period rates for all males. In the census years for which there are Massachusetts and U.S. data the two series move in parallel, with Massachusetts TB mortality consistently greater. Both series exhibit a monotonic decline, but that for the United States is interrupted in 1945.

Several million men were "missing" from the civilian population in 1945, serving overseas. (This is apparent in Table A.4 of Appendix A, which gives estimates of the population of the conterminous United States.) Improved diagnostic techniques made it possible to screen out most of the potential servicemen who were afflicted with tuberculosis (Aronson, 1946; Long and Jablon, 1955), so while few stateside TB deaths were averted during this period, the base population shrank dramatically. Were those overseas "returned" to the base population, the decline in TB mortality for the U.S. data would be smooth; the 'X' in Figure 1 denotes the approximate location of the corresponding adjusted

---

[8] We have chosen to work with sex-specific data since little is gained by combining the sexes if their patterns of within-cohort age-specific TB mortality differ (Frost, 1939; Springett, 1950).

[9] An alternative approach beyond our present means would be to analyze separately the data series for each state, thus allowing for different starting points and maximizing coverage of the United States over time. This would suffer the same limitation constraining the analyses we present, which is that the data amount to systematic samples of the annual time series, rather than age-specific rates in consecutive years. This absence of period detail hampers model evaluation.

Figure 1. Lung Tuberculosis Mortality by Year: Males,
Massachusetts, 1920–1970; White Males, United States, 1935–1975

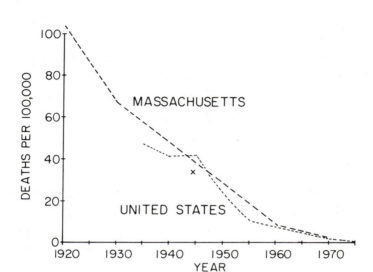

rate. No similar change is required for the Massachusetts series, in which
data are reported at ten-year intervals, but there remains the question of
the greater mortality in Massachusetts.

Rates for the two series need not be identical, of course, since for the
era under consideration TB mortality varied by state (Rich, 1951,
p. 206). Some of this part-whole difference is due to inclusion in the
Massachusetts data of mortality for nonwhites (composed largely of
blacks) as well as whites. Although blacks may have been no more likely
than whites to be infected with TB, the disease tended to be more acute
and run a shorter course among blacks during the years prior to the
chemotherapeutic revolution (Pope and Gordon, 1955). As a result, the

[9] (Cont.) For example, age-period-cohort analysis based on the Massachusetts data can
not reveal the impact of the 1918 influenza epidemic on TB mortality, nor could parallel
analyses of similar data from any other state, even though the U.S. annual time series
(which is not available disaggregated by age) suggests a decided effect (Rich, 1951, p. 898).
This kind of detail would be telling in the context of age-period-cohort specifications,
whereas it is unclear that disaggregation by state with quinquennial or decennial observations
would be nearly so revealing. For this reason we regard the paired analysis of the
Massachusetts and United States data as an acceptable compromise given our goals.

TB death rate among blacks over much of this period was four to five times that of whites (Roth, 1938; Edwards, 1940; Aronson, 1946). Relative to the U.S., however, Massachusetts has had a small black population, with 3% nonwhite in 1970 an all time high for this series (U.S. Bureau of the Census, 1973, p. 48).

Although the increase in the proportion nonwhite parallels the increase in the ratio of U.S. to Massachusetts mortality, it is doubtful that racial composition is the only source of differences between the two series. For example, a look at Tables 1 and 2 reveals instances in which the age-specific TB mortality rates for the U.S. actually exceed those for Massachusetts. Thus, the age structures of the two series must differ. It is likely that a variety of socioeconomic characteristics played a role in elevating Massachusetts TB mortality over that in the rest of the United States. The comparability of the two series we employ might be enhanced if the Massachusetts data were restricted to white males, but race-specific tabulations are not available in the early years for Massachusetts. Rather than truncate the lengthy perspective the Massachusetts series uniquely affords, we have elected to use data for males of all races.

4.2. Massachusetts

When we began work on the analysis reported here, one of our goals was to reanalyze Frost's (1939) data. These data were presented in five-year age groups for ages 0–4 and 5–9, and ten-year age groups thereafter. Since tuberculosis mortality declines precipitously between 0–4 and 5–9, and since it seemed possible that there might be similar five-year jumps elsewhere in the lifespan, we sought to divide the remaining age categories into five-year age groups as well. This would render them more comparable to the U.S. series. We thus began a search for Frost's sources and data, but could not find them for 1880, 1890 and 1900. Frost apparently adjusted data sent him by a colleague, but neither the data nor the precise method of adjustment are known to us. It is reasonably clear, however, that Frost's data for the three decades are *estimates* of total tuberculosis based on records for tuberculosis of the lung only (Frost, 1939, p. 95). We concluded that further analysis would best be served by compiling from extant sources our own series of Massachusetts mortality rates.

Table 1 presents age-specific pulmonary tuberculosis death rates for Massachusetts males from 1880 to 1970. These rates are based on the death counts and population totals found in Tables A.1 and A.2, respectively, of Appendix A. Apart from the extension of the series to 1970, these data differ from those used by Frost (1939) in two ways. First, whereas Frost studied mortality from all forms of TB, we restrict attention to lung TB—also called at times consumption, pulmonary consumption, consumption of the lungs, respiratory tuberculosis, pulmonary tuberculosis and phthisis. Regardless of changing names, the classification has remained consistent since 1880. The same is not true of nonrespiratory TB. In 1900 these other forms of tuberculosis were classified as scrofula, goitre, mensenterica and hydrocephalus; in 1910 they were tuberculosis of the larynx, tuberculosis of meninges, abdominal tuberculosis, Pott's disease, cold and by congestion, white tumors, tuberculosis of other organs, generalized tuberculosis and scrofula. Moreover, the age patterns of these nonpulmonary tuberculoses vary from that of lung tuberculosis, being concentrated in most cases at early ages. Frost's rates, particularly for the early ages, were much distorted by changing classifications of nonpulmonary tuberculoses. Restricting our analysis to lung TB reduces the chances that any period effects we may find are due to classification changes, and is consistent with the dominant choice in recent research (e.g., Spicer, 1954; Stevens and Lee, 1978).

The second major departure from Frost (1939) is that ages 0–4 and 5–9 have been collapsed into a single 0–9 category, despite the existence of data for these five-year age groups. Since they are the only five-year age groups for which data exist over the entire ninety year period, little is gained by maintaining the distinction. Even if it were maintained, individuals in separate five-year groups would be absorbed into ten-year groups as they aged into their tenth year.[10] Because the extreme early peak in overall TB mortality is greatly attenuated when the scope of analysis is limited to lung tuberculosis mortality, the retention of information for ages 0–4 and 5–9 is much less important than it would otherwise be.

---

[10] Fienberg and Mason (1978, pp. 41–42) describe the problem this creates and the absence of a satisfactory solution. Sacher (1960) derives separate estimates of effects for ages 0–4 and 5–9, but does not say how.

4.3. United States

Table 2 presents age-specific pulmonary tuberculosis death rates for white males in the United States from 1935 to 1975. The rates are formed from the counts of deaths and population found, respectively, in Tables A.3 and A.4 of Appendix A. Since no censuses were taken in the years 1935, 1945, 1955, 1965 and 1975, population figures for those years are necessarily estimates. Such estimates can vary with the official source consulted. We have studied some "worst case" examples of varying population estimates and determined that the choice of estimate has virtually no effect on the pattern of rates. This is a consequence of the extremely large size of the denominator (the population) relative to the numerator (deaths from lung tuberculosis). The data shown in Table 2 are presumably similar to those analyzed (but not presented) by Stevens and Lee (1978).

Inspection of the age-specific rates for 1940, 1945 and 1950 makes it clear that the break in the decline of TB mortality shown in Figure 1 is due to ages 15–39 in 1945. Tables A.3 and A.4 show further that the increase in TB mortality rates for these ages is artifactual, and must be a consequence of the shifting population base noted earlier. We have been unable to locate appropriate age-specific totals for white males serving overseas in 1945, and have interpolated our own adjusted base figures by aging forward to 1945 the appropriate five-year age groups in 1940 and allowing for immigration.[11] If the resulting adjusted rates were substituted for the observed rates, the decline in TB mortality would be unbroken.

An important advantage of the U.S. data over those to be analyzed for Massachusetts is the more refined grouping by five-year age intervals combined with the greater frequency of observation. The major disadvantage is that the data cover only forty years, as compared with ninety for Massachusetts. Whereas Massachusetts has had fairly complete reporting of deaths since at least 1865 (Shryock and Siegel, 1975, p. 29), the registration area of the United States came to encompass the conterminous forty-eight states only in 1933. Registration data for the United States prior to 1933 are biased to the extent that states entering

---

[11] The adjusted population totals are as follows: ages 15–19—5,200,000; ages 20–24—5,400,000; ages 25–29—5,100,000; ages 30–34—4,900,000; ages 35–39—4,500,000. The adjusted rates are then: ages 15–19—7.08; ages 20–24—17.24; ages 25–29—24.69; ages 30–34—30.96; ages 35–39—41.62.

Table 1. Deaths Due to Lung Tuberculosis (per 100,000) by Age: Males, Massachusetts, 1880-1970, with Deviations of Predicted from Observed Rates (in Parentheses)

Age	1880	1890	1900	1910	1920	1930	1940	1950	1960	1970
0-9	95 (3)	76 (0)	43 (-8)	27 (-1)	14 (2)	7 (4)	4 (2)	1 (1)	0 (0)	0 (0)
10-19	120 (-10)	109 (-7)	85 (5)	51 (-6)	37 (8)	17 (4)	4 (1)	1 (-1)	0 (0)	0 (0)
20-29	439 (27)	357 (3)	277 (-1)	188 (-15)	133 (-1)	74 (5)	33 (1)	7 (-4)	1 (-2)	0 (0)
30-39	373 (-15)	362 (1)	285 (12)	234 (6)	151 (-3)	106 (5)	51 (-7)	24 (-2)	4 (-1)	2 (0)
40-49	358 (0)	330 (9)	241 (-23)	229 (17)	164 (0)	111 (1)	86 (5)	43 (-3)	6 (-6)	3 (0)
50-59	352 (-10)	313 (-1)	252 (4)	229 (13)	161 (0)	120 (-4)	94 (0)	67 (0)	18 (-3)	7 (0)
60-69	449 (10)	327 (0)	266 (17)	226 (16)	158 (-12)	91 (-34)	110 (2)	89 (9)	38 (5)	12 (0)
70+	527 (0)	305 (-14)	229 (20)	146 (-23)	115 (-17)	87 (-20)	79 (-9)	84 (10)	50 (18)	15 (0)

Source: Rates are constructed from Tables A.1 and A.2; residuals (in parentheses) are differences between observed rates and fitted rates transformed from model VII, Table 3.

Table 2. Deaths Due to Lung Tuberculosis (per 100,000) by Age: White Males, United States, 1935–1975, with Deviations of Predicted from Observed Rates (in Parentheses)

Ages	1935	1940	1945	1950	1955	1960	1965	1970	1975
0-4	5.27	4.15	2.55	1.39	0.34	0.14	0.06	0.09	0.04
5-9	1.44 (0.00)	1.03	0.72	0.27	0.09	0.05	0.01	0.03	0.00
10-14	2.28 (-0.31)	1.81 (0.33)	1.00	0.53	0.03	0.05	0.01	0.02	0.01
15-19	13.04 (-1.29)	8.63 (0.09)	8.61 (1.47)	1.94	0.17	0.10	0.09	0.04	0.03
20-24	32.57 (-2.18)	22.63 (2.27)	35.85 (0.26)	5.20 (-0.28)	0.74	0.32	0.12	0.09	0.05
25-29	46.92 (1.81)	33.63 (2.49)	38.30 (-0.30)	8.88 (0.29)	1.87 (-0.84)	1.02	0.25	0.15	0.07
30-34	56.11 (-0.30)	42.38 (2.32)	39.98 (-1.54)	12.44 (0.58)	3.33 (-0.58)	1.38 (-0.62)	0.57	0.43	0.13
35-39	69.35 (1.88)	49.69 (-2.12)	46.29 (0.53)	20.02 (1.42)	5.32 (-0.72)	2.63 (-0.59)	1.46 (-0.16)	0.73	0.30
40-44	79.50 (-0.59)	63.15 (-2.65)	55.82 (4.60)	28.93 (0.53)	8.92 (-1.14)	4.51 (-0.76)	2.77 (0.00)	1.23 (0.16)	0.64
45-59	88.55 (-0.84)	73.34 (-3.30)	69.17 (5.33)	37.25 (-1.01)	14.35 (-0.72)	8.64 (0.02)	4.25 (-0.20)	2.24 (0.45)	0.96 (0.18)
50-54	91.59 (-3.59)	86.88 (-3.60)	82.53 (3.87)	50.85 (0.40)	22.33 (0.86)	13.72 (0.07)	7.82 (0.14)	3.25 (0.19)	1.97 (0.59)
55-59	98.44 (0.98)	97.13 (0.36)	94.44 (1.17)	61.74 (-0.68)	25.93 (-2.51)	19.55 (0.01)	12.50 (0.26)	5.78 (0.47)	2.55 (0.19)
60-64	93.73 (4.16)	99.62 (2.82)	92.51 (-4.92)	70.83 (-1.48)	35.20 (0.83)	25.50 (0.22)	16.67 (-0.44)	8.14 (-0.11)	4.10 (0.09)
65-69	95.83 (8.93)	97.24 (3.46)	95.82 (-6.93)	80.97 (1.33)	44.44 (2.46)	30.44 (-1.78)	21.67 (-1.67)	11.61 (-0.56)	5.19 (-1.37)
70-74	101.66 (13.01)	97.36 (6.83)	90.28 (-8.77)	81.15 (-2.42)	50.67 (4.66)	40.53 (1.38)	29.06 (-0.53)	11.29 (-5.23)	7.37 (-2.26)
75+	87.61 (0.00)	82.36 (-11.49)	81.46 (-15.71)	80.17 (-1.70)	53.44 (4.38)	48.65 (5.05)	39.36 (2.81)	23.81 (2.50)	14.77 (1.49)

Source: Rates are constructed from Tables A.3 and A.4; residuals (in parentheses) are differences between observed rates and fitted rates transformed from model x, Table 6.

the registration area later have mortality differing from those entering earlier. Because of this potential bias we have taken 1935 as the starting date of the U.S. series.

5. ANALYSIS OF TUBERCULOSIS MORTALITY– MASSACHUSETTS, 1880–1970

Data similar to those for Massachusetts introduced above were first analyzed by Frost (1939). He observed that among males the peak age at death appeared to be rising over time: In 1880 the peak was among men ages 20–29; by 1920 it was at ages 40–49, and in 1930 peak mortality occurred at ages 50–59. By reorganizing the data Frost was able to show that age-specific mortality patterns within birth cohorts had actually remained unchanged over time. In each cohort peak mortality was consistently at ages 20–29, and actually declined thereafter with age. The secular decline in TB mortality was responsible for the apparent shift in the age pattern of the disease when arrayed by periods, since at any given point in time the people at older ages were by definition from older, higher mortality cohorts.

The same trends can be seen in our series of Massachusetts data. Figure 2 plots lung TB mortality rates by age for each of the nine decennial years represented in Table 1. By 1960 mortality is highest at ages 70 and above. When these rates are replotted by cohort as in Figure 3, the pattern that Frost observed appears. Our reconstitution of the series has retained the most salient and compelling features of the original version.

Although often reprinted and much discussed, the Massachusetts data have never been modelled within a multivariate framework save by Sacher (1957; 1960; 1977). We have already discussed Sacher's analysis and some of its drawbacks, chief among them being his choice of identifying constraints. In addition, the data he analyzed included only the years through 1940. The Frost-Merrell series (Frost, 1939; Merrell, 1947) Sacher used terminated before the introduction of effective chemotherapy and thus before clearly interpretable period effects were likely to have been apparent. The following analysis of our revised and extended Massachusetts lung TB mortality series for 1880–1970, described in Section 4, therefore begins with a rationale for our choice of identifying restriction, and is unique in its estimation of period effects for the years subsequent to World War II.

5.1. Placement of Identifying Constraint

Fitting an identified age-period-cohort model with discrete effects (expression (5)) involves placement of an identifying constraint. We shall consider the possibility of placing an equality restriction on adjacent age contrasts, period contrasts, and cohort contrasts.[12] Where should such a restriction be placed? We immediately rule out an equality restriction on the cohort contrasts. Since we seek ultimately to explain cohort mortality there can be no gain in limiting its variability through an equality restriction (but cf. Sacher, 1960, pp. 256–257). We could equate the contrasts for two or more of the periods prior to 1950, as there is no strong reason to suspect meaningful period variability before then. In particular, the available data do not include 1918, the year of the influenza epidemic, nor do they include the years of either world war. Moreover, our focus on pulmonary tuberculosis limits the possibility that period effects are interpretable as changes in methods of diagnosis and death registration (Sacher, 1957; Stevens and Lee, 1978, p. 122). Nevertheless, we will not initially equate the pre-1950 period contrasts because we wish to demonstrate that differences among them are insubstantial. As for the post-1940 period, the significant medical innovation that took place would make any restrictions on these years counter-productive.

This leaves age contrasts to work with. Here we appeal to the data. Historically, lung TB mortality rates have been relatively low in the early ages, with the peak coming in early adulthood. Figures 2 and 3, which array age-specific lung TB mortality rates by period and cohort, respectively, indicate that the rates for the early ages are fairly close,

---

[12] Equality restrictions are preferable to inequality restrictions, which place an additional burden on the analyst: When a coefficient β_j is set equal to $k\beta_j$, $k \neq 1$, the choice of normalization for the set of dummy variables affects the pattern of estimates. In particular, dummy coding (one dummy per classification excluded from the equation) and effect coding (one dummy per classification subtracted from the others and then omitted) no longer yield equivalent results. Since it is highly unlikely that the analyst would have any *a priori* notion of which coding scheme is the more substantively appropriate, only chance or habit would dictate which pattern of results was analyzed.

Figure 2. Lung Tuberculosis Mortality by Age within Years:
Males, Massachusetts, 1880–1970

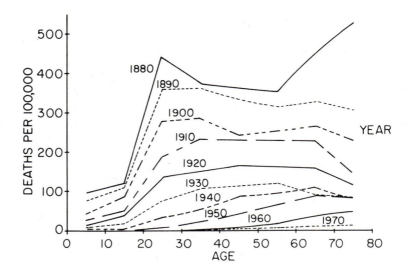

Figure 3. Lung Tuberculosis Mortality by Age for Selected Cohorts:
Males, Massachusetts, 1880–1970

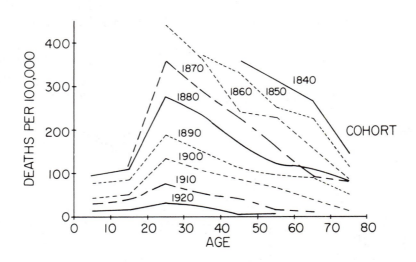

whether looked at from a cohort or a period perspective. We therefore equate the contrasts for ages 0–9 and 10–19. For the present this is a choice of convenience. We can not argue on theoretical grounds that it is an appropriate one, let alone the most appropriate one. Frost's (1939) data show that mortality is high at ages 0–4, and low at ages 5–9. Springett's (1950) comparative data for the British Isles and northern Europe typically show high mortality at ages 0–4, a sharp drop from 5 to 14, and a rise again over ages 15–25. Longitudinal data on tuberculosis incidence among Puerto Rican children (Comstock *et al.*, 1974) evince the same pattern. In fact, the graph of mortality from birth through age 20 is bimodal.

Why then do we place an equality restriction on the initial age groups? First, our data are for pulmonary tuberculosis mortality, not for incidence and not for TB mortality of all kinds. Tuberculosis mortality at young ages is dominated by nonpulmonary forms of the disease. For example, from the Massachusetts Registration Report of 1880, only 361 of the 929 tuberculosis deaths reported by Frost for ages 0–19 in Massachusetts in 1880 could have been pulmonary, as compared with 702 of 709 at ages 20–29, and 471 of 478 at ages 30–39. This dominance is accentuated during infancy: From the Massachusetts Registration Report of 1900 we know that in that year about 83% of infant tuberculosis mortality was from Tabes Mensenterica, a nonpulmonary classification. Consequently the drop in our data from ages 0–4 to 5–9 is less severe, and resembles in magnitude the rise in mortality at ages 15–19. Since our data occur at intervals of ten years (for reasons given earlier), the averages of mortality at ages 0–9 and 10–19 are similar, even though they are the result of contrary within-category trends. Again, this can be seen in Figures 2 and 3. Close observation reveals that rates at ages 10–19 are in general slightly greater than those at ages 0–9. Nonetheless, we prefer an equality restriction to an inequality restriction, in part for methodological reasons (see footnote 12), but mainly because within cohorts the rates are close.[13] For immediate purposes it is worth noting that equating the pre-1950 period contrasts on the grounds that there is no substantive reason for letting them vary (we consider this a strong justification) yields results in no appreciable way different from those obtained by equating the contrasts for the first two age groups.

[13] We experimented with inequality restrictions; see footnote 16.

Equating the coefficients of the first two age categories $(\beta_1 = \beta_2)$ is sufficient for the estimation of a just-identified age-period-cohort model in the form of expression (5). The actual three-way model we estimate, however, contains a second equality restriction and is thus over-identified. Note that in the upper-right corner of Table 1 (or Table A.1 of the Appendix) there are no deaths reported in the three cells for the cohorts of 1960 and 1970, and in two of the cells for the 1950 cohort.[14] The three corner cells require special treatment, since otherwise fitted logits or log rates for these cells would be undefined. To facilitate estimation of all parameters in the age-period-cohort specification applied to the entire data array, we impose an equality restriction on the effects of being born in 1950, 1960 and 1970 $(\delta_{15} = \delta_{16} = \delta_{17})$. Both the constraint and the data are consistent with our expectation that cohort differences will be greatly reduced and then eliminated for those born during the course of the chemotherapeutic revolution and thereafter.[15]

5.2. Results

In addition to the age-period-cohort model of expression (5), we estimate six reduced models: one for each of the dimensions ignoring the other two, and one for each of the three possible pairs of dimensions. No constraints on coefficients are necessary to identify these models, other than the usual normalization. In total there are four sets of coefficients for each dimension: one for the gross contrasts, a set for each dimension net of each of the other two taken separately, and one for each dimension controlling the other two simultaneously. Table 3 presents the coefficient estimates. We shall emphasize those of models I–III, and VII.

---

[14] As a matter of convention, when specific cohorts are named, the labelling will be given by the last year of the range covered. Thus, for example, the 1970 cohort refers to those born during the years 1961–1970 in the Massachusetts data, and to those born during the years 1966–1970 in the U.S. data.

[15] Note that owing to the zero-cells the equality restriction on the three cohorts is by itself an insufficient identifying restriction. It is also worth observing that an alternative to the strategy we have followed might be to model untransformed rates descriptively. We have not done so, preferring to employ the computations suitable for maximum likelihood estimation of the logit model, in order to produce results within a familiar statistical framework, and in order to maintain continuity with the procedure we would use if we had more obviously sampled data rather than population totals. The computational algorithm we use is iteratively reweighted least squares (Nelder and Wedderburn, 1972) as realized in the GLIM program (Baker and Nelder, 1978).

The coefficients in Table 3 are dummy variable coefficients, and have been normalized by the usual convention of omitting a dummy variable for each classification in each equation. Equality restrictions have been imposed either by omitting two or more dummy variables in a classification (e.g., the first two age categories in model VII) or by adding together the dummy variables whose coefficients are to be equated (the last three cohort dummy variables in each equation).

Comparisons between the coefficients of successive categories within classifications are of particular interest. These comparisons indicate changes in mortality from one age group to the next, from one decennium to the next, and from one cohort to the next. Figures 4–6 present the coefficients graphically, to facilitate inspection of the trends.

Figure 4 plots the gross age coefficients and also the net coefficients controlling period and cohort. A constant of 1.0 has been added to make the figure more legible. The zero-order relationship between age and tuberculosis mortality is characterized by a rapid rise in mortality rates between ages 10–19 and 20–29 and a plateau thereafter. In other words, lung TB mortality appears constant in adulthood and high relative to childhood and adolescence. Of necessity the pattern of logit coefficients for the gross age effects resembles a weighted average over periods of the age-specific mortality profile in Figure 2. Controlled for the effects of period and cohort (using model VII), the age pattern of lung TB mortality declines monotonically following a peak at ages 20–29. This is the expected finding. Note the flatness of the estimated mortality profile for ages 0–9 and 10–19—a consequence of the equality restriction permitting estimation of the age-period-cohort model.

Figure 5 presents the mortality profile for cohorts, both gross and net of age and period. Controlled or not, the chance of dying from respiratory tuberculosis declines with each successive cohort, at least through 1950. Most striking is the similarity of the two lines: the pattern of cohort mortality remains virtually the same even after controlling age and period. This was not the case for age, the marginal pattern of which did not hold up after the other two dimensions were controlled.

Figure 6 presents the period contrasts. As expected, the gross period effects suggest a secular decline in tuberculosis mortality. The full age-period-cohort model tells another story. Once age and cohort are controlled there are only minor period effects. From 1880 to 1950, the estimated net effects of period increase, although only to a small degree

Table 3. Logit Coefficients for Eight Models of Lung Tuberculosis Mortality: Males, Massachusetts, 1880–1970

	I [A]	II [P]	III [C]	IV [AP]	V [AC]	VI [PC]	VII [APC]	VIII [APC]
Constant	-8.64	-5.86	-5.24	-7.41	-4.74	-5.24	-4.33	-4.87
Age:								
0-9	0.00*			0.00*	0.00*		0.00*	0.00*
10-19	0.52			0.52	0.07		0.00*	0.08
20-29	1.93			1.82	0.97		0.83	0.99
30-39	1.98			1.92	0.73		0.53	0.76
40-49	1.89			1.94	0.43		0.16	0.47
50-59	1.87			2.01	0.18		-0.14	0.24
60-69	1.90			2.12	-0.05		-0.42	0.04
70+	1.73			2.04	-0.50		-0.91	-0.37
Period:								
1880		0.00*		0.00*		0.00*	0.00*	0.00*
1890		-0.13		-0.16		0.00	0.17	0.00*
1900		-0.40		-0.43		-0.10	0.22	0.00*
1910		-0.64		-0.68		-0.14	0.33	0.00*
1920		-1.01		-1.05		-0.26	0.36	0.00*
1930		-1.44		-1.49		-0.41	0.38	0.00*
1940		-1.78		-1.88		-0.45	0.52	0.01
1950		-2.26		-2.37		-0.55	0.64	0.05
1960		-3.42		-3.46		-1.20	0.22	-0.44
1970		-4.55		-4.58		-1.72	-0.08	-0.82
Cohort:								
1810			0.00*		0.00*	0.00*	0.00*	0.00*
1820			-0.31		-0.59	-0.31	-0.68	-0.56
1830			-0.52		-0.99	-0.49	-1.15	-0.94
1840			-0.59		-1.24	-0.55	-1.46	-1.18
1850			-0.62		-1.46	-0.55	-1.75	-1.38
1860			-0.63		-1.64	-0.52	-1.99	-1.55
1870			-0.91		-1.88	-0.76	-2.32	-1.78
1880			-1.17		-2.09	-0.98	-2.60	-2.00
1890			-1.53		-2.45	-1.23	-3.03	-2.35
1900			-1.97		-2.87	-1.55	-3.48	-2.73
1910			-2.60		-3.53	-2.09	-4.17	-3.36
1920			-3.43		-4.38	-2.81	-5.06	-4.17
1930			-4.71		-5.71	-3.98	-6.39	-5.42
1940			-5.70		-6.72	-4.85	-7.30	-6.25
1950			-7.81[**]		-8.54[**]	-6.54[**]	-9.02[**]	-7.85[**]
1960			-7.81[**]		-8.54[**]	-6.54[**]	-9.02[**]	-7.85[**]
1970			-7.81[**]		-8.54[**]	-6.54[**]	-9.02[**]	-7.85[**]
Deviance	16530	7206	2603	1185	264.8	1884	144.6	163.5
DF	72	70	65	63	58	56	50	54

*Dummy variable omitted for purposes of estimation.

**Coefficients constrained to be equal.

Note: "Deviance" is minus twice the maximized log-likelihood, and is asymptotically distributed as chi-square (Nelder and Wedderburn, 1972)

Figure 4. Age Effects: Coefficients for the Log-Odds of Dying from Lung Tuberculosis: Males, Massachusetts, 1880–1970

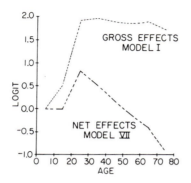

Figure 5. Cohort Effects: Coefficients for the Log-Odds of Dying from Lung Tuberculosis: Males, Massachusetts, 1880–1970

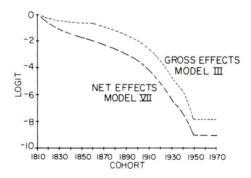

Figure 6. Period Effects: Coefficients for the Log-Odds of Dying from Lung Tuberculosis: Males, Massachusetts, 1880–1970

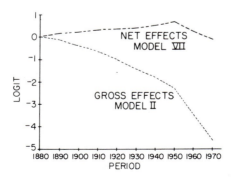

and in barely perceptible year to year steps. After 1950 there is a marked decline in period-specific mortality effects, exceeding in twenty years the gradual increase of 1880–1950. The data in Table 1 give the distinct impression that tuberculosis mortality declined period by period. Examining these rates is comparable to studying the gross effects profile in Figure 6. What Table 1 does not reveal, but is clear in the net effects profile in Figure 6, is that for most of the interval from 1880 to 1970 there are no substantial period effects.

5.3. Discussion

Estimation of an age-period-cohort model has allowed us to capture simultaneously and unambiguously the major patterns in respiratory tuberculosis for the past 100 years. The fit is good, whether summarized in terms of the likelihood ratio statistic or assayed by inspection of the residuals. Table 1 shows that the differences between observed and fitted rates are generally small and that there is no discernible pattern to them. Our results are also sturdy; over-identifying the model with an equality restriction on all period contrasts prior to 1940 (which is consistent with Frost's (1939) age-cohort interpretation of the 1880–1930 series) has no appreciable effect on fit or interpretation, as can be seen in comparing the coefficients of model VIII with those of model VII in Table 3. Although the actual coefficients appear different, the first differences between successive contrasts differ only slightly across models VII and VIII, and the pattern of effects is similar. Indeed, the first two age coefficients of model VIII, which are not constrained, are virtually identical. Whether, in light of the unexpected increase in period effects observed in model VII, the restriction of these effects is justified is not immediately clear; we consider this question further in our discussion of the interpretation of the estimated effects.[16]

---

[16] In his consideration of this result during his remarks at the SSRC Conference, Warren Sanderson suggested that the linear restriction we employed might be the source of this problem, and that an inequality restriction on the age effects might be preferable to the equality restriction we used. To check this possibility we estimated equations for a variety of models in which the coefficient for the second age-group (10–19) was set equal to that for the first age-group (0–9) times some constant k ($k \neq 1$); i.e., an inequality restriction. For reasonable values of $k > 1$, estimates of coefficients were similar to those obtained with an equality restriction ($k = 1$). However, for values of $1 > k > 0$, the pattern of estimated coefficients was highly unstable and uninterpretable. Since Figures 2 and 3 suggest that rates at ages 0–9 are generally slightly lower than those at ages 10–19, only moderate values of $k > 1$ are consonant with the data.

A useful next step would involve linking these results to possible interpretations of the decline of tuberculosis mortality. The age, period and cohort coefficients derived from our model are only manifestations of presumably real factors underlying trends in the etiology of the disease. Although we can not validate the interpretations of the age, period and cohort dimensions suggested earlier, we can use the results obtained thus far, in combination with external evidence, to qualify further our understanding of the reasons for the decline in TB mortality. In the discussion below we review some evidence on changes in nutritional level as a cause of the decline of TB in Massachusetts, we examine the possibility of a competing risks argument concerning this decline in light of the age pattern of TB mortality, and we point to the need for—and ultimately carry out—additional analysis to strengthen the interpretation of the period effects.

Cohorts and Nutrition. Tuberculosis mortality in Massachusetts declined monotonically for cohorts born over a period of at least 150 years. Did the nutritional status of the population improve concomitantly? Reasonable measures of nutrition would include such physical characteristics of the population as age at menarche and adult height. We have no time series for these characteristics directly applicable to Massachusetts, and doubt that it would be possible to construct one. Sokoloff and Villaflor's (1979) analysis of colonial and revolutionary muster rolls suggests, however, that such a series may be unnecessary. Their data reveal that by the time of the Revolution native-born American recruits had virtually attained the heights of modern-day Americans. Unfortunately these data do not include men born in Massachusetts, but they do include soldiers from the rest of the New England states. Their mean height was 67.9 inches, a bit less than that of native-born American southerners, but greater than that of the British soldiers, greater also than the average height of foreign-born soldiers fighting in support of the Revolution, and comparable to the average of 68.2 inches for both northern Civil War and World War II recruits. It is thus unlikely that the nutritional level of the native-born population of Massachusetts steadily and markedly improved as TB mortality declined there.

The nutrition thesis does not, of course, require a continuous improvement in diet for its presumed effect to be manifest. An increase need not have taken place in Massachusetts, but rather between Britain and Massachusetts. It may be that almost from its establishment as a colony, nutritional levels in Massachusetts were higher than in Britain. In effect, it could well be that a subpopulation of Britain experienced a substantial increase in nutrition by migrating to an area where land and game were relatively plentiful. This could have set the decline of TB in motion.

If this speculation about differences between countries in nutrition is correct for the colonial years, then it should also be true later on. Massachusetts has always had a fairly large immigrant population, and it is possible that data on the foreign-born provide additional evidence with which to qualify the nutrition thesis. Sokoloff and Villaflor's (1979) data are consistent with the observation that immigrants are generally less well nourished during childhood and presumably *in utero*. To the extent that undernourishment is more characteristic of immigrants, the percent foreign-born in a cohort may affect that cohort's susceptibility to TB. In particular, we would expect that as immigrants are added to the population, they slow or conceivably reverse the rate of decline in TB mortality: Although the immigrants' diet improves, each immigrating cohort brings with it a more severe legacy of tuberculosis than is present for the corresponding cohort in Massachusetts. This improved diet partially offsets the greater susceptibility to TB. All other things equal, then, increases over cohorts in the percent foreign-born would decrease the rate of decline in Massachusetts TB mortality. And, were the percent foreign-born large enough, the decline would be interrupted.

All other things are not equal, however, and any attempt to match the percent foreign-born with the observed pattern of cohort coefficients must be accompanied by the realization that the possible effects of immigration reflect more than the hypothesized lower levels of nutrition in the countries of origin. Immigrants to Massachusetts were typically concentrated in the cities, where crowding was the worst and labor the most strenuous, conditions which would spread the infection and increase TB mortality (Pope and Gordon, 1955, p. 326; Sydenstricker, 1974). This privation could have induced more TB mortality within cohorts than could be accounted for by any hypothesized nutritional differences in the lives of the native-born and the foreign-born. For this reason alone (and there are surely others), results consistent with the pattern initially conjectured would be no more than suggestive. Similarly, however, failure of the data to reveal the expected pattern would not constitute definitive evidence against the nutrition hypothesis: We lack cause-specific mortality rates, for example, which are not reported separately for the native-born and the foreign-born; the population of Massachusetts (whether native-born or foreign-born) is not closed to out-migration; the foreign-born population is heterogeneous and changing over time.

What data on the foreign-born we have been able to extract from official sources are listed in Table 4, which arrays the percent foreign-born by age in Massachusetts for the cohorts represented in our data. The percentages are displayed as age by cohort, with period found along the lower left to upper right diagonals. There is a fairly stable pattern within cohorts of increasing numbers of foreign-born to ages 30–39, with the percentages remaining stable thereafter. This is consistent with the well known greater probability of migration among young men, but is inconsistent with the assumed greater TB mortality among the foreign-born—which would bring about a steady decline in percent foreign-born after age forty (by which point immigration would have greatly diminished). The problem here, of course, is that since the population is not closed to migration, there may actually be excess mortality among the foreign-born at older ages, but also further in-migration, occurring at a rate which roughly offsets this mortality. With these data there is no way to be sure.

Assuming that the maximum percent foreign-born observable within each cohort adequately characterizes cohort composition with respect to nativity, the data show that percent foreign-born declines by cohort from 1900 to the present, and seems to have peaked among the cohorts of 1870, 1880 and 1890. The net cohort coefficients decline monotonically. Thus, within Massachusetts the immigrant stock of a cohort in no sense explains the decline over time of cohort-specific mortality. Closer inspection of Figure 5 reveals, however, that the pace of the decline in the cohort coefficients slows through the cohort of 1880 or 1890, and then accelerates rapidly. In fact, as Figure 7 indicates, there is a fairly strong correlation between the percent foreign-born in each cohort and the first differences of the cohort coefficients in model VII (Table 3): The larger the percent foreign-born, the slower the rate of decline in cohort TB mortality.

The correlation between the logit of foreign-born and the first-

Table 4. Percent Foreign-Born by Age for Various Cohorts: Massachusetts White Males, 1880-1970

	Cohort																
Age	1810	1820	1830	1840	1850	1860	1870	1880	1890	1900	1910	1920	1930	1940	1950	1960	1970
0-9								4.4	6.8	4.3	4.8	1.9	1.6	0.3	0.6	0.8	1.3
10-19							14.6	18.0	18.0	15.5	9.7	5.0	1.8	1.2	2.0	2.2	
20-29						25.4	37.2	37.1	42.6	29.3	18.6	5.4	3.5	3.9	4.5		
30-39					39.4	36.9	44.7	46.7	46.6	34.3	18.2	6.5	5.3	6.7			
40-49				42.0	43.5	40.1	47.6	47.4	47.2	33.7	18.9	8.0	7.0				
50-59			36.7	41.5	43.3	40.2	46.6	46.8	46.7	33.9	20.2	9.1					
60-69		30.0	36.5	41.1	42.5	40.1	46.7	46.8	47.1	34.0	20.1						
70+	20.9	25.6	31.4	38.1	40.3	39.5	45.2	47.0	45.2	36.2							

Sources: See Appendix B

Figure 7. First-Differences of Cohort Coefficients (Model VII) and
Logits of Cohort Foreign-Born: Males, Massachusetts,
Cohorts of 1820 to 1950

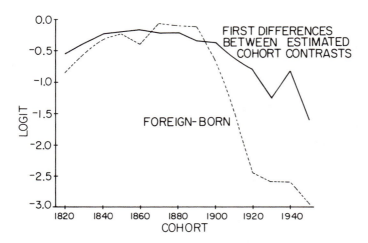

differences of the cohort coefficients is 0.93; it is 0.82 between the logit of
foreign-born and the cohort coefficients, although this second coefficient
is misleadingly high owing to the favorable location of two or three
points. (Only the cohorts of 1810–1950 were used in these calculations,
since for the cohorts born after 1950 there simply is no more registered
mortality.)   This result is consistent with the nutrition hypothesis,
assuming the percent foreign-born reflect differential nutritional levels
favoring Massachusetts over countries of origin, but may also have to do
with exposure of the foreign-born in Massachusetts to an unhealthy and
inhospitable urban environment.

The rationale for focusing on the relationship between percent
foreign-born and cohort coefficient first-differences is the following:
Imagine that the level of the kth cohort effect is a declining function—for
whatever reason—of the $(k-1)$th cohort mortality level, but in addition is
affected by the level of an exogenous variable, in this case the extent to
which the cohort is made up of persons of foreign nativity. We might
write this as (ignoring a stochastic error term)

$$Y_k = a + bY_{k-1} + c\,(\text{FB})_k,\qquad\qquad (6)$$

where Y_k is the logit coefficient for the kth cohort effect, and $(FB)_k$ is either (depending on the specification) the percent foreign-born in the cohort or the foreign-born logit. Alternatively, this difference equation can be rewritten as

$$Y_k - bY_{k-1} = a + c(FB)_k, \qquad (7)$$

which, if $b \simeq 1$, justifies the correlation of the first-differences of the cohort coefficients with the levels of nativity. Estimation of equation (6) with FB specified as a logit yields

$$\hat{Y}_k = -.13 + 1.03Y_{k-1} + .32(FB)_k$$

for Massachusetts, and, to anticipate somewhat, the comparable equation for the United States is

$$\hat{Y}_k = .21 + 1.02Y_{k-1} + .23(FB)_k.$$

These close approximations of b to unity support the plotting of the foreign-born logits against the cohort coefficient first-differences in Figure 7 (and later, in Figure 13).

Much of the discussion thus far has concentrated on establishing a framework in which improved nutrition could be seen to propagate cohort differences in TB mortality, and on attempting to evaluate evidence relevant to the possible impact of changing nutrition. In so doing the emphasis has taken on a historical flavor. It must be acknowledged, however, that tuberculosis is thought to occur in epidemics (Dubos and Dubos, 1952; Pope and Gordon, 1955), an analogy to waves spanning several hundred years from trough to trough having been suggested by Grigg (1958). In this context, the decline of the last century in the now developed countries is merely the waning of the most recent epidemic. Viewed in this more general perspective, a number of factors other than nutrition have been considered as possible causal agents of TB mortality. One of them—changes in the virulence of the bacillus—can be ruled out. More precisely, evidence over the past century demonstrates that the bacillus continues to act with great violence (Pope and Gordon, 1955, p. 321; Bushnell, 1920, pp. 156–166; Borrel, 1920). The generalization would be that the course of TB epidemics can not be accounted for by changes in the capacity of the bacillus to damage its host. Other potential causal agents include natural selection, improved living conditions as distinct from increased nutrition, and the development of resistance through mild infection in childhood. The evidence concerning these factors is piecemeal and kaleidoscopic, as it is also for the nutrition thesis. Assuming that these additional potential mechanisms can be linked with cohort variability, the problem of marshalling evidence to discriminate among various factors is vastly complex: Our perhaps too simplified model linking cohorts and nutrition (equation (1)) already requires two kinds of information for each cohort. Admitting other factors would increase the indeterminacy. Evidently spatial disaggregation will be necessary if further empirical research is to be decisive. But even this may be insufficient for the most recent historical period, because of the paucity of relevant numerical information, the tremendous migration within and between countries, and the transformation from agrarian to industrial societies.

Age and Competing Risks. The pattern of age coefficients estimated by our model is useful in ruling out a competing risks explanation of the change in the level of TB mortality. In a competing risks explanation the gain in the share of mortality attributable to one cause is offset by a drop in mortality due to others. Could it be that the increase in the risk of dying from other causes is responsible for the TB mortality decline? The answer is almost assuredly no. In 1866 tuberculosis was the leading cause of death in New York City, accounting for 19.8% of all deaths. At the turn of the century it was the second leading cause of death (behind pneumonia-influenza-bronchitis) in both New York City and the United States comprising, respectively, 13.2% and 11.3% of total mortality. By 1930, tuberculosis had become the sixth leading cause of death in the United States, and by 1970 did not appear among the ten leading causes of death (Omran, 1977). Diseases that gained in proportion of deaths over this period included heart disease, cancer and stroke; they made up 15.9% of all U.S. deaths in 1900, and 66.3% in 1970. These diseases are degenerative, claiming the majority of their victims at relatively advanced ages. Tuberculosis is concentrated primarily among children and young adults, with pulmonary tuberculosis responsible for most of the latter. It is thus unimaginable that increases in degenerative disease had any effect on the decline of TB mortality, although the converse is probably true. Only causes of death with age patterns similar to that of tuberculosis could plausibly be related to the TB mortality decline. Many infectious diseases are concentrated at young ages, but in general deaths due to communicable illness—bronchitis, pneumonia, diarrhea and so forth—declined at even greater rates than did tuberculosis mortality. Accidents and violence are also leading causes of death among young adults; however, they did not increase during this period.

Periods and Chemotherapy. The period contrasts are somewhat difficult to interpret, for there is no reason to anticipate their anomalous rise from 1880 through 1950. Before speculating about their meaning it is worth considering whether they bear interpretation. As mentioned earlier, the entire seventy year increase is less than the subsequent twenty year decline. The largest first-difference between successive coefficients (0.17, from 1880 to 1890) is smaller than any corresponding first-difference among the age or cohort coefficients. Moreover, this gentle upward trend contributes little to the fit due to the inclusion of period in the model: The difference in deviance statistics between model V, the age-cohort model, and model VII, the just-identified age-period-cohort model, is 120.2; the difference between model V and model VIII, which constrains six of these coefficients to be equal, is 101.3. Thus, only about 16% of the moderate contribution of period to the model can be attributed to the six periods in question.

If some of the environmental factors mentioned earlier as linked with cohorts were in fact operating to some degree in a period-specific matter, we would expect if anything a gentle *downward* slope across these coefficients, especially the more recent ones. Nothing in the literature suggests changes in the environment or the bacillus that would be conducive to a small but steady rise in TB mortality. For these reasons we are loathe to attach any significance to these pre-1950 period coefficients, although they do exist in a purely statistical sense and are admittedly quite puzzling. Instead, we focus our attention on the downturn in coefficients after 1950—a downturn that is quite evident irrespective of the equality restriction.

As expected on the basis of our discussion earlier, the period contrasts decline from 1950 to 1960, and from 1960 to 1970. Chemotherapy, which averts death at all ages, was introduced in two rounds following World War II. The effects of the first round of medication (Streptomycin, p-amino-salicylate and Isoniazid) cannot, however, be distinguished from the second during the 1960s (Ethambutol and Rifampin). Quinquennial data and five-year age groupings would help distinguish these two rounds of innovation. Application of the age-period-cohort framework to such data for Massachusetts would thus be a more stringent test of the interpretation made here of the period effects. Lacking these data for Massachusetts, we consider the data series for the U.S. discussed earlier. The five-year intervals and age groupings in the U.S. data also make them useful in determining whether the advent of successful medication drastically altered the classic age profile of lung tuberculosis mortality within cohorts. For these reasons we turn next to the forty year U.S. data series described earlier.

6. ANALYSIS OF TUBERCULOSIS MORTALITY–UNITED STATES, 1935–1975

To aid discussion of the U.S. mortality rates given in Table 3, Figures 8 and 9 present trace lines of the age-specific rates (scaled logarithmically) by period and cohort, respectively. In Figure 8 the age-specific profiles are stacked by period, with the most recent year at the bottom. The typical profile decreases from infancy and early childhood, and then increases from later childhood, so that the chance of dying from lung tuberculosis appears to be greater in old age than at younger ages. There are also cross-overs of profiles involving recent years and ages for which TB mortality almost vanishes, as well as the profile for 1945, which intersects those for 1940 and 1935. Although suggestive, not all of these characteristics can be taken at face value, as will be seen by examination of the cohort profiles.

Figure 9 arranges the age-specific mortality rates within birth cohorts. The profiles for the 1890–1930 cohorts stand out sharply from the profiles for the post-1930 cohorts, which have very low pulmonary TB mortality. For the 1890–1930 cohorts the typical pattern is one of peaking and then decline with age, which contradicts interpretation of the period profiles (Figure 8) in the way expected on the basis of experience with the Massachusetts data. There is for these cohorts, moreover, an initial increase followed by a steep decline, then a gentle decline or trough and finally a slightly steeper decline. The initial increase to the peak is

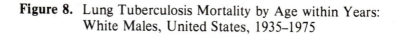

Figure 8. Lung Tuberculosis Mortality by Age within Years: White Males, United States, 1935–1975

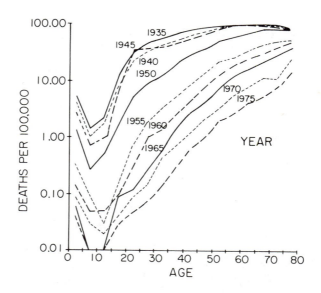

Figure 9. Lung Tuberculosis Mortality by Age for Selected Cohorts: White Males, United States, 1935–1975

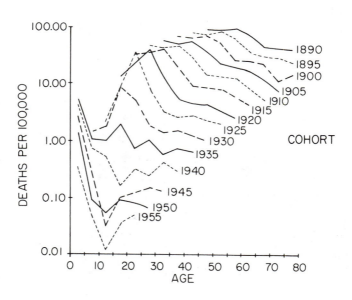

greatest for the 1930 cohort and declines monotonically the earlier the date of birth. To this pattern for the 1890–1930 cohorts there is a consistent five-year offset, lending Figure 9 a three-dimensional appearance and constituting prime evidence for the existence of period effects. Differences in the rate of initial increase for the 1890–1930 cohorts indicate that there are period-age interactions. This is consistent with the view that the increase is war related. Earlier, we noted that some of this was due to the shift of healthy young men from the civilian to the military population, and showed that adjusting for this shift yielded much lower rates. The need for a similar adjustment for men over age thirty-nine in 1935 is less obvious in the population totals displayed by Table A.4, and for this reason no adjustments have been made for older men of working age in 1945. In sum, there is a World War II effect with differential though consistent impact across ages in 1945. We can account for some of this interaction, but not all of it.

With demobilization there is a decrease in TB mortality which continues largely uninterrupted in the 1890–1930 cohorts. It is reasonable to infer that this decrease is compounded with the first wave of successful chemotherapeutic innovation in the treatment of tuberculosis. The trough, which occurs between 1955 and 1965, may reflect the dissipation of the impact of the initial round of treatment innovation, while the final decline, between 1965 and 1975, may reflect the advent of the second round of successful chemotherapeutic innovation.

The age pattern of mortality appears to deteriorate for cohorts born after 1930. A possible reason for this is that with the post-1930 cohorts TB mortality reached such low levels—rates of one or less per 100,000—that reporting errors could have visibly altered the pattern of age-specific rates. Additionally, and perhaps more importantly, people born after 1930, attaining early adulthood after 1950, would have been treated by the first effective medication in the history of the disease. That is, for the post-1930 cohorts the introduction of effective chemotherapy altered the classic within-cohort age-specific curve. This possibility was suggested earlier, in our discussion of the matching of chemotherapy with period effects.

The differentiation between the 1890–1930 and the post-1930 cohorts suggests that they require separate analytic treatment. For the post-1930 cohorts death due to lung tuberculosis has become a rare event and any modelling effort for this population would benefit from recognition of the decline. By the same token, since tuberculosis mortality has essentially vanished from this population, analysis of it would be motivated by concerns different from those providing the rationale for the work presented here.

In the analysis of the U.S. data below, we begin by applying the age-period-cohort framework to the 1935–1970 series and show that a just-identified specification fits the data poorly and yields implausible coefficients. We then show that including an age-period interaction for 1945 improves the fit but not the coefficients. Next, we separate the data for the post-1930 cohorts from the series and apply a just-identified age-period-cohort specification to the data for the 1890–1930 cohorts. Again the fit is poor and the coefficients implausible. Finally, we include an age-period interaction for 1945. This improves the fit and the coefficients.

6.1 Analysis

To identify the coefficients of the age-period-cohort model fitted to the U.S. data, we constrain ages 5–9 and 10–14 to have the same value. This is consistent with the logic underlying the identifying restriction employed in our analysis of the Massachusetts data: We would prefer that no constraints be placed on period or cohort effects, and, whether plotted by period or cohort, mortality is relatively low and similar at these young ages.

Our specification is again log-linear and, as in the case of Massachusetts, is estimated by maximum likelihood using iteratively reweighted least squares (Baker and Nelder, 1978). The response variable is the logarithm of the odds of dying of lung tuberculosis, based on the ratio of lung TB deaths (Table A.3) to the complement (Table A.4 less Table A.3). Table 5 displays the resulting coefficients for six reduced models, a full age-period-cohort specification, and another augmented by an adjustment variable for younger men in 1945. Of the first seven models, the full age-period-cohort specification is best-fitting even taking degrees of freedom into account, and we shall begin our discussion of the results with it.

In general, the patterns in the coefficients of model *vii* diverge from expectations. Turning first to the age effects, the chance of dying from lung tuberculosis is lowest at ages 5–14 and rises steadily thereafter to a peak at old age. This is the pattern suggested by inspection of the period-based age-specific mortality rates in Figure 8 and is consistent with the age coefficients of U.S. model *i*. It is at variance with the age effects for the Massachusetts full model and with what the eye can perceive in Figure 9. Period effects are also implausibly represented by the accounting model, with mortality declining monotonically from 1935 to 1975, and thus missing the pronounced increase in 1945 that is so evident in Figure 9. Finally, the coefficients for cohort effects increase through the cohort of 1905, not regaining the level of the 1860 cohort until the 1955 cohort, then decrease through the cohort of 1965 only to rise above the level of the 1860 cohort again. This is once more inconsistent with the Massachusetts results, and it is implausible on independent grounds, quite apart from distortion induced by the equally implausible age and period contrasts.

It is conceivable that our choice of identifying restriction is unfortunate, and is the source of the anomalous results obtained thus far for the U.S. data. Alternatives to the choice made for identifying the age-period-cohort model we have estimated would include different just-identifying restrictions as well as over-identifying restrictions. Since our interpretation of period effects is in terms of shifts in population between the military and the civilian sectors and in terms of medical treatment after World War II, it is reasonable to equate the period coefficients for 1935 and 1940. We have done so, and the patterns in the resulting coefficient estimates (not shown here) remain anomalous. The reduced models in Table 5 are also deficient, if not in the patterns of effects, then in goodness-of-fit. The over-identifying restrictions which define the reduced models are, moreover, less justified than the restrictions employed for the full models. In sum, we do not think that the choice of identifying restriction in the full model is the source of the problem.

Comparison of the observed and fitted rates based on model *vii* indicates that the residuals for younger men in 1945 include the largest in the entire data series. This is unsurprising, given that we have already shown that the denominators of the rates for men ages 15–39 are too small, due to the shift to the armed forces. To incorporate our understanding of this shift into the statistical analysis, we form an adjustment variable which is the ratio of the unadjusted to the adjusted rate (see note 11) for each age group in 1945. For age groups outside the

Table 5: Logit Coefficients for Eight Models of Lung Tuberculosis Mortality: White Males, United States, 1935-1975

	i [A]	ii [P]	iii [C]	iv [AP]	v [AC]	vi [PC]	vii [APC]	viii [APC]
Constant	-11.32	-7.66	-7.04	-10.24	-2.95	-7.04	-10.58	-6.93
Age:								
0-4	0.00*			0.00*	0.00*		0.00*	0.00*
5-9	-1.36			-1.33	-2.37		-1.77**	-1.85**
10-14	-0.87			-0.85	-2.90		-1.77**	-1.85**
15-19	0.90			0.90	-1.93		-0.32	-0.56
20-24	1.94			1.93	-1.60		0.50	-0.02
25-29	2.33			2.27	-1.87		0.70	0.09
30-34	2.54			2.46	-2.25		0.81	0.10
35-39	2.77			2.69	-2.55		1.00	0.22
40-44	3.00			2.92	-2.81		1.24	0.40
45-49	3.18			3.13	-3.05		1.50	0.56
50-54	3.35			3.33	-3.23		1.83	0.77
55-59	3.49			3.49	-3.41		2.16	0.99
60-64	3.55			3.57	-3.62		2.46	1.19
65-69	3.64			3.68	-3.79		2.82	1.44
70-74	3.68			3.76	-3.95		3.17	1.69
75+	3.69			3.85	-4.09		3.54	1.95
Period:								
1935		0.00*		0.00*		0.00*	0.00*	0.00*
1940		-0.13		-0.17		-0.01	-0.31	-0.20
1945		-0.12		-0.23		0.10	-0.49	-0.39
1950		-0.70		-0.78		-0.25	-1.16	-0.84
1955		-1.51		-1.58		-0.86	-2.06	-1.64
1960		-1.84		-1.92		-0.98	-2.48	-1.96
1965		-2.27		-2.31		-1.11	-2.93	-2.29
1970		-2.93		-2.99		-1.50	-3.61	-2.87
1975		-3.53		-3.62		-1.79	-4.19	-3.34

Table 5. (Cont.)

Cohort:

Cohort								
1860			0.00*		0.00*	0.00*	0.00*	0.00*
1865			0.04		-0.03	0.05	0.38	0.27
1870			0.04		-0.12	0.01	0.67	0.49
1875			0.03		-0.23	0.07	1.07	0.77
1880			-0.01		-0.39	0.12	1.46	1.06
1885			-0.09		-0.60	0.10	1.76	1.25
1890			-0.22		-0.85	0.05	2.03	1.41
1895			-0.45		-1.21	-0.11	2.18	1.46
1900			-0.71		-1.62	-0.30	2.29	1.46
1905			-0.96		-2.09	-0.54	2.32	1.40
1910			-1.24		-2.61	-0.77	2.31	1.27
1915			-1.59		-3.21	-1.08	2.21	1.03
1920			-2.09		-3.83	-1.56	2.07	0.69
1925			-2.70		-4.41	-2.14	1.97	0.37
1930			-3.55		-5.37	-3.02	1.52	-0.01
1935			-4.12		-6.63	-3.62	0.90	-0.68
1940			-4.64		-7.24	-4.05	0.71	-0.98
1945			-5.22		-7.92	-4.50	0.36	-1.77
1950			-5.69		-8.48	-4.73	0.42	-1.50
1955			-6.81		-9.69	-5.62	-0.02	-2.04
1960			-7.54		-10.39	-6.22	-0.27	-2.42
1965			-7.85		-10.98	-6.42	-0.41	-2.65
1970			-7.52		-11.01	-5.89	0.23	-2.11
1975			-7.58		-11.68	-5.80	0.15	-2.30
Adjustment								-2.06
Deviance	122800	123100	28400	13440	6308	4440	1728	638.5
DF	128	135	120	120	105	112	98	97

*Dummy variable omitted for purposes of estimation.

**Coefficients constrained to be equal.

Note: "Deviance" is minus twice the maximized log-likelihood, and is asymptotically distributed as chi-square (Nelder and Wedderburn, 1972)

15–39 range, the adjusted rate is identical to the unadjusted rate.[17] Extending model *vii* to include the adjustment for the shift to the military produces the values for model *viii* in Table 5. This one variable is responsible for a nearly two-thirds decrease in the deviance of model *vii*. Yet, despite this improvement in fit, the patterns of the coefficients remain implausible. The age coefficients increase monotonically from ages 5–14. The decreases in the period coefficients from 1935 to 1945 remain mysterious, there being no *a priori* reason to expect a decrease in the period coefficients for these years. The cohort coefficients retain the pattern observed in model *vii*, though now the mortality level of the 1860 cohort is regained by the cohort of 1930. In short, adjusting for the shift from the civilian to the military population greatly improves the fit of the age-period-cohort model, but has little impact on the patterns of the coefficients.

It is possible to further improve the fit of the augmented age-period-cohort model by including still more interaction terms. For this purpose we would divide the data series into the 1860–1930 cohorts and the 1935–1975 cohorts. Our initial discussion of the impact of the chemotherapeutic revolution suggested that for those born at or after the start of this era, the formerly seen age and cohort patterns should dissolve. The U.S. data graphed in Figure 9 support this expectation (see also Table 2). Moreover, the cohorts of 1940 and 1935 appear to be receiving considerable benefit from the modern era of medication. The 1940 cohort has thus far experienced TB mortality rates below one per 100,000 in all age groups except the first. The 1935 cohort attained adulthood around 1955, by which time effective medication had already become available. It is likely that for this reason the peaking of TB mortality in young adulthood is much attenuated for this cohort. Thus, both data and substantive reasoning suggest that the 1935–1975 cohorts require special consideration in further modelling of the U.S. series.

---

[17] For much of the analysis from this point on, we have used two alternatives to the adjustment variable described here. First, we have substituted the five adjusted rates for the deviant observed rates and then proceeded to fit age-period-cohort as well as reduced specifications. Second, we have used a dummy variable which distinguishes between ages 15–39 in 1945 and all other cells. Both alternatives yield the same conclusions, with negligible differences in fit and coefficients. We prefer the adjustment variable described in the text, since it seems appropriate to incorporate all of our knowledge into the analysis.

Since our main concern is to model TB mortality in the era when there still was some, rather than continue the analysis based on the entire series we have elected to concentrate on the data for the cohorts of 1860–1930. The question of further interactions for the 1860–1930 cohort is premature at this juncture, as it has yet to be demonstrated that this subset of the data requires them.

Table 6 presents the coefficients of four age-period-cohort models applied to the data for the 1860-1930 cohorts. Model *ix* identifies the coefficients by equating those for ages 5–9 and 10–14, as was also done in models *vii* and *viii*. In fact, model *ix* is defined identically to model *vii* except that age group 0–4 and cohorts 1935–1975 are missing. As can be seen, model *ix* fits the subsetted data poorly, and the pattern of its age coefficients is particularly troublesome, increasing monotonically from the earliest ages. Inspection of the residuals for this model indicates that those for ages 15–19 contain the largest in the data series. To compensate for this, model *x* augments model *ix* by including the adjustable variable, which again lowers the deviance by about two-thirds. Moreover, for the first time in model *x* we see coefficients that bear some resemblance to expectations. The age curve increases to ages 20–24, then declines and flattens with a slight upturn at the older ages. The period coefficients are essentially flat through 1945, after which they decline. The cohort coefficients increase slightly through the 1880 cohort and decline thereafter, regaining the level of the 1860 cohort by the time the 1890 cohort is encountered.

The near equality of the 1935 and 1940 period coefficients in model *x*, along with the prior expectation that these two coefficients should be equal, suggests that the age-period-cohort model could be identified using periods rather than ages, yielding coefficients much the same as those of model *x*. As the coefficient values for model *xi* show, this in fact happens. Indeed, it can be seen that the coefficients of age groups 5–9 and 10–14 are virtually identical in model *xi*. This suggests that the age-period-cohort model (with the adjustment variable) can be over-identified without degrading the fit or altering the patterns in the coefficients. Model *xii* equates the coefficients of the first two age groups and the first two periods. As expected, the coefficients change but little, and the fit not at all. The coefficients of models *xi* and *xii* are virtually identical, and little different from those of model *x*. It is surprising that the coefficients of model *x* are not closer yet to those of models *xi* and *xii*, but the differences appear to be of no practical importance.

Table 6. Logit Coefficients for Four Additional Models of Lung Tuberculosis Mortality: White Males, United States, 1935-1975, Cohorts Born 1930 and Earlier

	ix	x	xi	xii
Constant	-9.57	-5.87	-6.27	-6.25
Age:				
5-9	0.00*	0.00*	0.00*	0.00*
10-14	0.00*	0.00*	0.03	0.00*
15-19	1.36	1.16	1.22	1.20
20-24	1.97	1.49	1.57	1.55
25-29	1.93	1.35	1.46	1.44
30-34	1.82	1.12	1.27	1.24
35-39	1.78	1.01	1.18	1.16
40-44	1.80	0.96	1.16	1.13
45-49	1.84	0.88	1.11	1.09
50-54	1.94	0.87	1.12	1.10
55-59	2.04	0.85	1.14	1.12
60-64	2.12	0.82	1.13	1.11
65-69	2.26	0.84	1.18	1.16
70-74	2.39	0.85	1.22	1.20
75+	2.53	0.88	1.28	1.25
Period:				
1935	0.00*	0.00*	0.00*	0.00*
1940	-0.09	0.03	0.00*	0.00*
1945	-0.05	0.07	0.01	0.01
1950	-0.49	-0.15	-0.23	-0.23
1955	-1.16	-0.71	-0.82	-0.82
1960	-1.36	-0.79	-0.94	-0.93
1965	-1.57	-0.89	-1.06	-1.06
1970	-2.05	-1.25	-1.45	-1.45
1975	-2.42	-1.50	-1.72	-1.72
Cohort:				
1860	0.00*	0.00*	0.00*	0.00*
1865	0.16	0.04	0.07	0.07
1870	0.22	0.03	0.09	0.09
1875	0.40	0.08	0.17	0.17
1880	0.56	0.13	0.24	0.24
1885	0.65	0.09	0.24	0.24
1890	0.68	0.01	0.19	0.19
1895	0.62	-0.17	0.03	0.03
1900	0.50	-0.39	-0.16	-0.17
1905	0.30	-0.69	-0.43	-0.43
1910	0.07	-1.06	-0.77	-0.77
1915	-0.26	-1.53	-1.22	-1.22
1920	-0.62	-2.10	-1.76	-1.76
1925	-0.93	-2.64	-2.27	-2.27
1930	-1.58	-3.23	-2.83	-2.84
Adjustment	-	-2.05	-2.05	-2.05
Deviance	1559	481.8	481.8	481.8
DF	63	62	62	63

Note: "Deviance" is minus twice the maximized log-likelihood, and is asymptotically distributed as chi-square (Nelder and Wedderburn, 1972).
* Coefficient constrained to be zero.

Although including the adjustment variable for young men in 1945 improves the fit of the age-period-cohort model substantially, the deviance statistic remains high—about three times larger than obtained with the Massachusetts data, and much larger than would be considered acceptable with data from samples of moderate size. For a given pattern in the data, however, the deviance is a monotonically increasing function of the number of observations. In this instance the data set is extremely large. A different sense of the degree of fit of models x, xi, and xii, which all have the same deviance, is gained from computing the correlation between observed and expected values (frequencies, rates, or logits). For these models, no matter whether frequencies, rates or logits are used, the squared correlation between observed and expected values is all but perfect (0.99). By this criterion the fit is excellent and we might wish to describe and attempt interpretation of the coefficients. Before doing so, however, a further check of the fit may be useful. Table 2 includes the residuals (using model x); what can be gleaned from them?

Perhaps most strikingly, there is a concentration of relatively large residuals at ages 70–74 and 75 and over. Since some of the residuals for these two age groups are positive and others negative, their attribution to a common cause is uncertain. It should not escape notice, however, that the residuals for the 1865 and 1870 cohorts are among the largest.[18] Including three additional dummy variables to fit perfectly the cells of the 1865 and 1870 cohorts reduces the deviance to 344.6 (with 59 degrees of freedom), and in so doing changes little but the cohort coefficients in the augmented age-period-cohort model. We could proceed in like manner throughout the table—targeting deviant cells for special fitting. We lack the substantive grounds for doing so, however, and suggest that the degree of fit provided by the age-period-cohort model with an adjustment variable for young men in 1945 (model x, xi or

---

[18] The corresponding standardized residuals are not shown here. Table 2 presents fitting errors as differences between observed and fitted rates, since these seem more readily grasped. Although the standardized residuals provided by the GLIM program are approximately unit normal deviates under the assumptions of the model, they are also approximately equal to the difference of observed and fitted divided by the square root of the fitted frequency even if the assumptions of the model are not satisfied. Thus, the standardization adjusts for the differing magnitudes of the observed frequencies. It was with this interpretation in mind that we employed standardized residuals to scan for extreme outliers.

xii) is quite good, while reflecting as well all of the prior knowledge and theory we have been able to bring to bear on the prolem. Given this assessment of goodness-of-fit, we next describe and discuss the coefficients, for specificity using those of model *x*.

Figures 10–12 present the age, period and cohort coefficients graphically, using the conventions employed in displaying the results for Massachusetts. Figure 10 plots the net age coefficients, and displays the rapid ascent to a mortality peak in young adulthood, a subsequent drop, but then a slow increase to the open-ended age category. This final increase is unfamiliar and unexpected; it is not immediately clear whether it is real or reflects mis-specification in the model. There is no reason why the Massachusetts results, or those for other states or other nations, must be assumed valid while those for the United States should be considered otherwise. The pattern of decreasing TB mortality with age has often seemed, if anything, anomalous to researchers, which perhaps explains why analysts for so long continued to perceive the age relationship through cross-sectional, period, rates rather than through over-time, cohort, rates. Tuberculosis is a wasting disease, hence the slight increase in mortality with advanced age is plausible.

This look at the U.S. data was motivated by a concern for a more telling demonstration of period effects consistent with their explanation in terms of the chemotherapeutic revolution. Figure 11 graphs the period coefficients while also noting several key dates. The period trend is flat from 1935 to 1945, drops sharply for the next decade, declines more gently for another decade, and again drops rapidly in the final decade of the data. The two decades of greatest decline in TB mortality coincide with the most important developments in drug treatments. The five-year data for the United States are thus consistent with the ten-year data for Massachusetts, and with the interpretation we have advanced concerning the link between medication and period effects. In the terms of the age-period-cohort accounting framework, the impact of the medical revolution on tuberculosis mortality in twenty-five years can be thought of as equalling the maximum contrast between the safest and most dangerous ages with respect to TB. This result of course differs from that obtained with the Massachusetts data, which are based on wider age groups, and smooth the more extreme contrasts observable in the U.S. data.

Whereas for Massachusetts the cohort coefficients decline steadily in TB mortality, those for the United States display a slight increase from

Figure 10. Age Effects (Model *x*): Coefficients for the Log-Odds of Dying from Lung Tuberculosis, White Males, United States, Cohorts Born 1930 and Earlier

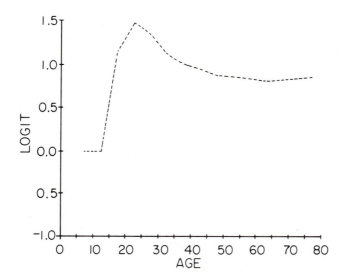

Figure 11. Period Effects (Model *x*): Coefficients for the Log-Odds of Dying from Lung Tuberculosis, White Males, United States, Cohorts Born 1930 and Earlier

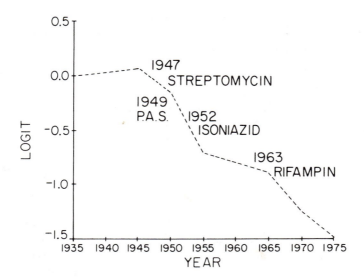

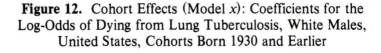

Figure 12. Cohort Effects (Model x): Coefficients for the Log-Odds of Dying from Lung Tuberculosis, White Males, United States, Cohorts Born 1930 and Earlier

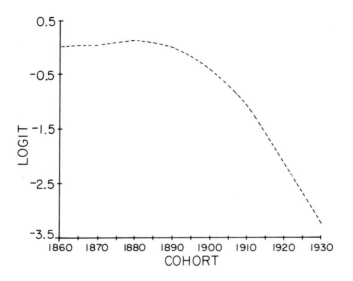

the 1860 to the 1885 cohort, and then an accelerating decline thereafter (Figure 12). The departure of the United States data from the monotonic decline witnessed in the Massachusetts data suggests that one or the other of the data sets has been modelled incorrectly, that there is something wrong with the data, or alternatively, that the differences between Massachusetts and the United States are real and need to be understood. We can not rule out the possibility of mis-specification, although our efforts thus far have been directed toward securing the most appropriate specification. Nor can we categorically rule out the possibility of errors in the data, though we have checked our own transcriptions and inspected the source figures for plausibility. Since there is little more we can do concerning mis-specification or other errors, we must consider the possibility that the differences between the Massachusetts and United States cohort trends are real.

At issue is the slight increase in mortality over the 1860–1885 U.S. cohorts, as contrasted with the monotonic decline over all Massachusetts cohorts. In our discussion of percent foreign-born, we suggested that increases in this variable could actually reverse the trend of declining cohort mortality and, short of a reversal, could slow the rate of decline.

We found for the Massachusetts data that there is a relationship between percent foreign-born and the successive first-differences, but none between percent foreign-born and the cohort contrasts. Quite apart from the difficulty of ascertaining the multiple meanings of percent foreign-born in an analysis as highly aggregated as this one, there remains the problem that Massachusetts experienced considerable out- as well as in-migration. It is possible that for this reason the pecent foreign-born, assuming it has something to do with cohort TB mortality and is not a purely accidental covariate, affected the rate of decline in Massachusetts, but did not bring about a temporary reversal in the decline. If that is so, the mechanism would require that some of those afflicted with TB would die elsewhere from the disease. Although there might be departures from the United States, we would expect that most of the mobility would be to internal destinations. Moreover, the United States has experienced little out-migration relative to Massachusetts, the climate of which has never been considered ameliorative with respect to tuberculosis. In short, the United States, more so than Massachusetts, approximates a population closed to out-migration. This could help explain the temporary reversal in cohort TB mortality for the United States. If the suggested interpretation of this difference is correct, there should be an observable association between the percent foreign-born and cohort TB mortality, along with the association previously observed between percent foreign-born and successive first-differences (i.e., rate of change in TB mortality).

Table 7 presents what information we have been able to assemble on the percent foreign-born by cohort. As before, the foreign-born composition of cohorts is stable by age forty. This consistency with the Massachusetts percent foreign-born does not rule out the line of reasoning we have suggested since what is at issue need not be differential migration within the United States by nativity, but could be movement of those with active cases of tuberculosis. The veil of aggregation in the Massachusetts data (for which there are no age-period-nativity-specific TB mortality rates) is less of a problem in the United States, since movement within the United States would not affect the country's TB mortality rates whereas it would those of particular states.

What, then, is the relationship between the percent foreign-born and cohort TB mortality for the United States? Using the percentage attained in age groups 30–34 or 35–39, the correlation between percent foreign-

Table 7. Percent Foreign-Born by Age for Various Cohorts: U.S. White Males, 1860-1970

Age	1860	1865	1870	1875	1880	1885	1890	1895	1900	1905	1910	1915	1920	1925	1930	1935	1940	1945	1950	1955	1960	1965	1970
																							Cohort
0-4	12.4		4.9		1.1		1.3		0.7		1.1		0.4		0.3		0.1		0.4		0.6		0.6
5-9		8.6		2.2		3.9		1.9		3.5		1.7		1.1		0.2		0.5		0.9		1.1	
10-14	27.1		17.4		9.8		4.5		4.5		3.5		1.4		0.5		0.7		1.5		1.4		
15-19		25.0		9.1		8.3		8.8		6.2		3.0		1.5		1.0		1.6		1.8			
20-24	26.9		25.1		14.4		20.1		11.3		6.7		1.9		1.7		2.6		2.7				
25-29		28.3		19.9		25.9		19.0		11.8		4.0		2.9		3.2		3.6					
30-34	27.2		29.4		26.7		25.1		15.8		7.5		2.9		3.5		4.8						
35-39		30.0		26.6		27.1		21.1		12.5		4.9		4.5		4.9							
40-44	26.5		27.9		26.1		25.3		16.4		8.4		4.0		4.8								
45-49		28.8		27.2		26.4		21.3		13.1		6.1		5.2									
50-54	25.8		26.7		25.3		25.6		16.7		9.3		4.5										
55-59		28.2		24.5		26.4		21.0		13.8		6.6											
60-64			26.2		25.7		25.3		16.7		9.6												
65-69		27.7		24.3		26.2		20.6		13.9													
70-74			27.7		24.9		24.3		16.8														
75+				24.7	24.7	22.9		21.7															

Sources: See Appendix B

born and the cohort contrasts is 0.91; that between percent foreign-born and the cohort successive first-differences is 0.99 (see Figure 13). These strong associations are not the result of strategically located points.

Such as they are, the data are apparently consistent with the conclusion that the cohort coefficients of model x (or models xi and xii—their correlations with percent foreign-born are the same) are numbers worthy of interpretation. Whether the specific interpretation rests ultimately on the nutrition thesis or is in some measure bound up with crowded and poor living conditions in ports of entry and the burgeoning industrial cities of the United States remains unclear. Nevertheless, this demonstration of the relationship between the percent foreign-born and cohort TB mortality as well as between the percent foreign-born and the rate of change in TB mortality further justifies the identification of the percent foreign-born variable as a causal agent in the trend, even if the specific mechanism remain to be determined and quantified. Thus, although our original motivation for considering the U.S. data was in terms of the relevance of its greater detail for the assessment of period effects, this series has also proven helpful in describing as well as understanding the trend in cohort TB mortality: The

Figure 13. First-Differences of Cohort Coefficients (Model x) and Logits of Cohort Foreign-Born: White Males, United States, Cohorts of 1865 to 1930

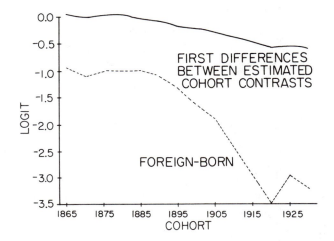

Massachusetts data have perhaps been reproduced so many times that they have taken on disproportionate importance. It is therefore noteworthy that differences between the U.S. and Massachusetts series have a plausible interpretation, and important as well that the line of reasoning used to account for the differences is connected with the initial attempt to examine the validity of the nutrition thesis. That use of the nativity variable is consistent with other scenarios for the decline of TB mortality is a salutary reminder that the nutrition thesis amounts conceptually to a bivariate relationship.

7. CONCLUSIONS

Our work on tuberculosis has mingled substantive with methodological considerations. We have analyzed data studied by others in similar form and borrowed conclusions based on one data series to inform analysis of the other. What are the bedrock conclusions, and what progress has been made? Although the separation is to a degree arbitrary, we first discuss the substance that has occupied us, and then take up the methodological aspects of the analysis.

7.1. Tuberculosis Mortality

We have argued that there are sound reasons for employing the age-period-cohort framework in the historical analysis of TB mortality. The reasons are that valid measurements of the phenomena thought to drive TB mortality are largely unavailable, and that the age, period and cohort dimensions can be construed plausibly to be linked uniquely to the underlying phenomena. For example, it appears appropriate to view medical innovation as linked to the period dimension and not the age or cohort dimensions. A comprehensive justification of the age-period-cohort framework is not present in prior writing on the subject, although the framework has been applied before and the potential trends associated with each of the accounting dimensions have been discussed separately.

We have shown that the application of an age-period-cohort model to the Massachusetts series yields patterns in the contrasts for each of the accounting dimensions which are consistent with our expectations and those of others based on inspection of the rates. That is, the model summarizes patterns apparent in the data. This is contrary to the one previous age-period-cohort analysis of the Massachusetts data, which, we have suggested, suffered from the use of inappropriate identifying restrictions and other problems.

By extending the Massachusetts series beyond its stopping point in earlier analyses, we have shown that the pattern of period effects is consistent with prior expectations concerning the impact of chemotherapeutic innovation.

By simultaneously articulating the meaning of age and cohort differences in TB mortality, we were able to indicate that any phenomenon affecting cohort susceptibility to tuberculosis—including level of nutrition—could exert continuous pressure on TB mortality, intermittent pressure, or even a once-only push. The Revolutionary War muster data suggest that in Massachusetts, if nutrition was the major factor contributing to resistance, a rise in its level must have taken place well before the nineteenth century. We suggested that the rise could have been not so much within Massachusetts as between Massachusetts and the European subpopulations supplying immigrants.

We were able to bring to bear additional fragmentary evidence concerning nutrition, in the form of data on the percent foreign-born, who may have been less well nourished prior to immigration. Although no more than suggestive at best, the data do not indicate that the influx of foreign-born even temporarily reversed the decline over cohorts in TB mortality, although changes in nativity seem to have impeded the decline in Massachusetts. Because of ambiguities in the interpretation of the percent foreign-born variable, this finding poses a riddle whose resolution should further clarify the role of changing nutrition in the decline of TB mortality.

We were able to show that the Massachusetts decline by cohort in TB mortality could not be attributed to changing risks in succumbing to major alternative causes of death.

Although the pattern in the period effects for the Massachusetts data is consistent with the role of effective medication, this pattern is not as convincing as it might otherwise be, due to the use of decennial data with ten-year age groups. For this reason we sought further confirmation of the interpretation of the period effects through the use of the U.S. data, which are reported quinquennially with five-year age-groups. The justification for the use of quinquennial data is that there were two rounds of chemotherapeutic innovation. Although the first round was a major success it could not have eradicated all TB mortality—if it had there would have been no need for further development of drugs for tuberculosis. Therefore, we thought it possible that there would be a levelling off in the period trend after the first round of new and effective drugs, followed by a later decline. This is the pattern of period effects that we looked for, and found by graphic display of the age-specific rates within cohorts for the U.S. series. This display also showed, especially for younger men, a prominent peaking in the age-specific rates across cohorts during 1945. Since there is no reason to expect that the chances of succumbing from tuberculosis would have made such an unprecedented leap, we noted its timing and checked the population base figures. These declined for younger men because of mobilization for World War II, while the actual number of deaths due to tuberculosis also declined, but to a lesser degree. The World War II age-period interaction has nothing to do with the processes fundamentally affecting TB mortality; nevertheless, it provides one more test of the adequacy of the age-period-cohort framework.

With the United States data we showed that the age pattern observed earlier, in the Massachusetts data, is modified. In particular, TB mortality does not decline to the oldest ages, but levels off and increases slightly with age, after reaching its maximum in earlier adulthood. Although we can not account for this pattern, it is no less plausible than that observed for Massachusetts, which is but one state of many. We found that the trend in the period coefficients is consistent with the pattern expected on the basis of innovation in chemotherapy. Finally, we obtained a cohort trend not quite seen earlier in the Massachusetts data, but plausible nevertheless. Again using percent foreign-born for cohorts, we showed that not only was the *rate* of decline over cohorts in TB mortality associated with the percent foreign born, but also the *level* of mortality. We suggested that a key difference between Massachusetts and the United States—degree of out-migration—might account for the association between percent foreign-born and the level of TB mortality in the United States, but not in Massachusetts. The meaning of the nativity variable in the context of this analysis is ambiguous, but the discussion of its meaning, its empirical juxtaposition with cohort mortality, and the results obtained all constitute progress in the study of the decline in TB mortality.

7.2. Methodology

Armed with strong prior expectations based on our knowledge of the epidemiology of tuberculosis, the findings of others, our results for the Massachusetts data, and our inspection of the U.S. series from several perspectives, we estimated an age-period-cohort model for the U.S. data and obtained uninterpretable coefficients for all three accounting dimensions. This is an important result: Application of a plausibly identified age-period-cohort model to data in which age, period and cohort patterns are distinctly visible does not necessarily yield the desired results. Proceeding further with the analysis we learned that omitted interactions can account for much distortion in the results of the included accounting categories. Thus, the choice of identifying restrictions is not the only sensitive characteristic of age-period-cohort models, and may not even be the most important. Including a single interaction variable, and excluding a group of recent cohorts from the data structure on the grounds that their rates were governed by a process different from that of the earlier cohorts, yielded results highly consistent with expectations.

The fragility of this process is striking. Without the extensive theoretical justification and the Massachusetts results, we would not have known that the initial age-period-cohort results for the U.S. series were implausible. It was this background that enabled us to examine the residuals for meaningful interactions, and led us to focus on the 1860–1930 cohorts. Indeed, without the prior examination of the data, and the even earlier formulation concerning the pattern to be expected for cohorts born in the era of modern medication, we would have had little justification for separating the younger cohorts from the older cohorts, the residuals for the younger cohorts not being notably large. In point of fact, we have not shown that it was necessary to focus on the older cohorts; only that when we do so the results essentially conform to theoretical expectations. It could be that an omitted interaction involving the older cohorts is the genuine cause of the distortions in the coefficients observed when the full data series is analyzed. Having exhausted our fund of knowledge about potential interactions, however, we are unable to explore this possibility. This illustrates what seems to be an especially challenging aspect of the age-period-cohort accounting framework. The importance of prior knowledge and theory is widely recognized and often given formal content in discussions of omitted variable bias (Theil, 1965). Although this kind of treatment is general and applies to the age-period-cohort accounting framework, it does so with a twist. Typically, omitted variables are thought of as additional additive factors. In the age-period-cohort accounting framework the analyst must examine residuals for what may be cell-specific causes of deviance, and in so doing must be able to conceive of fitting error as due to interactions which have meaningful interpretations.   Yet, interactions are among the most difficult relationships to understand.

The nature of the data structure also affects the potential for error in the analysis. In particular, the structure is necessarily unbalanced. This means that stochastic fluctuations in the data can have a differential impact depending on where they appear in the data structure, and can be more or less readily discerned depending on their location. For example, chance deviation in the count of a cell in the interior of an age-by-period array will have a relatively small effect on the coefficients of the corresponding age, period and cohort effects, since they will in all cases depend on several other cells as well. Moreover, with the other cells to counterbalance the deviant one, it is plausible that only the latter will have a large residual. An error in the lower-left or upper-right corners of the data structure will, by comparison, have greater but perhaps less detectable impact. As we move toward these corners in the design, each cell takes on a larger role in determining the estimate of the corresponding cohort parameter. There are fewer cells to "cancel-out" the error brought on by the offending cell; for this reason the remaining cells will also have large (oppositely signed) residuals. This phenomenon may be at work in the earliest cohorts of the U.S. data (see again Table 2; especially the residuals for the cohorts of 1865 and 1870). The problem exists no matter how the data are arrayed: In data collected by age across cohorts, cells in sparsely represented periods would be prone to similar difficulties.

The use of an interaction term to augment the age-period-cohort specification in our analysis of the U.S. data seems to us to mark a kind of progress, if perhaps only in our own thinking. So much attention has focussed on the identification problem caused by the inclusion of a third accounting dimension which is itself an interaction, that only recently have analysts considered the possibility of modelling other interactions. It is fortuitous in this connection that the major interaction we encountered has a straightforward substantive interpretation, since it enables us to satisfy the same standard of rigor in justifying its inclusion that we attempted to apply in justifying the simultaneous inclusion of age, period and cohort.

We consider, finally, whether the age-period-cohort accounting framework was a help or a hindrance. Could we have done without it? The answer must rest on an evaluation of the foregoing results. We found the accounting framework essential, and consider that more is now known about the decline in TB mortality than formerly. Our thinking about the mechanics of the decline and the factors possibly involved in the process was aided by the accounting framework. Imposing it on the problem of the TB mortality decline provides a perspective with which to organize the scatter of facts about the subject into a rich mosaic. Measurement of the factors hypothesized to be linked to the accounting categories is difficult. The one external variable we were able to bring into the analysis, percent foreign-born, can be only one of many theoretical possibilities. It is often said, though rarely if ever written, that the only fruitful way to conduct cohort analysis is to begin the analysis with measures of variables presumed to underlie the accounting categories. Even if that were usually possible, and it is not, we would find this no more justifiable than a recommendation never to carry out an analysis of variance or a multiple classification analysis. The use of the age-period-cohort accounting framework amounts to nothing more than the modelling of the kind of data structure used in analysis of variance or multiple classification analysis. Examination of these structures, even when there is a plenitude of data, can often be helpful in formulating subsequent analyses. This has been the role of the age-period-cohort accounting framework in this application. That the prospects for full mastery of the problem are bleak, if only because the data are inadequate, does not vitiate the usefulness of the framework, but remains a statement about the difficulty of the substantive problem.

Finally, also in discussion but not in writing, the view is sometimes advanced that the identification problem in the age-period-cohort accounting framework, which is avoided when at least one of the accounting categories can be replaced by a measured variable, renders the chance of obtaining correct results remote if not nil. Unquestionably identifying restrictions create limitations. As to the chances of securing an accurate representation of the facts, it must be pointed out that the claim of futility is not empirical and does not rest on irrefutable logic—it is, rather, an untested view. Our experience with the Massachusetts and United States data series suggests that the coefficients can be stable in the face of alternative, well justified, identifying restrictions. What seems at least as important if not more so is that omitted interactions can markedly distort the coefficients of the included variables. In that case, the use of measured variables will provide no particular advantage. Indeed, since measured variables are almost always ambiguous indicators in aggregated time-series analysis (as is the case, for example, with percent foreign-born), their use is by no means free from difficulty even if a particular data series contains no interactions.

APPENDIX A: BASIC DATA

Table A.1. Deaths Due to Lung Tuberculosis by Age: Males, Massachusetts, 1880-1970

Age	Year									
	1880	1890	1900	1910	1920	1930	1940	1950	1960	1970
0-9	168	152	115	84	51	26	11	5	0	0
10-19	193	219	194	146	118	62	16	2	0	0
20-29	702	792	737	586	427	233	116	20	3	1
30-39	471	609	656	640	458	338	154	82	13	5
40-49	349	406	386	480	410	310	253	124	20	9
50-59	240	262	267	309	284	252	222	176	48	20
60-69	197	175	168	173	155	119	171	166	77	24
70+	130	99	84	64	59	58	73	100	73	23

Sources: See Appendix B

Table A.2. Population by Age: Males, Massachusetts, 1880-1970

Age	Year									
	1880	1890	1900	1910	1920	1930	1940	1950	1960	1970
0–9	176,654	200,646	269,893	314,731	375,110	375,231	298,626	416,028	528,315	516,659
10–19	161,480	200,714	229,380	288,319	314,858	375,490	372,567	302,146	405,083	538,891
20–29	159,785	221,654	265,801	311,311	320,030	316,430	347,641	354,740	291,268	400,629
30–39	126,327	168,157	230,261	273,517	302,881	317,457	303,097	337,540	336,114	290,504
40–49	97,442	122,921	160,113	209,939	249,839	278,169	294,513	291,637	318,086	324,562
50–59	68,195	83,782	105,808	134,904	175,931	209,646	237,345	261,878	260,477	289,887
60–69	43,871	53,539	63,043	76,715	98,253	130,571	155,947	187,068	201,199	200,325
70+	24,686	32,475	36,750	43,697	51,202	67,049	92,843	119,330	145,693	157,941

Sources: See Appendix B

Table A.3. Deaths Due to Lung Tuberculosis by Age: White Males, Conterminous United States, 1935-1975

					Year				
Age	1935	1940	1945	1950	1955	1960	1965	1970	1975
0-4	240	195	148	101	28	10	5	7	3
5-9	76	49	38	16	7	4	1	3	0
10-14	127	95	50	26	2	4	1	2	1
15-19	686	476	368	91	8	6	7	3	3
20-24	1631	1157	931	260	32	15	7	6	4
25-29	2189	1645	1259	475	96	48	12	9	5
30-34	2414	1938	1517	632	180	72	27	21	8
35-39	2817	2114	1873	992	275	143	76	35	15
40-44	3211	2523	2325	1323	435	231	150	64	31
45-49	3231	2818	2688	1520	653	417	214	118	49
50-54	2833	2999	2933	1910	871	588	364	157	102
55-59	2530	2710	2869	2069	907	729	502	249	116
60-64	1913	2224	2322	2004	1085	796	561	297	160
65-69	1469	1689	1882	1800	1108	817	573	326	167
70-74	1043	1152	1208	1228	907	818	610	238	164
75+	919	957	1129	1302	1032	1073	1002	650	422

Sources: See Appendix B

Table A.4. Population (in Thousands) by Age: White Males, Conterminous United States, 1935-1975

	Year								
	1935	1940	1945	1950	1955	1960	1965	1970	1975
0-4	4,551	4,701	5,807	7,244	8,171	7,244	8,783	7,347	6,729
5-9	5,290	4,745	5,286	5,915	7,480	8,202	8,939	8,633	7,401
10-14	5,567	5,259	5,025	4,945	6,071	7,457	8,319	9,004	8,780
15-19	5,259	5,517	4,276	4,686	4,741	5,837	7,488	8,291	9,029
20-24	5,007	5,114	2,597	5,003	4,351	4,646	5,759	6,940	8,219
25-29	4,665	4,892	3,287	5,350	5,125	4,722	4,876	5,850	7,366
30-34	4,302	4,573	3,794	5,081	5,402	5,218	4,771	4,925	6,044
35-39	4,062	4,254	4,046	4,956	5,166	5,447	5,213	4,784	4,973
40-44	4,039	3,995	4,165	4,574	4,879	5,117	5,418	5,194	4,820
45-49	3,649	3,843	3,886	4,080	4,552	4,828	5,034	5,258	5,095
50-54	3,093	3,452	3,554	3,756	3,900	4,286	4,653	4,833	5,180
55-59	2,570	2,790	3,038	3,351	3,498	3,729	4,016	4,311	4,553
60-64	2,041	2,232	2,510	2,829	3,082	3,122	3,365	3,647	3,907
65-69	1,533	1,737	1,964	2,223	2,493	2,684	2,644	2,808	3,220
70-74	1,026	1,183	1,338	1,513	1,790	2,018	2,099	2,108	2,226
75+	1,049	1,162	1,386	1,624	1,931	2,206	2,546	2,730	2,858

Note: Figures for 1935, 1945, 1955, 1965, and 1975 are estimates.

Sources: See Appendix B

APPENDIX B

Sources for Table 4

1880 Department of the Interior, U.S. Census Office. Compendium of the Tenth Census, Part I. Washington, D.C.: Government Printing Office, 1883. Table XLII, pp. 626–627.

1890 Department of the Interior, U.S. Census Office. Report on Population of the United States at the Eleventh Census: 1890, Vol. I, Part 2. Washington, D.C.: Government Printing Office, 1895. Table 2, pp. 44–45.

1900 Department of the Interior, U.S. Census Office. Twelfth Census of the United States Taken in the Year 1900. Census Report, Vol. II, Population, Part II. Washington, D.C.: U.S. Census Office, 1902. Table 2, pp. 50–51.

1910 Department of Commerce. Thirteenth Census of the United States Taken in the year 1910. Vol. II, Population, Alabama-Montana. Washington, D.C.: Government Printing Office, 1913. Table 7, p. 866. Figure for ages 65–74 split at age 70 using foreign-born white ages 65–69 (both sexes) as shown in Table 13, p. 227 in Department of Commerce, U.S. Bureau of the Census. Fourteenth Census of the United States Taken in the Year 1920. Vol. II, Population, 1920, General Report and Analytical Tables. Washington, D.C.: Government Printing Office, 1922.

1920 Department of Commerce, U.S. Bureau of the Census. Fourteenth Census of the United States Taken in the Year 1920. Vol. II, Population, 1920, General Report and Analytical Tables. Washington, D.C.: Government Printing Office, 1922. Table 13, p. 227.

1930 U.S. Department of Commerce, U.S. Bureau of the Census. Fifteenth Census of the United States: 1930. Population, Vol. II, General Report, Statistics by Subjects. Washington, D.C.: U.S. Government Printing Office, 1933. Table 24, p. 615.

1940, 1950 U.S. Bureau of the Census. U.S. Census of Population: 1950. Vol. II, Characteristics of the Population, Part 21, Massachusetts. Washington, D.C.: U.S. Government Printing Office, 1952. Table 53, p. 111.

1960, 1970 U.S. Bureau of the Census. Census of Population: 1970. Vol. I, Characteristics of the Population, Part 23, Massachusetts.

Washington, D.C.: U.S. Government Printing Office, 1973. Table 138, p. 625.

Sources for Table 7

1880, 1890, 1900, 1910 Bureau of the Census. Thirteenth Census of the United States Taken in the Year 1910. Vol. I, Population, 1910, General Report and Analysis. Washington, D.C.: Government Printing Office, 1913. Table 33, pp. 322–325.

1920 Bureau of the Census. Fourteenth Census of the United States Taken in the Year 1920. Vol. II, Population, 1920, General Report and Analytical Tables. Washington, D.C.: Government Printing Office, 1922. Table 6, p. 159.

1930, 1940 U.S. Bureau of the Census. Sixteenth Census of the United States: 1940. Vol. II, Characteristics of the Population, Part I: United States Summary. U.S. Government Printing Office, Washington, D.C.: 1943. Table 7, p. 22.

1950 U.S. Bureau of the Census. U.S. Census of Population: 1950. Vol. II, Characteristics of the Population, Part I, United States Summary. U.S. Government Printing Office, Washington, D.C., 1953. Table 97, p. 1–172.

1960, 1970 U.S. Bureau of the Census. Census of Population: 1970. Detailed Characteristics. Final Report PC(1)-D1. United States Summary. U.S. Government Printing Office. Washington, D.C. 1973. Table 189, p. 1–591.

Population from Table A.4.

Sources for Table A.1

1880 State of Massachusetts. XXXIXth Registration Report. Table VIII, p. lxxxvi.

1890 State of Massachusetts. Registration Report. Table 105, p. 340.

1900 State of Massachusetts. Registration Report. Table IX, pp. 48–49.

1910 State of Massachusetts. Registration Report. Table IX, pp. 44–45.

1920 State of Massachusetts. Massachusetts Vital Statistics. Table 54, pp. 140–141.

1930 State of Massachusetts. Massachusetts Vital Statistics. Table 14, pp. 40–41.

1940 U.S. Department of Commerce. Bureau of the Census. Vital Statistics of the United States, Part I. Table 13, p. 325.

1950 U.S. Department of Health, Education, and Welfare. Public Health Service. National Office of Vital Statistics. Vital Statistics of the United States, Volume III. Table 56, p. 332.

1960 U.S. Department of Health, Education, and Welfare. Public Health Service. National Vital Statistics Division. Vital Statistics of the United States, Volume II, Mortality, Part B. Table 9–6, p. 9–230.

1970 U.S. Department of Health, Education, and Welfare. Public Health Service. Health Resources Administration. National Center for Health Statistics. Vital Statistics of the United States, Volume II, Mortality, Part B. Table 7–6, p. 7–294.

Sources for Table A.2

1950 U.S. Bureau of the Census. Census of Population, Vol. II, Part 21. Table 16, p. 42. (This reference contains population figures from the censuses of 1880 through 1950. Age unknowns exist through 1930; they are small in number, and have not been reclassified.)

1960 U.S. Bureau of the Census. Census of Population, Vol. I, Part 23. Table 16, p. 31.

1970 U.S. Bureau of the Census. Census of Population, PC(1)-B23. Table 20, p. 51.

Sources for Table A.3

1935 U.S. Department of Commerce. Bureau of the Census. Mortality Statistics. Table 7, pp. 202–203.

1940 U.S. Department of Commerce. Bureau of the Census. Vital Statistics of the United States, Part I. Table 11, pp. 212–213.

1945 Federal Security Agency. United States Public Health Service. National Office of Vital Statistics. Vital Statistics of the United States, Part I. Table 5, pp. 56–57.

1950 U.S. Department of Health, Education, and Welfare. Public Health Service. National Office of Vital Statistics. Vital Statistics of the United States, Volume III. Table 52, pp. 76–77.

1955 U.S. Department of Health, Education, and Welfare. Public Health Service. National Office of Vital Statistics. Vital Statistics of the

United States, Volume II. Table 53, pp. 52–53.

1960 U.S. Department of Health, Education, and Welfare. Public Health Service. National Vital Statistics Division. Vital Statistics of the United States, Volume II-Mortality, Part A. Table 5–9, pp. 5–48, 5–49.

1965 U.S. Department of Health, Education, and Welfare. Public Health Service. National Center for Health Statistics. Vital Statistics of the United States, Volume II-Mortality, Part A. Table 1–26, pp. 1–100, 1–101.

1970 U.S. Department of Health, Education, and Welfare. Public Health Service. Health Resources Administration. National Center for Health Statistics. Vital Statistics of the United States, Volume II-Mortality, Part A. Table 1–26, pp. 1–184, 1–185.

1975 U.S. Department of Health, Education, and Welfare. Public Health Service. National Center for Health Statistics. Vital Statistics of the United States, Volume II-Mortality, Part B. Table 7–5, pp. 7–134, 7–135.

Sources for Table A.4

1935 U.S. Bureau of the Census. Current Population Reports. Series P25, No. 311, 1965. "Estimates of the Population of the United States, by Single Years of Age, Color, and Sex: 1900 to 1959," pp. 52–53.

1940, 1945, 1950 U.S. Department of Health, Education, and Welfare. Public Health Service. National Office of Vital Statistics. 1950. Vital Statistics of the United States, Volume I. Table 2.21, p. 56.

1955 U.S. Department of Health, Education, and Welfare. Public Health Service. National Center for Health Statistics. 1955. Vital Statistics of the United States, Volume II-Mortality, Part A. Table 6–5, pp. 6–19.

1960 U.S. Department of Health, Education, and Welfare. Public Health Service. National Vital Statistics Division. 1960. Vital Statistics of the United States, Volume I-Natality, Table 5–3, pp. 5–13.

1965 U.S. Department of Health, Education, and Welfare. Public Health Service. National Center for Health Statistics. 1965. Vital Statistics of the United States, Volume II-Mortality, Part A. Table 6–2, pp. 6–16.

1970 U.S. Department of Health, Education, and Welfare. Public Health Service. Health Resources Administration. National Center for Health Statistics. 1970. Vital Statistics of the United States, Volume II-Mortality, Part A. Table 6–2, pp. 6–16.

1975 U.S. Department of Health, Education, and Welfare. Public Health Service. National Center for Health Statistics. Vital Statistics of the United States, Volume II-Mortality, Part A. Table 1–26, pp. 1–186 and 1–187.

REFERENCES

Andvord, K.F. (1930). What can be learned from following the development of tuberculosis from generation to generation? *Norsk Magazin for Laegenvidenskaben* **91**, 642–660.

Aronson, J.D. (1946). The occurrence and anatomic characteristics of fatal tuberculosis in the U.S. Army during World War II. *Military Surgeon* **99**, 491–503.

Bailey, N.T.J. (1975). *The Mathematical Theory of Infectious Diseases and its Applications.* 2nd ed. New York: Hafner Press.

Baker, R.J. and Nelder, J.A. (1978). *The GLIM System (Release 3) Manual.* Oxford, U.K.: Numerical Algorithm Group.

Barrett, J.C. (1973). Age, time and cohort factors in mortality from cancer of the cervix. *The Journal of Hygiene* **71**, 253–259.

Barrett, J.C. (1978a). The redundant factor method and bladder cancer mortality. *Journal of Epidemiology and Community Health* **32**, 314–316.

Barrett, J.C. (1978b). A method of mortality analysis: Application to breast cancer. *Revue d'Epidemiologie et Sante publique* **26**, 419–425.

Barrett, J.C. (1980). Cohort mortality and prostate cancer. *Journal of Biosocial Science* **12**, 341–344.

Borrel, A. (1920). Pneumonie et tuberculose chez les troupes noires. *Annales de L'institut Pasteur* **34**, 105–148.

Bushnell, G.E. (1920). *A Study of the Epidemiology of Tuberculosis.* New York: William Wood.

Cagan, P. (1971). Measuring quality changes and the purchasing power of money: An exploratory study of automobiles, in Z. Griliches (ed.), *Price Indexes and Quality Change.* Cambridge, Mass.: Harvard University Press, pp. 215–239.

Carr-Hill, R.A., Hope, K., and Stern, N.H. (1972). Delinquent generations revisited. *Quality and Quantity* **5**, 327–352.

Chapman, J.S. and Dyerly, M.D. (1964). Social and other factors in intra-familial transmission of tuberculosis. *American Review of Respiratory Disease* **90**, 48–60.

Chiang, C.L. (1980). *An Introduction to Stochastic Processes and Their*

Applications. Huntington, N.Y.: Krieger.

Chuang, J.-L.C. (1980). Analysis of categorical data with ordered categories. Ph.D. Dissertation. University of Minnesota.

Coale, A.J. (1972). *The Growth and Structure of Human Populations: A Mathematical Investigation.* Princeton, N.J.: Princeton University Press.

Coale, A.J. (1977). The development of new models of nuptiality and fertility. *Population* **32** (Special Number, September), 131–150.

Comstock, G.W. (1975). Frost revisited: The modern epidemiology of tuberculosis. *American Journal of Epidemiology* **101**, 363–382.

Comstock, G.W., Livesay, V.T. and Woolpert, S.F. (1974). The prognosis of a positive tuberculin reaction in childhood and adolescence. *American Journal of Epidemiology* **99**, 131–138.

Dubos, R.J. and Dubos, J. (1952). *The White Plague: Tuberculosis, Man and Society.* Boston: Little, Brown and Company.

Edwards, H.R. (1940). The problems of tuberculosis in New York City. *American Review of Tuberculosis* **41**, 8–23 (supp.).

Edwards, L.B. and Palmer, C.E. (1969). Tuberculosis infection, in A.M. Lowell, L.B. Edwards, and C.E. Palmer (eds.), *Tuberculosis.* Cambridge, Mass.: Harvard University Press, pp. 140–163.

Fienberg, S.E. and Mason, W.M. (1978). Identification and estimation of age-period-cohort models in the analysis of discrete archival data, in K. F. Schuessler (ed.), *Sociological Methodology 1979.* San Francisco: Jossey-Bass, pp. 1–67.

Fienberg, S.E. and Mason, W.M. (1985). Specification and implementation of age, period, and cohort models. This volume.

Frost, W.H. (1939). The age selection of mortality from tuberculosis in successive decades. *American Journal of Hygiene* **30**, 91–96.

Glenn, N.D. (1976). Cohort analysts' futile quest: Statistical attempts to separate age, period and cohort effects. *American Sociological Review* **41**, 900–904.

Greenberg, B.G., Wright, J.J. and Sheps, C.G. (1950). A technique for analyzing some factors affecting the incidence of syphilis. *Journal of the American Statistical Association* **25**, 373–399.

Grigg, E.R.N. (1958). The arcana of tuberculosis. *American Review of Tuberculosis and Pulmonary Diseases* **78**, 151–172, 426–453, 583–603.

Hagenaars, J.A. and Cobben, N.P. (1978). Age, cohort and period: A general model for the analysis of social change. *Netherlands Journal of Sociology* **14**, 59–91.

Hall, R.E. (1971). The measurement of quality change from vintage price data, in Z. Griliches (ed.), *Price Indexes and Quality Changes.* Cambridge, Mass.: Harvard University Press, pp. 240–272.

Hemminki, E. and Paakkulainen, A. (1976). The effect of antibiotics on mortality from infectious disease in Sweden and Finland. *American Journal of Public Health* **66**, 1180–1184.

Henry, L. (1976). *Population Analysis and Models.* New York: Academic Press.

Hinman, A.R., Judd, J.M., Kolnik, J.P., and Daitch, P.P. (1976). Changing risks in tuberculosis. *American Journal of Epidemiology* **103**, 486–497.

Kamat, S.R., Dawson, J.Y.Y., Devadatta, S., *et al.* (1966). A controlled study of the influence of segregation of tuberculosis patients for one year on the attack rate of tuberculosis in a 5-year period in close family contacts in South India. *Bulletin of the World Health Organization* **34**, 517–532.

Kermack, W.O., McKendrick, A.G., and McKinlay, P.L. (1934). Death rates in Great Britain and Sweden: Expression of specific mortality rates as products of two factors, and some consequences thereof. *Journal of Hygiene* **34**, 433–457.

Keyfitz, N. (1977). *Introduction to the Mathematics of Population with Revisions.* Reading, Mass.: Addison-Wesley.

Lancaster, H.O. (1978). World mortality survey. *Australian Journal of Statistics* **20**, 1–42.

Long, E.R. and Jablon, S. (1955). *Tuberculosis in the Army of the United States in World War II,* V. A. Medical Monograph. Washington, D.C.: U.S. Government Printing Office.

Lowell, A.M. (1969). Tuberculosis morbidity and mortality and its control, in A.M. Lowell, L.B. Edwards, and C.E. Palmer (eds.), *Tuberculosis.* Cambridge, Mass.: Harvard University Press, pp. 5–121.

Lowell, A.M. (1976). *Tuberculosis in the World: Trends in Tuberculosis Incidence, Prevalence, and Mortality at the Beginning of the 3rd Decade of the Chemotherapeutic Era,* HEW Publication No. CDC 76-8317. Washington, D.C.: U.S. Government Printing Office.

McKeown, T. (1976). *The Modern Rise of Population.* New York: Academic Press.

MacMahon, B., Pugh, T.F., and Ipsen, J. (1960). *Epidemiologic Methods.* Boston: Little, Brown and Company.

Mason, K.O., Mason, W.M., Winsborough, H.H., and Poole, W.K. (1973). Some methodological issues in cohort analysis of archival data. *American Sociological Review* **38**, 242–258.

Merrell, M. (1947). Time-specific life tables contrasted with observed survivorship. *Biometrics* **3**, 129–136.

Nelder, J.A. and Wedderburn, R.W.M. (1972). Generalized linear models. *Journal of the Royal Statistical Society, Series A* **135**, 370–384.

Omran, A.R. (1977). Epidemiologic transition in the U.S. *Population Bulletin* **32**, 3–42.

Pope, A.S. and Gordon, J.E. (1955). The impact of tuberculosis on human populations. *The American Journal of the Medical Sciences* **230**, 317–353.

Rich, A.R. (1951). *The Pathogenesis of Tuberculosis*, 2nd Edition. Springfield, Ill.: Charles C. Thomas.

Roth, R.B. (1938). The environmental factor in relation to high Negro tuberculosis rates. *American Review of Tuberculosis* **38**, 197–204.

Ryder, N.B. (1968). Cohort analysis, in D.L. Sills (ed.), *International Encyclopedia of the Social Sciences*. New York: Macmillan and Free Press, pp. 546–550.

Sacher, G.A. (1957). Basic mechanisms in radiobiology, Part 5, mammalian aspects, in H.J. Curtis and H. Quastler (eds.), *Nuclear Science Series, Report Number 21, Subcommittee on Radiobiology, Committee on Nuclear Science*. Publication Number 513 of National Academy of Sciences-National Research Council, Washington, D.C., pp. 121–125.

Sacher, G.A. (1960). Analysis of life tables with secular terms, in B.L. Strehler, J.D. Ebert, H.B. Glass, and N.W. Shock (eds.), *The Biology of Aging*. Washington, D.C.: The American Institute of Biological Sciences, pp. 253–257.

Sacher, G.A. (1977). Life table modification and life prolongation, in C.E. Finch and L. Hayflick (eds.), *Handbook of the Biology of Aging*. New York: Van Nostrand Rinehold, pp. 582–683.

Shryock, H.S. and Siegel, J.S. (1975). *The Methods and Materials of Demography, Volume 1*. Washington, D.C.: U.S. Government Printing Office.

Sokoloff, K.L. and Villaflor, G.C. (1979). Colonial and revolutionary muster rolls: Some new evidence on nutrition and migration in early America. Working Paper No. 374 of National Bureau of Economic Research, Inc., Cambridge, Massachusetts.

Spicer, C.C. (1954). The generation method of analysis applied to mortality from respiratory tuberculosis. *Journal of Hygiene* **54**, 361–368.

Springett, V.H. (1950). A comparative study of tuberculosis mortality rates. *Journal of Hygiene* **48**, 361–395.

Stevens, R.G. and Lee, J.A.H. (1978). Tuberculosis: Generation effects and chemotherapy. *American Journal of Epidemiology* **107**, 120–126.

Susser, M. (1973). *Causal Thinking in the Health Sciences.* New York: Oxford University Press.

Sydenstricker, E. (1974). The declining death rate from tuberculosis, in R.V. Kasius, (ed.), *The Challenge of Facts.* New York: Prodist, pp. 345–369.

Theil, H. (1965). *Economic Forecasts and Policy.* Amsterdam: North-Holland.

Toman, K. (1979). *Tuberculosis Case-Finding and Chemotherapy: Questions and Answers.* Geneva: World Health Organization.

Tukey, J.W. (1977). *Exploratory Data Analysis.* Reading, Mass.: Addison-Wesley.

U.S. Bureau of the Census (1973). *Census of the Population: 1970. Vol. I, Characteristics of the Population, Part 23, Massachusetts.* Washington, D.C.: U.S. Government Printing Office.

7. ANALYSIS OF AGE, PERIOD, AND COHORT EFFECTS IN MARITAL FERTILITY*

Robert A. Johnson[†]

1. INTRODUCTION

Biological factors in the age pattern of fecundity and cultural universals in the age pattern of fertility control result in uniformities in schedules of age-specific marital fertility across diverse human populations. Yet the fertility of married women at a given age depends not only upon age but also upon the previous experience of the cohort (cohort effect) and the social and economic conditions of the time (period effect).

With the expectation that both period and cohort affect age-specific fertility, demographers have used period and cohort schedules of fertility to supplement each other and have found that the two types of schedules of age-specific rates taken together may throw more light on the subject than either used in isolation.

Unfortunately, there have been few attempts by demographers to separate and *simultaneously* estimate age, period, and cohort effects in fertility using a single multivariate model (Pullum, 1980; Hobcraft, Menken, and Preston, 1982, reprinted in this volume). This is unfortunate because any assessment of the contributions of these factors should allow for their simultaneous influences in determining fertility. A

* This research was supported by Iowa State University. I wish to thank Kenneth Koehler, Robert A. Hackenberg, O.D. Duncan, Clifford Clogg, T. James Trussell, and Stephen Fienberg for helpful comments. The typing and illustrations were done by Gayle Abramsohn and Margie Krest. I am responsible for any errors or shortcomings. This paper was presented at the annual convention of the Population Association of America, Washington, D.C., March 26–28, 1981.

† School of Urban and Public Affairs, Carnegie-Mellon University.

multivariate analysis of the effects of age, period, and cohort, and of the interactions of these variables, might show the interpretations based upon separate univariate period and cohort analyses of the same data to be faulty. This paper proposes a class of loglinear models for simultaneously analyzing age, period, and cohort effects, and age-cohort and age-period interactions, in time series of schedules of age-specific marital fertility rates. The utility and properties of these models are illustrated by an analysis of ASMFRs computed from sample surveys of married women in Davao City, Philippines.

The approach draws heavily upon the research of Fienberg and Mason (1978) on the formal age-period-cohort identification problem in the general case of a time series of vectors of age-specific measurements. These authors show that the linear components of age, period, and cohort effects are not identified in time series of age-specific measurements without additional identifying assumptions. They also establish the types of additional assumptions necessary for identifying the linear components of these effects.

Fienberg and Mason (1978) make no assumptions in their discussion about the kind of phenomenon being studied and therefore introduce no assumptions from the theory of any particular substantive area. This paper uses the substantive assumption that age effects in marital fertility have a similar pattern in all populations. This assumption enables us to identify and estimate a specialized class of models which applies to time series of age-specific marital fertility schedules but which does not apply to any other subject matter.

The basic assumption is that age effects in the ratio of observed to "natural" marital fertility can be described by a particular family of two-parameter exponential decay models (Coale and Trussell, 1974). It follows that the identification problem can be resolved by specifying a class of loglinear models in which age is treated as a scaled variable (Haberman, 1978, 1979).

The simplification based upon subject matter theory enables us to consider a greater variety of age-period-cohort models than was possible in the general context considered by Fienberg and Mason (1978). In their general analysis, assumptions about the equality of effect parameters across ages, periods, or cohorts were suggested in order to identify separate age, period, and cohort effects. In our more specialized analysis, the assumption that age can be treated as a scaled variable allows us to identify not only separate age, period, and cohort effects but also interactions in the effects of period and age and in the effects of cohort and age.

The data for Davao, Philippines, 1971–1978, introduced in Section 4, provide an unusual record of the early fertility transition of a developing population. Future research should elaborate the analysis of changing marital fertility by comparing age-period-cohort effects across social classes, educational levels, ethnicities, types of contraceptive history, and other social variables conditioning change in marital fertility. The age-period-cohort models presented here can be readily extended to analyses with additional independent variables.

It would be useful to develop age-period-cohort models of nonmarital fertility (usually assumed rare in the Philippines) and age-period-cohort models of the pattern of marriage (once again, elaborated by important social variables) in order to provide an overall description of changing fertility in Davao. Our strict focus upon marital fertility entails that we do not address the interesting problem of the decomposition of age-period-cohort effects in overall fertility into components attributable to age-period-cohort patterns of marital fertility, age-period-cohort patterns of nonmarital fertility, and age-period-cohort patterns of marriage.

2. IDENTIFICATION OF AGE, PERIOD, AND COHORT EFFECTS IN MODELS WITH AND WITHOUT A SCALED AGE CLASSIFICATION

A basic result discussed by Fienberg and Mason (1978) is that the identification problem in age-period-cohort models is restricted to the linear components of age, period, and cohort effects. A simple data array involving measurements of only three ages, three periods, and five cohorts was used by Fienberg and Mason to illustate the identification problem and will be used here to illustrate the more complete analysis that is possible when age can be treated as a scaled classification.

Table 1 shows a period-by-cohort display of a data array with measurements for three ages, three periods, and five cohorts. The symbol f_{ijk} denotes the measurement of a dependent quantity for the ith age, jth period, and kth cohort. The dependent quantity f_{ijk} might be a count of the number of "events" (say the number of births) occuring in the ith age, jth period, and kth cohort. Alternatively, f_{ijk} might be the ratio of the counts of two mutually exclusive, exhaustive events (say the "odds" on a birth, the ratio of births to nonbirths), the ratio of odds ("odds-ratio") in two mutually exclusive categories, or a higher dimensional ratio of odds-ratios. In the application of this paper (Section 4), f_{ijk} denotes the ratio of observed births occurring to women in the ith age, jth period, and kth cohort to the number of births expected under natural fertility.

Table 1. Period-by-Cohort Display of a Data Array with Measurements for Three Ages, Three Periods, and Five Cohorts

				Cohort		
		1	2	3	4	5
	1	-	-	f_{113}	f_{214}	f_{315}
Period	2	-	f_{122}	f_{223}	f_{324}	-
	3	f_{131}	f_{232}	f_{333}	-	-

Note that one of the three subscripts in Table 1 is redundant since the values of any two of age, period, and cohort implies the value of the third variable. In the case of the general period-by-cohort display with J periods and K cohorts ($J=4$ and $K=15$ in the following), the age of persons in the jth period and kth cohort is $i=j+k-J$.

Table 2 shows two design matrices each of which defines the same age-period-cohort model for the logarithms of the means of the dependent quantities in Table 1. The first design matrix describes the age-period-cohort model using effect coding while the second design matrix describes the age-period-cohort model using orthogonal polynomial coding. The logs of the expectations of the f_{ijk} under the model index the rows of the design matrices. The columns of the design matrices are indexed by symbols for the parameters of the model: b, a_i, p_j, and c_k in the first statement of the model and b, a_i^*, p_j^*, and c_k^* in the second statement of the model; and also by the symbols of the corresponding variables described in the columns of the design matrices, A_i, P_j, and C_k in the first design matrix and A^i, P^j, and C^k in the second design matrix.

The model using the first design matrix (effect coding) is written as follows:

$$\log(Ef_{ijk}) = b + \sum_{i=1}^{2} a_i A_i + \sum_{j=1}^{2} p_j P_j + \sum_{k=1}^{4} c_k C_k , \tag{1}$$
$$i = 1,2,3; j = 1,2,3; k = 1,2,3,4,5; i = j+k-J.$$

In this parameterization, the fact that the parameters of the model are not identified is not readily apparent from the statement of the model.

Fienberg and Mason (1978, p. 23) therefore introduce an alternative statement of the model using the second design matrix (orthogonal polynomial coding):

$$\log(Ef_{ijk}) = b + \sum_{i=1}^{2} a_i^* A^i + \sum_{j=1}^{2} p_j^* P^j \sum_{k=1}^{4} c_k^* C^{k} , \tag{2}$$
$$i = 1,2,3; j = 1,2,3; k = 1,2,3,4,5; i = j+k-J.$$

Model (2) is empirically equivalent to model (1) because the parameters of any K-category classification can be exactly described by a polynomial of degree $K-1$.

Substitution of the identity $A = P-C$ in (2) suffices to prove it is the *linear* components of effects of age, period, and cohort (that is, the coefficients a_1^*, b_1^*, and c_1^* in (2), of the variables A, B, and C) which are not identified:

$$\log(Ef_{ijk}) = b + (a_1^*+p_1^*)P + (a_2^*+p_2^*)P^2 + (c_1^*-a_1^*)C + (a_2^*+c_2^*)C^2$$
$$+ c_3^* C^3 + c_4^* C^4 - 2a_2^* PC . \tag{3}$$

Estimation of the coefficients in (3) enables us to deduce the values of

Table 2. Design Matrices for an Age-Period-Cohort Model (Unscaled Effects) Applied to the Data Array in Table 1: Effect Coding and Orthogonal Polynomial Coding

A. First Design Matrix. Effect Coding

Parameter and Corresponding Independent Variable

Dependent Quantity	b	a_1	a_2	p_1	p_2	c_1	c_2	c_3	c_4
	1	A_1	A_2	P_1	P_2	C_1	C_2	C_3	C_4
$\log (Ef_{113})$	1	1	0	1	0	0	0	1	0
$\log (Ef_{214})$	1	0	1	1	0	0	0	0	1
$\log (Ef_{315})$	1	-1	-1	1	0	-1	-1	-1	-1
$\log (Ef_{122})$	1	1	0	0	1	0	1	0	0
$\log (Ef_{223})$	1	0	1	0	1	0	0	1	0
$\log (Ef_{324})$	1	-1	-1	0	1	0	0	0	1
$\log (Ef_{131})$	1	1	0	-1	-1	1	0	0	0
$\log (Ef_{232})$	1	0	1	-1	-1	0	1	0	0
$\log (Ef_{333})$	1	-1	-1	-1	-1	0	0	1	0

B. Second Design Matrix. Orthogonal Polynomial Coding

Parameter and Corresponding Independent Variable

Dependent Quantity	b	a_1^*	a_2^*	p_1^*	p_2^*	c_1^*	c_2^*	c_3^*	c_4^*
	1	A	A^2	P	P^2	C	C^2	C^3	C^4
$\log (Ef_{113})$	1	1	-1	1	-1	0	-2	0	6
$\log (Ef_{214})$	1	0	2	1	-1	1	-1	-2	-4
$\log (Ef_{315})$	1	-1	-1	1	-1	2	2	1	1
$\log (Ef_{122})$	1	1	-1	0	2	-1	-1	2	-4
$\log (Ef_{223})$	1	0	2	0	2	0	-2	0	6
$\log (Ef_{324})$	1	-1	-1	0	2	1	-1	-2	-4
$\log (Ef_{131})$	1	1	-1	-1	-1	-2	2	-1	1
$\log (Ef_{232})$	1	0	2	-1	-1	-1	-1	2	-4
$\log (Ef_{333})$	1	-1	-1	-1	-1	0	-2	0	6

a_2^*, p_2^*, c_2^*, c_3^*, and c_4^*. However, the *linear* components a_1^*, b_1^*, and c_1^* *cannot* be deduced.

The fact that it is only the linear components of the model that are inestimable implies that treating one (or more) of age, period, and cohort as a scaled classification will suffice to identify the model, provided only that the numerical scores assigned to the categories of the scaled classification are not generated from a linear transformation of age, period, or cohort.

Table 3 shows a design matrix for an age-period-cohort model applied to the data array in Table 1 in which age is treated as a scaled classification. On the basis of prior information, a numerical score, denoted by v_i, has been assigned to the *i*th category of age ($i = 1,2,3$). As indicated in Table 3, the assignment of scores generally allows not only the overall age effect a but also the age-period interaction effects $(ap)_j$ and the age-cohort interaction effects $(ac)_k$ to be identified. However, as described in the following, this will be true only if k, the number of cohorts in the data array, is sufficiently large.

In the general case of J periods and K cohorts (hence $I=K-J+1$ ages), the model defined by Table 3 can be written as follows:

$$\log(Ef_{ijk}) = b + av_i + \sum_{j=2}^{J} p_j P_j + \sum_{k=1}^{K-1} c_k C_k$$
$$+ \sum_{j=2}^{J} (ap)_j AP_j + \sum_{k=1}^{K-1} (ac)_k AC_k, \tag{4}$$

$$i = 1,...,I; j = 1,...,J; k = 1,...,K; i = j+k-J.$$

In models (3) and (4) and subsequently in this paper, the first period (base period) and the Kth cohort (oldest cohort) have been treated as the reference categories in the effects coding schemes for period and cohort (Table 3). This implies that the parameters p_1 and c_K are given by

$$p_1 = -\sum_{j=2}^{J} p_j \text{ and } c_K = -\sum_{k=1}^{K-1} c_k$$

and also that the parameters $(ap)_1$ and $(ac)_K$ are given by

$$(ap)_1 = -\sum_{j=2}^{J} (ap)_j \text{ and } (ac)_K = -\sum_{k=1}^{K-1} (ac)_k.$$

Table 3. Design Matrix for an Age-Period-Cohort Model with a Scaled Age Classification and Age-Period and Age-Cohort Interactions, Applied to the Data Array in Table 1

Dependent Quantity		Parameter and Corresponding Independent Variable												
	1	a	p_2	p_3	c_1	c_2	c_3	c_4	$(ap)_2$	$(ap)_3$	$(ac)_1$	$(ac)_2$	$(ac)_3$	$(ac)_4$
		A	P_2	P_3	C_1	C_2	C_3	C_4	AP_2	AP_3	AC_1	AC_2	AC_3	AC_4
$\log(Ef_{113})$	1	v_1	-1	-1	0	0	1	0	$-v_1$	$-v_1$	0	0	v_1	0
$\log(Ef_{214})$	1	v_2	-1	-1	0	0	0	1	$-v_2$	$-v_2$	0	0	0	v_2
$\log(Ef_{315})$	1	v_3	-1	-1	-1	-1	-1	-1	$-v_3$	$-v_3$	$-v_3$	$-v_3$	$-v_3$	$-v_3$
$\log(Ef_{122})$	1	v_1	1	0	0	1	0	0	v_1	0	0	v_1	0	0
$\log(Ef_{223})$	1	v_2	1	0	0	0	1	0	v_2	0	0	0	v_2	0
$\log(Ef_{324})$	1	v_3	1	0	0	0	0	1	v_3	0	0	0	0	v_3
$\log(Ef_{131})$	1	v_1	0	1	1	0	0	0	0	v_1	v_1	0	0	0
$\log(Ef_{232})$	1	v_2	0	1	0	1	0	0	0	v_2	0	v_2	0	0
$\log(Ef_{333})$	1	v_3	0	1	0	0	1	0	0	v_3	0	0	v_3	0

If we apply model (4) to $J \times K$ counterpart of the Table 1, then all of the parameters are identified except for one of the $(K-1)$ $(ac)_k$ parameters. The number of degrees of freedom available for testing the fit of the model to the data equals $JK - 2(J + K - 2) - J(J - 1)$. The number of degrees of freedom equals the number of cells in table (JK) minus the number of independent parameters that are estimated $(2(J + K - 2))$ minus the number of structural zeroes in the table $(J(J - 1))$. Clearly, in order to apply the model to an actual data array, we must have K sufficiently large that the number of cells which are not structural zeroes $(JK - J(J - 1))$ is equal to or greater than the number of effects to be estimated $(2(J + K - 2))$. ($K \geq 2 + J(J - 1)/(J - 2)$ is necessary and sufficient.)

In the application to the Davao, Philippines time series of age-specific marital fertility schedules in the following, model (4), termed the "P-C-AP-AC" model, is used as the base model in the analysis. Since there are 4 periods and 15 cohorts in this application (Table 6), the base model has 14 degrees of freedom.

3. AGE EFFECTS IN MARITAL FERTILITY: COALE AND TRUSSELL'S ANALYSIS

The application of age-period-cohort models with a scaled age classification to time series of age-specific marital fertility rates depends upon the assumption that marital fertility has a regular age pattern in all human populations. Strong support for this assumption comes from the important work of Coale and Trussell (1974) in constructing a family of model fertility schedules encompassing a broad range of human experience. These authors were able to formulate impressively simple models to describe regularities both in age patterns of marital fertility and in age patterns of nuptiality and then combined these models in order to generate the family of model fertility schedules.

This paper makes extensive use only of the Coale-Trussell marital fertility function. However, the Coale-Trussell nuptiality function could also be made to serve as the basis for a family of age-period-cohort models of nuptiality. The two models could then be combined in a single model in order to analyze overall fertility. Such a model might provide a more penetrating and accurate description of any data than the original Coale-Trussell model schedules. The reason is that the model schedules wrongly attribute all variations in an observed schedule of age-specific fertility rates to age effects in nuptiality and in marital fertility. The model schedules do not allow for period and cohort effects in marital fertility and in nuptiality and provide no mechanism for separating such period and cohort effects from genuine age effects.

Coale and Trussell propose that the ratio $r(i)/n(i)$ of observed marital fertility at age i, $r(i)$, to natural fertility at age i, $n(i)$, is given by the following two-parameter exponential decay model (Coale and Trussell, p. 187):

$$\frac{r(i)}{n(i)} = M \exp (m \cdot v(i)), \tag{5}$$

where $v(i)$ denotes a logarithmic departure from natural fertility at age i and M and m are parameters to be estimated from the data. Note that $v(i)$ is a nonpositive decreasing function of i and that M, m, and $n(i)$ are strictly positive.

The interpretation of (5) is that the age pattern of marital fertility increasingly departs from natural fertility as age increases. This departure is due to voluntary control of fertility. As Coale and Trussell explain (p. 188): "The factor M is a scale factor expressing the ratio of $r(i)$ to $n(i)$ at some arbitrarily chosen age ... The function $v(i)$ expresses the tendency for older women in populations practicing contraception or abortion to effect particularly large reductions of fertility below the natural level." The parameter m obviously indexes the *degree* of fertility control in marriage.

The authors (p. 189) validated the formulation (5) by showing its close fit to forty-three empirical marital fertility schedules taken from the 1965 U.N. Demographic Yearbook. These forty-three schedules covered a broad spectrum of diverse populations and were thought to be relatively free of age misreporting.

The functions $n(i)$ and $v(i)$ were also derived by Coale and Trussell from empirical data. The function $n(i)$ was calculated as the average of a number of fertility schedules designated by the French demographer Louis Henry as natural. The function $v(i)$ was obtained by calculations which employed the forty-three empirical schedules from the 1965 U.N. Demographic Yearbook (Coale and Trussell, 1974, p. 188).

Table 4 shows values of $n(i)$ and $v(i)$ taken from Coale and Trussell (1974). In anticipation of the application of these functions to the Philippines data in Section 4, the values of $n(i)$ and $v(i)$ in Table 4 are averages for the age intervals 20–21, 22–23,..., 42–43. In applying these functions in analyzing a particular data set, we must assume that the period and cohort effects present in each of the empirical marital fertility schedules which were averaged in deriving $n(i)$ and $v(i)$ were canceled out in the averaging process.

Table 4. Natural Fertility Rate $n(i)$ and Logarithmic Departure from Natural Fertility $v(i)$. Averaged for Two-Year Age Groups 20–21, 22–23,..., 42–43.[*] After Coale and Trussell (1974)

i	age group	$n(i)$	$v(i)$
1	20–21	0.476	−0.02
2	22–23	0.468	−0.08
3	24–25	0.458	−0.13
4	26–27	0.446	−0.28
5	28–29	0.432	−0.41
6	30–31	0.415	−0.56
7	32–33	0.395	−0.72
8	34–35	0.368	−0.86
9	36–37	0.334	−1.00
10	38–39	0.293	−1.14
11	40–41	0.227	−1.28
12	42–43	0.147	−1.42

[*] The averages are *weighted* averages of the single-year values reported by Coale and Trussell (p. 202). The weights were the relative frequencies of years of marital exposure in the Davao data for the pair of years in each two-year interval.

Combining (4) and (5) yields the complete specification of the base model, P-C-AP-AC, to be applied to Davao, Philippines data introduced in the following section:

$$\log \left(\frac{Eb_{ijk}}{n_{ijk}} \right) = b + av_i + \sum_{j=2}^{J} p_j P_j + \sum_{k=1}^{K-1} c_k C_k$$

$$+ \sum_{j=2}^{J} (ap)_j AP_j + \sum_{k=1}^{K-1} (ac)_k AC_k, \tag{6}$$

$$i = 1,...,I; \ j = 1,...,J; \ k = 1,...,K; \ i = j+k-J,$$

where b_{ijk} denotes the observed number of births to married women of the kth cohort in the jth period; n_{ijk} denotes the number of births expected under natural fertility at age i given the sample number of women-years of marital exposure of the kth cohort in the jth period; v_i denotes the logarithmic departure from natural fertility at age i, as shown in Table 4, and the remaining effects and variables are as indicated in Table 3.

In (6) the dependent quantities f_{ijk} in (4) have been set equal to ratio of actual births b_{ijk} to births expected under natural fertility n_{ijk}: $f_{ijk} = b_{ijk}/n_{ijk}$. It follows that f_{ijk} equals the dependent quantity $r(i)/n(i)$ in (5) because the denominators of both the observed marital fertility rate $r(i)$ and the natural fertility rate $n(i)$ equal N_{ijk}, the number of woman-years of marital exposure for the kth cohort in the jth period, and, hence, cancel in the division of the former rate by the latter rate.

Each n_{ijk} is computed by multiplying N_{ijk}, the number of woman-years of marital exposure of the kth cohort in the jth period, by $n(i)$, the natural fertility rate at age i (Table 4): $n_{ijk} = N_{ijk} \cdot n(i)$. Note that the n_{ijk} will be treated as fixed constants in our analysis, which gives rise to a class of *loglinear* models for the expected values of the (b_{ijk}/n_{ijk}) (namely, model (6) and special cases thereof). The numbers of births are assumed to be independent Poisson random variables in the statistical inferences of Section 4. It might be desirable in some applications to treat the n_{ijk} as well as the b_{ijk} as random variables, which would give rise to an analogous class of *logit* models for the $(b_{ijk}/(n_{ijk}-b_{ijk}))$.

Model (6) leads to a more refined statement of our criticism of Coale and Trussell (1974). Taking antilogarithms in (6) and adapting the parameterization of (5) implies:

$$\frac{Eb_{ijk}}{n_{ijk}} = M_{jk} \exp(m_{jk} \cdot v(i)), \qquad (7)$$

where

$$M_{jk} = \exp\left(b + \sum_j p_j P_j + \sum_k c_k C_k\right);$$

$$m_{jk} = a + \sum_j (ap)_j P_j + \sum_k (ac)_k C_k.$$

Equations (7) make clear that both the scale parameter M and the fertility control parameter m can depend upon both cohort and period. An approach to analysis which admits these possibilities and can separate out the effects of age, period, and cohort may offer a surer guide to the measurement of M and m.

4. APPLICATION TO DAVAO, PHILIPPINES SURVEY DATA

Table 5 presents a comparison using five-year age intervals of age-specific marital fertility rates and total marital fertility rates estimated for Davao, Philippines, 1971–1978, and age-specific marital fertility rates and total marital fertility rates estimated for the total Philippines and for metropolitan areas of the Philippines, 1968–1972. The rates for Davao were computed using the data from the pooled 1972, 1974, 1976, and 1979 Davao Surveys (Hackenberg, 1975). The rates for the total Philippines and for metropolitan areas of the Philippines were computed using the data from the 1973 National Demographic Survey (Concepcion and Smith, 1977).

The comparisons in Table 5 will serve both to illustrate some special characteristics of the population of Davao and to point out some apparent problems in using the Davao data to measure marital fertility at younger

Table 5. Age-Specific Marital Fertility Rates (per 1000 Woman-Years of Marital Exposure) and Total Marital Fertility Rates (per Married Life Cycle in the Hypothetical Cohort): Davao, Philippines, 1971–1978 and Republic of Philippines, 1968–1972. Pooled 1972, 1974, 1976, and 1979 Davao Sample Surveys and 1973 National Demographic Survey.*
(Base Numbers of Years of Marital Exposure in Parentheses)

| Age | ASMFRs by Year of Exposure |||||||| 1973 NDS* ||
	1971	1972	1973	1974	1975	1976	1977	1978	Total	Metro
15-19	314	363	314	304	397	321	378	537	449	413
	(283)	(253)	(236)	(184)	(171)	(81)	(74)	(54)		
20-24	398	397	398	388	352	412	365	411	443	459
	(1142)	(1053)	(1033)	(909)	(866)	(498)	(446)	(389)		
25-29	344	347	317	288	319	284	254	313	378	348
	(1362)	(1188)	(1311)	(1256)	(1355)	(701)	(746)	(709)		
30-34	260	255	235	187	204	174	196	193	307	246
	(1407)	(1315)	(1315)	(1147)	(1141)	(621)	(593)	(658)		
35-39	175	187	158	155	149	131	115	105	217	139
	(1074)	(1024)	(1080)	(1065)	(1138)	(632)	(671)	(649)		
40-44	79	75	74	62	52	48	45	63	108	85
	(866)	(831)	(891)	(787)	(781)	(439)	(463)	(505)		
45-49	20	13	18	11	5	9	3	10	24	11
	(586)	(526)	(558)	(530)	(614)	(341)	(376)	(412)		
TMFR	7.950	8.185	7.570	6.975	7.390	6.895	6.780	8.160	9.630	8.510

* The ASMFRs from the 1973 NDS, for Total Philippines and Metropolitan areas, are taken from Concepcion and Smith (1977) p. 68.

ages. We shall demonstrate that the types of models proposed herein can be used, independently of auxiliary data sources, to identify age ranges for which marital fertility rates computed from a particular data source are unrealistically high or low. In these models, unreliable ASMFRs appear as outliers from the expected curve of marital fertility implied by the entire time series of ASMFRs.

Davao, a commercial and industrial city of 509,000 (1975 estimate), is at the opposite end of the Philippines from Manila. A variety of data sources can be used to show that the island of Mindanao, of which Davao is an important regional center, has experienced rapid population growth during the entire twentieth century (Concepcion and Smith, 1977, pp. 8–13). This growth has been due to declining mortality, continued high fertility (attibutable not only to the low degree of fertility control in marriage but also to a pattern of marriage at younger ages than in the Philippines as a whole), and, significantly, to a large "frontier stream" of migration to Mindanao from the more settled islands of Luzon, Bicol, and the Visayas. In the 1972 Davao survey, about 80 percent of heads of households reported that they had been born outside Mindanao.

A case can be made using the Davao surveys that rapid population growth has stymied private and public efforts to raise the very low level of economic development of this city and has instead brought about a worsening in the scope and severity of poverty (Hackenberg, 1975). Since 1970, the Philippine government has promoted family planning in Davao. Data from the 1972, 1974, 1976 and 1979 Davao surveys will be used to analyze the pattern of change in marital fertility during the decade following the initiation of the program.

The four Davao sample surveys taken in 1972, 1974, 1976, and 1979 were independently drawn multi-stage equal probability samples of households using a PPS selection of census enumeration districts in the first stage. The data used in this report are (1) measures of births in years of marital exposure preceding the surveys, and (2) measures of the presence or absence of marital exposure during the years preceding the surveys. In each survey, these data were available only for the wives (living or deceased) of the heads of households. This restriction has implications for the analysis, to be discussed in the following.

The total number of married women in sample households of the four surveys who reported at least one year of marital exposure at an age between 15 and 49 during the period 1971–1978 was 7762. This total included 775 women in the 1972 survey, 754 women in the 1974 survey, 2857 women in the 1976 survey, and 3376 women in the 1979 survey. However, since women in the 1974, 1976, and 1979 surveys could report more than one year of marital exposure during the period 1971–1978 (a maximum of three years in the 1974 survey, five years in the 1976 survey, and eight years in the 1979 surveys), the total number of years of marital exposure represented in the bases of sample ASMFRs is substantially larger than the number of married women interviewed in these surveys. The total number of years of marital exposure at ages between 15 and 49 during the period 1971–1978 equals 41,357. This total includes 775 years reported by respondents to the 1972 survey, 2256 years reported by respondents to the 1974 survey, 13,420 years reported by respondents to the 1976 survey, and 24,906 years reported by respondents to the 1979 survey.

An inspection of the schedule of rates in Table 5 reveals two deficiences of the Davao data which require careful attention in our analysis. First, the reported ASMFRs for 1978 are unrealistically high when compared to the corresponding ASMFRs for the immediately preceding years and suggest an unrealistically sharp departure from the secular fertility decline evidenced by the ASMFRs for 1971–1977. Since the rates for years 1976–1978 are based entirely upon the 1979 survey, this discrepancy suggests that 1979 survey respondents overreported the number of births which occurred in the year immediately preceding that survey. Rates computed separately for the 1972, 1974, and 1976 surveys, and comparisons of rates estimated for the same year using different surveys, not shown here, show that overreporting of births in the year preceding the survey also contaminates the rates computed separately from the 1972, 1974, and 1976 surveys.

In the following analysis, births and years of marital exposure are pooled for the two year periods 1971–1972, 1973–1974, 1975–1976, and 1977–1978. This reduction provides an *ad hoc* correction not only for the pattern of overreporting but also for the autocorrelation of birth reports in successive years of the fertility histories of individual women. Annual birth reports in the fertility histories of individual Davao women follow an approximate first-order autoregressive scheme, leading to a violation of the assumption that the numbers of observed births in different periods and cohorts are independent Poisson random variables.

A second deficiency of the Davao data is revealed by the comparison of estimated Davao ASMFRs to the ASMFRs for the total Philippines and metropolitan areas of the Philippines based on the 1973 NDS (Concepcion and Smith, 1977, p. 68). The Davao rates for ages 15–19, and to a lesser extent ages 20–24, are unrealistically low. One explanation for this discrepancy is that those women with marital exposure who were not the wives of household heads, hence not represented in these data, are likely to have been young women. An alternative explanation is found in the attenuation of birth reporting with distance in time from the interval reported and the correlation of distant intervals with young ages.

Because of the unreliablilty of estimated rates at the youngest ages (15–19) and the imprecision of estimated rates at the oldest ages (45–49), the following analysis is restricted to age intervals 20–21, 22–23,..., 42–43. Still, a pattern of unreliability in the estimated ASMFRs at ages 20–21, 22–23, 24–25, 26–27, and, to a lesser extent 28–29, emerges with considerable force in the estimated parameters of age-period-cohort models applied to the data array in Table 6.

Table 6 shows that the period-by-cohort display of observed births b_{ijk}, births expected under natural fertility n_{ijk}, the ratio f_{ijk} of b_{ijk} to n_{ijk}, the logarithmic departure v_i from natural fertility at age i, and pooled sample woman-years of marital exposure N_{ijk} for periods 1971–1972, 1973–1974, 1975–1976, and 1977–1978 and ages 20–21, 22–23,..., 42–43. The design matrix for applying P-C-AP-AC to this 4×15 array is directly analogous to the design matrix presented in Table 3 for the 3×5 array.

Figure 1 displays the hierarchies of models, nested sequences of special cases of P-C-AP-AC, which can be obtained by setting one or more sets of parameters, p_j, c_k, $(ap)_j$, and $(ac)_k$, equal to zero in (6). Recall that the parameters in the base model can be divided into two sets: (i) those contributing to the Coale-Trussell scale parameter M, namely, b, the p_j, and the c_k, and (ii) those contributing to the Coale-Trussell fertility control parameter m, namely, a, the $(ap)_j$, and the $(ac)_k$ (see eqs. (7)).

Each of these two sets of parameters can be subdivided into a constant effect (b in the first set and a in the second set), parameters representing the effects of period (p_j in the first set and $(ap)_j$ in the second set), and parameters representing the effects of cohort (c_k in the first set and $(ac)_k$ in the second set). The hierarchies of models displayed in Figure 1 are generated by successively setting combinations of the four non-constant sets of parameters, p_j, c_k, $(ap)_j$, and $(ac)_k$, equal to zero.

For example, the four models shown on the second level of Figure 1, P-C-AP, P-AP-AC, C-AP-AC, and P-C-AC, are each obtained by setting

Table 6. Period-By-Cohort Display of Observed Number of Births b_{ijk}, Births Expected Under Natural Fertility n_{ijk}, Ratio f_{ijk} of b_{ijk} to n_{ijk}, Logarithmic Departure from Natural Fertility v_j, and Number of Woman-Years of Marital Exposure N_{ijk}. Pooled 1972, 1974, 1976, and 1979 Davao, Phillippines Sample Surveys. Age Groups 20–21,..., 42–43. Periods 1971–1972, 1973–1974, 1975–1976, 1977–1978

Period j		1	2	3	4	5	6	7
								Cohort k
1 (1971-72)	Age				20-21	22-23	24-25	26-27
	b_{ijk}				269	405	411	342
	n_{ijk}				301	471	490	430
	f_{ijk}				0.894	0.860	0.839	0.795
	v_j				-0.02	-0.08	-0.13	-0.28
	N_{ijk}				633	1007	1072	964
2 (1973-74)	Age			20-21	22-23	24-25	26-27	28-29
	b_{ijk}			261	329	389	302	261
	n_{ijk}			288	383	514	466	397
	f_{ijk}			0.906	0.859	0.757	0.648	0.657
	v_j			-0.02	-0.08	-0.13	-0.28	-0.41
	N_{ijk}			605	818	1121	1046	919
3 (1975-76)	Age		20-21	22-23	24-25	26-27	28-29	30-31
	b_{ijk}		151	218	282	312	186	133
	n_{ijk}		202	286	330	406	334	276
	f_{ijk}		0.748	0.762	0.855	0.768	0.557	0.482
	v_j		-0.02	-0.08	-0.13	-0.28	-0.41	-0.56
	N_{ijk}		425	611	720	911	773	665
4 (1977-78)	Age	20-21	22-23	24-25	26-27	28-29	30-31	32-33
	b_{ijk}	79	157	167	161	171	120	91
	n_{ijk}	100	178	236	236	283	223	184
	f_{ijk}	0.790	0.882	0.708	0.682	0.604	0.538	0.495
	v_j	-0.02	-0.08	-0.13	-0.28	-0.41	-0.56	-0.72
	N_{ijk}	210	378	516	531	655	538	465

Table 6 (Cont.)

8	9	10	11	12	13	14	15
28-29	30-31	32-33	34-35	36-37	38-39	40-41	42-43
328	305	284	224	163	104	80	40
462	452	435	383	271	228	171	100
0.710	0.675	0.653	0.585	0.601	0.456	0.468	0.400
-0.41	-0.56	-0.72	-0.86	-1.00	-1.14	-1.28	-1.42
1070	1089	1101	1039	812	778	751	680
30-31	32-33	34-35	36-37	38-39	40-41	42-43	
217	214	188	142	98	75	32	
405	385	376	311	297	158	98	
0.536	0.556	0.500	0.457	0.473	0.475	0.327	
-0.56	-0.72	-0.86	-1.00	-1.14	-1.28	1.42	
976	976	1020	929	707	696	663	
32-33	34-35	36-37	38-39	40-41	42-43		
145	113	124	78	36	23		
287	264	252	195	111	74		
0.505	0.428	0.492	0.400	0.324	0.311		
-0.72	-0.86	-1.00	-1.14	-1.28	-1.42		
728	718	755	666	487	502		
34-35	36-37	38-39	40-41	42-43			
66	52	59	31	17			
186	173	159	103	51			
0.355	0.301	0.371	0.301	0.333			
-0.86	-1.00	-1.14	-1.28	-1.42			
460	519	543	456	346			

Figure 1. Hierarchies of Age-Period-Cohort Models with a
Scaled Age Classification. (In Parentheses: Likelihood
Ratio Chi-Square Statistic and Number of Degrees of Freedom
for the Data in Table 6)

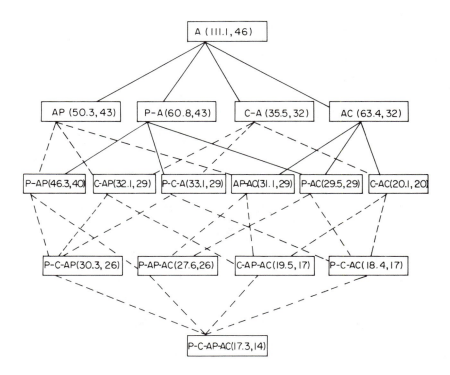

one of the four sets of parameters equal to zero. The P-C-AP model is
obtained by setting the $(ac)_k$ equal to zero, implying that fertility control
does not depend on cohort. The P-AP-AC model is obtained by setting
the c_k equal to zero, implying that the overall level of fertility does not
depend on cohort. Similarly, C-AP-AC implies that fertility level does
not depend on period (i.e., the p_j equal zero) and P-C-AC implies that
fertility control does not depend upon period (i.e., the $(ap)_j$ equal zero.)

Each of these four models can be further simplified in three ways by
setting one of the *remaining* three sets of parameters equal to zero, which
gives rise to the six models shown on the third level of Figure 1. For
example, the model P-C-A, which implies that fertility control depends

neither on cohort nor on period (i.e., the counterpart of Fienberg and Mason's age-period-cohort model for the case of a scaled age classification), is obtained by setting the $(ap)_j$ equal to zero in P-C-AP, or, alternatively, by setting the $(ac)_k$ equal to zero in P-C-AC. Note, however, that P-C-A *cannot* be obtained either by setting parameters equal to zero in P-AP-AC or by setting parameters equal to zero in C-AP-AC.

Each of the six models in which two of the four sets of parameters equal zero can be further simplified by setting one of the two remaining sets of parameters equal to zero, giving rise to the four models, AP, P-A, C-A, and AC, displayed on the fourth level of Figure 1. Finally, the simplest model in all of the hierarchies, A, specifies that all four sets of parameters equal zero, i.e., that neither fertility level nor fertility control depend either on period or on cohort. This model, which fits only two parameters, b and a, is the model of marital fertility which is implicit in the Coale-Trussell model fertility schedules.

The goodness-of-fit of each of the models displayed in Figure 1 to the data displayed in Table 6 can be tested using a likelihood ratio chi-square test. Following Haberman (1978, pp. 124–133), we assume that the number of observed births b_{ijk} is a Poisson random variable for each period j and cohort k and that these Poisson random variables are independently distributed. (Note that the ratio of b_{ijk} to n_{ijk}, births expected under natural fertility, is a fertility rate expressed as per natural units of marital exposure.)

Under this assumption, maximum likelihood estimates of the expected numbers of births under each of the models depicted in Figure 1 can be computed using either iterative proportional fitting or the Newton-Raphson algorithm. The advantages of Newton-Raphson, equivalent to an iterative cycle of weighted least squares regressions, are quicker convergence and provision of the estimated asymptotic covariance matrix of the parameter estimates as a by-product of the calculations. Accordingly, we relied upon the Newton-Raphson computer program FREQ written by Haberman (1979, Appendix, pp. 571–578). The basic input for this program consists of the observed births, the expected births under natural fertility (z_{ijk} in Haberman's notation), and the design matrix for a particular model.

Given the estimated expected numbers of births (cell frequencies), the goodness-of-fit of the model to the data can be tested using the likelihood-ratio test statistic:

$$L^2 = 2 \sum_{j,k} b_{ijk} \log \left(\frac{b_{ijk}}{\hat{b}_{ijk}} \right),$$

where b_{ijk} is the observed number of births and $\hat{b}_{ijk}$ the estimated expected number of births in the kth cohort in the jth period. Under the null hypothesis that the model is true, this statistic has an asymptotic chi square distribution with number of degrees of freedom equal to the number of cells in the table that are not structural zeroes (e.g., 48 cells in Table 6) minus the number of independent parameters in the model (equal to the number of columns in the design matrix).

In parentheses following the mnemonics of each model in Figure 1 are shown the observed value of L^2 and the number of degrees of freedom obtained when that model is applied to the data in Table 6. Clearly, the base model P-C-AP-AC provides a good fit since $L^2 = 17.3$ with 14 degrees of freedom has attained significance p > 0.25. Generally, by the criterion of such "unconditional" tests of goodness-of-fit, only three of the models in Figure 1, namely, P-A, AC, and A, can be rejected at significance level $\alpha = 0.05$.

In addition to the unconditional tests, conditional tests of goodness-of-fit (difference chi-square tests) play a role in model selection. Two models are said to be nested if the simpler of the two models (i.e., the one with fewer parameters) is a *special case* of the more complicated model (i.e., the one with more parameters). In other words, two models are nested if one of the two models can be obtained by setting one or more parameters (or linear combinations of parameters) in the other model equal to zero. Hence, as previously indicated, P-C-AP and P-C-A are nested in Figure 1 but P-AP-AC and P-C-A are not nested in Figure 1.

If two models, say Model 1 and Model 2, are nested and the more complicated of the two models, say Model 1, fits the data, then the difference of the likelihood ratio statistics of the two models, $L_2^2 - L_1^2$, can be used to test the hypothesis that the parameters included in Model 1 but not included in Model 2 are equal to zero. Under the null hypothesis that Model 2 is true, $L_2^2 - L_1^2$ has an asymptotic chi-square distribution with number of degrees of freedom equal to the difference, $df_2 - df_1$, of the numbers of degrees of freedom of the two models.

In Figure 1, one or more lines (either dotted or solid) connecting the mnemonics of two models indicates that these two models are nested. One or more *dotted* lines connecting the mnemonics of two models indicates that the simpler (higher level) model departs insignificantly in goodness-of-fit from the more complicated (lower level) model on the basis of a conditional goodness-of-fit test. For example, since the difference between the likelihood ratio statistics for P-C-AP and P-C-A equals $33.1 - 30.3 = 2.8$, which, compared to a chi-square distribution with $29 - 26 = 3$ degrees of freedom, has attained significance $P > 0.40$, the line connecting P-C-AP and P-C-A is dotted rather than solid. It happens that, in the application to Table 6, the same pattern of dotted and solid lines is obtained irrespective of whether one employs significance level $\alpha = 0.01$ or significance level $\alpha = 0.20$.

The basic strategy of model selection can now be discerned. In the interest of parsimony, the selection rises to as high a level as possible above the base model, along all permissible sequences of dotted lines. The aim is to select the most parsimonious model(s) which depart(s) insignificantly in goodness-of-fit from the base model and from lower level nested models and which provide(s) a satisfactory global fit to the data. The upward flow of the model selection must stop at any model which has no higher level special cases departing insignificantly in goodness-of-fit from that model.

In the application to Table 6, the stategy leads to the selection of three models, AP, C-A, and P-AC. These models are not nested and therefore cannot be directly compared using a goodness-of-fit test. The three models simply represent alternative, statistically defensible interpretations of the same data. Generally, AP is attractive because it is more parsimonious (using only $48 - 43 = 5$ independent parameters) than either C-A or P-CA while C-A and P-AC are attractive because they fit the data somewhat more closely than AP.

The choice of a single model to describe and report the data should depend not only upon statistical tests but also upon the substantive interpretations which can be given to the estimated parameters of the selected models. Table 7 shows the estimated effect parameters for each of the selected models and, in addition, the estimated effect parameters for a "modified P-AC" model, to be described in the following. In Table 7, the parameter estimates for each model have been normalized using the conventional constraints:

$$\sum_{j=1}^{4} p_j = \sum_{k=1}^{15} c_k = \sum_{j=1}^{4} (ap)_j = \sum_{k=1}^{15} (ac)_k = 0.$$

Note that the estimated parameters in the left-hand panel of Table 7 comprise the set contributing to the estimated Coale-Trussell scale parameters M_{jk} and that the estimated parameters in the right-hand panel of Table 7 comprise the set contributing to the estimated Coale-Trussell fertility control parameters m_{jk} (see equations (8)).

The parameter estimates for AP, C-A, and P-AC suggest very different interpretations of the pattern of change in marital fertility in Davao City. The estimates for the AP model attribute reductions in marital fertility entirely to approximately linear period increase in fertility control from $\hat{m}_{1k} = 0.664 - 0.220 = 0.444$ in 1971–1972 to $\hat{m}_{4k} = 0.663 + 0.193 = 0.856$ in 1977–1978. Hence, AP may appear dubious because it does not provide either for changes in the overall level of fertility or for cohort effects in fertility control.

The C-A model, on the other hand, explains the decline in marital fertility entirely in terms of essentially monotonic cohort declines in the overall level of fertility. Acceptance of C-A is tantamount to assuming that any increases in contraceptive usage due to the Philippine family planning program have affected only the level and not the shape of the marital fertility curve. The model implies, unrealistically, that the Coale-Trussell fertility control parameter m has remained fixed across cohorts and periods at the surprisingly *high* level of 1.271.

Only the P-AC model represents a substantively plausible interpretation of the data, but, in the parameter estimates for this model, there are unmistakable indications of the deficiencies of the Davao data in measuring marital fertility at the younger ages. P-AC implies that the level of fertility has declined monotonically from 1971–1972 to 1977–1978 and that fertility control has varied across cohorts. However, the estimates of parameters $(ac)_1$, $(ac)_2$, $(ac)_3$, $(ac)_4$, and $(ac)_5$ are *impossibly* low. Indeed, the estimates of $(ac)_1$, $(ac)_2$, $(ac)_3$, and $(ac)_4$ for the P-AC model in Table 7 imply levels of the fertility control parameter m_{jk} which

Table 7. Maximum Likelihood Parameter Estimates* for the AP, C-A, P-AC, and Modified P-AC Models for the Data Shown in Table 6

	Model					Model			
Effect	AP	C-A	P-AC	mod** P-AC	Effect	AP	C-A	P-AC	mod** P-AC
b	-0.151	0.272	-0.276	0.122	a	0.664	1.271	-0.768	0.987
p_1	-	-	0.177	0.094	$(ap)_1$	-0.220	-	-	-
p_2	-	-	0.048	0.004	$(ap)_2$	-0.037	-	-	-
p_3	-	-	-0.037	-0.027	$(ap)_3$	0.065	-	-	-
p_4	-	-	-0.188	-0.071	$(ap)_4$	0.193	-	-	-
c_1	-	-0.483	-	-	$(ac)_1$	-	-	-10.65	-
c_2	-	-0.422	-	-	$(ac)_2$	-	-	-3.28	-
c_3	-	-0.407	-	-	$(ac)_3$	-	-	-0.14	-
c_4	-	-0.313	-	-	$(ac)_4$	-	-	0.20	-
c_5	-	-0.301	-	-	$(ac)_5$	-	-	0.82	-
c_6	-	-0.302	-	-	$(ac)_6$	-	-	1.31	0.388
c_7	-	-0.170	-	-	$(ac)_7$	-	-	1.28	0.218
c_8	-	-0.122	-	-	$(ac)_8$	-	-	0.139	0.222
c_9	-	0.015	-	-	$(ac)_9$	-	-	1.34	0.102
c_{10}	-	0.200	-	-	$(ac)_{10}$	-	-	1.24	-0.094
c_{11}	-	0.250	-	-	$(ac)_{11}$	-	-	1.30	-0.086
c_{12}	-	0.435	-	-	$(ac)_{12}$	-	-	1.24	-0.201
c_{13}	-	0.464	-	-	$(ac)_{13}$	-	-	1.30	-0.180
c_{14}	-	0.540	-	-	$(ac)_{14}$	-	-	1.32	-0.183
c_{15}	-	0.616	-	-	$(ac)_{15}$	-	-	1.34	-0.186

* In these parameter estimates, the following constraints have been imposed:
$$\sum_j p_j = \sum_k c_k = \sum_j (ap)_j = \sum_k (ac)_k = 0.$$
** In addition to the parameters shown, modified P-AC fits parameters corresponding to dummy variables for ages 1 through 5 (20-21, 22-23, 24-25, 26-27, and 28-29, respectively). The estimates of these parameters are a_1 = -0.282, a_2 = -0.237, a_3 = -0.222, a_4 = -0.127, and a_5 = -0.087. Modified P-AC has 29 degrees of freedom and L^2 = 33.4.

are less than zero. (For example, $\hat{m}_{j1} = \hat{b} + \hat{(ac)}_1 = -0.768 - 10.65 = -11.42$.) Since a value of m equal to zero corresponds to the complete absence of fertility control, the estimates of $(ac)_k$ for the first five cohorts suggest that the data seriously underrepresent the numbers of births occurring in these cohorts. Since these are the youngest cohorts represented in these data (ranging from 14–15 in 1971–1972 to 22–23 in 1971–1972), the inference of data deficiencies based upon P-AC accords with the inference from Table 5 that the Davao data underestimate the ASMFRs of younger women.

One approach to modifying the P-AC model in order to take these data deficiencies explicitly into account is to incorporate additional parameters which correct for the underestimation of the birth rate at ages 20–21, 22–23, 24–25, 26–27, and 28–29. The "modified P-AC" model in Table 7 omits the five parameters $(ac)_1$, $(ac)_2$, $(ac)_3$, $(ac)_4$, and $(ac)_5$ in P-AC and adds the five parameters a_1, a_2, a_3, a_4, a_5 which are the effects of dummy variables indexing the age groups 20–21, 22–23, 24–25, 26–27, and 28–29, respectively.

The modified P-AC model is written as follows:

$$\log \left(\frac{Eb_{ijk}}{n_{ijk}} \right) = b + \sum_{i=1}^{5} a_i A_i + \sum_{j=2}^{4} p_j P_j$$

$$+ av_i + \sum_{k=6}^{14} (ac)_k v_i , \tag{8}$$

$$i = 1,...,12; \; j = 1,...,4; \; k = 1,...,15; \; i = j+k-J,$$

where $A_i = 1$ if age equals i; $A_i = 0$ otherwise, and the remaining effects are as defined in previous models. Applied to the data in Table 6, modified P-AC has $L^2 = 33.4$ with 29 degrees of freedom.

Including the dummy effects for age groups 1 through 5 functions to elevate the estimated ASMFRs in these younger age groups to the levels expected on the basis of the average curve of marital fertility in the older age groups. The estimated parameters a_1, a_2, a_3, a_4, and a_5 gauge the degrees of underestimation of fertility in age groups 20–21, 22–23, 24–25, 26–27, and 28–29, respectively. These parameter estimates are $a_1 = -0.282$, $a_2 = -0.237$, $a_3 = -0.222$, $a_4 = -0.127$, and $a_5 = -0.088$. Hence, as expected from the comparison with the 1973 NDS (Table 5), the older the age group the more accurate are the data.

The remaining estimated parameters of modified P-AC, shown in Table 7, suggest a substantively plausible inerpretation of change in marital fertility in Davao. The scale of fertility declined regularly but rather modestly across periods while fertility control increased more sharply from the oldest cohort to the cohort aged 24–25 in 1971–1972 (cohort 6, the youngest cohort for which these data seem reasonable).

Table 8 displays the estimates of the Coale-Trussell indexes M and m which are implied by the modified P-AC parameter estimates in Table 7.

Table 8. Estimates of Coale and Trussell's Indexes M_{jk} (Scale Factor) and m_{jk} (Fertility Control) Using the Modified P-AC Model Applied to the Data Array in Table 6.* Cohorts Aged 24–25 to 42–43 in 1971–1972

Cohort k	Age in 1971–72	Period j							
		1 1971–72		2 1973–74		3 1975–76		4 1977–78	
		M	m	M	m	M	m	M	m
6	24–25	1.241	1.375	1.134	1.375	1.100	1.375	1.052	1.375
7	26–27	1.241	1.205	1.134	1.205	1.100	1.205	1.052	1.205
8	28–29	1.241	1.209	1.134	1.209	1.100	1.209	1.052	1.209
9	30–31	1.241	1.089	1.134	1.089	1.100	1.089	1.052	1.089
10	32–33	1.241	0.893	1.134	0.893	1.100	0.893	1.052	0.893
11	34–35	1.241	0.902	1.134	0.902	1.100	0.902	1.052	0.902
12	36–37	1.241	0.786	1.134	0.786	1.100	0.786	1.052	0.786
13	38–39	1.241	0.807	1.134	0.807	1.100	0.807	–	–
14	40–41	1.241	0.804	1.134	0.804	–	–	–	–
15	42–43	1.241	0.801	–	–	–	–	–	–

* The estimates of M_{jk} and m_{jk} are computed by applying the equations $M_{jk} = \exp(b + p_j + c_k)$ and $m_{jk} = a + (ap)_j + (ac)_k$ to the parameter estimates in Table 7.

The indexes are presented only for the cohorts with reliable data (cohorts 6 through 15), although M and m can also be computed for cohorts 1 through 5. (The value of $\hat{M}_{jk}$ for $1 \leq k \leq 5$ equals exp $(0.122 + \hat{p}_j + \hat{a}_i)$ and the value of $\hat{m}_{jk}$ for $1 \leq k \leq 5$ equals 0.987.) The levels of $\hat{m}$ reported in Table 8 can be understood in the context of the Coale-Trussell model schedules. Compared to most of the model tables reported by these authors (1974, pp. 205–258), fertility control in Davao in 1977–1978 was still at a moderately low level despite the inference from Table 8 that substantial increases in m occurred during the eight years following the initiation of the Philippine family planning program in 1970.

In general, such indirect inferences about the time path of fertility regulation should be supplemented, whenever possible, with direct measures of change in contraceptive practices. It is encouraging that the inference from modified P-AC of rapidly increasing fertility control in Davao is fully consistent with evidence from direct measurements of contraceptive practices included in the Philippine Areal Fertility Surveys (Hackenberg et al., 1981).

This section has illustrated the application of age-period-cohort loglinear models with a scaled age classification in the analysis of age-specific marital fertility schedules. Through an analysis of survey data from Davao, Philippines, we have shown that the proposed class of models has utility both in identifying alternative, statistically defensible interpretations of a data set and in detecting data deficiencies. As in the case of any statistical models, valid conclusions need not follow from the application of our models in the absence of judicious attention to the character of data deficiencies.

REFERENCES

Coale, A.J. and Trussell, T.J. (1974). Model fertility schedules: Variations in the age structure of childbearing in human populations. *Population Index* **40**, 185–257.

Concepcion, M.B. and Smith, P.C. (1977). *The Demographic Situation in the Philippines: An Assessment in 1977*. Honolulu, Hawaii: Papers of the East-West Population Institute, No. 44.

Fienberg, S.E. and Mason, W.M. (1978). Identification and estimation of age-period-cohort models in the analysis of discrete archival data, in K.F. Schuessler (ed.), *Sociological Methodology, 1979.* San Francisco: Jossey-Bass, pp. 1–67.

Haberman, S.J. (1978). *Analysis of Qualitative Data. Vol. 1: Introductory Topics.* New York: Academic Press.

Haberman, S.J. (1979). *Analysis of Qualitative Data. Vol. 2: New Developments.* New York: Academic Press.

Hackenberg, R.A. (1975). *Fallout from the Poverty Explosion: Economic and Demographic Trends in Davao City, 1972–1974,* Monograph No. 2. Davao City, Philippines: Davao Action Information Center.

Hackenberg, R.A., Magalit, H.F., and Ring, M.R. (1981). *Philippine Population Growth in The the 1970's: Socioeconomic Change and Demographic Response.* Davao City, Philippines: Davao Research and Planning Foundation.

Hobcraft, J., Menken, J., and Preston, S. (1982). Age, period, and cohort effects in demography: A review. *Population Index* 4, 4–43. Reprinted in this volume.

Pullum, T.W. (1980). Separating age, period, and cohort effects in white U.S. fertility, 1920–1970. *Social Science Research* 9, 225–244.

8. DYNAMIC MODELING OF COHORT CHANGE: THE CASE OF POLITICAL PARTISANSHIP*

Gregory B. Markus[†]

This article describes an alternative to typical cohort analysis procedures for modeling developmental processes using cohort data. The alternative strategy, a dynamic modeling approach, is illustrated by an analysis of trends in the strength of partisan identification in the United States 1952–1978. The proposed model accounts for observed variation in partisan strength by age and cohort without any need to include those variables in the model itself.

1. INTRODUCTION

In 1959, William Evan proposed that a technique developed by demographers and called "cohort analysis" might be applied to questions concerning long-term opinion change. In the two dozen years since that suggestion was advanced, cohort analysis has been employed to study a wide range of sociopolitical attitudes and behaviors, including foreign policy opinions (Cutler, 1970a), political alienation (Cutler and Bengston, 1974), ideological orientations (Glenn, 1974), voting (Glenn and Grimes, 1968; Hout and Knoke, 1975), and most especially, partisan attachments (Crittenden, 1962; Cutler, 1970b; Glenn, 1972; Glenn and Hefner, 1972; Knoke and Hout, 1974; Abramson, 1976, 1979; Converse, 1976). During the same period the term "cohort analysis" has come to denote not a

* The author is grateful to Philip E. Converse for his contributions to this investigation. The data on which the study is based were obtained from the Inter-university Consortium for Political and Social Research. Reprinted from *American Journal of Political Science*, **27**, (1983), 717–739.

† Department of Political Science, The University of Michigan.

single, well-defined method of analysis but any of a wide array of approaches, ranging from the most casual "eyeballing" of tabular displays to fairly rigorous multiple regression and log-linear estimation procedures (Mason *et al.*, 1973; Fienberg and Mason, 1978).

The purpose of this paper is to describe an alternative strategy for the analysis of cohort data, a dynamic modeling approach that, it will be argued, is better suited to the study of many nondemographic variables than are the methods commonly employed. This strategy will be illustrated by an analysis of trends in the strength of partisan identification in the United States 1952–1978.

2. BACKGROUND

Cohort analysis is a method—or set of methods—for studying longitudinal patterns of change. As such, it is related to panel analysis but with the difference that in the latter the same individuals are observed through time, while in the former differing (but, presumably, representative) samples of cohort members are observed. Cohorts may be defined with reference to any of a number of variables (e.g., persons who were married in a given time interval or individuals who attended college in a particular year). But the most commonly used variable for demarcating cohorts is date of birth. Thus, for example, we may have as units of analysis the cohorts of persons born in the years 1901–1910, 1911–1920, 1921–1930, and so on. The span of years for each cohort may be dictated by theoretical concerns or by data constraints.[1]

Regardless of the particular method adopted by the researcher, the goal of cohort analysis, broadly speaking, is to assess the extent to which variation in a criterion measure (for example, percentage voting or mean years of education) observed on cohorts over time is attributable to *period*, *age*, and *cohort* effects, or possibly to interactions of the three. Period effects are fluctuations in the data that are due to idiosyncratic events or circumstances occurring at particular time points. Age effects

---

[1] More detailed discussions of cohort analysis may be found in Mason *et al.* (1973), Converse (1976), and Glenn (1977).

refer to long-term movements that are associated with progression through the life cycle, although not necessarily with aging *per se*. And cohort or, as they are sometimes called, generation effects are defined to be enduring intercohort distinctions that are attributable to the common "imprinting" of cohort members. With regard to attitudinal dependent variables, generation effects are often presumed to be the result of cohort members having shared similar socializing experiences, especially during late adolescence and early adulthood (Mannheim, 1952; Ryder, 1965).

Paralleling the usual analysis of variance model, the Age-Period-Cohort (APC) model for the three "main effects" may be summarized as

$$Y_{ijk} = \mu + \alpha_i + \beta_j + \gamma_k + e_{ijk}, \tag{1}$$

where Y_{ijk} is the dependent variable score for the ith cohort at age j in period k; μ is the grand mean; α_i is the effect of being in cohort i; β_j is the effect associated with age j; γ_k is the effect for period k; and e_{ijk} is a random disturbance. The task that remains is to devise a means for providing reliable estimates of the effects.

2.1. The APC Model and Political Partisanship

The literature on cohort analysis has not always been distinguished by careful reasoning or methodological rigor; and nowhere is this more apparent than in the case of cohort analyses of political partisanship. In one of the first of such studies, Crittenden (1962) purported to find evidence of a positive relationship between aging and movement toward Republican identification. Although the raw cohort values exhibited no such trend, Crittenden argued that once adjustments for generally pro-Democratic "period effects" were introduced, the hypothesized pattern emerged. This judgment went largely unchallenged until 1970, when Cutler pointed to a number of basic inadequacies in Crittenden's method, in particular a failure to consider the possibility of generational effects. An exchange between Crittenden and Cutler followed, and other scholars soon joined the fray. In the ensuing debate, analysts ransacked cohort data on both the strength and direction components of partisan identification. Some authors (e.g., Knoke and Hout, 1974) claimed to show support for life-cycle hypotheses, while most others (e.g., Glenn, 1972; Abramson, 1976) argued for a generational effects interpretation.

Almost none of this work, however, displayed a proper appreciation of the mathematical truth made explicit by Mason *et al.* in 1973: the APC model is intrinsically underidentified. As it stands, the three effects in Equation (1) *cannot* be estimated uniquely. This is because once the values of any two factors, such as age and period, are known, the value of the third factor is completely determined. For instance, there is only one birth cohort (1921–30) that can be of age 30–39 in period 1960. If the possibility of interactions of age, period, and cohort is also admitted, then the situation becomes further underidentified.

As Mason *et al.* pointed out, if one main effect can be plausibly set to zero or if effects associated with particular ages, periods, or cohorts are assumed to be equal or to have particular functional forms, then the APC model may be identified, permitting unique estimates of the effects within the constrained model. To take an example (based on Abramson, 1983, pp. 56–61), if one were studying education levels of adult cohorts in the U.S., one could probably assume with confidence that period effects were essentially nil (i.e., there were no uniform shifts in the education levels of all cohorts for particular years) and that aging effects were of a particular functional form (monotonic nondecreasing, since—critics of higher education notwithstanding—one does not become less educated with age).[2]

The Mason *et al.* exposition was important, because it unambiguously described the fundamental problem of cohort analysis and possible routes to a solution. But estimation of the APC model with respect to nondemographic dependent variables has remained problematic because (1) there are generally few plausible grounds for imposing strong identifying restrictions *a priori* and (2) even where simplifying assumptions can be made, often the result is merely to transform a formally indeterminate problem into a nearly indeterminate one (i.e., one in which the estimates of effects are highly sensitive to minor variations in the data).[3]

---

[2] The aging effect could be obscured if cohorts were affected by systematic mortality. If women tend to be less educated than men and if they also tend to live longer than men, then cohorts traced beyond age 65 or so might well appear to be declining in education. If a cohort analyst finds that differential mortality rates pose a threat to valid inference, a statistical correction should be introduced. See Riley (1973) for further comment on this and related topics.

[3] This dilemma is conceptually identical to the distinction between a perfectly multicollinear set of predictors versus a highly, but not perfectly, multicollinear set. In the former case, no consistent estimation is possible; in the latter, consistent estimation is possible, but the standard errors of the resulting coefficient estimates will be quite large.

In a review of the Mason *et al.* exposition and related work, Glenn (1976, p. 903) concluded that purely statistical attempts to overcome the identification problem will be of doubtful value, because solutions will likely depend "at least as much on knowledge of theories of aging and recent history as on technical expertise." Baltes, Cornelius, and Nesselroade (1980, pp. 68–69) concurred, arguing that analysis of cohort data "should be guided more by theoretical considerations about the developmental phenomena and less by mathematical-statistical decisions inherent to the matrix provided by age, cohort, and time of measurement. This is particularly true in applications ... where the immediate task is one of accurate identification of intra-individual change."

In this vein, the APC model is not well suited to the analysis of many sociopolitical phenomena for three reasons. First, the APC model is primarily an accounting equation rather than an explanatory one. That is, its purpose is to partition variation into distinct bundles (age, period, cohort); it is rarely purported to represent in mathematical form the underlying process generating the observed data. Second, and very much related, the variables in the APC model are often of little substantive interest in their own right. More often, age, birth date, and period of observation are simply used as surrogates for unspecified and unmeasured variables of ultimate theoretical concern. Finally, the APC model is static, whereas developmental processes of attitude formation and change are generally dynamic, that is, past attitudes affect current ones in a nontrivial fashion.

For certain types of substantive problems—especially those in which one main effect may be confidently ruled out *a priori*—the APC model may well be of value. But a model that is suited to demographic variables such as fertility or literacy rates is not necessarily appropriate for the analysis of attitudes and behavior that arise from qualitatively different kinds of processes. For the latter, the researcher would probably do better to construct a model that reflects substantive ideas, however tentative, about the underlying causal process. If such a model can be crafted, it will lead to richer insights about observed age, period, and cohort differences than could be achieved by artificially imposing the APC analytic paradigm onto the research problem.

This alternative perspective will be demonstrated by using both cohort and individual-level data to develop and evaluate a dynamic model of strength of partisan identification in the United States.

3. A MODEL OF PARTISAN STRENGTH

Virtually all cross-sectional surveys of mass political attitudes have displayed a persistent positive relationship between age and the strength of subjective identification with a political party. The pattern of this association typically follows the path as shown in Figure 1, partisan strength increasing as a function of age with a slight but perceptible negative acceleration.

Explanation of this cross-sectional correlation may proceed along either (or both) of two avenues. Perhaps older citizens are more staunchly partisan because the repeated use of party labels to interpret and understand the political world through the years reinforces and strengthens one's partisan ties (Campbell *et al.*, 1960; Converse, 1969). On the other hand, it may be argued that the stronger partisanship of older people is a reflection of their socialization in an era in which partisan debate was more vigorous and partly cleavages better defined than they have been in recent years (Burnham, 1965, 1969; Abramson, 1976).

The first explanation of the age-partisanship association is one of age effects. In this explanation the relationship is not presumed to be a function of chronological age itself, however. Age merely serves as an imperfect surrogate for a more abstract concept of ultimate interest, which might be termed "the length of time that a person has felt some psychological attachment to a particular party" (Converse, 1976, p. 47; Shively, 1979). How adequate age is as an indicator of this "length of time" depends on how well age correlates with it in given cases. It correlates with it very poorly in political systems where parties and democratic process have just begun in the recent past. It also correlates poorly with it among individuals who are immigrants at adult ages, or among persons who have in middle age been converted to some new party persuasion. Since the party system in the United States is of considerable vintage, and immigration and conversions are relatively rare, age is not obviously an unsatisfactory operationalization of the concept in this context. Nevertheless, the important point remains that mere chronological age within an APC model lacks any direct correspondence to the developmental process implied by any plausible substantive theory.

In much the same way, the APC model also fails to reflect substantive hypotheses about the formation of enduring intercohort attitudinal

Figure 1. Mean Partisan Strength by Age: 1952–1964.
Source: Converse (1976, p. 48)

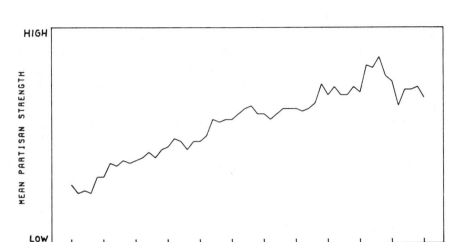

distinctions as embodied in the second, cohort effects, explanation. That is, with respect to partisanship (and probably most other attitudinal variables, as well) mere membership in a particular birth cohort is not presumed to be an ultimate causal factor. Instead, an explanation geared to cohort phenomena typically asserts that abiding observed cohort differences are the result of significant variations among birth cohorts in terms of their life histories of attitude-relevant events and experiences. Particularly with respect to psychological orientations, cohort effects are often interpreted in terms of classical theories of the formation of sociopolitical generations (Mannheim, 1952; Ryder, 1965). Such theories posit that the socializing experiences of late adolescence and early adulthood are of crucial importance in forming political outlooks because of the heightened sensitivity of cohort members during this formative life stage. According to this view, subsequent circumstances may to some extent modify orientations developed earlier, but the cohort will continue to bear the imprint of shared initial socializing experiences.

Thus far it has been suggested that the APC model does not correspond directly to either life cycle or generational hypotheses of substantive interest. There is another related disjuncture between substantive theory and such a statistical model. As mentioned earlier, the

APC model is static, but the development of partisan attitudes is undeniably dynamic, current attitudes reflecting, more or less, past attitudes. A characteristic of dynamic processses is that they posses a "memory," such that the impact of an exogenous event (a so-called period effect) upon the dependent variable is not limited to a single time point. Instead, some trace of the event is reflected in the process outcome for some span of time, the imprint of the event gradually dying out.

Consider a simple dynamic model of partisan strength of the form:

$$S_{it} = \beta_0 + \beta_1 S_{it-1} + u_{it}, \quad 0 < \beta_1 < 1, \tag{2}$$

where S_{it} is the mean partisan strength for cohort i at time t, S_{it-1} is the same variable lagged one time point, and u_{it} is a stochastic disturbance.[4] If initial partisan strength is less than its eventual equilibrium value, and if the disturbances have an expected value of zero, then Equation (2) will generate a time path for S_{it} much like that depicted in Figure 1, tapering toward an asymptote equal to $\beta_0/(1-\beta_1)$. This can be shown by taking the expected value of Equation (2), and noting that $E(S_{it}) = E(S_{it-1}) = \mu$:

$$E(S_{it}) = \beta_0 + \beta_1 E(S_{it-1}) + E(u_{it}) .$$

Thus the common limiting value is

$$\mu = \frac{\beta_0}{1 - \beta_1} .$$

If more than one cohort is observed through time, it is possible to modify Equation (2) to distinguish between period-specific shifts in partisan strength that are uniform across all cohorts and the idiosyncratic

---

[4] Higher order autoregressive models, which include additional lagged S_i values, are alternatives, in principle. With regard to partisan strength, however, there is presently neither sufficient theoretical nor empirical justification for resorting to these more elaborate models.

disturbances in the partisan strength of individual cohorts. A simple way to do this is by incorporating a set of dummy variables into the model:

$$S_{it} = \beta_1 S_{it-1} + \sum_{k=1}^{t} \alpha_k D_{kt} + u_{it}. \tag{3}$$

The coefficients on the dummy variables can be thought of as being period-specific constant terms representing the immediate net impact on all cohorts of the relevant events and experiences occurring in each period. Ideally, one would prefer to specify the exogenous events (elections, economic recessions, wars, government scandals) and relevant experiences (evaluating partisan candidates, following political campaigns, voting) that systematically influence individual partisan complexions of cohorts. In the absence of such measures, the dummy variables serve as surrogates for the composite of the unspecified events and experiences.

With a bit of algebraic manipulation,[5] Equation (3) can be restated as

$$S_{it} = \beta_1^t S_{i0} + \sum_{l=0}^{t-1} \beta_1^l \alpha_{t-l} + \sum_{l=0}^{t-1} \beta_1^l u_{it-l}. \tag{4}$$

Although Equations (3) and (4) are alternative ways of stating the same model, the equations serve different purposes. For estimating the β and α parameters, Equation (3) is preferable because of its comparatively parsimonious form. Equation (4), on the other hand, provides a clearer picture of the theoretical generating process implied by the model.

The first component on the right-hand side of Equation (4) is analogous to a cohort effect. It shows that the current partisan strength of a cohort bears some trace of its initial strength of partisanship (i.e., at $t=0$). The influence of initial partisanship diminishes with time, because the weight β_1^t decreases as t increases. If the autoregressive parameter β_1 is relatively large (i.e., approaching unity), it implies that partisan attitudes are persistent, and the partisan complexions of cohorts change slowly with time. On the other hand, a small autoregressive parameter (one near zero) would imply that initial differences in the partisanship of adjacent cohorts would soon fade if the cohorts were subsequently exposed to a common stream of events and experiences.

The second component is a series of weighted period effects. The weights decrease geometrically as the amount of time lag (l) between the

[5] See Appendix A.

current period and the period in which a particular effect occurred increases. Hence, the model postulates that each period-specific input is not immediately "forgotten" after it occurs but rather exerts a gradually diminishing influence over time.

Both period and cohort effects are represented in the model, but age effects are not. By excluding an age-trend variable (or a set of dummy variables for age), the model asserts that there are no deterministic life-cycle effects. Instead, gains (or losses) in partisan strength over the life cycle are presumed to be a function of the initial partisanship of a cohort and its history of relevant events and experiences as subsumed in the period variables and the disturbance terms.

4. EVALUATION OF THE MODEL

4.1. Data Base

The cohort data for this investigation are derived from the National Election Study surveys conducted biennially since 1952 by the University of Michigan's Survey Research Center and Center for Political Studies. For each time point, respondents have been classified into age catergories of four-year intervals. For presidential election years, the 13 age categories begin with persons 25–28 years of age and end with the group 69–72. For nonpresidential contests, the first of 12 groups is aged 27–30 and the last is 71–74. This staggering of age categories enables us to trace four-year cohorts through the progression of biennial elections. More finely incremented classifications would have reduced the cell sizes to unacceptably small numbers, ballooning the sampling error in the aggregate estimates. Broader age categories would result in proportionally fewer data points with which to evaluate the fit of the model. As it turns out, the age groups are fairly uniform in size; each cohort data point is based on an average of 108 respondents, with a standard deviation of 37. Cohorts are not observed prior to age 25 because of known biases in the representativeness of the sample for persons below that age (Converse, 1976, pp. 47–51).

The cohort data provide a useful basis by which to evaluate the proposed model of partisan development. Ultimately, however, the developmental process takes place at the level of the individual, not the cohort. The information provided in a cohort matrix is utilized in developmental studies simply because suitable longitudinal individual-level data are unavailable.[6] Fortunately, the series of National Election Studies does permit a glimpse into the dynamics of the partisanship of the individual as well as the cohort. This is true because the series contains within it two true panels: one covering 1956–1958–1960 and a second for the years 1972–1974–1976. Although the terms spanned by these panels are relatively short, this limitation is mitigated by the increased cross-sectional variation obtained by shifting the analysis to the level of individuals. In the presentation to follow, this variation is exploited to gain an advantage on certain key modeling questions, allowing movement back and forth between aggregate and microdata analysis.

4.2. Operational Measures

Partisan Strength. The measure of strength of partisan attachments is derived from a set of questions that have been asked in identical form in all of the National Election Studies.[7] The questions lead to a classification of respondents into four levels of partisan strength (in increasing order): independents, independents who lean toward a party, party identifiers, and strong party indentifiers. In the present study, the numerical scores of 1, 4, 5, and 10, respectively, are assigned to the categories. These values are consistent with Weisberg's analysis of metric data on partisan stimuli from the 1976 National Election Study (see also Miller and Miller, 1977).

Specifically, Weisberg analyzed the difference between feeling thermometer scores assigned to the stimuli "Republicans" and "Democrats" by respondents in each of the seven categories of party identification, from strong Republican to strong Democrat. A feeling

---

[6] It may be worth pointing out that it is not the lack of individual-level data that renders the APC model underidentified. Whether we speak of individuals or cohorts, the linear dependence of age, period, and "vintage" obtains.

[7] Respondents are first asked: "Generally speaking, do you usually think of yourself as a *Republican*, a *Democrat*, an *Independent*, or what? If the answer is Democrat or Republican: Would you call yourself a *strong* (Republican/Democrat) or a *not very strong* (Republican/Democrat)? If Independent: Do you think of yourself as closer to the Republican or to the Democratic party?"

thermometer is a technique by which respondents assign a value from 0 to 100 degrees depending on how warm or favorable they feel toward the stimuli. The mean difference scores for the 1976 data were:

	Strong Rep.	Rep.	Rep. Leaner	Indep.	Dem. Leaner	Dem.	Strong Dem.
Thermometer Difference	26	9	6	−3	−12	−15	−30

The transformation

$$\frac{|DIFF + 3|}{3} + 1$$

corresponds almost exactly to the scoring convention employed in the present analysis.

The aggregate movement of partisan strength 1952–1978 is displayed in Figure 2. As Converse (1976, p. 31) noted, the data exhibit a fairly flat plateau from 1952–1964, a sharp drop between 1964 and 1966, and a downward drift for the remainder of the series. Accounting for this temporal movement within the context of a model that is also consistent with the positive cross-sectional correlation between age and partisanship is the goal of much of the analysis to follow.

5. ESTIMATION

Applying simple least squares procedures to Equation (3) would yield biased parameter estimates because of measurement and sampling error in the lagged partisan strength regressor. In particular, the estimate of the autogressive parameter would be seriously biased downward (Johnston, 1972, pp. 281–283). One method of obtaining consistent (but typically inefficient) parameter estimates entails an instrumental variables

Figure 2. Mean Partisan Strength for All Cohorts: 1952–1978

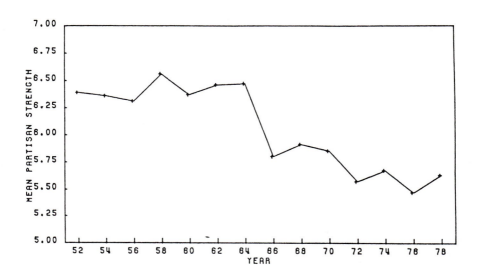

procedure, as employed in Jackson's studies of the dynamics of partisan identification (Jackson, 1975; Franklin and Jackson, 1983). Alternatively, Wiley and Wiley (1970) have shown that an adjustment can be made for the bias, provided that three waves of panel data are available. Since [8] such data were available (1956–1958–1960 and 1972–1974–1976) they were exploited to obtain a consistent estimate of the autoregressive parameter. Once this was accomplished, that estimate was inserted into Equation (3) and the period effects coefficients were calculated by using the cohort data.

The Wiley-Wiley estimates of measurement reliability and the autoregressive parameter are shown in Table 1. The estimates are quite stable, despite the fact that the two panels are embedded in quite

[8] The Wiley-Wiley model may be viewed as a special case of a LISREL model (Jöreskog, 1973), and the estimates obtained by the Wiley-Wiley procedure are identical to those that would be obtained for that model by LISREL. Since the model is a saturated one (i.e., one that contains as many parameters to be estimated as there are unique elements in the three-wave variance covariance matrix, that matrix is reproduced exactly.

Table 1. Wiley-Wiley Estimates of Partisan Strength
Reliability and Autoregressive Coefficients

	Reliability[*]	Autoregression
1972–1974	0.54, 0.58	1.00
1974–1976	0.58, 0.55	0.93
1956–1958	0.60, 0.58	0.92
1958–1960	0.58, 0.60	0.97
Average	0.58	0.95

[*] The method yields a separate reliability estimate for each year.

different historical contexts. The calculated reliability of the partisan strength measure is approximately 0.58, and, consequently, the autoregressive coefficient is revised upward to about 0.95. These values square nicely with previous work on the "unfolded" seven-step party identification measure, for which the adjusted autoregressive parameter was estimated to be approximately 0.97 (Converse and Markus, 1979). It is also consistent with the plot shown in Figure 1; a two-year lag autoregressive process fitted by ordinary least squares to those data yields an estimated coefficient of 0.932 (standard error = 0.056) and an R^2 of 0.92.[9]

One implication of this result is that any difference between the mean partisan strength of a cohort entering adulthood and that of the remainder of the electorate will tend to persist for some time. For example, even after eight elections, or 16 years, about two-thirds (0.95^8

[9] Bias due to individual-level measurement error and sampling fluctuations are not a problem in this instance, since the data points in Figure 1 are means based on fairly large numbers of cases, roughly, 1,000 to 2,000 (Blalock, 1961, pp. 158–162).

= 0.663) of the initial difference would remain. Thus, the possibility of fairly robust "cohort effects" is a logical consequence of the estimated structure of the model itself without resort to the atheoretical birth-cohort demarcators of the APC accounting equation.[10]

5.1. Estimation of Period Effects

Although the panel data were more suitable than the highly aggregated cohort information for purposes of estimating the stability of partisan strength, the former are of little direct use for gauging the magnitude of whatever period-specific variations in partisanship occurred throughout the complete span of elections under study. To accomplish that task, we must turn to the cohort matrix.

Period effects were estimated by fitting Equation (3) to the cohort data ($N = 150$) with the autoregressive coefficient fixed at its previously estimated value of 0.95.[11] These estimated period effects are best interpreted relative to some meaningful baseline. The reference value used in Figure 3 is the period input required to maintain the fairly stable mean partisan strength of the 1952–1964 era.[12] Approximate bounds based on one and two standard errors are also shown.

The analysis indicates that after an era of modest, predominantly partisan-reinforcing period effects, a substantial negative shock occurred in the period bounded roughly by the 1964 and 1966 national elections. This shock was followed by a brief positive rebound and another span of small, primarily negative period inputs.

Identification of the substantive events underlying these period effects is necessarily speculative at this stage, but, as suggested elsewhere

---

[10] If the estimated value of .95 for the autoregressive coefficient were revised by ± 0.05, the fraction of initial cohort differences that would remain after 16 years would range from 1.00 to 0.43. Although this is a broad range, the central idea that nontrivial cohort differences would remain is sustained.

[11] If the autoregressive parameter is left free to be estimated from the cohort data along with the period effects, the OLS estimate of β_1 is 0.71. As expected, this estimate is smaller than that derived by the Wiley-Wiley procedure, a reflection of the bias due to measurement and sampling errors. On the validity of making individual-level inferences from cohort-level estimates, see Firebaugh (1978).

[12] This value can be easily determined by using the equation for the equilibrium value of an autoregressive function with constant input, setting the equilibrium to the 1952–1964 mean of 6.42, and calculating the necessary value of the period input required to maintain that equilibrium: $6.42(1 - 0.95) = 0.32$.

Figure 3. Estimated Period Inputs, 1954–1978

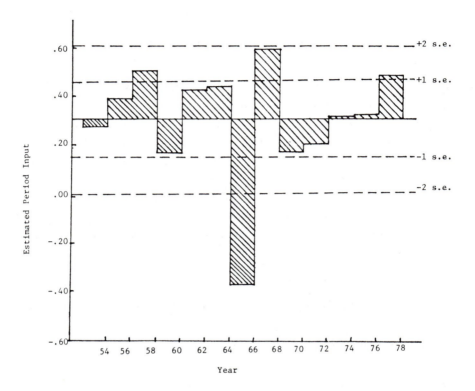

(Converse, 1976, pp. 94–111), there is good reason to believe that the large negative shock—crudely located by our data as occurring between November 1964 and November 1966—had racial issues as a prime cause. A review of events of that period recalls that the civil rights offensive at Selma, Alabama, with its accompanying police violence and vigilante murders, took place January through March 1965. A string of violent and near-violent mass encounters followed, culminating with the Watts riot in August of that same year. Glenn (1972) also isolated a sharp decline in partisanship in the South just prior to 1966, attributing it partly to the temporary attraction of southern whites to the independent candidacy of George Wallace. Interpreting the 1968 rebound is more problematic, but data reported by Abramson (1979) suggest that the gains in partisan strength occurred primarily among blacks, possibly in response to the Humphrey candidacy (see, also, Converse, 1976).

The Vietnam War undoubtedly began to intrude upon the public conscience in 1966, and much of the sustained 1969–1973 minor shock probably derived from disillusionment with the escalation and subsequent drawn out disengagement from that conflict. What may seem puzzling, though, is that Figure 3 betrays no distinct ripple attributable to the Watergate affair. In fact, other survey evidence indicates that the disclosure of the Nixon Administration's misdeeds did have an appreciable impact on partisan identification. The impact was decidedly directional, however: the 1972–1974 panel data show that while the proportion of strong Republicans declined by about 2 percent (from 12 to 10 percent) during that period, the proportion of strong Democrats increased by almost 5 percent. The net impact on overall partisan strength levels was, therefore, small at best.[13]

6. GOODNESS OF FIT

Figures 4A–4D show the partisan histories for cohorts spaced 12 years apart, beginning with the cohort born 1896–1899 and ending with the 1932–1935 birth cohort. Cohorts beyond those annual boundaries cannot be traced for more than a few elections with the data at hand. Predictions generated by the model are also displayed in these figures.[14] Comparable results were obtained for the other cohorts (not shown here).

---

[13] Wattenberg (1981), working with open-ended "party image" material from the National Election Study series, has recently shown that over the whole time span from 1952 to 1976, there has been a moderately steady shift from persons evaluating the major parties positively to evaluations that are more balanced or ambivalent, but not necessarily more negative. The one aberrant period in these quadrennial measurements is a very marked increase in negative evaluations between 1964 and 1968, a surge of negativism that has since abated. This surge seems to coincide in time with the one major "shock" visible in Figure 3, which also occurred between 1964 and 1968, and registered in the strength of partisanship, as well as in the more cognitive party images.

[14] The presence of measurement error in the partisan strength variable induces a negative serial correlation in the disturbance term which is taken into account in generating the forecasts.

Figure 4. Actual and Predicted Partisan Strength
for Selected Cohorts

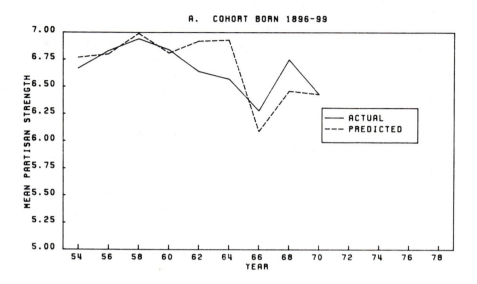

A. COHORT BORN 1896-99

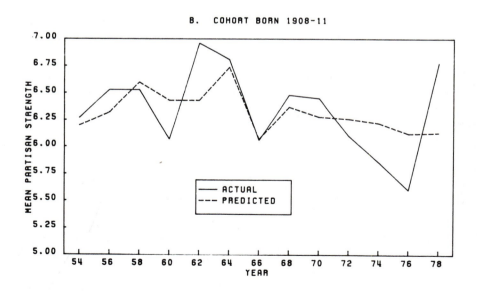

B. COHORT BORN 1908-11

Figure 4 (Cont.)

C.   COHORT BORN 1920-23

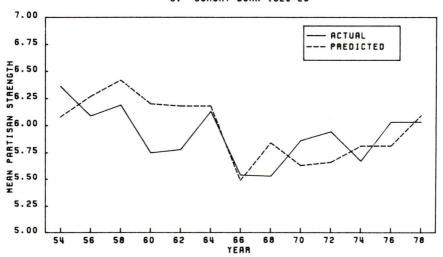

D.   COHORT BORN 1932-35

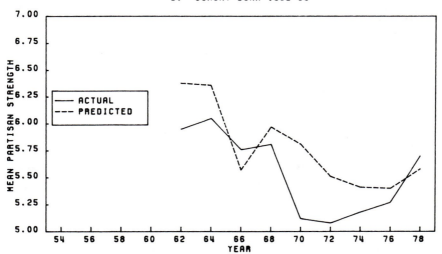

Examination of these time plots suggests that the model fits well for cohorts raised in quite disparate eras. More quantitative analysis indicates that the model accounts for virtually all of the covariation between partisanship and age or cohort. The squared correlation between age and forecast errors is 0.04, as compared with the initial age-partisanship squared correlation of 0.45 (as estimated with the cohort data). Similarly, an analysis of variance of forecast errors as a function of cohort membership is utterly nonsignificant ($\eta^2 = 0.11$, F < 1.0), despite an initially significant relationship between cohort classification and partisan strength ($\eta^2 = 0.74$, F = 21.8). The mean squared error of prediction is 0.11, and the correlation between observed and predicted partisanship among cohorts is 0.85.[15] In sum, then, the model not only fits the cohort data quite well, it also accounts for observed variation in partisan strength by age and cohort without any need to include those variables in the model itself.

7. AN ALTERNATIVE MODEL SPECIFICATION

As mentioned earlier, one explanation of persisting cohort differences in political attitudes is that such differences stem from the unique historical circumstances surrounding each cohort's movement through adolescence and early adulthood. According to this view, individuals' political attitudes are particularly susceptible to the influences of events occurring during those life stages and are progressively less mutable as the individuals age.

A reasonable translation of this thesis into mathematical form is a model in which the weights for the period effects decrease and the autoregressive parameter increases with age. Carlsson and Karlsson (1970) explicity incorporated this idea into their proposed "fixation model" of attitude change, and Jackson (1975) and Franklin and Jackson

---

[15] If β_1 in Equation (3) is estimated by OLS along with the period effects coefficients, MSE = 0.12, and R^2 = 0.83.

(1984) applied a similar model in two investigations of the dynamics of party identification—with somewhat mixed results. Jackson (1975) found evidence of age-related variations in the parameters for partisans but not for Independents. Franklin and Jackson (1984), using a different estimation procedure but comparable data, supported the hypothesis of age-dependent increases in the autoregressive parameter but not the hypothesis of declining impacts of current inputs with age.

Faced with these inconclusive results, we evaluated the fixation model with the panel and cohort data. The first step involved replicating the Wiley-Wiley estimation of the autoregressive parameter, but this time dividing the panels into five successive age groups. Predictably, parameter estimates based on the panel subsamples fluctuate more than do estimates based on the entire samples. The fluctuations, however, are utterly unrelated to age: across the four two-wave panels, the mean correlation between age and estimated autoregressive parameter is only 0.09. The same pattern is obtained if ordinary least squares estimates are used rather than the Wiley-Wiley values.

The next step was to determine whether the impact of period effects declined with age. As in the initial estimation of period effects, the cohort data were used for this purpose. More specifically, for each period residuals from the model with age-invariant coefficients were regressed on age to ascertain whether there were any systematic age trends in the residuals. For only one period (1954) of the thirteen is there a statistically significant trend in the residuals, and even in that case it is fairly weak. Consequently, there appears to be no compelling reason to opt for a model with either age-dependent period or autoregressive coefficients, as long as we restrict our attention to individuals age 25 or older. That restriction, however, may be an important one, and it will be elaborated upon below.

8. CONCLUSIONS

This analysis shows that a fairly simple and theoretically derived dynamic model fits well to trends in cohort partisanship for the 1954–1978 period and squares neatly with what can be learned about individual dynamics from patches of panel data as well. One of the charms of such a model is that a number of implications about period, age, and cohort effects on partisan strength may be deduced from it.

8.1. Age Effects

In the usual APC model, any observed covariation between chronological age and partisan strength is represented deterministically, either by a trend line or by a series of dummy variable step functions. In contrast, the model developed here does not include age as an independent variable at all. Instead, age-related gains (or, under some circumstances, losses) in partisan strength are a consequence of the structure of the model and the nature of the inputs. We regard this feature as an advantage of the present model, since age as a variable has no direct theoretical meaning in a model of the development of partisan strength.

It follows from this line of argument that, strictly speaking, a question about whether age effects are small or large is in a very real sense the wrong question to ask, since age by itself exerts no independent influence on partisanship. A more properly specified query would be of the form: "If a cohort entered adulthood with a mean partisan strength of such and such and if period inputs over the life cycle followed such and such a pattern, what would be the expected change in partisan strength?" This question may not be as pat as the previous one, but it hews more closely to the fundamental idea that the output of a dynamic process (such as partisan development) is a function of the structure of the model and the nature of the inputs (cf. Cortes, Przeworski, and Sprague, 1974). Moreover, the proper question invites a proper answer. Once the initial conditions and the stream of inputs are specified, the path of partisan development and the expected equilibrium can be determined precisely.

8.2. Cohort Effects

Just as the dynamic model does not include age as a regressor, neither does it include dummy variables denoting particular cohorts. The logic behind this decision parallels that regarding age effects: mere membership in a cohort is not in itself a very rich or useful explanatory variable; instead we should ask what factors may give rise to intercohort variations in partisanship and model those factors appropriately.

It was possible that, consistent with the fixation model, the weights attached to period inputs might be age dependent. However, empirical evidence lent little support to this hypothesis, and the application of a model with constant weights was found to fit both cohort and true panel data quite satisfactorily. Virtually all of the observed intercohort variation in partisan strength is accounted for by the model without the resort to cohort dummy variables.

Even without age-dependent coefficients, the large estimated autoregressive parameter implies that a kind of cohort effect can obtain, since, *ceteris paribus*, initial differences between cohorts will be partially conserved by the "memory" of the dynamic model. This idea is illustrated in Figure 5. In that figure are plotted the observed mean partisan strength scores at age 25–28 for the seven cohorts for which data are possessed. There is a good deal of variability in these initial values—a prerequisite for cohort effects by any definition. With those values as starting points, the paths of expected gains in partisan strength were traced under the assumption that total period inputs are held constant for all cohorts at a level equivalent to that of the 1956–1964 era. As can be seen in the figure, traces of the original intercohort distinctions are retained well into middle age, although, according to the model, initial differences become progressively diluted in the stream of common historical experiences shared by cohorts whose life spans overlap appreciably.

There is one other important point to be noted with respect to cohort effects. We are able to monitor cohorts reliably only from age 25 onward; yet it is precisely the age interval from about 17–24 that is of crucial interest to theories of generation formation. It is possible that the generating process evaluated in this paper does not extend backward into that age span in a straightforward fashion. There is, in fact, some evidence to support the hypothesis that it does not. The Jennings-Niemi panel study is based on a national sample of young adults and their parents who were interviewed in 1965 (when the youth were high school seniors) and again in 1973. Analysis of these data (Markus, 1979) indicates that opinions on the Vietnam War and on race relations had a significantly greater impact on the partisan orientations of the young adults than on those of their parents. The persistence of partisan attitudes was also substantially lower for the filial generation. There is, therefore, reason to believe that a quite different set of weighting

Figure 5. Simulated Cohort Partisan Strength
Under Constant Period Inputs

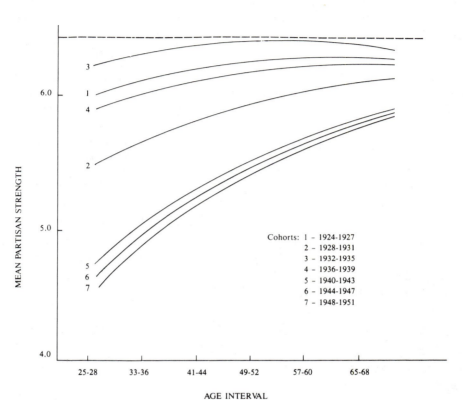

coefficients governs the model during the theoretically crucial formative
years of adolescence and early adulthood.

8.3 Period Effects

Of the three main effects in the APC model, only period effects were
explicity incorporated into the developmental model of partisan strength.
This was because there were substantive reasons to believe that
partisanship would respond to variations in those short-term political
forces generated by wars, recession, presidential elections, and other
events of national significance. There is however no precise way within

the model of attaching a single numerical value to the relative importance of these period impacts on partisanship. This is probably no great loss, since the intrusion of events powerful enough to make much difference in the system is both "lumpy" in time and, one would suppose, randomly distributed in time as well. Therefore, the meaning of any such precise figure would be stringently limited to the peculiarities of the time interval on which it is based. Bearing this in mind, with respect to the cohort data over the specific 1954–1978 interval, with the autoregressive coefficient fixed at 0.95, one sees that the period variables accounted for about 14 percent of the total variation in partisan strength.

8.4. Suggestions for Future Study

In closing, it is worth reiterating that the purpose of this article was to describe an alternative strategy to the traditional APC accounting model and, secondarily, to illustrate that strategy with a brief examination of the strength of partisan identifications in the United States. That illustation by no means exhausts the substantive questions concerning the dynamics of partisanship. In particular, although the incorporation of dummy period variables into the model was useful for suggesting what sorts of events might give rise to uniform cohort shifts in strength of partisanship, a complete investigation would go beyond that step by attempting to specify explicitly the relevant events and experiences and incorporating measures of those factors into the model in place of the dummy surrogates. In addition, a thorough explication of the origins of differences in partisanship between cohorts would go beyond the present example to focus on the origins of intergenerational differences in partisan attitudes during adolescence and early adulthood. The results of such studies could then be incorporated into the simple dynamic model of strength of partisanship, thereby increasing the explanatory power of that model.

APPENDIX A: DERIVATION OF EQUATION (4)

The simplest, although not the most elegant, way of deriving Equation (4) from Equation (3) is outlined as follows. By Equation (2),

$$S_{i1} = \beta_1 S_{i0} + \alpha_1 + u_{i1},$$

and

$$S_{i2} = \beta_1 S_{i1} + \alpha_2 + u_{i2}.$$

By substitution,

$$S_{i2} = \beta_1 (\beta_1 S_{i0} + \alpha_1 + u_{i1}) + \alpha_2 + u_{i2}$$
$$= \beta_1^2 S_{i0} + \beta_1 \alpha_1 + \alpha_2 + \beta_1 u_{i1} + u_{i2}.$$

Similarly,

$$S_{i3} = \beta_1 S_{i2} + \alpha_3 + u_{i3}$$
$$= \beta_1 (\beta_1^2 S_{i0} + \beta_1 \alpha_1 + \alpha_2 + \beta_1 u_{i1} + u_{i2}) + \alpha_3 + u_{i3}$$
$$= (\beta_1^3 S_{i0} + \beta_1^2 \alpha_1 + \beta_1 \alpha_2 + \alpha_3 + \beta_1^2 u_{i1} + \beta_1 u_{i2} + u_{i3};$$

or, in general,

$$S_{it} = \beta_1^t S_{i0} + \sum_{l=0}^{t-1} \beta_1^l \alpha_{t-l} + \sum_{l=0}^{t-1} \beta_1^l u_{it-l}. \tag{4}$$

REFERENCES

Abramson, P.R. (1976). Generational change and the decline of party identification in America: 1952–1974. *American Political Science Review* **70**, 469–478.

Abramson, P.R. (1979). Developing party identification: A further examination of life-cycle, generational, and period effects. *American Journal of Political Science* **23**, 78–96.

Abramson, P.R. (1983). *Political Attitudes in America*. San Francisco: Freeman.

Baltes, P.B., Cornelius, S.W., and Nesselroade, J.R. (1980). Cohort effects in developmental psychology, in J.R. Nesselroade and P.B. Baltes (eds.), *Longitudinal Research in the Study of Behavior and Development.* New York: Academic Press, pp. 61–87.

Blalock, H.M., Jr. (1961). *Causal Inferences in Nonexperimental Research.* New York: Norton.

Burnham, W.D. (1965). The changing shape of the American political universe. *American Political Science Review* **59**, 7–28.

Burnham, W.D. (1969). *Critical Elections and the Mainsprings of American Politics.* New York: Norton.

Cambell, A., Converse, P.E., Miller, W.E., and Stokes, D.E. (1960). *The American Voter.* New York: Wiley.

Carlsson, G. and Karlsson, K. (1970). Age, cohorts, and the generation of generations. *American Sociological Review* **35**, 710–718.

Converse, P.E. (1969). Of time and partisan stability. *Comparative Political Studies* **2**, 139–171.

Converse, P.E. (1976). *The Dynamics of Party Support.* Beverly Hills, CA: Sage.

Converse, P.E. and Markus, G.B. (1979). Plus ca change ... : The new CPS election study panel. *American Political Science Review* **73**, 32–49.

Cortes, F., Przeworski, A., and Sprague, J. (1974). *Systems Analysis for Social Scientists.* New York: Wiley.

Crittenden, J. (1962). Aging and party affiliation. *Public Opinion Quarterly* **26**, 648–657.

Cutler, N.E. (1970a). Generational succession as a source of foreign policy attitudes: A cohort analysis of American opinion, 1946–1966. *Journal of Peace Research* **7** (1), 33–47.

Cutler, N.E. (1970b). Generation, maturation, and party affiliation: A cohort analysis. *Public Opinion Quarterly* **33**, 583–588.

Cutler, N.E. and Bengston, V.L. (1974). Age and political alienation: Maturation, generation, and period effects. *Annals of the American Academy of Political and Social Science* **415**, 160–175.

Evan, W.M. (1959). Cohort analysis of survey data: A procedure for studying long-term opinion change. *Public Opinion Quarterly* **23**, 63–72.

Fienberg, S.E. and Mason, W.M. (1978). Identification and estimation of age-period-cohort models in the analysis of discrete archival data, in K.F. Schuessler (ed.), *Sociological Methodology, 1979.* San Francisco: Jossey-Bass, pp. 1–67.

Firebaugh, G. (1978). A rule for inferring individual-level relationships from aggregate data. *American Sociological Review* **43**, 557–572.

Franklin, C.H. and Jackson, J.E. (1983). The dynamics of party identification. *American Political Science Review* **77**, 957–973.

Glenn, N.D. (1972). Sources of the shift to independence: Some evidence from a cohort analysis. *Social Science Quarterly* **53**, 494–519.

Glenn, N.D. (1974). Aging and conservatism. *Annals of the American Academy of Political and Social Science* **415**, 176–186.

Glenn, N.D. (1976). Cohort analysts' futile quest: Statistical attempts to separate age, period, and cohort effects. *American Sociological Review* **41**, 900–904.

Glenn, N.D. (1977). *Cohort Analysis.* Beverly Hills, CA: Sage.

Glenn, N.D. and Grimes, M. (1968). Aging, voting, and political interest. *American Sociological Review* **33**, 563–575.

Glenn, N.D. and Hefner, T. (1972). Further evidence on aging and party identification. *Public Opinion Quarterly* **36**, 31–47.

Hout, M. and Knoke, D. (1975). Change in voter turnout, 1952–1972. *Public Opinion Quarterly* **39**, 52–68.

Jackson, J.E. (1975). Issues and party alignment, in L. Maisel and P.M. Sacks (eds.), *The Future of Political Parties.* Beverly Hills, CA: Sage, pp. 101–123.

Johnston, J. (1972). *Econometric Methods*, 2nd ed. New York: McGraw-Hill.

Jöreskog, K.G. (1973). A general method for estimating a linear structural equation system, in A. Goldberger and O.D. Duncan (eds.), *Structural Equation Models in the Social Sciences.* New York: Seminar Press, pp. 85–112.

Knoke, D. and Hout, M. (1974). Social and demographic factors in American political party affiliations, 1952–1972. *American Sociological Review* **39**, 700–713.

Mannheim, K. (1952). The problem of generations, in P. Kecskemeti (ed.), *Essays on the Sociology of Knowledge.* London: Routledge and Kegan Paul.

Markus, G.B. (1979). The political environment and the dynamics of public attitudes: A panel study. *American Journal of Political Science* **23**, 338–359.

Mason, K.O., Mason, W.M., Winsborough, H.H., and Poole, W.K. (1973). Some methodological issues in cohort analysis of archival data. *American Sociological Review* **38**, 242–258.

Miller, A.H., and Miller, W.E. (1977). Partisanship and performance: "Rational" choice in the 1976 presidential election. Paper presented at the annual meeting of the American Political Science Association, Washington, D.C., September.

Riley, M.W. (1973). Aging and cohort succession: Interpretations and misinterpretations. *Public Opinion Quarterly* **37**, 35–49.

Ryder, N.B. (1965). The cohort as a concept in the study of social change. *American Sociological Review* **30**, 843–861. Reprinted in this volume.

Shively, W.P. (1979). The development of party identification among adults: Exploration of a functional model. *American Political Science Review* **73**, 1039–1054.

Wattenberg, M.P. (1981). The decline of American party politics: Negativity or neutrality? *American Political Science Review* **75**, 941–950.

Weisberg, H.F. (1980). A multidimensional conceptualization of party identification. *Political Behavior* **2** (1), 33–60.

Wiley, D.E. and Wiley, J.A. (1970). The estimation of measurement error in panel data. *American Sociological Review* **35**, 112–117.

9. GENERATIONS, COHORTS, AND CONFORMITY*

Otis Dudley Duncan[†]

This paper offers further analyses of data generated by a survey question that has been studied in some earlier reports (Duncan, Schuman, and Duncan, 1973; Duncan, 1975; Duncan and Duncan, 1978). The question reads:

Which statement do you agree more with?

The younger generation should be taught by their elders to do what is right.

The younger generation should be taught to think for themselves even though they may do something their elders disapprove of.

Reasons for devoting more attention to this item include these: (1) The question is intrinsically an interesting one. In the entire adult population, the responses are about equally favored. But there are pronounced differences in the percentages by age and education. Evidently, the question gets at a real issue, however that issue is conceptualized. (2) Earlier analyses were incomplete or inept. (3) It is now possible to supplement the data from the 1956 and 1971 surveys of the Detroit Area Study (DAS) with data from the 1976 survey.

One takes a risk in assuming specific conceptual interpretations of a single survey question. But there is a great temptation to accept that risk here, for the YG question seems on its face to go directly to the heart of the value conflict analyzed by Kohn (1969, p. 35):

... middle-class parents are more likely to value self-direction; working-class parents are more likely to value conformity to external authority. ...

* This research was supported by National Science Foundation Grant No. SOC77-27365. Charles Brody, James A. McRae, Jr., and Dolores Vura assisted with computations and analysis. They also made helpful suggestions, as did Melvin Kohn, Clifford Clogg, and Duane Alwin.

† Department of Sociology, University of California, Santa Barbara.

self-direction focuses on *internal* standards for behavior; conformity on *externally* imposed rules. ... Self-direction does not imply rigidity, isolation, or insensitivity to others; on the contrary, it implies that one is attuned to internal dynamics—one's own, and other people's. Conformity does not imply sensitivity to one's peers, but rather obedience to the dictates of authority.

Table 1. Association of Response to Younger Generation Question with Goals in Childrearing, 1971

Goal[a]	n	Odds, *think: do right* Observed	Fitted[b]
To obey	454	0.40	0.42
To be well liked or popular	31	0.41	0.42
To think for himself	975	1.8	1.8
To work hard	132	0.48	0.42
To help others when they need help	217	0.71	0.71

[a] "If you had to choose, which thing on this list would you pick as the most important for a child to learn to prepare him [*sic*] for life?"
[b] Derived from a partitioning of the YG by Goals in Childrearing table, wherein only the contrasts shown here are significant.

A little light is shed on the meaning of the YG response categories in cross-classifying them by responses to another question on goals in rearing children (Table 1). One of those goals, "to think for himself," is virtually synonymous with the *think* response to YG. But it is not so obvious which of the other four goals have the most in common with *do right*. As it turns out, the goals to obey, to be well liked, and to work hard are about equally incompatible with *think*, but to help others is significantly less so.

It is interesting that a factor analysis of the Goals in Childrearing question by Alwin and Jackson (1982b) found a "latent factor ... quite similar in meaning to that found in our earlier analysis of Kohn's measures." But the strongest evidence for YG as a measure of Kohn's concept comes from 1980 General Social Survey data, which became available after this study was completed (see the Appendix).

This report will not recapitulate all of Kohn's research on social correlates of conformity. Our primary concern is with the factor, birth year, and its interpretation in terms of age and cohort. But we shall look at sex, color, education, and income as determinants of response as a preliminary to the consideration of age/cohort effects. Methods suited to the analysis of categorical data, as presented by Goodman (1978), facilitate the analysis.

1. CORRELATES OF RESPONSE

The report on sex can be brief. No main effect of sex on the YG response was detected in 1956, 1971, or 1976. Moreover, a thorough search revealed no interaction of sex with other factors (such as age, color, and education) with respect to YG response (Duncan and Duncan, 1978, pp. 261–266).

Results for color are more interesting. The observed odds suggest that between 1956 and 1971 blacks gained in proportion endorsing self-direction, while there was little change for whites. A formal analysis of the data in Table 2 confirms the significance of this differential change. The 1971 and 1976 data, however, are consistent with the supposition of no further differential change by color. The restricted three-way interaction conveyed by the fitted odds puts the ratio of the black to the white odds on *think* at 0.82 in 1956 and 1.30 in both 1971 and 1976. The civil rights movement of the 1960s, one infers, involved blacks in a general reduction in their evaluation of conformity to external authority. As we note later on, this shift was not confined to the younger cohorts of blacks.

A basis for expecting the odds on *think* to vary positively with education is provided by Kohn's (1969, p. 190) discussion:

> Education is important because self-direction requires more intellectual flexibility and breadth of perspective than does conformity; tolerance of

Table 2. Response to Younger Generation by Color,
1956, 1971, and 1976

Year	Color	Younger Generation Do Right	Think	Odds on think Observed	Fitted
1956	Black	75	55	0.73	0.73
	White	331	295	0.89	0.89
1971	Black	175	224	1.26	1.22
	White	734	681	0.93	0.94
1976	Black[a]	161	226	1.40	1.47
	White	242	284	1.17	1.13

[a] Data include responses of a supplementary sample of black respondents.

nonconformity, in particular, requires a degree of analytic ability that is difficult to achieve without formal education.

Even this unequivocal statement may not lead us to anticipate how strong the education effect on YG response really is. For summary purposes we cite the results of a logit regression analysis where $Y = $ log odds on *think* and $X = $ educational attainment, coded in equal steps, $0 \leq X \leq 7$, according to the progression, 0–4, 5–7, 8, 9–11, 12, 13–15, 16, and ≥ 17 years of school completed. Color and year are categorical covariates. The simplest model including all significant effects fits quite satisfactorily: Berkson's logit chi-square statistic $X_B^2 = 41.72$, d.f. $= 40$, P > 0.25. There is no significant variation in slope by year or color. For whites in 1956 we have $\hat{Y} = -1.32 + 0.363X$. For blacks in that year the intercept is -1.30. (Hence the color differential for 1956 noted earlier is fully explained by education.) The 1971 and 1976 intercepts for whites are -1.48 and -1.33, respectively, and the intercepts for blacks are 0.45 higher in each year. (Hence the differential change by color noted earlier is *not* explained by education; the antilog of $0.45 - 0.02 = 0.43$ is 1.54, very slightly lower than the ratio of the two odds ratios 1.30 and 0.82 given before.) To give some sense of the magnitude of the education effect, we compute $\hat{Y}$ for $X = 0$, 4, and 7 and transform the estimated logit into the percentage responding *think* among whites in 1976. We find 21% at the lowest education level, 53% of high school graduates, and 77% of persons with postgraduate university attainment endorsing this response alternative. The estimate of the education effect, incidentally, is little influenced by the inclusion of color as a covariate, even though the estimate of the color effect is considerably changed by holding constant education.

Kohn (1969, pp. 133–135) indicates that income has little relationship to class values, once education and occupational status are taken into account. We reconsider this matter in some detail, inasmuch as the results are quite striking.

Table 3. Response to Younger Generation Question by
Family Income, 1956 and 1971

Income[a] ($1,000)		1956		1971		Fitted odds, *think: do right,* Model H_3
1956	1971	Do Right	Think	Do Right	Think	
0–2	0–3	39	14	81	43	0.47
2–4	3–6	79	48	130	96	0.69
4–7	6–10	152	145	196	188	0.96
7–10	10–15	80	87	228	239	1.06
≥10	≥15	46	47	209	284	1.30
No answer		10	9	65	55	0.85

[a] The 1956 and 1971 intervals are roughly equivalent in terms of an adjustment for change in the consumer price index.

Response to the YG question is classified by family income in Table 3. The income classes are designed to produce rough comparability in terms of real income. The analysis of this table is straightforward; the most relevant models are listed in Table 4. Comparing H_1 and H_2 we observe a significant change in the distribution of (real) income between 1956 and

1971.   The effect of income on response is found significant by the comparison of the likelihood-ratio chi-square statistics: $L^2(H_2) - L^2(H_3)$ = 45.15, d.f. = 5. But there is no significant year effect, whether income effects are (H_3 vs. H_5) or are not (H_2 vs. H_4) in the model. Moreover, the excellent fit of H_5 leaves little room for the supposition that there is a three-way interaction—that is, a change between 1956 and 1971 in the income effect.   Since we accept the hypotheses of no change in income effect and no year effect, fitted counts under Model H_3 are relevant for estimating the income effect.   See last column of Table 3.   Disregarding the *no answer* category, the income effect is monotonic: the higher the income, the greater the odds on *think*.

Table 4. Results of Fitting Alternative Models
to the Data in Table 3

Model	Marginals Fitted[a]	d.f.	L^2
H_1	$\{I\}, \{Y\}, \{R\}$	16	197.73
H_2	$\{IY\}, \{R\}$	11	48.72
H_3	$\{IY\}, \{RI\}$	6	3.57
H_4	$\{IY\}, \{RY\}$	10	45.96
H_5	$\{IY\}, \{RI\}, \{RY\}$	5	2.54

[a] *I*: Income, *Y*: Year, *R*: Response to YG question.

Since the earlier analysis showed a pronounced effect of education on response, and since the correlation of education and income is well known, it seemed advisable to determine whether the apparent income effect is, in a sense, spurious.   The relevant cross-classification is the four-way table, $\{REIY\}$, where *R* is response, *E* is education (0–4, 5–7, 8, 9–11, 12, 13–15, 16, ≥17 years of schooling), *I* is income (categories listed in Table 3), and Y is year. This large table is not shown, and we shall mention only a few of the models that were fitted to it. When all pairwise associations (two-way marginals) are in the model (H_6), we have an acceptable fit: $L^2 = 122.35$, d.f $= 113$, $P > 0.25$. (There are 113 rather than 117 d.f., because all four cells pertaining to the highest education and lowest income category in both years are empty; hence these cells have fitted zeroes under the model.) If the year effect, represented by $\{RY\}$, is dropped from the model, we have Model H_7 with $L^2 = 122.84$, d.f. $= 114$, so that there is no significant deterioration of fit. If, in addition, the income effect $\{RI\}$ is omitted, we obtain Model H_8, with $L^2 = 129.53$, d.f. $= 119$. Again, the deterioration in fit is not significant: $L^2(H_8) - L^2(H_7) = 6.69$, d.f. $= 5$. However, none of the other two-way marginals can be omitted without incurring an unacceptable worsening of the fit.

Table 5. Estimates of Effect of Income on Response to Younger Generation Question (Relative Odds on *think*)

Income ($1,000) 1971	Gross Effect	Net Effect[a]	Induced Effect[a] 1956	Induced Effect[a] 1971
0– 3	1.0	1.0	1.0	1.0
3– 6	1.5	1.2	1.3	1.3
6–10	2.0	1.5	1.5	1.4
10–15	2.3	1.4	1.8	1.7
≥15	2.8	1.3	2.3	2.0

[a] See text for method of computation.

The substantive meaning of these results is explored in Table 5. In the first column, Gross Effect, we see the fitted odds from Table 3 re-expressed on a relative basis; the odds for each income category are divided by the odds for the lowest income class. The second column, Net

Effect, is based on odds under H_6, which includes an income effect that is the same at all levels of education in both years. Note that the pattern of relative odds is no longer monotonic and the effect is greatly attenuated. It is this very weak income effect that is dropped from H_8, in which the relative odds for every income class is, of course, 1.0. But it is important to note that H_8 merely explains or accounts for the association of YG response with income; it does not somehow make that association disappear. To bring out this point, we compute the so-called Induced Effect of income in the last two columns of Table 5. We sum the *fitted* counts under H_8 over categories of education to produce a three-way table, Response by Income by Year. Odds on *think* are then computed for each Income-by-Year combination; and these odds are expressed on a relative basis. The induced effect is quite pronounced, though not as large as the gross effect. Indeed, *to a very rough approximation*, Gross Effect = Net Effect × Induced Effect. The very fact that the last term is not quite the same in the two years demonstrates that the equation is not algebraically correct. Another way to state the point is to observe that "there is no calculus of path coefficients" (Fienberg 1980, p. 120) for categorical variables.

The practicing research worker does not often actually see examples of the textbook case in which controlling a single "third variable" practically eliminates an apparent association between two other variables. Hence, it may be worthwhile to ponder this particular result. Our education variable is, of course, a set of classes pertaining to the highest grade in the regular school and college system completed by the respondent. Why that variable should make any difference in attitudes or in response to YG is not really self-evident, although survey analysts are so accustomed to substantial associations of opinions with schooling that they come to take them for granted. And one reason for the prevalence of such associations may be that the opinions survey investigators like to study are precisely those on issues related to modern values (Yorburg, 1974, pp. 88ff). Now, at least two kinds of things happen in greater or lesser degrees as a consequence of continuation in school. One is increased exposure to a literature written by exponents of modern values and to the knowledge on which the technological support of those values is based. Thus, one result of education is enlightenment, which seems to entail or give rise to a state of mind or cast of intellect which one can describe as cultural tolerance. At least, S.M. Lipset (1960) has so described it. A distinct effect of schooling is that it provides skills and credentials which gain the educated person entree into the higher status and better paying occupations, so that (*ceteris paribus*) the well-educated person can expect over his life cycle to accumulate greater wealth and to enjoy more of the other rewards of status than the less educated one. This (again, *ceteris paribus*) will give him a greater stake in the economic-political status quo and make him less willing to see large-scale governmental intervention in the processes of income distribution made in the name of general welfare.

Consider three kinds of opinion questions that might be found in the entire universe of questions that could on some basis be described as reflecting "liberalism." If the question is one that gets at an issue whose resolution is implicit in how culturally tolerant the respondent is, a type-A question in Figure 1A, then the liberal response will be associated with years of schooling, since the intervening paths are positive. If the question is of type C, however—if it raises an issue about government intervention in the distributive process—the response will be negatively associated with schooling, since the product of the signs of intervening paths is negative. A type-B question that manages to mix the two kinds of issue in a double-barreled or ambiguous wording (a proposition, say, to the effect that not only are all men/women equal, but the government should take steps to equalize them) will have an unpredictable but probably low association with schooling, since the two causal chains by which education produces its effect on response are offsetting. (See also Kohn, 1969/1977, p. xlii.)

The diagram is specialized to the case at hand in Figure 1B. Our finding is that YG response is associated with both education and income, but that the association with income is (almost wholly) spurious. We infer that YG is a type-A question. Highly educated people endorse *think* (not all of them do so, of course, but the preponderant fraction) because they are tolerant, because they have been enlightened by exposure to knowledge, arguments, and role models favorable to the modern ideal that tolerates, among other things, people thinking for themselves.

Our study of income in relation to YG does not, therefore, lead to an improved "explanation" of variation in response to that question (in the usual, vulgar sense of raising the coefficient of determination). But it does give us an enlarged perspective on the statistical result already obtained, to wit, the positive regression of *think* on educational attainment. We have verified that YG is a type-A question.

Figure 1. How Schooling Affects Opinions

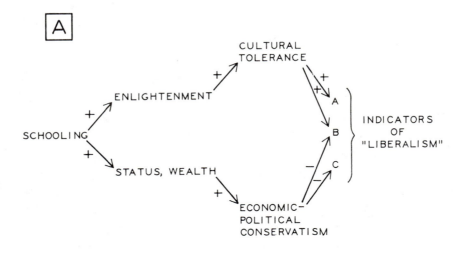

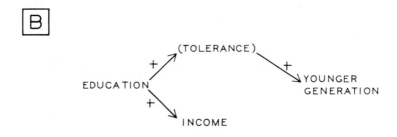

2. AGE OR COHORT EFFECTS

In most respects, the YG question seems like a good indicator for Kohn's distinction between self-direction (*think*) and conformity to external authority (*do right*). But there is one aspect of the question that perhaps limits its generality as an indicator. In the *think* response that is offered, the reference to external authority is specifically and particularly to the authority held by the older generation: "... think for themselves even though they may do something their elders disapprove of." What would be the effect on response of substituting "peers," or a synonym thereof, for "elders"? That question cannot now be answered statistically, for lack of data, but it seems likely that YG response is affected by respondent's age to a greater degree than one would infer from Kohn's conceptual distinction per se. No elaborate argument to this effect seems necessary. Its major premise is just the empirical generalization, "Legally and factually in all societies the age groups have been stratified, with different rights, duties, status, roles, privileges, disfranchisements" (Sorokin, 1947, p. 281). The minor premise is that one is the more likely to identify with the interests of the "elders" the more advanced one's age is.

The argument evidently would predict a monotonic decrease in the odds on *think* with increasing age, other factors aside. Perhaps a more complicated argument, relating to the second derivative of the age-*think* function, would appeal to the association of respondent's age with the probability of experiencing parenthood or, more specifically, of acting out the role of "elder" vis-a-vis various categories of younger persons.

There is also an argument for cohort effects on YG response. Kohn (1969, pp. 193–194) notes:

> ... a major historical trend probably has been—and will continue to be—toward an increasingly self-directed populace. It is well known that educational levels have long been rising and are continuing to do so. What is not so well recognized is that levels of occupational self-direction have also been rising, and almost certainly will continue to rise.

Education is, of course, the paradigmatic example of a cohort-differentiating characteristic (Duncan, 1968; Fienberg and Mason, 1978). The case is not so clear for occupation, although some measure of continuity across the main portion of the working life is recognized as normal, especially for men (Blau and Duncan, 1967), so that cohorts are semi-permanently distinguished by their occupational profiles. Kohn's projection, if translated into a statement about cohort differentiation, leads to the expectation of a positive association of the odds on *think* with year of birth. Given the rather smooth upward trend of educational attainment over all the cohorts represented in the DAS populations—and in the absence of definite expectations concerning possible intercohort discontinuities due to pulsatory influences of other cohort-differentiating factors—there is little basis for a prediction more specific than the one just suggested.

On a preliminary consideration of the matter we find, therefore, that age and cohort effects both are expected to produce a positive relationship of proportion responding *think* to birth year. If the relationship in each case is strictly linear, there is no possibility of distinguishing empirically between age and cohort effects, no matter how many survey years are represented in the data. If these effects are detectably nonlinear, the mathematical possibility of estimating them, using data from repeated cross-sectional surveys, does exist in principle (Fienberg and Mason, 1978). With only three surveys, unequally spaced in time, available for the present analysis, and lacking any solid theoretical basis for specifying nonlinear effects, one would be optimistic indeed in expecting real assistance from this theorem.

Our objective, then, is not to make a unique estimate of age and/or cohort effects, but to experiment with alternative "readings" of the data in the hope of learning a little about the course of social change in the period under study. "Cohort analysis," after all, is a means and not an end in itself.

Figures 2 and 3 summarize parallel analyses treating age and cohort as the independent variables. In each case, the effects are represented by a quintic equation and the fitting makes use of orthogonal polynomials. The objective was not to specify a theoretically defensible functional form but to smooth the data in a reasonably flexible way. In the event, the quintic term was not statistically significant in either analysis. But for the age analysis the cubic term was significant and in the cohort analysis the quartic term was significant, as judged by the increment to X_B^2 resulting from deletion of the particular term. The departures from linearity in both analyses, though statistically significant, are not such as to encourage thoughts of estimating age and cohort effects in a single model. Both data plots show a gentle undulation but no substantial departure from monotonicity. The goodness-of-fit statistics provide little reason to prefer one of the plots over the other. In the age analysis, Figure 2, we have $X_B^2 = 13.53$, d.f. = 20, and in the cohort analysis, Figure 3, $X_B^2 = 16.11$, d.f. = 26. (The cohort analysis has a few more data points than the age analysis, inasmuch as the 1971 and 1976 surveys provide some age detail above 65 but the 1956 survey does not.)

One important feature is common to the two analyses. The linear component of age or cohort interacts with year, and this interaction is significant in both analyses. Indeed, in both of them, one could accept a model with the 1956 and 1976 or the 1971 and 1976 curves parallel. That is, we can be reasonably sure that there was a shift in the age or cohort pattern between 1956 and 1971, but a subsequent further shift (apparently, a shift back toward the 1956 pattern) is not unequivocally demonstrated.

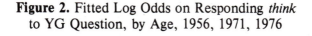

Figure 2. Fitted Log Odds on Responding *think*
to YG Question, by Age, 1956, 1971, 1976

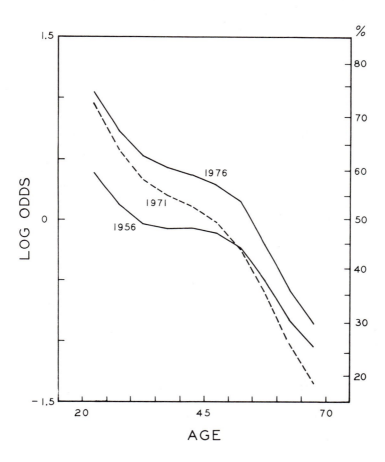

As it appears in the age analysis, the 1956–1971 shift can be described as a further polarization of the age groups. Whereas, in 1956, the age curve was relatively flat from ages 30 to 50, in 1971, there was a pronounced gradient of response in all segments of the age range. From the viewpoint of the cohort analysis this same interaction meant that there was an actual decrease in the log odds on *think* for all the cohorts represented in the 1956 survey and the magnitude of the decrease was an inverse linear function of birth year. The older cohorts greatly reduced their endorsement of *think*, while cohorts aging from 21–24 to 36–39 between 1956 and 1971 hardly changed at all. It is only a happenstance

Figure 3. Fitted Log Odds on Responding *think*
to YG Question, by Birth Cohort, 1956, 1971, 1976.
Cohort 1 Was Born Before 1891, Cohort 14 in 1950 or
Later. (Inset: Cohort Effects Imputed to Education; See Text)

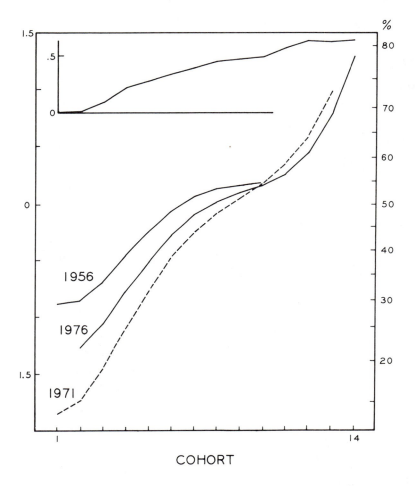

COHORT

that the three curves come together for this particular cohort, as though it
were the fulcrum of change. The statistical models do not impose this
coincidence.

As a matter of convenience, the overall pattern of change from 1956
to 1971 is, therefore, more readily described in terms of the cohort
results. But the 1971–1976 change is (seemingly) simpler to summarize
with the age results, inasmuch as the 1976 age curve lies above the 1971
curve at all ages.

In pondering such a remark, it is well to keep in mind the double (or multiple) meaning of the concept "change." In both figures, the term refers to the vertical distance separating a pair of curves. If they are age curves, then "change" really refers to the *replacement* of one group of people aged x to $x + 5$ in one year by a different group having the same age in a later year. In this case, change is best described as *inter*cohort change or change due to cohort succession. This kind of change can occur, of course, even if not one individual actually alters her or his response during the time period in question. The vertical distances between the cohort curves (Figure 3), on the contrary, register actual *net* changes for the same populations of people born during the interval of birth years b to $b + 5$ (failures of cohort closure due to migration and mortality being neglected). In some ways the cohort description seems more natural, since it brings to mind some individuals changing their responses from *do right* to *think* and others changing in the opposite direction with the preponderance being in one direction or the other. In addition to the dynamics of individual change (which one might hope to analyze with panel data, if such were available), the cohort description also draws attention to the "new" cohorts. In 1971, the three cohorts having entered the adult population since 1956 all had higher odds on *think* than any of the older cohorts in either 1956 or 1971. Thus, this source of aggregate change for the whole population dramatically counterbalanced the *intra*cohort shifts favoring *do right* over *think*. The imagery suggested here is that "new" and "old" cohorts, during the 1960s, were involved in a negative feedback relationship. The demand for autonomy on the part of the former was countered by an intensified insistence of the latter on their own authority. If the 1976 estimates shown in Figure 3 are to be believed, this confrontation left its mark on the cohorts, albeit in somewhat attenuated form.

Statistical reasons have been stated for foregoing an attempt to estimate a combined age-cohort-period model of the kind proposed by Fienberg and Mason (1978). But there are evidently *substantive* reasons as well for doubting the suitability of such a model when all the effects are additive (in the logarithmic formulation). We find either age-by-period or cohort-by-period interactions that authentically reflect the "climate of the period" spanned by the 1956 and 1971 surveys. Models that feature this kind of historicity have something to be said for them (Converse, 1976, and Glenn, 1977), however attractive the elegance of the additive three-factor model.

Thus far, the age/cohort analyses have proceeded without explicit reference to the mechanisms that supposedly generate the age or cohort effects. It is not obvious how one might model the age effects, particularly if the three DAS surveys are the only sources of data. But at least one cohort-differentiating factor—to wit, education—can be brought into the picture. We consider the cross-classification of YG response by age by survey year by education (with the two lowest and the two highest of the eight education classes described earlier being combined). In a standard multiway contingency analysis we find separate effects of the three factors on response. The response-by-age-by-year interaction is not significant, no doubt because it uses 21 d.f. rather than the single d.f. for the linear version described earlier.

Now let us suppose that the true model for this cross-classification is the one depicted schematically in Figure 4. There really are cohort effects—even though cohort as such is not an explicit factor in the statistical analysis—but they come about entirely via education as a cohort-differentiating variable. The figure allows direct effects of year and age on response. If Figure 4 were a path diagram, each arrow would correspond to a single coefficient and it would be easy to eliminate education from the diagram by substitution, thereby deriving the reduced-form equation. Note that no year or age effects on education are allowed, Fienberg and Mason (1978) notwithstanding, in the interest of simplicity. Of course, "there is no calculus of path coefficients" in the analysis of categorical variables (Fienberg, 1980, p. 120). Hence we offer a heuristic and mathematically inexact (though suggestive) calculation. From the model for the four-way table we calculate the net education effects in terms of log odds on *think*. Then we construct the two-way table, education by cohort, from the aggregated data for the three surveys. We allow the cohorts to have the ages pertaining to one of the survey years, say 1976, and compute the weighted mean education effect for each cohort, using its education distribution as weights. The resulting pattern of cohort differences in YG response induced by education is shown as the inset in Figure 3.

Very nearly the same set of induced cohort effects is obtained by an alternative method. Rearrange the multiway tabulation, response by age by year by education to obtain the response by *cohort* by year by education cross-classification. Estimate first the gross effects of cohort (education omitted from the model) and second the net effects of cohort (in a model with additive cohort, year, and education effects). The set of

Figure 4. Schematic Model for Cohort Effects
Entirely Attributed to Education

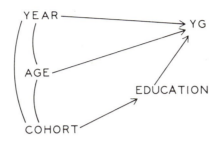

differences, gross minus net, is so similar to the pattern in the Figure 3 inset that the two cannot be distinguished graphically.

Evidently, the pattern of education-induced cohort effects provides a lower-bound estimate of "true" cohort effects (barring some kind of perverse mechanism for offseting age and cohort effects). If occupation works like Kohn asserts, if cohorts are semi-permanently differentiated by occupational profile, and if occupation effects are not themselves wholly induced by education, then the trajectory of cohort effects has a somewhat steeper gradient than is shown in the inset, Figure 3. The same argument applies, *mutatis mutandis*, to any other proposed cohort-differentiating factor.

With all reasonable allowance for such factors, the gap between the "cohort effects" estimated in the main portion of Figure 3 and the education-induced cohort effects seems much too large to be explained without allowing age (or the variables for which age is a proxy) to have a distinct effect on response. The observation would have to be weaker if instead of *response* (to the YG question) we read "self-direction vs. conformity" (or an ideal indicator of Kohn's distinction). As noted earlier, the YG question does explicitly allude to *age* stratification, thereby reducing its generality as an indicator of Kohn's variable. What we cannot know is whether an ideal indicator would show the very interesting age-by-year or cohort-by-year interaction we found for YG itself. Perhaps it would. The main empirical support for this conjecture is the result for color. *All* blacks, regardless of age, acted like "new cohorts" between 1956 and 1971. If the cohort analysis in Figure 3 is repeated with the data further subdivided by color, we again find the color-by-year interaction already described. The black-white difference in log odds on *think* is 0.51 higher in 1971 or 1976 than in 1956, for all birth cohorts. But if the main effects of cohort per se are allowed to vary by color (and this decision is supported by a statistically significant color effect on the cubic term), we do not see for blacks quite so dramatic a contrast between the three or four most recent cohorts and all their predecessors as we note in Figure 3 or the very similar figure for white respondents separately.

3. BETWEEN GENERATIONS

In the work reported thus far the notion of generation enters only by way of the YG question wording. A more direct look at the "generation gap" is made possible by a second question, asked of half the respondents in 1971 and all of them in 1976:

> How do you think your (father/mother) [parent of the same sex as respondent] would have answered this question when you were growing up? Which one would (he/she) have agreed with more?

The cross-classification of the two responses, YG by Par YG, is shown in Table 6 for the four-category sex-by-color cross-classification. The table omits the seven respondents in each year who answered *do right* to YG but *think* to Par YG. The complete tabulation, then, aggregating over sex and color would show, for 1971, 464 responding *do right* to both questions, 7 *do right* to YG but *think* to Par YG, 292 *think* to YG but *do right* to Par YG, and 146 *think* to both questions. Corresponding frequencies are 384, 7, 339, 165 in 1976. There is clearly a strong intergenerational transmission of this attitude (taking responses at face value). The odds ratio measuring association of YG and Par YG is estimated at 33.1 from the 1971 data, 26.7 from the 1976 data. (The difference is not significant, nor do we find any significant variation in this measure of association across categories of sex, color, age, or education.) There is equally clearly a large amount of intergenerational mobility with respect to the attitude (again, taking Par YG responses at face value). The mobility is almost wholly in one direction: from the endorsement of conformity (*do right*) which is attributed to the parent to the preference for self-direction (*think*) on the part of the respondent.

Table 6. Response to Younger Generation Questions, by Sex and Color, 1971 and 1976, with Fitted Counts Under Preferred Model

Year	Color	Sex	YG: Par YG:	Response[a] Do Right Do Right	Think Do Right	Think Think
				(1)	(2)	(3)
					observed counts[c]	
1971	White	Men		171	93	58
		Women		215	121	61
	Black	Men		35	28	12
		Women		43	50	15
1976	White	Men		105	77	46
		Women		123	101	58
	Black	Men		57	51	23
		Women		99	110	38
					fitted counts[b]	
1971	White	Men		169.4	100.4	52.2
		Women		208.9	123.7	64.4
	Black	Men		33.7	31.0	10.4
		Women		48.5	44.6	14.9
1976	White	Men		106.5	75.1	46.5
		Women		131.7	92.8	57.5
	Black	Men		51.8	56.6	22.6
		Women		97.6	106.8	42.6

[a] See text for question wording.

[b] Model fits three-way marginals, {Sex × Color × Year}; one-way marginals, {Response}; linear effect of year on response; constrained color effect on response contrasting middle with two end categories. L^2 = 6.57, d.f. = 12. $P > 0.75$.

[c] 1971 data for Form B respondents only. 1976 data include supplementary black sample. In each year 7 respondents were classified *do right* on YG and *think* on Par YG. They are omitted from the reported analyses.

An earlier analysis (Duncan, 1975, Figure 5–2) suggested that part of the generation gap implied by this mobility is a function of a difference in perception or definition between parent and offspring. It seems likely that a goodly number of parents who would, themselves, have chosen *think* are classified in the *do right* category by their proxies. Even so, the cohort effects noted earlier, *though not synonymous with the generation gap*, suggest that not all that gap is to be so explained.

Now, the seven respondents (it is only a coincidence that the number was the same in the two samples) in each year who gave the highly deviant response, *do right* for themselves and *think* for their parents, represent a most interesting phenomenon—a retreat to conformity. One would like to know more about such people. But it will require larger samples than these to produce reliable estimates of their characteristics and orientations. With the clear recognition that a category of great conceptual interest is being dropped, we omit these respondents from all subsequent analyses. In that event, the YG-by-Par-YG response is reduced to a miniature two-item Guttman scale and some special constraints of interest for an ordered trichotomy (Duncan, 1979b) may be entertained.

Table 7. Comparison of Alternative Models
for the Data in Table 6

Model	Factors Included[a]	d.f.	L^2
(1)	None	14	32.93
(2)	Sex	12	29.69
(3)	Color	12	13.79
(4)	Year	12	20.81
(5)	Sex, Color	10	11.56
(6)	Sex, Year	10	17.81
(7)	Color, Year	10	5.78
(8)	Sex, Color, Year	8	3.60
(7*)	Constrained effects, linear for Year, middle vs. ends for Color	12	6.57

[a] All models fit three-way marginals, {Sex × Color × Year}, and one-way marginals, {Response}. In all models with two or three factors, effects are additive (in the log-linear representation of the model), because no significant joint effects of factors were detected.

The analysis of Table 6 is summarized in Table 7. We again find no sex effect on response or interaction of sex with another factor in regard to the response. The year effect is nicely represented as linear: the ratio of the fitted 1976 count to the fitted 1971 count of respondents in any one of the sex/color categories (say, white men) is 1.19 times as great for response category (2) as for category (1) and, again, 1.19 times as great for category (3) as for category (2), following the numbering of the columns of Table 6. Thus between 1971 and 1976 there was a net shift toward self-direction, as measured by this three-category scale.

The color effect is not, however, linear in the same sense. On the contrary, we find the fitted ratio of blacks to whites (within either sex in either year) to be 1.55 times as great in the middle response category as in either of the extreme categories. Thus, the experience of an inter-generational discrepancy is relatively more common among blacks than among whites. (We can only conjecture that this color effect appeared after 1956, bearing in mind the year-by-color interaction for YG reported earlier.)

Sample data on education by three-category response are shown in Table 8. From the work reported earlier, we may surely infer the general pattern of this relationship. But the truly elegant form of the relationship is one that we have learned to specify only recently (Haberman, 1974; Duncan, 1979a; Goodman, 1979). The uniform-association model of the response-by-education association states that the odds ratio defined for the four cells falling in any pair of adjacent rows and any pair of adjacent columns has a constant value, θ. Thus, to summarize this three-way table we need in our model only one d.f. for the education effect and one d.f. for the year effect. The linear year effect is here estimated as $\hat{\beta} = 1.17$ (slightly different from 1.19 in the sex/color analysis) and the uniform-association parameter as $\hat{\theta} = 1.32$. Comparisons among the models listed in Table 9 show that fit is not significantly improved by inclusion of additional parameters for either association.

The uniform-association parameter, we note in passing, serves the same function here as the usual "measure of association" recommended for contingency tables in elementary statistics textbooks. There is one vital distinction, however. We only use θ to measure association after determining that a very strong model of the *structure* of the association is appropriate. The usual "measure of association" (of whatever variety) can be computed for any table of the requisite form, whatever the underlying structure of association. That is why Plackett (1974, p. 27) said of such measures, "They are purely descriptive and have no real interpretation."

Table 8. Response to Younger Generation Questions, by Education, 1971 and 1976, with Fitted Counts Under Preferred Model

Year	Response YG	Par YG	0-4	5-7	8	9-11	12	13-15	16	17+	Total
						observed counts					
1971	Do Right	Do Right	22	39	46	107	161	60	16	13	464
	Think	Do Right	3	11	14	67	109	53	18	17	292
	Think	Think	1	3	1	23	51	28	18	21	146
1976	Do Right	Do Right	8	21	39	73	89	45	15	7	297
	Think	Do Right	0	7	6	45	101	48	17	15	239
	Think	Think	0	3	7	14	46	38	11	11	130
						fitted counts[a]					
1971	Do Right	Do Right	20.6	39.0	40.7	115.6	159.8	57.1	16.4	11.9	461.1
	Think	Do Right	4.7	11.7	16.2	61.0	111.7	52.9	20.1	19.3	297.6
	Think	Think	0.7	2.2	4.1	20.4	49.4	31.0	15.6	19.8	143.2
1976	Do Right	Do Right	6.1	21.6	32.4	70.8	104.9	46.2	11.4	6.3	299.7
	Think	Do Right	1.6	7.6	15.1	43.9	86.2	50.2	16.5	12.1	233.2
	Think	Think	0.3	1.7	4.5	17.2	44.8	34.6	15.1	14.6	132.8

[a] For H_{15} in Table 9.

Table 9. Comparison of Alternative Models
of Association for the Data in Table 8

Model[a]	Fits	d.f.	L^2
H_{14}	{Education × Year}, {Response × Year} (independence of Education and Response within years)	28	164.84
H_{15}	{Education × Year}, {Response}, uniform association ($\hat{\theta} = 1.32$) common to the two years, linear year effect ($\hat{\beta} = 1.18$)	28	33.68
H_{16}	{Education × Year}, {Response × Year}, uniform association ($\hat{\theta} = 1.32$) common to the two years	27	33.28
H_{17}	{Education × Year}, {Response × Year}, uniform association within years ($\hat{\theta} = 1.33$ in 1971, 1.32 in 1976	26	33.23
H_{18}	{Education × Year}, {Response × Year}, linear education effects within years	24	28.88

[a] Relationships between models: $H_{14} \Rightarrow H_{16}$; $H_{15} \Rightarrow H_{16}$; $H_{16} \Rightarrow H_{17} \Rightarrow H_{18}$.

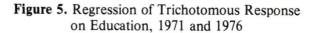

Figure 5. Regression of Trichotomous Response
on Education, 1971 and 1976

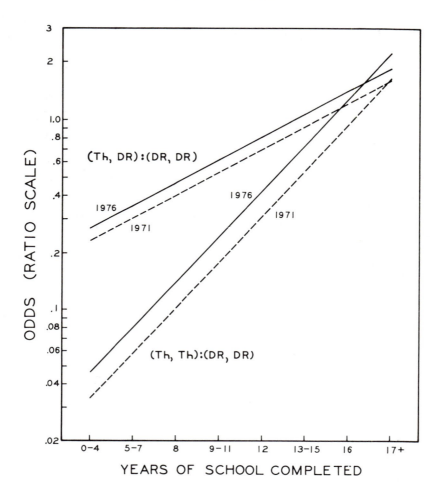

Figure 5 makes explicit the meaning of the two main structural features of our model. Any odds on one response relative to another will have a linear regression on education (after taking logs) and the slope will be $\log \theta$ if the response categories are adjacent and $h \log \theta$ if they are h steps apart. (Here, of course, we have $1 \leq h \leq 2$.) The parameter for the year effect, β, controls how far apart the 1976 and 1971 regressions are. That distance is again a function of the separation of the response categories.

Education differentiates cohorts but so do age and possibly other factors. It is not a foregone conclusion, therefore, that a model of the response-by-cohort association will have the same form as the one for response by education. But the data in Table 10 suggest that this is indeed the case. In fact, we learn from Table 11 that there is no significant net year effect, linear or otherwise, when the response-by-cohort association is taken to be uniform and the cohort-by-year distributions are fitted with no constraints on their form. The preferred model for Table 10 is, therefore, a pure cohort-effects model. Failure to detect a year effect can also be read as failure to detect an age effect. For after all, each cohort aged by 5 years between the two surveys.

We are making no strong theoretical claims here. The samples are small and the time period covered is limited. But the results in this section surely permit the suggestion that the momentum of intercohort change is sustained not only by rising levels of educational attainment but also by the intergenerational transmission of value orientations. The basis for a conjecture, like Kohn's, as to future trend of self-direction/conformity seems secure. In that event, we would do well to ask, what crisis or as yet embryonic trend could confound all our expectations?

4. SUMMARY

Our generation has a younger one
Whose moral norms and values we propose
To fix, if that can feasibly be done.

But strategy dictates that no one knows
The true agenda. Teach the kids to think
They think without the aid of parents. Pray
When thinking for themselves they never link
Their premises to what the elders say.

Well-educated cohorts will respond,
When queried in a calm unbiased way,
That any error honestly incurred
By cogitating children is beyond
Account. They know full well it would betray
The game to let displeasure be inferred.

Table 10. Response to Younger Generation Questions, by Birth Cohort, 1971 and 1976, with Fitted Counts Under Preferred Model

Year	Response YG	Par YG	70+	65 -69	60 -64	55 -59	50 -54	45 -49	41 -44	36 -40	31 -35	26 -31	21 -25	Total
							observed counts							
1971	Do Right	Do Right	85	41	52	56	46	45	39	36	31	33	...	464
	Think	Do Right	15	12	16	25	34	41	20	40	35	54	...	292
	Think	Think	5	1	6	8	13	24	10	15	27	37	...	146
1976	Do Right	Do Right	35	26	28	30	33	27	16	22	35	21	19	292
	Think	Do Right	13	6	13	23	21	21	15	22	34	35	34	237
	Think	Think	3	3	6	5	14	13	9	11	19	23	24	130
							fitted counts[a]							
1971	Do Right	Do Right	75.4	36.7	47.2	52.7	50.7	54.4	30.6	35.8	31.9	36.6	...	452.0
	Think	Do Right	24.7	14.0	21.1	27.5	30.9	38.8	25.5	34.7	36.2	48.4	...	301.8
	Think	Think	4.9	3.3	5.7	8.7	11.4	16.8	12.9	20.5	24.9	39.0	...	148.1
1976	Do Right	Do Right	36.6	23.8	30.0	34.4	37.0	30.2	17.8	21.6	30.2	23.3	19.2	304.1
	Think	Do Right	12.0	9.1	13.4	17.9	22.6	21.5	14.8	21.0	34.2	30.9	29.8	227.2
	Think	Think	2.4	2.1	3:6	5.7	8.4	9.3	7.5	12.4	23.6	24.9	28.0	127.9

Age in 1976

[a] For H_{20} in Table 11.

Table 11. Comparison of Alternative Models of Association for the Data in Table 10

Model[a]	Fits	d.f.	L^2
H_{19}	{Cohort $\times$ Year}, {Response $\times$ Year} (independence of Cohort and Response within years)	38	202.70
H_{20}	{Cohort $\times$ Year}, {Response}, uniform association ($\hat{\theta}$ = 1.17) common to the two years (no year effect on response)	39	39.53
H_{21}	{Cohort $\times$ Year}, {Response}, uniform association within years ($\hat{\theta}$ = 1.169 in 1971, 1.167 in 1976)	38	39.52
H_{22}	{Cohort $\times$ Year}, {Response $\times$ Year}, uniform association common to the two years ($\hat{\theta}$ = 1.17)	37	37.78
H_{23}	{Cohort $\times$ Year}, {Response $\times$ Year}, uniform association within years ($\hat{\theta}$ = 1.20 in 1971, 1.13 in 1976)	36	33.14

[a] Relationships between models: $H_{19} \Rightarrow H_{22} \Rightarrow H_{23}$; $H_{20} \Rightarrow H_{21} \Rightarrow H_{23}$; $H_{20} \Rightarrow H_{22} \Rightarrow H_{23}$.

A question on whether the younger generation (YG) should be taught to think for themselves or do what their elders believe is right is a plausible indicator of Kohn's conceptual variable, self-direction/conformity. Odds on *think* vary positively with education and income, though the latter association is spurious. Between 1956 and 1971 blacks and new cohorts entering the Detroit adult population showed substantial increases in odds on *think*. Formal separation of age and cohort effects does not seem feasible, although there is reason to suppose both are present. Between 1956 and 1971 the age or cohort gradient became more pronounced, perhaps because the legitimacy of authority was under debate during the period. Respondents' reports on their parents' views may exaggerate the generation gap but suggest, nevertheless, a preponderantly one-way intergenerational movement toward *think*. The relationships of the joint YG-by-Parent-YG response to education and cohort are nicely summarized by the uniform-association model. Intergenerational and intercohort continuities thereby detected afford a basis for trend extrapolation which, however (like all extrapolation), should be viewed skeptically.

APPENDIX

A more searching examination of the properties of YG as an indicator of Kohn's self-direction/conformity dimension is possible with data available for the first time in the 1980 General Social Survey (NORC, 1980). The objective is to compare the evidence Kohn used to get at parental evaluation of self-direction with the evidence provided by YG. Responses to the Kohn items (listed in Table 12) are obtained by presenting to each respondent a list of 13 "qualities" and asking him or her to designate the "three ... most desirable for a child to have," the "most desirable ... one of these three," the three considered "least important," and the one "least important of all." Each item is thereby placed in one of five categories, with the middle category pertaining to items not mentioned as one of the three most desirable or the three least desirable. Kohn (1969) assigned the integers 1 to 5 to these categories and used them as scores in carrying out a factor analysis of the responses of some 1,500 fathers of children aged 3–15 in a national sample taken by

Table 12. Coefficients Pertaining to Kohn's Items and
Younger Generation Question as Indicators of
Self-Direction

Parental Value, Child's Being/Having	1964 Fathers (1)	1973		1973, 75, 76, 78		1980, All Adults			(SE)
		Fathers (2)	Adults (3)	Fathers (4)	Mothers (5)	Form X (6)	Form Y (7)	Both (8)	
a. Considerate of others	0.43	0.40	0.36	0.169	0.103	0.232	0.160	0.192	(.093)
b. Interested in how and why things happen	0.51	0.50	0.54	0.311	0.441	0.587	0.389	0.488	(.071)
c. Responsible	0.28	0.42	0.44	0.238	0.261	0.475	0.471	0.473	(.092)
d. Self-control	0.29	0.34	0.26	0.115	0.060	-0.050	0.034	-0.008	(.101)
e. Good sense and sound judgment	0.30	0.51	0.45	0.349	0.382	0.418	0.421	0.419	(.076)
f. Good manners	-0.56	-0.51	-0.48	-0.280	-0.308	-0.471	-0.550	-0.510	(.084)
g. Neat and clean	-0.62	-0.36	-0.47	-0.129	-0.271	-0.555	-0.359	-0.457	(.111)
h. A good student	-0.35	-0.25	-0.18	-0.178	-0.085	-0.272	-0.006	-0.136	(.091)
i. Honest	-0.07	-0.21	-0.13	-0.132	-0.151	-0.201	0.030	-0.092	(.074)
j. Obedient to his parents	-0.34	-0.62	-0.58	-0.397	-0.346	-0.683	-0.604	-0.639	(.084)
k. (Acting) as a boy (girl) should	-0.05	-0.28	-0.34	-0.141	-0.132	-0.266	-0.216	-0.240	(.069)
l. (Trying) hard to succeed	0.07	-0.06	-0.01	0.080	0.029	0.244	-0.133	0.061	(.082)
m. (Getting) along well with other children	0.17	0.09	0.07	-0.006	0.018	-0.064	-0.063	-0.063	(.101)
(n)	(1,499)	(216)	(1,500)	(721)	(1,069)	(487)	(484)	(971)	

Sources and notes: (1) Kohn (1969, Table 4-3), repeated in Kohn (1976, Table 1); correlation of item score with factor score for self-direction/conformity factor. (2) and (3) Kohn (1976, Table 1); factor loading, item on first principal component. (4) and (5) Alwin and Jackson (1982, Tables 2 and 3); factor loading, signs reversed, of item on common factor, modified factor analysis. (6), (7), (8) Association of YG with Kohn item (natural log of estimated uniform association parameter). Standard error in parentheses for estimates in column (8).

NORC in 1964. See column (1) of Table 12. The work was replicated with data from the 1973 General Social Survey (GSS), using the principal component method of factor analysis. In 1973, "fathers" refers to fathers of children aged 6–17, and the questions pertain to children in general, rather than to a specific child (as was the case in the 1964 study). Columns (2) and (3) record the results of the replication (Kohn, 1976). In columns (4) and (5) are shown results of a factor analysis of 1973, 1975, 1976, and 1978 GSS data by Alwin and Jackson (1982a). Their modification of the usual factor analysis procedure was intended to circumvent the ipsative property of Kohn's item scores (the sum of scores on all 13 items is 39 for each respondent). Inasmuch as the conceptual discussion by Kohn (1969) was based on results from the 1964 survey, it is those results that are of greatest relevance in the present context, where we want to see how well YG gets at what Kohn thought his items were getting at. Kohn (1977, p. xxix) cites additional evidence of "factorial invariance" beyond that in our columns (1) through (5).

In the last three columns of Table 12 we look at the problem in quite a different way. We are no longer concerned with the internal structure of responses to Kohn's items, but with the association of each of these items, by itself, with YG. The basic data are counts in the 2 × 5 table, YG by the five categories of a given Kohn item. There are, therefore, 13 distinct analyses of such tables, although their results are not statistically independent, in view of the dependency generated by the design of Kohn's partial ranking procedure and by the use of the same respondents in each analysis. The measure of association is the natural logarithm of the estimated uniform association parameter for the 2 × 5 table. (This measure, of course, is not comparable as to metric with the correlations in the first five columns; the log of the association parameter has no upper or lower limit.) We looked for differences between data from Form X, where questions were worded in almost the same way as in Kohn's original work, and Form Y, where "a child" replaced "he" in the wording of each item. Only for the item Succeed is there an indication that the association is affected by form. But we cannot actually reject (at the 0.05 level) the hypothesis that this item is independent of YG on both forms. Hence, for this item as well as all others, we confine attention to the result reported in column (8).

For all items but one the uniform association model fits the data acceptably well (at the 0.05 level). For 8 of the 13 items the estimate of the uniform association parameter differs significantly from zero; see estimated standard errors in parentheses in column (8), obtained in fitting the model with program FREQ of Haberman (1979, Appendix). The other minor exception to the favorable results on fit of the model pertains to the Kohn item Neat and Clean, for which $L^2 = 16.57$, d.f. = 7, for the model fitting marginals of that item by form, YG by form, and one uniform association parameter common to the two forms. Allowing that parameter to differ by form yields $L^2 = 14.51$, d.f. = 6, again an unsatisfactory fit. But we note that for the last two categories of this item (4—second or third least important, 5—the one least important) there is no association with YG. Combining these two categories, we find $L^2 = 8.35$, d.f. $= 5$, $0.1 < P < 0.2$.

The appraisal of these results is unambiguous. The item-to-YG associations in column (8) parallel the response structure of Kohn's 1964 data about as well as any of the replications of the 1964 material. The Spearman rank correlation between columns (1) and (8) is 0.88. Rank correlations betweeen columns (1) and the four succeeding columns are 0.90, 0.91, 0.85, and 0.90, respectively. Moreover, column (8) correlates with them to the extent of 0.97, 0.98, 0.94, and 0.97. Four of Kohn's items, Interested, Responsible, Good Sense, and Considerate, have significant positive associations with the *think* response to YG. Kohn found only one other item, Self-control, with a positive factor loading over 0.2. Another four Kohn items, Obedient, Good Manners, Neat and Clean, and Acts Like a Boy (Girl), have significant negative associations with *think* (i.e., positive associations with *do right*). In the 1964 data, all these have negative factor loadings, although the loading is small in absolute value for Acts Like a Boy (Girl). Kohn's results suggest a substantial negative relationship between self-direction and Good Student. The sign of the association in column (8) is right, although it does not attain significance at the 0.05 level.

There are, no doubt, nuances of Kohn's concept and of his indicators of self-direction/conformity that are beyond our grasp. But it seems clear that YG does very well as a single, dichotomous indicator of that concept. In any event, the results in column (8) enrich the earlier discussion of this issue based on Table 1 of the text.

REFERENCES

Alwin, D.F. and Jackson, D.J. (1982a). The statistical analysis of Kohn's measures of parental values, in K.G. Jöreskog and H. Wold (eds.), *Systems Under Indirect Observation*, Part I. Amsterdam: North-Holland, pp. 197–223.

Alwin, D.F. and Jackson, D.J. (1982b). Adult values for children: An application of factor analysis to ranked preference data, in R.M.

Hauser, D. Mechanic, A.O. Haller, and T.S. Hauser (eds.), *Social Structure and Behavior: Papers in Honor of William H. Sewell.* New York: Academic Press, pp. 311–329.

Blau, P.M. and Duncan, O.D. (1967). *The American Occupational Structure.* New York: Wiley.

Converse, P.E. (1976). *The Dynamics of Party Support: Cohort Analyzing Party Identification.* Beverly Hills, Calif.: Sage.

Duncan, B. (1968). Trends in output and distribution of schooling, in E.B. Sheldon and W.E. Moore (eds.), *Indicators of Social Change.* New York: Russell Sage Foundation.

Duncan, B. and Duncan, O.D. (1978). *Sex Typing and Social Roles.* New York: Academic Press.

Duncan, O.D. (1975). Measuring social change via replication of surveys, in K.C. Land and S. Spilerman (eds.), *Social Indicator Models.* New York: Russell Sage Foundation.

Duncan, O.D. (1979a). How destination depends on origin in the occupational mobility table. *American Journal of Sociology* **84**, 793–803.

Duncan, O.D. (1979b). Constrained parameters in a model for categorical data. *Sociological Methods and Research* **8**, 57–68.

Duncan, O.D., Schuman, H., and Duncan, B. (1973). *Social Change in a Metropolitan Community.* New York: Russell Sage Foundation.

Fienberg, S.E. (1980). *The Analysis of Cross-Classified Categorical Data.* (2nd edition.) Cambridge, Mass.: MIT Press.

Fienberg, S.E. and Mason, W.M. (1978). Identification and estimation of age-period-cohort models in the analysis of discrete archival data, in K.F. Schuessler (ed.), *Sociological Methodology 1979.* San Francisco: Jossey-Bass, pp. 1–67.

Glenn, N.D. (1977). *Cohort Analysis.* Beverly Hills, Calif.: Sage.

Goodman, L.A. (1978). *Analyzing Qualitative/Categorical Data.* Cambridge, Mass.: Abt Books.

Goodman, L.A. (1979). Simple models for the analysis of association in cross-classifications having ordered categories. *Journal of the American Statistical Association* **74**, 537–552.

Haberman, S.J. (1974). Log-linear models for frequency tables with ordered classifications. *Biometrics* **30**, 589–600.

Haberman, S.J. (1979). *Analysis of Qualitative Data, Vol. 2, New Developments.* New York: Academic Press.

Kohn M.L. (1969). *Class and Conformity.* Homewood, Ill.: Dorsey Press. (2nd edition, Chicago: University of Chicago Press, 1977.)

Kohn, M.L. (1976). Social class and parental values: Another confirmation of the relationship. *American Sociological Review* **41**, 538–545.

Lipset, S.M. (1960). *Political Man.* Garden City, N.Y.: Doubleday.

NORC (National Opinion Research Center) (1980). *General Social Surveys: 1972–1980: Cumulative Codebook.* Storrs, Conn.: Roper Public Opinion Research Center.

Plackett, R.L. (1974). *The Analysis of Categorical Data.* New York: Hafner Press.

Sorokin, P.A. (1947). *Society, Culture, and Personality.* New York: Harper.

Yorburg, B. (1974). *Sexual Identity: Sex Roles and Social Change.* New York: Wiley.

10. SIMULTANEOUS ANALYSIS OF LONGITUDINAL DATA FROM SEVERAL COHORTS*

Karl G. Jöreskog

Dag Sörbom

1. INTRODUCTION

A number of different research designs for data collection, analysis, and interpretation has been proposed for the study of developmental change (see e.g., Baltes, 1968; Schaie, 1965, 1977; Schaie and Baltes, 1975). In Schaie's (1965) general developmental model, the individual's psychological response under study may be characterized by the cohort (C) to which the individual belongs, the period or time of measurement (T), and the age (A) of the individual at the time of measurement. Much of the discussion in the developmental change literature is focussed on separately identifying the effects of age, time, and cohort on the response. Because $A = T - C$ for all observations these effects will necessarily be confounded in all studies which employ linear models of the response function. Fienberg and Mason (1978; 1985, in this volume) discuss this problem in the case of categorical response and show that, with a response function more general than the linear, it is possible, under certain restrictions, to separately identify and estimate all three effects.

In this chapter we examine continuous response variables and focus attention on longitudinal sequences and one of Schaie's research designs,

* This research was supported by the Bank of Sweden Tercentenary Foundation under project *Methodology of Evaluation Research*, Karl G. Jöreskog, project director.

† Both authors are affiliated with the Department of Statistics, University of Uppsala, Uppsala, Sweden.

namely the cross-sequential one. The cross-sequential design involves a cohort × occasions data set based on independent samples, drawn from several successive cohorts. These samples are then measured longitudinally over a number of time periods.

As pointed out by several writers, notably Bock (1979) and Rogosa (1979), a basic distinction among designs, from a statistical point of view, depends on whether the same people or different people are measured at different occasions and whether or not measurement scales are commensurate at each time point. If the people are different or if the measures are different at different occasions the design is not a true longitudinal design (Bock, 1979). Longitudinal data often require complex multivariate statistical models and techniques for their analysis. Data from independent samples (even from the same cohort) at different occasions are considerably easier to analyze and may often be analyzed by standard statistical techniques such as ANOVA and MANOVA.

Most behavioral or social scientists work with concepts and constructs that are not directly measurable. Although such hypothetical concepts or constructs or, as we shall call them, latent variables cannot be directly measured, a number of variables can be used to measure various aspects of these latent variables more or less accurately. The observed variables may be regarded as indicators of the latent variables. Each indicator has a relationship with the latent variable but one indicator alone may be a poor measure of the latent variable. By using several indicators of a latent variable we get a better measurement of it.

One reason for using latent variable models in behavioral and social science applications is that they explicitly incorporate the concept of measurement error (observational error) in the observed variables. Most measurements used in the behavioral, social, and economic sciences contain sizeable errors which, if not taken into account, may bias resulting conclusions. Measurement errors occur because of imperfection in the various measurement instruments (tests, questionnaires, scales, etc.) used to measure such concepts as people's behavior, attitudes, feelings, and motivations. Even if one could construct valid measurements of these concepts it would still be impossible to obtain perfectly reliable measurements. Special care must be taken to obtain measurements that really measure the latent variables that one is interested in measuring.

In this paper we assume that a single latent variable is measured at each occasion. The limitation to a single variable is only for the purpose of keeping the exposition clear and the model within a reasonable level of complexity. The *measurement model*, a term to be defined subsequently, for this single latent variable has location and scale parameters that are assumed to be invariant over time as well as over cohorts. This assumption enables us to use the same scale in examining changes in the latent variable over time and differences in the latent variable between cohorts. To explain the values of the latent variable we build a *structural model* which contains a mean structure and a covariance structure. The mean structure is interpreted in terms of cohort (or age) effects and time effects. The covariance structure is an autoregressive model which explains the latent variable at time t by the value of the latent variable at time $t - 1$ and by other observed explanatory variables.

The LISREL VI computer program of Jöreskog and Sörbom (1984) is used to estimate all the models discussed in this chapter. The program also provides a χ^2-measure of goodness of fit of the model. As explained elsewhere (Jöreskog, 1978b, p. 448) the values of χ^2 must be interpreted very cautiously because of the sensitivity of χ^2 to such basic assumptions as linearity, additivity, multinormality, independence of observations and homoscedasticity of error terms. Deviations from these assumptions tend to increase the value of χ^2. Often one can only use differences in χ^2-values between alternative models to decide which of a number of alternative models fits the data best. If there is evidence to reject a given model due to poor fit to the data, the program provides modification indices to suggest which part of the model is causing the poor fit. If, on the other hand, the model fits the data well, the standard errors of the estimated parameters can be used to eliminate parameters which are insignificant, thereby simpifying the model further.

2. GENERAL MODELS

Suppose we have observations on a number of individuals over T periods of time from each of G cohorts. At each occasion we have measurements on the same p variables. Let $y^{(g)}_{\alpha it}$ be the observed score of individual α from cohort g on variables i at time period t, where $\alpha = 1,2,...,N_g$, $i = 1,2,...,p$, $t = 1,2,...,T$ and $g = 1,2,...,G$. Initially, we consider a single cohort and omit the superscript g. For an arbitrary randomly selected individual α we omit the index α and write his scores on the p variables at occasion t as a random vector

$$\mathbf{y}_t = (y_{1t}, y_{2t}, ..., y_{pt})'.$$

The vector $\mathbf{y}_t$ may represent scores on a number of psychological variables (e.g., mental abilities or personality characteristics), educational variables (e.g., aptitude or achievement measures) or sociological variables (e.g., attitude or aspiration scales). We assume that the p variables are fallible measures of a single latent variable denoted by η_t but one can also deal with the case of several latent variables and the case when each observed variable is an errorfree measure (see Jöreskog and Sörbom, 1976, 1977; Jöreskog, 1978a, 1979).

2.1. Measurement Model

The measurement model specifies how the p response variables $\mathbf{y}_t$ are used to measure the latent variable at occasion t. The measurement model can be used to study measurement properties such as validity and reliability of the response variables and how these vary over time and over cohorts. The measurement model is of the form

$$\mathbf{y}_t = \nu + \lambda\eta_t + \epsilon_t, \tag{1}$$

where ν is a vector of location parameters representing the general level of the response variables, λ is a vector of scale parameters (factor loadings), and ϵ_t is a vector of random error terms (measurement errors). The vectors ν and λ are regarded as properties of the measures being used and are therefore assumed to be invariant over time as well as over cohorts.

It is assumed that ϵ_t is uncorrelated with η_t and that $E(\epsilon_t) = \mathbf{0}$ for every cohort. Furthermore, it is assumed that ϵ_{is} and ϵ_{jt} are uncorrelated for $i \neq j$, for all s and t, where ϵ_{is} and ϵ_{jt} are the ith element and jth element of ϵ_s and ϵ_t, respectively. These assumptions are made to allow for specific factors in each response variable that do not contribute to correlations between the observed variables within occasions but do affect the correlations between the same variable over different occasions. It has been demonstrated elsewhere (Jöreskog, 1979; Jöreskog and Sörbom, 1976, 1977) that such correlations are usually present in empirical longitudinal data.

Both the origin and the unit of measurement of η_t are arbitrary but η_t may be defined on a scale which is common to all occasions and all cohorts. To do so, one can fix the origin so that $E(\eta_1) = 0$ for *one* cohort and the unit of measurement so that one element of λ is one. Then the means and variances of η_t are identified for all t and all cohorts.

Combining the response variables over all occasions into one vector and writing the measurement models for all occasions simultaneously, we have, as illustrated with $T = 4$,

$$
\begin{pmatrix} y_1 \\ y_2 \\ y_3 \\ y_4 \end{pmatrix} = \begin{pmatrix} \nu \\ \nu \\ \nu \\ \nu \end{pmatrix} + \begin{bmatrix} \lambda & 0 & 0 & 0 \\ 0 & \lambda & 0 & 0 \\ 0 & 0 & \lambda & 0 \\ 0 & 0 & 0 & \lambda \end{bmatrix} \begin{pmatrix} \eta_1 \\ \eta_2 \\ \eta_3 \\ \eta_4 \end{pmatrix} + \begin{pmatrix} \epsilon_1 \\ \epsilon_2 \\ \epsilon_3 \\ \epsilon_4 \end{pmatrix} \tag{2}
$$

or

$$
\mathbf{y} = (\mathbf{1} \otimes \nu) + (\mathbf{I} \otimes \lambda)\eta + \epsilon , \tag{3}
$$

where $\mathbf{1}$ is a $T \times 1$ column vector of ones and $\mathbf{I}$ is a $T \times T$ identity matrix and $\otimes$ denotes the Kronecker product. In (3), $\mathbf{y}$ and ϵ are vectors of order pT whereas η is a vector of order T.

Let $\kappa = E(\eta)$ and let $\Phi(T \times T)$ and $\theta(pT \times pT)$ be the covariance matrices of η and ϵ, respectively. Then the mean vector $\mu = E(\mathbf{y})$ of all observed response variables is

$$
\mu^{(g)} = (\mathbf{1} \otimes \nu) + (\mathbf{I} \otimes \lambda)\kappa^{(g)} \tag{4}
$$

and the covariance matrix $\Sigma = \text{Cov}(\mathbf{y})$ is

$$
\Sigma^{(g)} = (\mathbf{I} \otimes \lambda)\Phi^{(g)}(\mathbf{I} \otimes \lambda)' + \theta^{(g)} . \tag{5}
$$

In (4) and (5) we have included the superscript g on κ and Φ to indicate that the mean vector and covariance matrix of η, and therefore also the mean vector and covariance matrix of $\mathbf{y}$, in general, will be different for different cohorts. This may in principle hold also for the θ but it may be of interest to see to what extent θ is invariant over cohorts. In fact, it is possible to test the hypothesis of invariant θ's. In view of the assumptions made about the ϵ-terms, θ is of the form

$$\theta \;=\; \begin{bmatrix} \theta_{11} & & & \\ \theta_{21} & \theta_{22} & & \\ \theta_{31} & \theta_{32} & \theta_{33} & \\ \theta_{41} & \theta_{42} & \theta_{43} & \theta_{44} \end{bmatrix},$$

where all θ_{ij} are diagonal matrices of order $p \times p$.

2.2. Structural Model

The structural model is used to describe how the latent variable η_t depends on other variables whose effects are to be estimated and studied. The structural model is

$$\eta_t = \alpha_t + \beta_t \eta_{t-1} + \gamma_t' \mathbf{x}_t + \zeta_t, \tag{6}$$

where $\mathbf{x}_t$ is a vector of explanatory variables. Explanatory variables may be background variables such as sex, education, experience and income, or measures of environmental effects, or effects associated with the time of measurement. Some or all of these variables may be constant over time. However, their effects γ_t are in general expected to depend on time. We assume that the explanatory variables $\mathbf{x}_t$ are exactly measured although the case of fallible variables can also be handled (Jöreskog, 1979; Jöreskog and Sörbom, 1977). For convenience, we assume that the variables $\mathbf{x}_t$ are measured in deviations from the cohort means, so that $E(\mathbf{x}_t) = 0$ for all cohorts. The coefficients α_t, β_t and γ_t may in general depend on the cohort being measured. The coefficients α_t represent effects of cohort and time, each confounded by age. The α_t-coefficients reflect changes in level (means) over time. The β_t-coefficient is usually called a stability coefficient, because it reflects the extent to which η_t can be predicted from η_{t-1}, high values of β_t being associated with high stability of η_t. The last term ζ_t in (6) is a random disturbance term representing the combined effects of all variables influencing η_t and not included in $\mathbf{x}_t$. It is assumed that ζ_t is uncorrelated with $\mathbf{x}_t$ and η_{t-1} and that $E(\zeta_t) = 0$ for all t and all cohorts.

Equation (6), which is defined for $t = 2,3,...,T$, specifies a first order autoregressive structure for η_t but higher order autoregression may also be used. It is convenient to define η_1 as

$$\eta_1 = \kappa_1 + \gamma_1{}'\mathbf{x}_1 + \zeta_1 \tag{7}$$

with $E(\eta_1) = \kappa_1$. Then (6) defines a recursive sequence for the means $\kappa_t = E(\eta_t)$, $t = 2,3,...,T$,

$$\kappa_t = \alpha_t + \beta_t \kappa_{t-1} . \tag{8}$$

In general, all three quantities κ_t, α_t and β_t may depend on the cohort.

Equation (7) and equation (6) for $t = 2,3,...,T$ may be combined into a single matrix equation, which, in the case of $T = 4$, will be

$$\begin{bmatrix} 1 & 0 & 0 & 0 \\ -\beta_2 & 1 & 0 & 0 \\ 0 & -\beta_3 & 1 & 0 \\ 0 & 0 & -\beta_4 & 1 \end{bmatrix} \begin{bmatrix} \eta_1 \\ \eta_2 \\ \eta_3 \\ \eta_4 \end{bmatrix} = \begin{bmatrix} a_1 \\ a_2 \\ a_3 \\ a_4 \end{bmatrix} + \begin{bmatrix} \gamma_1' & 0' & 0' & 0' \\ 0' & \gamma_2' & 0' & 0' \\ 0' & 0' & \gamma_3' & 0' \\ 0' & 0' & 0' & \gamma_4' \end{bmatrix} \begin{bmatrix} \mathbf{x}_1 \\ \mathbf{x}_2 \\ \mathbf{x}_3 \\ \mathbf{x}_4 \end{bmatrix} + \begin{bmatrix} \zeta_1 \\ \zeta_2 \\ \zeta_3 \\ \zeta_4 \end{bmatrix} ,$$

where $\alpha_1 = \kappa_1$, or

$$\mathbf{B}\eta = \alpha + \Gamma\mathbf{x} + \zeta . \tag{9}$$

Taking the expectation of (9) and premultiplying by $\mathbf{B}^{-1}$ gives the mean vector κ of η as

$$\kappa = \mathbf{B}^{-1}\alpha . \tag{10}$$

Similarly, the covariance matrix Φ of η can be obtained from (9) after premultiplication by $\mathbf{B}^{-1}$. This gives

$$\Phi = \mathbf{B}^{-1}\Gamma\Sigma_{xx}\Gamma'\mathbf{B}'^{-1} + \mathbf{B}^{-1}\Psi\mathbf{B}'^{-1} , \tag{11}$$

where Σ_{xx} is the covariance matrix of $\mathbf{x}$ and Ψ is the covariance matrix of ζ. The latter is assumed to be diagonal.

It can be shown that all parameters that we have introduced are identified by means of the mean vector μ of $\mathbf{y}$ and the variances and covariances of all the observed y- and x-variables. The proof of this is rather complicated, however, and will be omitted here.

3. STRATEGY OF ANALYSIS

In the previous section we described a general model for the analysis of longitudinal data from several cohorts. The general model contains a large number of submodels as special cases, any one of which may be suitable for the particular data at hand. It is important to have a strategy for analyzing the data that leads to the most suitable model in the sense that it contains as few parameters as possible while at the same time fitting the data well and giving meaningful results. How this can be done will be discussed and illustrated in this section.

Table 1. Short-Term Longitudinal Sequences Design
for the Study of Adolescent Development

Cohort			Age			
	13	14	15	16	17	18
1959	1972					
1958	1971	1972				
1957	1970	1971	1972			
1956		1970	1971	1972		
1955			1970	1971	1972	
1954				1970	1971	1972
1953					1970	1971
1952						1970

The strategy of analysis will be discussed in general terms but it will also be illustrated using some sequential longitudinal data gathered and previously analyzed by Nesselroade and Baltes (1974) in a study of adolescent development.[1] They analyzed their data by means of a cross-

---

[1] We are grateful to Professors Nesselroade and Baltes for making these data available to us.

sequential design, as shown in Table 1. Here we use only the core longitudinal samples enclosed in the broken parallelogram, i.e., the cohorts 1954, 1955, 1956, and 1957, which will be labeled cohorts 4, 3, 2, and 1, respectively. For these data the number of cohorts $G = 4$ and the number of time periods $T = 3$. The four sample sizes are $N_1 = 214$, $N_2 = 211$, $N_3 = 212$ and $N_4 = 141$. The measurements used by Nesselroade and Baltes were 40 measures of primary mental abilities and personality characteristics. However, for illustrative purposes, we shall only use three of the primary mental ability tests, namely Number facility, Letter series, and Word grouping from the Primary Mental Abilities test (Thurstone and Thurstone, 1962). Thus $p = 3$ in our illustative examples.

3.1. Testing the Measurement Model

The starting point for the analysis is a test of the measurement model (3) without assuming any structure on η, i.e., by letting Φ in (5) be a free covariance matrix. To test the measurement model in a single cohort one fixes the first element of κ to zero and the first element of λ to one. The test of the measurement model is essentially a test of the hypothesis that ν and λ are invariant over time so that η is measured on the same scale at all occasions. Should this hypothesis be rejected one must either let ν or λ vary over time or introduce more latent variables η. Note that the hypothesis also includes a correlation structure for the error terms ϵ such that these are correlated over time for the same variables but uncorrelated for different variables. This specification is equivalent to the inclusion of correlated test-specific factors, in addition to the measurement error, one for each observed variable.

For an analysis of the data of cohort 1 (1957) the obtained $\chi^2 = 39.5$ with 23 degrees of freedom indicates a reasonable fit. In principle one could proceed to test the measurement model for the other cohorts also. However, this would yield different vectors ν and λ for different cohorts and we are more interested in the hypothesis that the measurement model is invariant over all cohorts as well as over all occasions. To test the hypothesis of a cohort invariant measurement model one must do a simultaneous analysis of the data, constraining ν and λ to be the same in all cohorts. In this analysis all the means of η in all cohorts can be estimated except for a single additive constant. It may be chosen, for example, such that the first element of κ is zero for the first cohort. The test gives $\chi^2 = 198.6$ with 104 degrees of freedom. Although the outcome is significant at conventional levels of significance the residuals are generally small and in view of the earlier remark about the sensitivity of χ^2 the fit must be regarded as a reasonably good one.[2] We shall therefore consider the measurement model to be invariant over occasions as well as over cohorts. The conclusion is that changes in the latent variable η over time can be studied on the same scale for all cohorts. The estimated means of the latent variables are given in Table 2 and the profile of these means for the different cohorts is shown in Figure 1.

Table 2. Estimated Mean Values Under Measurement Model

| | Time of Measurement | | |
Cohort	1970	1971	1972
1957	0.000	2.253	3.938
1956	1.040	3.387	4.776
1955	2.339	4.332	5.518
1954	2.825	4.684	5.898

3.2. Testing the Structural Model

Once a reasonable measurement model has been established one can proceed to investigate the structural model (6). In doing so one assumes that the measurement model holds and is invariant over occasions and cohorts and imposes additional structure on the mean vector κ and covariance matrix Φ of η.

If the vector α in (9) is unconstrained and free to vary over cohorts,

---

[2] For these data there is a slight skewness in the variables and the independence of observations may be questionable.

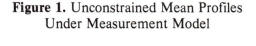

Figure 1. Unconstrained Mean Profiles
Under Measurement Model

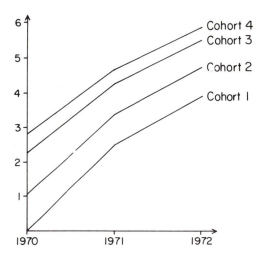

the structure on the means does not impose any restrictions. With $\alpha_1 = 0$ for cohort 1 there will be a one-to-one correspondence between all the α's and all the κ's. However, when $T \geq 3$, the hypothesis of first order autoregression in (6) imposes restrictions on the covariance matrix Φ. A reasonable starting point for the investigation of the structural model is to test whether these restrictions hold. For our illustrative data we do not use any explanatory variables $\mathbf{x}$. A test of the hypothesis of autoregression in cohort 1 gives an overall $\chi^2 = 39.7$ with 24 degrees of freedom. This should be compared with the corresponding values for the measurement model reported earlier: $\chi^2 = 39.5$ with 23 degrees of freedom. Hence with a $\chi^2 = 39.7 - 39.5 = 0.2$ with 1 degree of freedom the hypothesis of first order autoregression cannot be rejected. The estimates of the stability coefficients are $\hat{\beta}_2 = 1.09$ and $\hat{\beta}_3 = 0.93$ with standard errors 0.09 and 0.06, respectively. It is clear that these are not significantly different from one. An analysis with $\beta_2 = \beta_3 = 1$ gives an overall $\chi^2 = 41.7$ with 26 degrees of freedom. A test of the hypothesis gives $\chi^2 = 2.0$ with 2 degrees of freedom. Hence this hypothesis cannot be rejected.

In general, each of the hypotheses

$$H_\beta: \beta_2 = \beta_3 = \ldots = \beta_T = \beta \; ,$$

say, and

$$H_\alpha : \alpha_2 = \alpha_3 = \ldots = \alpha_T = \alpha \, ,$$

say, may be of interest. If H_β holds, then

$$\kappa_t = \beta^{t-1}\kappa + \beta^{t-2}\alpha_2 + \beta^{t-3}\alpha_3 + \ldots + \beta\alpha_{t-1} + \alpha_t, \qquad (12)$$

where $\kappa = \kappa_1$. In analyzing a single cohort, κ is not identified separately from the α's but can be assigned an arbitrary value, for example, zero. However, when we analyze several cohorts simultaneously, as we will do later, all the κ's can be identified except for an additive constant, which may be chosen so that $\kappa = 0$ in one cohort. If H_α holds also, then

$$\kappa_t = \beta^{t-1}\kappa + \alpha\frac{\beta^{t-1} - 1}{\beta - 1} \, , \beta \neq 1 \, . \qquad (13)$$

If, in addition, $\beta = 1$, (12) and (13) becomes

$$\kappa_t = \kappa + \sum_{i=2}^{t} \alpha_i \qquad (14)$$

and

$$\kappa_t = \kappa + (t - 1)\alpha \, . \qquad (15)$$

Hypothesis H_β has implications also for the covariance structure of η. Let $\phi_t = \mathrm{Var}(\eta_t)$ and $\psi_t = \mathrm{Var}(\zeta_t)$, $t = 1,2,\ldots,T$, with ψ_1 defined as ϕ_1. There is a one-to-one correspondence between $(\phi_2,\phi_3,\ldots,\phi_T)$ and $(\psi_2,\psi_3,\ldots,\psi_T)$ for given $\phi_1 = \psi_1$ and $\beta_2,\beta_3,\ldots,\beta_T$, and

$$\phi_t = \beta_t^2\phi_{t-1} + \psi_t \, , t = 2,3,\ldots,T \, . \qquad (16)$$

The covariance matrix of η, illustrated here for $T = 4$, is

$$\phi = \begin{bmatrix} \phi_1 & & & \\ \beta_2\phi_1 & \phi_2 & & \\ \beta_2\beta_3\phi_1 & \beta_3\phi_2 & \phi_3 & \\ \beta_2\beta_3\beta_4\phi_1 & \beta_3\beta_4\phi_2 & \beta_4\phi_3 & \phi_4 \end{bmatrix} . \qquad (17)$$

Such a covariance structure is called a Markov simplex (Jöreskog, 1970). The corresponding correlation matrix is

$$
\mathbf{P} = \begin{bmatrix} 1 & & & \\ \rho_2 & 1 & & \\ \rho_2\rho_3 & \rho_3 & 1 & \\ \rho_2\rho_3\rho_4 & \rho_3\rho_4 & \rho_4 & 1 \end{bmatrix},
\tag{18}
$$

where $\rho_t = \beta_t(\phi_{t-1}/\phi_t)^{1/2}$, $t = 2,3,...,T$. The matrix ϕ has $2T - 1$ elements. Under H_β there will be just $T + 1$ parameters. If $\beta = 1$ under H_β the covariance structure is a Wiener simplex (Jöreskog, 1970), i.e.,

$$
\phi = \begin{bmatrix} \phi_1 & & & \\ \phi_1 & \phi_2 & & \\ \phi_1 & \phi_2 & \phi_3 & \\ \phi_1 & \phi_2 & \phi_3 & \phi_4 \end{bmatrix},
\tag{19}
$$

with T parameters. Since, in this case,

$$
\phi_t = \psi_1 + \psi_2 + ... + \psi_t,
$$

the variances are non-decreasing over time. If H_β holds with $\beta \neq 1$ and in addition

$$
H_\phi: \phi_1 = \phi_2 = ... = \phi_T
$$

holds, the covariance structure is a stationary Markov simplex with two parameters, i.e., the variances of η_t are stationary. The means of η_t can still vary over time as in (13).

Returning to our illustrative data, after having established that H_β holds with $\beta = 1$, we next test the hypothesis H_α, i.e., $\alpha_2 = \alpha_3$. The test gives $\chi^2 = 5.5$ with 1 degree of freedom. This is significant at the 5% level but not at the 1% level. Figure 1 shows that α_3 is smaller than α_2 in all cohorts. It seems safer to reject the hypothesis than to accept it. We therefore take the means to be described by (14) and the covariance structure by (19). Finally we test the hypothesis H_ϕ, i.e., $\phi_1 = \phi_2 = \phi_3$. This gives $\chi^2 = 14.2$ with 2 degrees of freedom and the hypothesis is rejected. The variance of η_t is increasing over time.

Table 3. Mean Values According to Final Wiener Model

| | Time of Measurement | | |
Cohort	1970	1971	1972
1957	0	α_2	$\alpha_2 + \alpha_3$
1956	$\kappa^{(2)}$	$\kappa^{(2)} + \alpha_2$	$\kappa^{(2)} + \alpha_2 + \alpha_3$
1955	$\kappa^{(3)}$	$\kappa^{(3)} + \alpha_2$	$\kappa^{(3)} + \alpha_2 + \alpha_3$
1954	$\kappa^{(4)}$	$\kappa^{(4)} + \alpha_2$	$\kappa^{(4)} + \alpha_2 + \alpha_3$

We now analyze all the cohorts simultaneously. We assume that H_β holds with $\beta = 1$ in all cohorts and test the hypotheses that α_2 and α_3 are the same for all cohorts. All the means are then generated by five parameters namely α_2, α_3, $\kappa^{(2)}$, $\kappa^{(3)}$ and $\kappa^{(4)}$, remembering that $\kappa^{(1)} = 0$. According to this model the means of η_t will be as given in Table 3. The overall χ^2 for this model is $\chi^2 = 236.4$ with 122 degrees of freedom. The estimates of the mean parameters, with standard errors in parenthesis, are

$$\hat{\alpha}_2 = 2.10 \ (0.09) \ , \ \hat{\alpha}_3 = 1.35 \ (0.08),$$

$$\hat{\kappa}^{(2)} = 1.04 \ (0.34) \ , \ \hat{\kappa}^{(3)} = 2.13 \ (0.33) \ , \ \hat{\kappa}^{(4)} = 2.55 \ (0.40) \ .$$

The α's can be interpreted as effects of the time of measurement. The effect of a change in time of measurement from 1970 to 1971 is $\hat{\alpha}_2 = 2.10$ and the corresponding effect from 1971 to 1972 is $\hat{\alpha}_3 = 1.35$, a somewhat smaller effect. The κ's can be interpreted as cohort effects or age effects. The effect of cohort g (1957 − g) relative to cohort 1 (1957) is $\hat{\kappa}^{(g)}$, $g = 2, 3, 4$. Since the cohorts used in the study are from successive years it would be of interest to see to what extent also the effects $\kappa^{(g)}$ are equidistant, i.e., to test the hypothesis

$$H_\delta: \delta^{(2)} = \delta^{(3)} = ... \delta^{(G)} = \delta ,$$

say, where

$$\delta^{(g)} = \kappa^{(g)} - \kappa^{(g-1)} , g = 2, 3, 4 .$$

This cannot be done in LISREL but one can estimate the standard errors of $\hat{\delta}^{(g)}$. The estimates of $\delta^{(g)}$ and their standard errors are

$$\delta^{(2)} = 1.04 \ (0.34) , \delta^{(3)} = 1.09 \ (0.36) , \delta^{(4)} = 0.42 \ (0.42)$$

The evidence concerning H_δ obtained from these estimates is somewhat ambiguous. It is clear that $\delta^{(2)} = \delta^{(3)}$ but $\delta^{(4)}$ is probably smaller and perhaps zero, i.e., there is a constant increase from cohort 1 to cohort 2 and from cohort 2 to cohort 3, but a smaller increase from cohort 3 to cohort 4. However, we shall retain the model with five parameters for the means. The estimates of the twelve means under this model are given in Table 4 (compare Table 2).

The LISREL estimates of the location ν and scale λ parameters for the observed variables in the final structural model are

$$\hat{\nu} = \begin{vmatrix} 9.95 & (0.24) \\ 7.95 & (0.20) \\ 13.57 & (0.20) \end{vmatrix}, \quad \hat{\lambda} = \begin{vmatrix} 1.00 & \\ 0.86 & (0.03) \\ 0.86 & (0.03) \end{vmatrix} .$$

The element $\lambda_1 = 1.00$ is specified a priori to fix the unit of measurement of η.

Table 4. Estimated Mean Values Under Final Wiener Model

	Time of Measurement		
Cohort	1970	1971	1972
1957	0.000	2.096	3.450
1956	1.035	3.131	4.485
1955	2.126	4.222	5.576
1954	2.546	4.642	5.996

Table 5. LISREL Estimates of ϕ_T, $t = 1, 2, 3$ for Final Model

	Time of Measurement		
Cohort	1970	1971	1972
1957	7.30	8.32	9.46
1956	11.40	13.10	13.62
1955	10.50	10.99	12.02
1954	13.42	13.71	14.69

Other parameters of the final structural model are given in Table 5 which gives the LISREL estimates of the variances ϕ_t, $t = 2,3,...,T$ for each cohort. It is seen that the variance of η_t is strictly increasing in each cohort. There is also a clear increasing trend over cohorts for each time of measurement. With the exception of cohort 3 (1955) the variances are increasing over cohorts. Thus, both the means and variances of this measure of mental ability are increasing with age. Older age groups are more heterogenous in mental ability than younger age groups.

4. SUMMARY AND DISCUSSION

In this paper we have developed a general model for the description of developmental change in data obtained from several cohorts. The model has the following features:

1. It is formulated in terms of latent variables or hypothetical construct variables.

2. It takes into account measurement errors in the observed variables.

3. It takes proper account of the longitudinal nature of the data, i.e., the fact that observations are dependent rather than independent over time.

4. It consists of two parts: (a) the measurement model describing the measurement properties of the variables used; and (b) the structural model describing change in level and structure of the latent variables.

The model is general and flexible and includes many submodels as special cases. A strategy for choosing a suitable model among all possible submodels was discussed and illustrated above. All submodels can be estimated by means of the LISREL VI computer program which gives standard errors of all estimated parameters. If the model does not fit the data the program also gives information about which part or assumption of the model is most likely causing the poor fit.

The model, its estimation and testing and the strategy of data analysis were illustrated using data on adolescent mental ability development reported by Nesselroade and Baltes (1974). These data are from four cohort samples, each measured at three occasions. Our analysis shows that the measurement for the mental ability variables can be taken to be invariant over cohorts and occasions, thereby providing a single scale for the study of changes over time of latent variable (mental ability) and differences between cohorts. Our analysis further shows that there are significant effects of cohort and time but no significant cohort by time interaction effect. The twelve means in the cohort by occasion design can be described by five parameters, three describing cohort differences and two describing differential change over time.

The covariance structure of the latent variables was studied also. The analyses revealed that changes in the latent variable over time are best described by a first order autoregressive process: only the immediately preceding value of the latent variable is needed to determine the current value of the latent variable. However, the stability coefficients turn out to be not only stationary over time but in fact equal to one in all cohorts. As a consequence of this, the illustrative data are best described by a Wiener process in which a random component is added to the current value of the latent variable at each occasion. Therefore the variance of the latent variable is increasing over time, i.e., latent ability tends to be more heterogenous as age increases. Thus, based on these data, both means and variances of latent ability increase over time for all cohorts.

REFERENCES

Baltes, P.B. (1968). Longitudinal and cross-sectional sequences in the study of age and generation effects. *Human Development* **11**, 145–171.

Bock, R.D. (1975). *Multivariate Statistical Methods in Behavioral Research.* New York: McGraw-Hill.

Bock, R.D. (1979). Univariate and multivariate analysis of variance of time-structured data, in J.R. Nesselroade and P.B. Baltes (eds.), *Longitudinal Research in the Study of Behavior and Development.* New York: Academic Press.

Fienberg, S.E. and Mason, W.M. (1978). Identification and estimation of age-period-cohort models in the analysis of discrete archival data, in K. Schuessler (ed.), *Sociological Methodology 1979.* San Francisco: Jossey-Bass, pp. 1–67.

Fienberg, S.E. and Mason, W.M. (1985). Specification and implementation of age, period and cohort models. This volume.

Jöreskog, K.G. (1970). Estimation and testing of simplex models. *British Journal of Mathematical and Statistical Psychology* **23**, 121–145.

Jöreskog, K.G. (1978a). An econometric model for multivariate panel data. *Annales de l'INSEE* **30–31**, 355–366.

Jöreskog, K.G. (1978b). Structural analysis of covariance and correlation matrices. *Psychometrika* **43**, 443–477.

Jöreskog, K.G. (1979). Statistical estimation of structural models in longitudinal-developmental investigations, in J.R. Nesselroade and P.B. Baltes (eds.), *Longitudinal Research in the Study of Behavior and Development.* New York: Academic Press.

Jöreskog, K.G. and Sörbom, D. (1976). Statistical models and methods for test-retest situations, in D.N.M. de Gruijter and L.J.Th. van der Kamp (eds.), *Advances in Psychological and Educational Measurement.* London: Wiley, pp. 135–157.

Jöreskog, K.G. and Sörbom, D. (1977). Statistical models and methods for analysis of longitudinal data, in D.J. Aigner and A.S. Goldberger (eds.), *Latent Variables in Socioeconomic Models.* Amsterdam: North-Holland, pp. 285–325.

Jöreskog, K.G. and Sörbom, D. (1984). *LISREL VI: Analysis of Linear Structural Relationships by the Method of Maximum Likelihood.* Chicago: Scientific Software, Inc.

Nesselroade, J.R. and Baltes, P.B. (1974). Adolescent personality development and historical change: 1970–1972. *Monographs of the Society for Research in Child Development* **39**. Chicago: The University of Chicago Press.

Rogosa, D. (1979). Causal models in longitudinal research, in J.R. Nesselroade and P.B. Baltes (eds.), *Longitudinal Research in the Study of Behavior and Development.* New York: Academic Press.

Schaie, K.W. (1965). A general model for the study of developmental problems. *Psychological Bulletin* **64**, 92–107.

Schaie, K.W. (1977). Quasi-experimental research designs in the psychology of aging, in J.E. Birren and K.W. Schaie (eds.), *Handbook of the Psychology of Aging.* New York: Van Nostrand-Reinhold, pp. 39–58.

Schaie, K.W. and Baltes, P.B. (1975). On sequential strategies in developmental research. *Human Development* **18**, 384–390.

Thurstone, L.L. and Thurnstone, T.G. (1962). *SRA Primary Mental Abilities.* Chicago: Science Research Associates.

11. STATISTICS AND THE SCIENTIFIC METHOD

David A. Freedman[†]

Regression models have not been so useful in the social sciences. In an attempt to see why, such models are contrasted with successful mathematical models in the natural sciences, including Kepler's three laws of motion for the planets.

1. INTRODUCTION

In the social sciences today, much effort is spent running regressions. As far as I can see, the return on this intellectual investment has been meager.[1] If so, this raises two very difficult questions: Why is it that regression models have had so little success? And why are they so popular? As a partial answer, it may help to look at some mathematical models that have succeeded. I have chosen a few, largely on the basis of familiarity. They are not regression models. They happen to belong to the natural sciences rather than the social sciences.

The comparison between typical regression models in the social

Department of Statistics, University of California, Berkeley. I would like to thank the following persons for their help with the essay—in one or two cases, rendered despite serious disagreement with some of the contents: Persi Diaconis, Morris Eaton, John Heilbron, David Hopelain, David Lane, Thomas Rothenberg, Richard Sutch, Amos Tversky. Research partially supported by NSF Grant MCS-80-02535.

[1] For some evidence to support this assertion, see Freedman (1981, 1983a) or Freedman, Rothenberg, and Sutch (1983). Also see Baumrind (1983), Brown and Koziol (1983), Christ (1975), Hendry (1980), Karlin (1979), Kiefer (1979), Leamer (1983), Ling (1983), Lucas (1975), Lucas and Sargent (1978), Zarnowitz (1979). For related discussions on handling experimental data, see Hausman and Wise (1982) or Zeisel (1982). For complementary discussions, see Sims (1980, 1982).

sciences and a select handful of the great natural science models may seem unfair or even irrelevant. Hence it requires some justification. The point is not to demonstrate the superiority of natural science: there are plenty of bad models in biology or physics, and much good work in economics or psychology. The idea is rather to examine some highly successful mathematical models for natural phenomena, in order to understand the sources of their strength. The history will be interesting in its own right, and may—or may not—shed some light on the present issue: Why have mathematical methods succeeded so well in the physical sciences, and not so well in the social sciences?

My view is that regression models are in vogue in the social sciences largely because of the success of other kinds of mathematical models in the natural sciences. However, these notions of "model" seem so different to me that covering both by the same term may be a source of real confusion. Saying clearly what the differences are is not so simple, but the following headings seem relevent: natural law, originality, depth, prediction, stochastics, measurement, and replication. In brief, my points will be as follows:

On Natural Law. The great models in the natural sciences result from a search for truth, namely the laws governing the phenomena under investigation. Such a model expresses in definite mathematical form the investigator's idea as to how the phenomenon really behaves. By comparison, social scientists who do regressions are usually fitting curves: they are modeling the data (see Neyman, 1977). It should come as no surprise when such curves lose their fit after a short time. An investigator who is not looking for the truth will not find it.

On Originality. The great models are brilliantly original; no two are alike. Each one was discovered through an act of intellectual creativity of high order. Regression models, by comparison, are right off the shelf.

On Depth. In the natural sciences, the great models reflect profound insight, and show real intellectual elegance. Typically the model succeeds in explaining some very diverse set of facts on the basis of a few simple axioms—including facts not available when the model was developed. However, much hard thinking is needed to get from the axioms defining the model to the conclusions about the world. With regression models, there is seldom much real difference between the inputs and the outputs.

On Prediction. Models in the natural sciences are expected to make sharp and nontrivial predictions about the future, predictions which can be verified by direct observation. Some models even give a large measure of control over the phenomena. Models which fail such tests eventually get scrapped. For a brilliant, if sometimes perverse account, see Kuhn (1970). In the social sciences, regression models are seldom exposed to this kind of risk. But models which are not subjected to rigorous empirical testing cannot be expected to have much empirical content. And the standard statistical tests are usually irrelevent, as will be argued below: the main reason is that the tests themselves make assumptions which are not tenable.

On Stochastics. There are great stochastic models in the natural sciences, and a lot of attention goes into testing their basic assumptions. After all, it is the assumptions which define the model. Regression models too make quite strict assumptions, explicitly or implicitly, about the stochastic nature of the world. In most social-science applications, these assumptions do not hold water. Neither do the resulting models.

On Measurement. The great models in the natural sciences involve variables which have been defined clearly and measured carefully. Such claims can be made for few regression models in the social sciences. Good models are hard to build on the basis of bad data.

On Replication. In the natural sciences, the crucial experiments to validate important models get replicated as a matter of course. In the social sciences, few regressions get replicated. This comes back to the point that few social science regression models are exposed to rigorous empirical testing.

I hope this paper will not be construed as making invidious comparisons between the social sciences and the natural sciences: there are plenty of bad models in the natural sciences. It is not an attack on the social sciences, or even on the use of quantitative methods in the social sciences. Indeed, statistics are clearly very useful in descriptive work; so are survey methods. My critique is much narrower: the focus is on regression models and variants like structural equation models. The criticisms seem to apply to many of the papers in the present volume; for specifics, see the Appendix or Freedman (1983b).

2. SOME MODELS IN THE
NATURAL SCIENCES

In 1609, Kepler published his laws of planetary motion: the first law, for
instance, is that planets move in elliptical orbits with the sun at one focus.
These laws constitute a "model" for the solar system.[2] I use
quotation marks because Kepler viewed his laws not as a model, but as a
description of how the planets actually moved in space. The story of
Kepler will be discussed in more detail in Section 7, to show his attitude
toward natural law, as well as the originality, depth and power of his
discovery.

Kepler gave a brilliantly simple description of a very complicated set of
planetary motions. Twenty years later, the "Rudolphine Tables" were
published; these used Kepler's laws to predict the positions of the planets
in the sky, and were an immediate practical success. The earlier
Ptolemaic and Copernican tables were often in error by up to 5 degrees in
predicting planetary positions; the Keplerian tables reduced the error by a
factor of 30, to below 10 minutes of arc.[3] Still, the mechanism behind
Kepler's laws was unknown. Half a century later, Newton provided the
mechanism, whose centerpiece was the law of gravity. Newton's theory
looks very different from the facts it explains. The law of gravity, for
example, is that any two bodies attract each other with a force
proportional to the product of their masses, divided by the square of the
distance between them. This does not seem to have much to do with an
ellipse. However, Newtonian mechanics implies Kepler's laws (including
the elliptical orbits) by a strict mathematical argument. To bring off this
argument, Newton was obliged to invent large parts of what is now called
"the calculus." In this example, the inputs to the model are very
different from the outputs, and a lot of hard thinking is needed to get

---

[2] The language of "laws" and "models" does not cohere so well. For present purposes, I
will construe a "law" as one of the axioms defining a model. However, such axioms are also
truths about the world—although not necessarily self-evident ones. This is an old-fashioned
view. Friedman (1953) argues that useful theory about the world can be developed from
axioms which are false as statements about the world. But this is only another proof of how
clever Milton Friedman really is. Other investigators would be well advised not to accept the
handicap imposed by false assumptions.

[3] See Gingerich (1971).

from the axioms to the conclusions.

The word "gravity" is so much a part of our vocabularies now that the idea may be difficult to appreciate. But in its time it was brilliantly original. In fact, it was almost unthinkable for many of Newton's contemporaries, and rather hard even for Newton himself, because it involved the idea of action at a distance.

Newtonian mechanics has come to dominate our view of the physical world, and has given us substantial mastery over the world. Guided by Newton's theory, investigators can discover new planets by the anomalies created in the orbits of the old ones[4]; and in this century, astronauts land on the moon. The great models have empirical consequences.

Of course, Newtonian mechanics is not the last word. Einstein discovered that Newton's laws were only a first approximation, applicable to relatively small masses moving at negligible fractions of the speed of light. But Newton's mysterious force of gravity turns out to be a consequence of the very geometry of space—and the tensor calculus.

This brief history may indicate some of the originality, diversity, and depth of the great mathematical models in physics, as well as their explanatory power. There are similar stories in biology. In 1865, Gregor Mendel proposed a statistical model to explain the mechanism of heredity.[5] Seed color in peas, to take a famous example, was postulated to depend on a pair of "entities," one from each parent. The transmission of these entities from one generation to the next obeyed carefully formulated probabilistic laws, which successfully explained a maze of empirical data. In this century, the physiological basis for the model has been thoroughly explored, and most of it can now be photographed under

---

[4] See Grosser (1962). The existence and position of the planet Neptune was deduced by Leverrier, from a study of anomalies in the motion of Uranus. Neptune was first observed (through a telescope) by Galle. Two quotes:

It is impossible to satisfy the observations of Uranus without introducing the action of a new Planet, thus far unknown...Here are the elements of the orbit which I assign to the body...

Leverrier to Galle, September 18, 1846

The Planet whose position you have pointed out *actually* exists...

Galle to Leverrier, September 25, 1846

[5] Some references are Judson (1979), Rosenberg (1979), Freedman, Purves, and Pisani (1978, Chapter 25). An interesting sidelight is that Mendel's theory was overlooked for nearly half a century, and then rediscovered independently by some ordinary, working scientists. The triumph is of method, as well as genius.

an electron microscope. A cell divides: and a chromosome is either on one side of the line or the other, with a 50-50 chance. There is even a successful model for the structure of the chromosome itself: the Watson-Crick double helix. Again, it is hard to over-estimate the degree of understanding and control that Mendelian genetics gives us. In the third world, for example, millions of people live on the "miracle rice" developed at the International Rice Research Institute, using Mendel's principles. The genetic model too captured the truth. It was strikingly original and very deep. Its conclusions are quite different from its assumptions. And it has great explanatory power.

3. REGRESSION MODELS IN THE SOCIAL SCIENCES

In social-science regression analysis, the approach is very different. Usually the idea is to fit a curve to the data, rather than figuring out the process which generated the data. As a matter of fact, investigators often talk about "modeling the data." This is almost perverse: surely the object is to model the phenomenon, and the data are interesting only because they contain information about that phenomenon. Whatever it is that most social-science investigators are doing when they construct regression models, discovering natural laws does not seem to be uppermost in their minds.

The next point to make is that most statistical models in the social sciences bear a strong resemblance to one another. Investigators have the normal curve and regression, the multinomial distribution and logits, time series and autoregression, used over and over again. Indeed, the choice of statistical model is usually governed not by logic of the situation but by the layout of the data files in the computer.

What about the use of social-science regression models to make predictions? In such models, there is very little difference between the inputs and the outputs. Investigators postulate a linear relationship between the dependent variable and some explanatory variables, which may even include thinly disguised versions of the dependent variable itself. They fit the model by least squares, and theorize retrospectively about the coefficients. (If the coefficients come out wrong, they respecify the equations.) Sometimes they use the model to do simulations—for a world which will be never observed. And that is where such modeling exercises usually seem to stop. This kind of work is unlikely to lead to any real advances in the understanding of social phenomena.

4. STOCHASTICS

Even off-the-shelf statistical models make quite strong assumptions about the processes generating the data, and are likely to produce nonsense if these assumptions fail. However, it is rare indeed to find an investigator who takes these assumptions seriously—or who backs off when confronted with the fact that the assumptions are clearly violated by the phenomenon under analysis. Specific examples will be discussed in the Appendix. In Mendelian genetics, by contrast, the stochastic assumptions are taken very seriously indeed. Maybe that is one reason why statistical models work so much better in genetics than in the social sciences.

5. MEASUREMENT

In the natural sciences much importance is attached to careful measurement work. The key variables get defined very cleanly. A lot of ingenuity, and years of patient work, go into determining the fundamental parameters of physical models: these parameters get connected to observable quantities. And the investigators often manage to design the experiments so that measurement error is held to a very low level indeed.

I will cite two important physical constants that seem almost impossible to measure. The first is the charge on the electron. How can you measure something that small? Millikan did it, using a drop of oil. Or what about the speed of light, which is practically infinite? Michelson is famous because he measured it. See Franklin (1980), Holton (1978), Livingston (1973), and Swenson (1972).

With social-science regression models, it is altogether different. Few investigators do careful measurement work. Instead, they factor-analyze questionnaires. If the scale is not reliable enough, they just add a few more items. Such techniques are not serious, by comparison with the sort of measurement work done in the natural sciences.[6]

6. REPLICATION

In the natural sciences, most of the crucial experiments and observations are replicated not just once but dozens and hundreds of times. The really classic ones even get incorporated into high school and college lab courses. Replication is another characteristic feature of the natural sciences.

In the social sciences, by comparison, few studies are done more than once. But replication is a relevent idea, even for investigators fitting regression models to observational data. After running the regressions, the investigators can collect some more data and see if the equations survive. Econometricians are almost forced into this, because year by year new data comes pouring in. And the half-life of a coefficient in an econometric model is measured in months, not years. I do not wish to be unkind, but the contrast is stark. Astronomers still use Kepler's model. He got it right.

7. SOME RESPONSES

There are three standard objections to my line of argument:

- Natural scientists can do controlled experiments; social scientists cannot.

- Social scientists deal with more complicated problems than

---

[6] For a well-known critical review of the accuracy of economic data, see Morgenstern (1963).

natural scientists.

■ Social science models should not be judged so harshly, because the investigators are only doing data analysis.

My reactions are as follows.

On Controlled Experiments.   Astronomy, for example, is mainly observational.   And learning theorists in psychology do a lot of experimentation on human subjects.   Controlled experiments are very useful, but not crucial.

On Complexity. Some problems in the natural sciences now look very clean and simple, but only because of the analytical work that has been done.   To appreciate this point, imagine trying to figure out the orbit of Mars for yourself. You go out on a clear night, look up into the sky, and see thousands of points of light. Which one is Mars? To begin closer to the beginning, which ones are the planets and which are the stars? Continuing to watch for several hours might only confuse matters further: for the pattern of the stars will gradually change as the night wears on. Even recognizing this change depends on prior knowledge; for it is hard to see the shifting pattern of the stars without using the constellations.

It took many thousands of years of patient study before astronomers were able to recognize the existence of the planets ("planet" derives from a greek word meaning "wanderer"), or stars which moved against the background created by the constellations of fixed stars. And even after astronomers recognized the fixed stars and the planets, they needed a theory to enable them to measure positions in the sky. Such a theory was developed by the Greeks, who imagined the stars as fixed to a heavenly sphere, with the earth at its center. This sphere revolved once a day. The sun moved along the sphere in a path called the *ecliptic*, completing one circuit every year.[7] And each planet moved along the heavenly sphere in its appointed orbit. This theory now seems quaint or even absurd. But in its time it was a brilliant advance, for it permitted astronomers to record the positions of the planets by separating their movement against the stars from the apparent daily rotation of the

---

[7] The *Signs of the Zodiac* are the constellations through which the sun moves, along the ecliptic. Today, the ecliptic is defined as the apparent path of the sun against the fixed stars.

heavens. So when Brahe and Kepler went to work, they could draw on centuries of skillful observation and theorizing. The main elements of the problem had been identified, and some techniques for making relevent measurements had been well developed.

One conclusion from this history: before scientists can make good measurements, they need to have a clear idea of what it is they are going to measure. In other words, good measurements often depend on good theory (e.g., see Koopmans, 1947). A second conclusion: insofar as the problem of the planetary motions now looks clean and simple, that is the result of many centuries of hard work. A final conclusion: the social sciences may well be at the pre-Keplerian stage of investigation—the equivalent of figuring out which are the planets and which are the fixed stars. If so, using sophisticated analytical techniques like regression is bound to add to the confusion. The problem is to define the basic variables, to figure out ways of measuring them, to perceive the main empirical regularities. Estimating coefficients by least squares before the basic variables have been understood is like using a scalpel to clear a path through the jungle.

On Data Analysis. "Data analysis" is one of the current slogans in statistics, but it is not a fair description of the kind of statistical work usually done in the social sciences. Data analysts emphasize close inspection of the numbers, displayed graphically. Conventional methods involve histograms, scatter diagrams, and residual plots. The more radical ones involve the stem-and-leaf, hinges, and hanging root-a-grams. But all data analysts draw pictures. In the social sciences, graphical analyses of the data are quite rare. Data analysts work very hard to develop models for their data, and run diagnostics to see if the models are sensible. They spend endless hours dealing with outliers, or changes in the relationships from one region to another, or non-linearities. In the social sciences, this kind of analysis too is quite rare. Data analysts seldom make conventional statistical tests, like t, χ^2, or F, because such tests are valid only under severely restrictive mathematical assumptions. There are few statistical papers in the social sciences without a battery of such tests.[8]

---

[8] The paper by Duncan in this volume is an example of what can be done by using simple, and appropriate, statistical techniques for looking at data.

The conclusion seems inescapable. In general, social scientists who run regressions are not doing data analysis. Instead, they are mechanically applying regression models in situations where the assumptions do not hold. The computer outputs—the parameter estimates, the standard errors, the *t*-tests—are usually devoid of scientific meaning. Rather than facing up to this issue, however, the investigators just label the outputs as "descriptive statistics." This is a swindle. If the assumptions of the regression model do not hold, the computer outputs do not describe anything: they are mere numerical artifacts.

8. THE STORY OF KEPLER[9]

One of the great mysteries of the ancient world was how to explain the motions of the planets, for their apparent paths in the sky were extremely complicated. The problem was made even more difficult by the doctrines of Aristotle and Plato, who held that the earth was stationary at the center of the universe, and furthermore that the planets went around the earth in perfect circles at constant speed—*the rule of absolute motion.* By ignoring some of these obstacles, the Greek astronomer Ptolemy (second century A.D.) perfected an astronomical system which explained the apparent paths of the planets reasonably well.

Ptolemy had to depart from Aristotelian physics in several ways. Perhaps most important was his use of the epicycle and equant. Take Mars as an example. Ptolemy postulated that this planet moved at constant speed in a circle called the *epicycle* (Figure 1). The center *C* of this epicycle moved in a larger circle (the *eccentric*) around the earth. However, Ptolemy placed the center of this larger circle in space off the earth, and he did not make *C* move at constant speed around this center. Instead, he introduced another point called the *equant.* In his scheme, the radius vector joining *C* to the equant swept out equal angles in equal

---

[9] I am grateful to John Heilbron, Professor of History, University of California at Berkeley, for his help with this section. Needless to say, I am responsible for all the faults which remain. Some references are: Butterfield (1949), Dreyer (1953), Koestler (1963), Koyre (1973), Kuhn (1969), Russell (1964), Wilson (1968, 1972).

amounts of time. As we know today, Ptolemy was forced into these complications because Mars goes around the sun, not the earth, and does not follow a circular orbit.

Figure 1. Ptolemy's Theory (for a detailed explanation, see the discussion in the text).

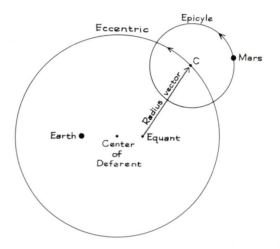

Using a half-dozen equants and two dozen epicycles, Ptolemaic astronomers were able to account fairly well for most of the observed planetary motions. However, there were always some discrepancies between the predictions and the observations. These discrepancies were especially noticeable for the motions in latitude, that is, north or south of the ecliptic. The observed changes in the distances between the planets and the earth, indicated by changes in their apparent brightness, also presented a serious problem for the theory. For these reasons, and perhaps because of the artificiality of their constructions, Ptolemaic astronomers tended to regard their system as a device for predicting the apparent positions of the planets, and not as a true description of paths in space.

In the Middle Ages, however, many astonomers took Ptolemy very literally indeed. They equipped the heavens with crystalline spheres revolving on spheres to carry the planets along the epicycles. There were endless arguments about how many spheres were needed, how they fitted together, whether motion could be transferred from one to another, and how many angels were needed to keep the spheres going. This state of affairs went on until the time of Copernicus (1473–1543).

As most high school texts explain, Copernicus rebelled against the Ptolemaic system, and taught that the earth went around the sun. However, it was not that simple. What Copernicus seems mainly to have rebelled against was Ptolemy's use of equants, regarding them as a violation of Aristotle's rule of absolute motion. As Copernicus himself put it, according to Koestler (1963, p. 145)

> Having become aware of these defects, I often considered whether there could perhaps be found a more reasonable arrangement of circles...in which everything would move uniformly about its proper center, as the rule of absolute motion requires.

After many years of labor, Copernicus found such a system. Part of it—the orbit of the earth—is illustrated in Figure 2. As this shows, Copernicus imagined the earth to move at constant speed in a perfect circle around the point C, completing one orbit each year. This imaginary point in turn moves at constant speed in a perfect circle around the point B, completing one orbit every 3434 years. Copernicus is not done yet, for B also moves at constant speed in a perfect circle around the sun, completing its orbit in about 53,000 years.

The other planets all move on similar nests of circles, ultimately centered on the imaginary point C, the moving center of the earth's orbit. Copernicus says with evident pleasure (Dreyer, 1953, p. 343)

> Thus Mercury runs in all on seven circles, Venus on five, the earth on three, and round it the moon on four, lastly Mars, Jupiter and Saturn on five each. Thus altogether thirty-four circles suffice to explain the whole construction of the world and the whole dance of the planets.

Koestler (1963, p. 572) has complained that when Copernicus got down to brass tacks, he actually needed forty-eight circles. Whether this is true or not, the verdict of Butterfield (1949, p. 30) seems right:

> When you go down, so to speak, for the third time, long after you have forgotten everything else in this lecture, there will still float before your eyes that hazy vision, that fantasia of circles and spheres which is the trademark of Copernicus.

The next figure in the story is Tycho Brahe (1546–1601). Brahe recognized that in order to solve the mystery of the planetary motions, thousands of very accurate observations of their positions would be needed, over a period of many years. He devoted his life to this task,

Figure 2. The Copernican Theory of the Orbit of the Earth.
This Figure is Adapted from Dreyer (1953, p. 332)

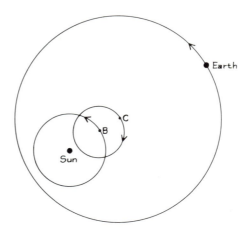

and his achievement marks the beginning of modern observational
astronomy.   This approach was strikingly different from that of
Copernicus, who so far as is known made only twenty-seven observations
on the planets.[10] Eventually, Brahe tried to use his observations to piece
together a theory of the solar system. He made all the planets except the
earth revolve around the sun—while the sun went around the earth.

Now I introduce Johannes Kepler (1571–1630). Kepler went to Prague
in 1600 to join Brahe, who had just moved there from Denmark. Kepler
spent many years trying to fit Brahe's data on Mars by means of circular
orbits. But even with the best such orbit, the theoretical position of Mars
on a certain date proved to be eight minutes of arc away from the
position observed by Brahe. Now eight minutes of arc is a very small
angle. It is the apparent size of a penny held at a distance of ten yards
from the observer. As in Figure 3, a penny held ten yards from the eye

---

[10] And, in fact, many of the Copernican epicycles were needed to get the theory to
conform to certain observations made by the Arab astronomers—observations which have
since been shown to be wrong. It is hard to build a good model on the basis of bad data.

covers both the actual position, and the theoretical position of Mars computed from the circular orbit. However, Kepler knew that Brahe was very unlikely to have made a measurement error that large. (Brahe's observations of the planetary positions were accurate to within four minutes of arc or so.) So this small difference forced Kepler to break with the tradition of circular orbits, and in time led him to discover the true shape of the planery orbits. As Kepler said (Dreyer, 1953, p. 385):

> To us Divine goodness has given a most diligent observer in Tycho Brahe, and it is therefore right that we should with a grateful mind make use of this gift to find the true celestial motions.

Figure 3. Eight Minutes of Arc is the Apparent Size of a Penny Held Ten Yards from the Eye. The Figure is Not Drawn to Scale, and the Angle Shown is About 100 Minutes of Arc

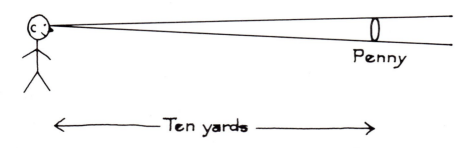

What Kepler found was that the planets really move in elliptical orbits. As Figure 4 shows, an ellipse can be drawn by tying a loop of string around two nails, tucking a pencil into the loop, and tracing a curve with the string held taut. Each nail is a focus of the ellipse. The *major axis* goes through the foci of the ellipse; the minor axis passes half-way between the foci, being perpendicular to the major axis and somewhat shorter (Figure 4). The ellipse was discovered by mathematicians in ancient Greece, while they were investigating cones; before Kepler, there was absolutely nothing to connect this curve to the paths of the planets in the sky.

Figure 4. The Ellipse. The Points S and F Are the
Foci of an Ellipse; as P Moves Around the Ellipse,
the Sum of the Distances PS + PF Remains Constant

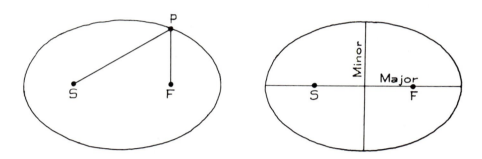

Kepler's first two laws can be stated as follows:

- Each planet (including the earth) moves around the sun in an elliptical orbit, with the sun at one focus.

- A planet moves in its orbit at varying speeds, in such a way that if it is joined to the sun by an imaginary line, this line will sweep out equal areas in equal times (Figure 5).[11]

A theory assuming circular orbit for Mars causes only a small discrepancy between predictions and observations, because the elliptical orbit of Mars is in fact nearly circular: the ratio of the minor axis to the major is 199 to 200, compared to a ratio of one for a perfect circle.[12]

Kepler's attitude belongs to the great age of science. He was looking for the true path of Mars in space, rather than a device for computing apparent positions. Indeed, he seems to have been the first astronomer to define the problem that way. He was willing to spend years on the search and in the end go against centuries-old physical doctrine, because

---

[11] The first law governs the shape of the orbit; the second, the rate of motion along the orbit. The third law is that the square of the period of rotation is proportional to the cube of the average distance from the sun.

[12] Using an eccentric circle, with speed regulated by an equant, makes the circular motion even closer to the elliptical one—down to the eight minutes of arc.

Figure 5. Kepler's First Two Laws. Mars Moves in an Elliptical Orbit with the Sun at One Focus. The Shaded Area Is Swept Out by the Radius Vector as the Planet Moves from P_2 to P_1. Equal Areas Are Swept Out in Equal Times.

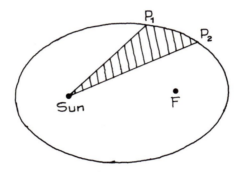

he was certain that the true shape of the path would be accessible to the human mind. And his theory had to explain all of Brahe's observations on Mars. Not some of them, or most of them, all of them. He was guided by faith that some natural law would be found to govern the shape of the orbit, if he could only see what that shape was.

I sometimes have a nightmare about Kepler. Suppose a few of us were transported back in time to the year 1600, and were invited by the Emperor Rudolph II to set up an Imperial Department of Statistics in the court at Prague. Despairing of those circular orbits, Kepler enrolls in our department. We teach him the general linear model, least squares, dummy variables, everything. He goes back to work, fits the best circular orbit for Mars by least squares, puts in a dummy variable for the exceptional observation—and publishes. And that's the end, right there in Prague at the beginning of the 17th century.

APPENDIX:
DISCUSSION OF THE JÖRESKOG-SÖRBOM PAPER

My major criticism of this paper has to do with the underlying model, which the authors do not spell out in anything like enough detail. Once stated clearly, the main assumptions may seem quite implausible. If so the analysis is without adequate foundation. Let me now state the assumptions explicitly, following the Jöreskog-Sörbom notation as closely as possible. We have children indexed by c, each child belonging to some cohort g; tests i are administered at times t. Thus, y_{cit}^g denotes the score obtained by child c in cohort g on test i at time t. There are four cohorts, three tests, and three times.

The model is summarized in two equations:

$$y_{cit}^g = \nu_{it}^g + \lambda_{it}^g \eta_{ct}^g + \epsilon_{cit}^g, \tag{1}$$

$$\eta_{ct}^g = \alpha_t^g + \beta_t^g \eta_{ct-1}^g + \delta_{ct}^g. \tag{2}$$

Here, η_{ct}^g is a latent variable, intended to represent child c's "intelligence" at time t. The coefficients ν_{it}^g and λ_{it}^g in (1) relate the scale of the latent variable η to the scale of the observable test scores y. The coefficients are assumed constant across children within cohorts. For the bulk of the paper, they are assumed constant across times and cohorts as well. Equation (2) states that η evolves in an autoregressive way. Again, the coefficients are assumed constant across children.

To finish specifying the model, it is necessary to spell out the assumptions governing the "errors" ϵ and δ in (1) and (2). I believe that the assumptions needed to justify the statistical manipulations are the following:

1. Children are independent, and within cohorts identically distributed, i.e., the vectors

$$\{y_{cit}^g, \eta_{ct}^g, \epsilon_{cit}^g, \delta_{ct}^g : i, t = 1, 2, 3\}$$

   are independent across c's, with a multivariate distribution dependent only on g.

2. The ϵ's are independent of the δ's.

3. The ϵ's are independent across tests; however, dependence is allowed within child and test across times: so ϵ_{cis}^g and ϵ_{cit}^g

have non-zero covariance which depends on g, i, s and t, but not on c.

4. The δ's are independent across time; the variance of δ_{ct}^g is allowed to depend on g and t, but not c.

5. All variables are jointly Gaussian—that is, multivariate normal.

6. The ϵ's and δ's all have mean 0.

These assumptions are not subject to direct empirical verification, mainly because η is unobservable. However, they are inherently implausible. To begin at the beginning, why should a child's intelligence be representable as a single number? Many specialists in factor-analytic theories of intelligence would reject this idea, leaving η without much appeal as a construct. And whatever η may be, why would it obey equation (2), especially with all the other assumptions on the errors?

The major assumption in the paper is perhaps (1), that children are independent, and identically distributed within cohorts. Without independence, the statistical computations reported by Jöreskog and Sörbom have little meaning. Of course, their computer package LISREL will do the arithmetic in any case. If the independence assumption is wrong, however, the estimates may be biased—or meaningless.

Jöreskog and Sörbom do not discuss the sample design. With, e.g., a conventional cluster sample, some of the children in the study must have known each other, played together, gone to school together, or even come from the same family. Under such circumstances, independence is most unlikely. Ignoring these inter-child correlations biases the estimates. Building them into the model makes it under-identified.[*]

Next, consider the hypothesis in (1) that within cohorts, children are identically distributed. Casual empiricism and psychological doctrine alike suggest that different children evolve in different ways—so the coefficients in (1) and (2) as well as the covariances of the errors may really depend on the child in question. Again, if the model is modified to allow this kind of person-to-person variation, it becomes under-identified. But without this modification, the parameters may lose their meaning.

For the sake of argument, let us set all this aside for a moment, and

---

[*] Jöreskog and Sörbom concede, in a footnote, that the independence "may be questionable."

look at assumption (3), that the "measurement errors" ϵ in test scores are uncorrelated across tests. This assertion too is quite implausible. Suppose, for instance, that a child is depressed one year: this could easily lower all the test scores—producing correlated ϵ's. Other sources of correlation are easy to imagine. Building inter-test correlations into the model makes it under-identified: leaving them out biases the estimates.

Finally, consider assumption (5), that the variables are jointly Gaussian. Like (1), this is a strong assumption, and it is not stated explicitly in the paper. But in the absence of this assumption, the log-likelihood χ^2-tests in the paper have no scientific foundation.

These log-likelihood tests are the principal mode of statistical analysis used by Jöreskog and Sörbom, so they are worth considering in some detail. To begin with, such tests cannot give any absolute, overall check on the fit of the model to the data. The reason is that log-likelihood tests are always nested, with some general hypothesis H_{gen} and a more specific hypothesis H_{spec}. The log-likelihood test takes H_{gen} for granted, and asks whether the data are relatively more or less likely under H_{spec}. To spell out the mechanics a bit, let $L_{\theta}(x)$ be the likelihood of the (multivariate) data x if the vector of parameters is θ. The test statistic is

$$T = 2 \log \sup_{\theta \in H_{gen}} L_{\theta}(x) - 2 \log \sup_{\theta \in H_{spec}} L_{\theta}(x).$$

And this is a measure of relative likelihood. It is a well accepted part of the statistical folklore that asymptotically, on the null hypothesis, T follows the chi-squared distribution. This can be proved rigorously when

- the likelihood function is smooth;
- H_{gen} and H_{spec} are open subsets of Euclidean spaces;
- the parameter vector corresponding to the null hypothesis is an interior point of H_{spec}.

See Cox and Hinkley (1974, pp. 331 and 355); or Kendall and Stuart (1961, Vol. II, p. 231).

Jöreskog and Sörbom do not cite any specific theorems whose assumptions are satisfied in their application. Even if T is asymptotically chi-squared on the basis of some unspecified theorem, there still are some formidable technical problems. Each data point (the test scores for one child) is nine-dimensional: three tests by three times. So there are nine means, nine variances, and $1/2 \cdot 8 \cdot 9 = 36$ covariances to estimate for each cohort, from about 200 children per cohort. This only works out to four data points per parameter. The asymptotic theory, with sample sizes going to infinity, may not offer any very reliable guide to the sampling distribution of T in the present application. Finally, the joint distribution of scores can hardly be exactly jointly Gaussian. Minor departures from normality may have a major impact on the distribution of T.

Now let me waive all such technical objections to the log-likelihood tests. The substantive interpretation in the Jöreskog-Sörbom paper still presents real difficulties. For instance, consider testing the hypothesis H_{spec} that the "factor loadings" ν_{it}^g and λ_{it}^g in (1) are constant across cohorts g and occasions t. According to Jöreskog and Sörbom:

> The test gives $\chi^2 = 198.6$ with 104 degrees of freedom. Although the outcome is significant at conventional levels of significance the residuals are generally small and in view of the earlier remark about the sensitivity of χ^2 the fit must be regarded as a reasonably good one. We shall therefore consider the measurement model to be invariant over occasions as well as over cohorts.

In fact, the p-value of this test is 10^{-7}: i.e., if H_{spec} were right, and the asymptotic theory were valid, we would have only one chance in ten million of getting a χ^2-value as big as or bigger than the one reported by Jöreskog and Sörbom. The only reasonable conclusion is that H_{spec} is wrong: the factor loadings depend on cohort and occasion.

Social scientists often argue that with large sample sizes, the χ^2-test is bound to reject; so χ^2-points per degree of freedom is used as a measure of goodness of fit. I am somewhat sympathetic to this argument, when the model has any prior claim on our sympathy. However, the Jöreskog-Sörbom model is not simple, elegant and useful. It does not have any theoretical justification. The only possible defense is empirical: it fits the facts. However as the χ^2-test shows, H_{spec} does *not* fit the facts—even if we take H_{gen} for granted.

I now wish to sum up the statistical part of the discussion. The model used by Jöreskog and Sörbom is very incompletely specified in their paper. When completely specified, its major assumptions turn out to be untestable and in important ways implausible. If these assumptions are wrong, the parameter estimates and associated standard errors may be severely biased—and perhaps meaningless. Even if the assumptions are right, presently available statistical theory does not justify the paper's principal mode of analysis: log-likelihood χ^2-tests. Clearly, Jöreskog and

Sörbom have gone off on their own. A final summary point: waiving all technical questions about these χ^2-tests, they flatly contradict the specific hypothesis of the "measurement model," namely, constant factor loadings: the p-value is about 10^{-7}. Thus, the entire analytic apparatus used by Jöreskog and Sörbom is faulty, from top to bottom.

Having summarized the statistical discussion, I want to make a nonstatistical comment. Nothing seems to ride on the statistical analysis, because all the inferences are about unobservables: the parameters governing the postulated stochastic distribution of the unobservable variable η. The paper does not say anything about any quantity that could be observed. Not only is the technical foundation of the analysis somewhat shaky, but its scientific value remains questionable—until the unobservables are tied into a theory which is open to empirical testing.

REFERENCES

Baumrind, D. (1983). Specious causal attribution in the social sciences: The reformulated stepping-stone theory of heroin use as exemplar. *J. of Personality and Social Psychology*, to appear.

Brown, C.C. and Koziol, J.A. (1983). Statistical aspects of the estimation of human risk from suspected environmental carcinogens. *SIAM Review* **25**, 151–181.

Butterfield, H. (1949). *The Origins of Modern Science*. London.

Christ, C. (1975). Judging the performance of econometric models of the United States economy. *International Economic Review* **16**, 54–74.

Cox, D. and Hinkley, D. (1974). *Theoretical Statistics*. London: Chapman and Hall.

Dreyer, J.L.E. (1953). *A History of Astronomy From Thales to Kepler*. New York: Dover.

Franklin, A. (1980). *Historical Studies in Physical Science* **11**, Part 11.

Freedman, D., Purves, R., and Pisani, R. (1978). *Statistics*. New York: Norton.

Freedman, D. (1981). Some pitfalls in large econometric models: A case study. *Journal of Business* **54**, 479–500.

Freedman, D. (1983a). Structural-equation models: A case study. Technical Report No. 22, Department of Statistics, University of

California, Berkeley.

Freedman, D. (1983b).   Comments on a paper by Markus.   Technical Report, Department of Statistics, University of California, Berkeley.

Freedman, D., Rothenberg, T., and Sutch, R. (1983).   On energy policy models. *Journal of Business and Economic Statistics* **1**, 24–36.

Friedman, M. (1953).   *Essays in Positive Economics.* Chicago: University of Chicago Press.

Gingerich, O. (1971).   *Sky and Telescope* **42**, 328–333.

Grosser, H. (1962).   *The Discovery of Neptune.*   Cambridge, Mass.: Harvard University Press.

Hausman, J. and Wise, D. (1982).   Technical Problems in social experimentation: Cost versus ease of analysis, N.B.E.R. Working Paper No. 1061.

Hendry, D. (1979). Econometrics—alchemy or science? *Economica* **47**, 387–406.

Holton, G. (1978).   Subelectrons, presuppositions, and the Millikan-Ehrenhaft dispute, in R. McCormmach et al. (eds.), *Historical Studies in the Physical Sciences* **9**. Baltimore: Johns Hopkins University Press.

Judson, H.F. (1979).   *The Eighth Day of Creation.* New York: Simon and Schuster.

Karlin, S. (1979).   Comments on statistical methodology in medical genetics, in *Genetic Analysis of Common Diseases: Application to Predictive Factors in Coronary Disease.*   New York: Alan R. Liss, pp. 497–520.

Kendall, M.G. and Stuart, J.R. (1961).   *The Advanced Theory of Statistics.* London: Griffin.

Kiefer, J. (1979).   Comments on taxonomy, independence, and mathematical models (with reference to a methodology of Machol and Singer). *Mycologia* **LXXI**, 343–378.

Koestler, A. (1963).   *The Sleepwalkers.* New York: Grosset and Dunlap.

Koopmans, T.C. (1947).   Measurement without theory. *Review of Economics and Statistics* **29**, 161–172.

Koyré, A. (1973).   *The Astronomical Revolution.*   Ithaca, N.Y.:   Cornell University Press.

Kuhn, T.S. (1969).   *The Copernican Revolution.* New York: Random House.

Kuhn, T.S. (1970).   *The Structure of Scientific Revolutions.*   Chicago: University of Chicago Press.

Leamer, E. (1983).   Taking the con out of econometrics. *American*

Economic Review, 31–43.

Ling, R.F. (1983). Review of *Correlation and Causation* by Kenny. *J. Am. Statist. Assoc.* **77**, 489–491.

Livingston, D. (1973). *Master of Light.* New York: Scribners.

Lucas, R.E. (1975). Macro-economic policy-making: A critique. *J. of Monetary Economics.*

Lucas, R.E. and Sargent, T.J. (1978). After Keynesian macro-economics, in *After the Phillips Curve: Persistence of High Inflation and High Employment.* Conference Series No. 19. Boston: Federal Reserve Bank of Boston, pp. 49–72.

Morgenstern, O. (1963). *On the Accuracy of Economic Observations*, 2nd ed. Princeton, NJ: Princeton University Press.

Neyman, J. (1977). Frequentist probability and frequentist statistics. *Synthese* **36**, 97–131.

Rosenberg, E. (1979). *Cell and Molecular Biology.* New York: Holt, Rinehart and Winston.

Russell, J.L. (1964). Kepler's laws of planetary motion, 1609–1666. *British Journal of the History of Science* **2**, 1–24.

Sims, C.A. (1980). Macro-economics and reality. *Econometrica* **48**, 1–48.

Sims, C.A. (1982). Scientific standards in econometrics modelling. Paper presented at the *Symposium on the Developments in Econometrics and Related Fields.* Netherlands Econometric Institute.

Swenson, L. (1972). *The Ethereal Aether.* Austin: University of Texas Press.

Wilson, C. (1968). Kepler's derivation of the elliptical path. *Isis* **59**, 5–25.

Wilson, C. (1972). How did Kepler discover his first two laws? *Scientific America.*

Zarnowitz, V. (1979). An analysis of annual and multiperiod quarterly forecasts of aggregate income, output, and the price level. *Journal of Business* **52**, 1–34.

Zeisel, H. (1982). Disagreement over the evaluation of a controlled experiment. *American Journal of Sociology* **88**, 378–389.

12. REPLY TO FREEDMAN

Karl G. Jöreskog

Dag Sörbom[†]

In our paper we proposed a general methodology for analyzing longitudinal data from several cohorts. This methodology is general and flexible and can accommodate many different models for this kind of data. The main purpose of the proposed methodology is to find a model which takes the intrinsic structure of the data collection design into account (i.e., the fact that repeated measurement on the same individuals are used and that comparable cohorts are used) and at the same time fits a given set of data reasonably well.

We illustrated the general methodology using a small data set. We pointed out that this was merely an illustration. Freedman criticizes our analysis of these data and rejects essentially all assumptions on which this analysis was based. We admit (as we did in a footnote to our paper) that the assumptions (3) and (7) of independently and identically distributed observations and of multivariate normality, probably do not hold for these data. This will affect the interpretation of χ^2 (more on this later) but will not necessarily severely bias the parameter estimates.

Other assumptions considered by Freedman may bias parameter estimates but most such assumptions are in fact testable within the framework of our methodology, quite the contrary to what Freedman states.

Freedman remarks "Why should a child's intelligence be representable as a single number?" Of course, we don't believe that intelligence in a general context is a single latent trait. And, of course, our general methodology is not restricted to a single latent variable but allows for several latent variables at each occasion. We point out "In this paper we assume that a single latent variable is measured at each occasion. The

---

[†] Both authors are affiliated with the Department of Statistics, University of Uppsala, Uppsala, Sweden.

limitation to a single variable is only for the purpose of keeping the exposition clear and the model within a reasonable level of complexity." In our illustration we use three PMA tests as indicators of latent ability η. With only three observed variables, the unidimensionality of η cannot be contradicted since the model is just identified.

Freedman goes on to criticize the assumption that the ϵ are uncorrelated across tests. He says that this assertion is quite implausible. It seems that Freedman misses the main idea of latent variable modelling. The latent variables are supposed to account for the intercorrelations among the observed variables, in the sense that, when the latent variables are partialed out from the observed variables, there are no more intercorrelations left (see, e.g., Jöreskog, 1979). Hence, by definition, the ϵ are uncorrelated among themselves and also uncorrelated with the latent variables. This definition also takes care of the dimensionality problem for the latent variables. If one latent variable is not sufficient to account for the intercorrelations, two or more latent variables must be added so that indeed the ϵ become uncorrelated. In our paper we assume that the ϵ are uncorrelated across tests within occasions but because of memory and other retest effects we do not assume that the ϵ are uncorrelated across occasions. In our illustration, the assumption that the ϵ are uncorrelated within occasions is justified, as we have already argued, since we are using only three observed variables to measure one latent variable.

The main point of Freedman's critique is our use of χ^2 for assessing the fit of the model. When testing the hypothesis that the measurement model is the same for all cohorts we say "the test gives $\chi^2 = 198.6$ with 104 degrees of freedom. Although the outcome is significant at conventional levels of significance, the residuals are generally small and, in view of the earlier remark about the sensitivity of χ^2, the fit must be regarded as a reasonably good one." Our point is that one should not regard χ^2 strictly as a χ^2-variate with a given degrees of freedom. As we have written elsewhere (see Jöreskog and Sörbom, 1981, pp. I. 38–40):

> "Although the χ^2-measure may be derived theoretically as a likelihood ratio test statistic for testing the hypothesis that Σ is of the form implied by the model against the alternative that Σ is unconstrained, it should be emphasized that such a use of χ^2 is not valid in most cases for several reasons. Firstly, in most empirical work the model is only tentative and is only regarded as an approximation to reality. From this point of view the statistical problem is not one of testing a given hypothesis (which a

priori may be considered false) but rather one of fitting the model to the data and to decide whether the fit is adequate or not. Instead of regarding χ^2 as a test statistic one should regard it as a goodness (or badness) of fit measure in the sense that large χ^2-values correspond to bad fit and small χ^2-values to good fit. The degrees of freedom serves as a standard by which to judge whether χ^2 is large or small. The χ^2-measure is sensitive to sample size and very sensitive to departures from multivariate normality of the observed variables. Large sample sizes and departures from normality tend to increase χ^2 over and above what can be expected due to specification error in the model. One reasonable way to use χ^2-measures in comparative model fitting is to use χ^2-differences in the following way. If a value of χ^2 is obtained, which is large compared to the number of degrees of freedom, the fit may be examined and assessed by an inspection of the covariance residuals, the normalized residuals and the modification indices (see below). Often these quantities will suggest ways to relax the model somewhat by introducing more parameters. The new model usually yields a smaller χ^2. A large drop in χ^2, compared to the difference in degrees of freedom, indicates that the changes made in the model represent a real improvement. On the other hand, a drop in χ^2 close to the difference in number of degrees of freedom indicates that the improvement in fit is obtained by "capitalizing on chance," and the added parameters may not have real significance and meaning."

The fact that χ^2 cannot be used to test hypotheses in a rigorous statistical sense, does not invalidate the use of χ^2 as goodness-of-fit measure. This measure has proven to be very useful for discriminating between models that fit a given set of data very badly and those that fit much better. We should also like to point out that the fit of the model can be assessed by many other means. The χ^2-measure is only one measure of overall fit. A more detailed assessment of fit can be obtained by inspection of residuals, normalized residuals and modification indices (see Jöreskog and Sörbom, 1981). Ultimately the decision to accept or reject a given model is up to the subjective judgement of the investigator who knows the data best and who has all the information from the analysis.

As for our illustrative example, we still contend that the model we arrived at in our paper is a reasonably simple and parsimonious description of the complex data. It is possible, of course, to improve the fit of the model but only at the expense of adding many more parameters. For example, one can allow the measurement model to be different for different cohorts. However, the differences between cohorts turn out to be fairly small in general. Even if such differences were statistically significant (assuming that this could be rigorously tested) they don't seem to be practically important.

REFERENCES

Jöreskog, K.G. (1979). Basic ideas of factor and component analysis, in K.G. Jöreskog and D. Sörbom, *Advances in Factor Analysis and Structural Equation Models*. Cambridge, Mass.: Abt Books, pp. 5–20.

Jöreskog, K.G. and Sörbom, D. (1981). *LISREL-Analysis of Linear Structural Relationships by the Method of Maximum Likelihood*. Chicago: International Educational Services.

13. COMMENTS ON AND REACTIONS TO FREEDMAN, STATISTICS AND THE SCIENTIFIC METHOD*

Stephen E. Fienberg[†]

1. INTRODUCTION

Mindless applications of regression models to poorly measured data in the social sciences are what Freedman deplores. I yield to nobody in my opposition to mindlessness—in the natural sciences as in the social sciences—and I am steadfastly in favor of good measurement of theoretical relevant constructs. But frequently the lines between mindlessness and wise exploration, between measurement guided by lame-brained theories and that inspired by a truly visionary world view are unclear, distinguishable only through the myopia-correcting lenses of hindsight. Freedman uses such hindsight to discern and describe some examples of mathematical models in the natural sciences that have succeeded admirably, and he contrasts them to "typical regression models in the social sciences." He suggests the comparison may be unfair and even cruel: In this suggestion he is correct; The comparison is certainly unfair. While social science comes off second-best by design, surely the tables would be turned were we to take shoddy examples of physical science and compare them with the best of theory-guided social science research, whether or not it uses regression analysis. But in addition the comparison is somewhat misleading, in that in some cases the description of the natural scientist at work is taken sufficiently out of context as to

* Research partially supported by National Science Foundation Grant SES80-08573 to the University of Minnesota. Several friends and colleagues provided comments and materials on which this paper is based. Special thanks go to Clark Glymour, Judith Tanur, and Luke Tierney.

† Departments of Statistics and Social Sciences, Carnegie-Mellon University.

give a biased picture of the conduct of good natural science and of great natural scientists.

It is not my purpose here to defend the role of statistical modelling and analysis in the social science, for despite Freedman's attack the best of this work will stand the test of time. Rather, I wish to point out that the natural and social sciences have much more in common than Freedman would lead us to believe. Moreover, I will suggest that the very examples Freedman singles out as great science contain many of the flaws that he attributes primarily to the social sciences. Finally, I will touch briefly on the problems of statistical analyses without stochastics, a matter of relevance to science in general, and to certain examples in this volume, in particular.

2. ON THE ORIGINS OF STATISTICS

The history of statistics and the development of statistical methods is a long and varied one, although the formal structure that we now take for granted was developed only in the past century. Thus Kepler and Newton could not avail themselves of regression and other statistical models, and we can only speculate on whether these models and methods would have helped or hindered the scientists of the 17th century. Modern statistics grew out of two separate but related traditions: (1) mathematical and philosophical research on probability theory and the foundations of statistical inference, (2) empirical research on social and biological measurements. Much of the statistical work in the social sciences, of which Freedman is so critical, has its roots in both of these statistical traditions. Indeed, the interwining of these roots goes back to such distinguished mathematicians as Poisson and LaPlace, both of whom used observation data (and modelling of those data) to estimate the probability that jurors err in arriving at a verdict of guilty.

One of the founders of modern day social statistics was Adolphe Quetelet (1797–1874). Originally trained in mathematics, astronomy, and physics, he turned his energies in the 1820's to the establishment of an observatory in Brussels. This led him to visit Paris where Poisson, LaPlace, and Fourier introduced him to probability and statistical methods. They also introduced him to the idea of using observational data to model social phenomena. On his return to Brussels, Quetelet embarked on essentially a new career organizing the collection of statistical data and using the data to develop principles of social theory. His training in mathematics and probability helped him to structure these efforts. It may be of special interest to the readers of this volume that in his early memoir on crime, Quetelet used what we now know of as the life cycle perspective. Thus his work provides one of the earliest versions of the type of modelling which is under discussion at this conference. It was also Quetelet who suggested that social phenomena in general are extremely regular, and that these regularities can be discovered empirically through the applications of statistical techniques (for further details see Landau and Lazarsfeld, 1978).

3. ON MEASUREMENT AND REPLICATION IN THE NATURAL SCIENCES

Freedman singles out several examples of models in the natural sciences that he urges us to examine with great care:

> The great models in the natural sciences involve variables which have been defined very clearly and measured very carefully... . Good models are hard to build on the basis of bad data. ... In the natural sciences, the crucial experiments to validate important models get replicated as a matter of course.

As does Freedman, we save Kepler's work for a separate section, and turn here to a brief discussion of the work of Mendel and Millikan.

In 1865, Gregor Mendel reported on the results of his experiments on the hybridization of garden peas to illustrate the probabilistic model now known as the theory of Mendelian inheritance. Although most biologists accept Mendel's model as being essentially correct, and although the description of Mendel's experiments suggest the appropriateness of a multinomial sampling model for the counts of offspring, a careful examination of Mendel's data suggests that something is amiss. The chi-square tests of fit for the model in all cases are too small, i.e., the variability in the reported experimental data is consistently smaller than that which we expect for genuine data (e.g., see the discussion in Bishop,

Fienberg, and Holland, 1975, pp. 327–328). Sir R.A. Fisher (1936), who was one of the first to spot this problem with the quality of Mendel's measurements, notes:

> One natural cause of bias of this kind is the tendency to give the theory the benefit of doubt when objects such as seeds, which may be deformed or discolored by a variety of cause, are being classified....Although no explanation can be expected to be satisfactory, it remains a possibility among others that Mendel was deceived by some assistant who knew too well what was expected. This possibility is supported by independent evidence that the data of most, if not all; of the experiments have been falsified so as to agree closely with Mendel's expectations.

It seems that Mendel got the statistical model of genetics correct (at least for the simplest systems of hereditary theory), but we should be careful in looking to him for a model of careful measurement to be emulated.

Perhaps physics presents the examples for us to follow. Freedman cites the example of Millikan who measured the charge on the electron in his now famous oil drop experiment. The very article that Freedman suggests we read to learn about how Millikan did it, by Holton (1978), provides evidence contrary to Freedman's thesis. In Holton (1978), we learn that Millikan's 1910 *Science* paper on the oil drop experiment gives a final mean value of e based on 27 observations, even though 40 observations were available. Not surprisingly it was the 13 most extreme values that were dropped, and thus Millikan's reported probable error is a substantial underestimate of what he actually observed. If we are to believe that Millikan got the answer, then we are indeed fortunate that he did not share in Freedman's nightmare regarding the dropping of outliers!

The actual details of Millikan's selective use of data on the oil drop experiments are even clearer from Holton's report on notebooks from the 1911–1912 experiments. Marginal notes such as the following appear throughout the notebooks:

> Error high will not use.
> Beauty. Publish this surely, beautiful!
> Very low. Something wrong.
> Will not work out.
> Agreement poor.
> Perhaps publish.
> $e = 4.98$ which means that this could not be an oil drop.

In all, Millikan published the data on only 58 drops out of about 140 documented in the notebooks. Selective reporting of data is, of course, a standard practice in physics and chemistry, and one which makes sense if we are aware of artifacts that mess up delicate instrumentation and if we have a theory into which to place the measurements. But what if Millikan did not know the correct answer? Then where would we have been led by his selection of data? The physics literature contains many examples of those who got it wrong, and accurately so!

Actually Millikan didn't quite get it correct anyway. Indeed, his calculations were based on the charge of any object being an integer multiple of e—a matter now brought into dispute by those who claim to have found evidence to support the existence of free quarks. It is a tribute to Millikan's experimental work that a modified version of his oil drop experiment is being used today in the hunt for quarks.

One other example from the astronomy and physics literature illustrates further the problems of measurement and selective reporting of data. On the basis of his general theory of relativity, Einstein predicted in 1916 that starlight is bent by the gravitational field of the sun. His theory predicted a deflection of 1.74", compared with the value of 0.87" predicted by Newtonian theory. To confirm this prediction, Arthur Stanley Eddington, with the support of the Astronomer Royal, Sir Frank Watson Dyson, organized a pair of expeditions in March 1919 to make appropriate measurements during the eclipse of the sun. One expedition went to Sobral, Brazil and the other led by Eddington to the Island of Principe, off the coast of West Africa. At Sobral two sets of measurements were taken and at Principe one.

Earman and Glymour (1980) report the following values for these three sets for the deflection at the limb of the sun (the measurements are in second of arc):

Data Set	Mean Deflection	S.D.
1 Principe astrographic	1.61"	0.444"
2 Sobral astrographic	0.86"	0.48"
3 Sobral 4-inch	1.98"	0.178"

The Sobral astrographic measurement is almost identical to the Newtonian value of 0.87", while the Sobral 4-inch provides support for the Einstein value of 1.74″. Eddington's Principe measurements yielded a value close to the Einstein prediction, but only about 1.7 standard deviations away from the Newtonian value. What should a good scientist conclude from such data?

Dyson's and Eddington's conclusions were unequivocal. In reports before an extraordinary joint meeting of the Astronomical and Royal Societies on November 6, 1919, they announced that Einstein's prediction had been confirmed, and cited only the Sobral 4-inch and Principe results for support. In this and subsequent reports on the expeditions Eddington never mentioned the Sobral astrographic results at all. For further details, see Earman and Glymour (1980).

What lessons can we learn from these stories about Mendel, Millikan, and Eddington? Surely it is not that the discoveries for which they are now famous are the result of the collection of data with very low measurement error—for each in his own way appears to have reported data selectively, making the measurement error appear substantially lower than what the full data suggest. That each one ultimately proved to be correct (or at least almost so) suggests that we should admire them for their ingenuity. But in judging science how are we to distinguish those who are correct from those who aren't? How are we to decide between Millikan and Ehrenhaft, between Eddington and those whose earlier measurements supported Newtonian theory, unless we know the truth already? The landscape of natural science history is littered with far more examples of "good measurement" in support of what we now take to be preposterous theories, than it is decorated with success stories such as those associated with names such as Mendel, Millikan, and Eddington.

4. ON KEPLER

Freedman's story of Kepler makes for fascinating reading, and is by and large correct—Kepler did indeed find that the planets move in elliptical orbits. The question we need to ask is: "By what means was Kepler led to go from circular to elliptical orbits?" Kepler clearly argues, as Freedman suggests, that the discrepancy of 8′ of arc was sufficient to discard the circular orbit theory. His first departure from the circle, however, was not to the ellipse, but to the ovoid which coincides with the circle at the apsides, as deplicted here in Figure 1 (Hanson, 1969).

Figure 1.

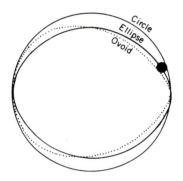

Fortunately for Kepler and for us, the ovoid in Figure 1 did not have a tractable geometric form, and so Kepler was led to approximate it by an ellipse[1]:

> The general geometric properties of the perfect ellipse are manifested in the actual ovoid curve, from which it is but insensibly different...

Careful measurement didn't help here; Brahe's data didn't allow Kepler to distinguish between the fit of the ovoid and the fit of the ellipse. Thus it was only indirectly that Kepler arrived at the idea of using an elliptical orbit with the sun at one of the foci. If the ovoid had been more tractible geometrically, Kepler might not have got it right!

Once he was led to consider the ellipse, how did Kepler actually fit it to the data? Why, with a crude form of statistical analysis not unlike a least-squares algorithm (Sheynin, 1973). To check on the fit of various models he corrected his data by small arbitrary quantities, within the "bounds" of the known accuracy of the observations:

> One could be suspicious of the liberty with which I have made small changes to the given quantities, and might believe that with this liberty to change things we don't like about the observations one could, in the end, arrive at the entire eccentricity of Tycho. Well, one should try

---

[1] This passage is quoted from a translation by Hanson (1969, p. 79.)

this, and when one compares these changes with ours, one should judge which of the two are within the range of observational error. Yes, one should be very careful that one doesn't, raised by the success of a single such step, find oneself all the more embarrassed when, after additional steps, one finds the apogee of the sun in the most out-of-the-way locations.[2]

To pursue the matter further, let us consider an argument presented by Glymour (1983). Suppose that Kepler, true to Freedman's nightmare, had learned about linear models and had done his regressions obtaining the best circular orbit for each planet.

> ...His other laws remain the same, one might suppose, save perhaps that he publishes confidence intervals. Would it have made any difference for the subsequent history of physics? Probably not. Elliptical orbits are a consequence of Newtonian celestial mechanics, and Newton himself made much of the fact that he was able to derive from his law of gravitation the conclusion that the planets move in elliptical orbits. Yet in *arguing* for the law of gravitation, Newton assumed that the planetary orbits are *circular*, which he fully knew to be false. Kepler's circular orbits would have done no harm at all.
>
> Glymour (1983)

As a footnote to the story of Kepler we should also note that he contributed at least one other theory regarding astronomy, besides the laws discussed by Freedman. In his *Mysterium Cosmographicum*, Kepler explained the existence of *just* six planets and their mutual disposition. He did so by inserting the five regular solids (cube, tetrahedron, dodecahedron, icosahedron, and octahedron) between the planet spheres, and then analyzing the resulting discrepancies as given in Table 1 (as reproduced in Sheynin, 1973). Sheynin (1973) reconstructs Kepler's argument as follows:

> Kepler explicity noticed that four (out of five) discrepancies are positive and one negative, and he divided all of them into three groups according to their absolute values. Thus, two of them are small, another two are large and one is intermediate. All this is sound, but now Kepler introduces duality: the cube and the octahedron are dual, and therefore the corresponding discrepancies are positive (and small); dual, also are the dodecahedron and the icosahedron, and also positive (and large) are the corresponding discrepancies; lastly, the tetrahedron is dual to itself, and the corresponding discrepancy is the only negative one (and intermediate).

---

[2] This passage is a translation of a quote from Kepler given by Sheynin (1973, 1975) in German.

If this is to be viewed as great science, then we might well have benefited from Kepler's enrolling in the Imperial Department of Statistics in the court of Prague, as he does in Freedman's nightmare.

Table 1. Discrepancies between calculations and observations
(from Kepler as given by Sheynin, 1973)

1. Saturn-Jupiter	(cube)	2
2. Jupiter-Mars	(tetrahedron)	−16
3. Mars-Earth	(dodecahedron)	36
4. Earth-Venus	(icosahedron)	43
5. Venus-Mercury	(octahedron)	4

5. ON STATISTICAL ANALYSIS WITHOUT FORMAL STOCHASTICS

In his comments Freedman attacks the use of statistical models in the social sciences in part because of the stochastic assuptions, which he argues are rarely taken seriously. Such an attack, while quite accurate in many respects, deserves to be launched on the natural and medical sciences as well. Yet in both the natural and the social sciences there are examples of good statistical analysis where appropriate attention is given to the stochastics and their correctness. We must not lose sight of this fact.

Many of the data sets analyzed here at this conference, and throughout the social science literature, consist of population data. Thus, the usual justifications of stochastic components used to model the related underlying phenomena, namely urn models or sampling procedures, are absent. Using maximum likelihood estimation based on a ficticious model and conventional test statistics as data analytic devices in such settings seems to me to be just as useful as hinges, froots, and flogs with median polish. The key here is recognizing that the "parameter estimates" are simply the result of a form of curve fitting, and that p-values associated with test statistics have no direct probability interpretation. Relating such quantities to the assumed but non-existent stochastics often provides a convenient frame of reference. Indeed, residual analyses in such a situation can often be used to provide empirical support for stochastic assumptions about the discrepancies between observations and model predictions.

There are two other devices that can be used in support of statistical analysis without formal stochastics, especially in population settings:

(1) superpopulation descriptions,
(2) randomization arguments.

Both types of devices involve viewing results related to the population and model in question as coming from some type of sampling or urn-like model, quite possibly hypothetical. The more complex the model the harder it is mathematically and/or statistically to show how such devices justify the use of standard statistical methods. Fortunately, mathematical statisticians have recently turned their attention to such problems (e.g., see Freedman and Lane, 1983, and Levin and Robbins, 1981).

Finally, as a Bayesian statistician I feel quite comfortable making careful subjective assessments about error terms in models and assigning my own probability distributions to quantities. Urn models, whether actual or hypothetical, are simply not necessary for stochastic components in models. I know that Freedman does not share this Bayesian perspective.

6. SOCIAL SCIENCE THEORY AND MEASUREMENT

Freedman argues that good measurements are critical to good science, and to make good measurement you need good theory. He adds that in this respect the social sciences may well be at the pre-Keplerian stage of investigation. I take issue with such a suggestion. As Prewitt (1980) points out, many persons miss "the fact that the great discoveries of social science quickly become conventional wisdom," much as Freedman reminds us that the now taken-for-granted concept of gravity was startling in its own time. Similarly, Prewitt adds:

> ...The workings of the unconscious were not so obvious before Freud made them so. The unanticipated costs of market economies predated the economic concept of "externalities," but labeling the obvious with this concept has substantially increased our understanding of resource depletion and environmental damage. No doubt there were some who intuitively sensed the social power of reference groups before the work of Herbert Hyman and Samuel A. Stouffer, but it was scientific documentation of the obvious that created this useful concept.
>
> If social science discovers the obvious, and thereby renders it accessible, it also disproves the obvious. It evaluates the truth of conventional wisdom, often finding that accepted assumptions are wrong. In a now-famous 1949 review of The American Soldier, Paul F. Lazarsfeld presented a long list of "obvious facts" about the military in World War II. He pointed out that better educated soldiers were more likely to have psychological problems than less educated ones, that soldiers from rural areas had fewer complaints about the hardships of army life, and that soldiers stationed in Europe were more likely to want to return to the States during the fighting than after the Germans surrendered. He then pointed out that in the case of each of these "facts," exactly the opposite was found by Stouffer and his associates to be true...
>
> The social sciences seldom get credit for their counterintuitive findings, as legion as they are, because people quickly rearrange their belief systems, claiming that they "knew it all along." Even this obvious fact was not so obvious before psychology began to develop theories of dissonance reduction.

A recent report on behavioral and social science research (Adams et al., 1982) not only reinforces this perspective but also documents the important roles that statistical planning and analysis play in major advances in various areas.

Moreover, good social scientists are as concerned with quality measurements as are good natural and physical scientists. Currently, much effort is expended in improving questionnaires and in reducing nonsampling errors in social surveys, and in improving the measurement of program effects in social experiments. Tanur (1982) documents many recent advances in these areas. This paper has been reproduced with several others in Part II of Adams et al., 1982. See also Fienberg, Singer, and Tanur (1985) for a more detailed discussion of large-scale social experiments.

Freedman may well be correct that the running of large numbers of regressions is unlikely to lead to the next great step foward in the social sciences, but I believe that looking back to the great discoveries of the natural sciences may be of even less help. As Converse (1982) suggests:

> ...there are to me manifest differences in the textures of different subject matters, and it seemed to me that the raw materials of social science—any of them—are much more complex in their structure than the things Newton had to work with...I wasn't even certain that there might ever be a culmination in social science like the Newton one, at least in pure form, or that we would wither on the vine without it...Waiting for Newton [is] like waiting for Godot.

What is needed in the social sciences, and I believe Freedman and I agree on this, is careful measurements of social phenomena, measurements guided by evolving theory and analyzed by means of mathematical and statistical models thoughtfully constructed. Such efforts are currently under way on several research frontiers, and some of these are reported in this volume.

REFERENCES

Adams, R.M., Smelser, N.J., and Treiman, D. (eds.) (1982). *Behavior and Social Science Research: A National Resource*, Parts I and II, Washington, D.C.: National Academy Press.

Bishop, Y.M.M., Fienberg, S.E., and Holland, P.W. (1975). *Discrete Multivariate Analysis: Theory and Practice*. Cambridge, Mass: M.I.T. Press.

Converse, P.E. (1982). Response to lecture by Professor Cronbach, in W.H. Kruskal (ed.), *The Social Sciences, Their Nature and Uses*. Chicago: University of Chicago Press, pp. 83–94.

Earman, J. and Glymour, C. (1980). Relativity and eclipses: The British eclipse expeditions of 1919 and their predecessors, in G. Heilbron *et al.* (eds.), *Historical Studies on the Physical Sciences* **11**. Berkeley, Calif.: University of California Press, pp. 49–85.

Fienberg, S.E., Singer, B., and Tanur, J.M. (1985). Large scale social experimentation in the U.S.A., in A.C. Atkinson and S.E. Fienberg (eds.), *A Celebration of Statistics: The ISI Centenary Volume*. New York: Springer-Verlag (forthcoming).

Fisher, R.A. (1936). Has Mendel's work been rediscovered? *Annals of Science* **1**, 115–137.

Freedman, D.A. (1985). Statistics and the scientific method. (This volume).

Freedman, D.A. and Lane, D. (1983). Significance testing in a non-stochastic setting, in P. Bickel, K. Doksum, J.L. Hodges Jr. (eds.), *A Festschrift for Erich L. Lehmann.* Beimont, Calif.: Wadsworth, pp. 184–208.

Glymour, C. (1983). Social sciences and social physics. *Behavioral Science* **28**, 126–134.

Hanson, N.R. (1969). *Patterns of Discovery.* Cambridge: Cambridge University Press.

Holton, G. (1978). Subelectrons, presuppositions, and the Millikan-Erenhaft dispute, in R. McCormmach *et al.* (eds.), *Historical Studies in the Physical Sciences* **9**. Baltimore, MD: Johns Hopkins University Press, pp. 25–83.

Landau, D. and Lazarsfeld, P.F. (1978). Quetelet, Adolphe, in Wm. Kruskal and J.M. Tanur (eds.), *International Encyclopedia of Statistics* **2**. New York: Macmillan and the Free Press, pp. 824–834.

Levin, B. and Robbins, H. (1981). Urn models for regression analysis, with applications to employment discrimination studies. Unpublished manuscript.

Prewitt, K. (1980). Annual Report of the President 1979–1980: The council and the usefulness of the social sciences. *Annual Report 1979–1980.* New York, NY: Social Science Research Council, xiii–xxvii.

Sheynin, O.B. (1973). Mathematical treatment of astronomical observations (a historical essay). *Arch. Hist. Exact. Sci.* **11**, 97–126.

Sheynin, O.B. (1977). J. Kepler as a statistician. *Bulletin of the Int. Stat. Inst.* (Proceedings of the 40th Session), 341–354.

Sheynin, O.B. (1978). Kepler, Johannes, in Wm. Kruskal and J.M. Tanur (eds.), *International Encyclopedia of Statistics* **1**. New York: Macmillan and the Free Press, pp. 487–488.

Tanur, J.M. (1982). Advances in methods for large scale surveys and experiments, in *Five Year Outlook on Science and Technology.* Washington, DC: National Science Foundation, pp. 589–619.

14. A REJOINDER TO FIENBERG'S COMMENTS

David A. Freedman[†]

1. THE NATURAL-SCIENCE EXAMPLES

In our various ways, Fienberg and I are both addressing the relevance of standard statistical models to social science research. I found it convenient to make part of my argument in terms of a comparison between the use of models in the natural sciences and in the social sciences. Fienberg seems to disagree more with my history lesson than with its conclusions, but that may be a matter of rhetoric—on both sides.

His counter-argument on the history comes down to this: natural scientists too have feet of clay. Mendel censored his data; my hero Kepler indulged in metaphysical speculations: and the list could easily be extended.[1] On the other hand, despite their sins, natural scientists have discovered very powerful mathematical models, which make sharp predictions about the future, and unify many apparently disparate phenomena, including facts unknown when the model is formulated.[2]

[†] Department of Statistics, University of California, Berkeley. The rules of engagement require me to refer to my good friend and generous opponent Steve by his surname. They also prevent me from responding to the comments by Jöreskog and Sörbom.

[1] Note, however, that Kepler's contemporaries found it easy to distinguish his three laws from the metaphysics. There are significant differences between the modeling traditions in the natural sciences and in the social sciences: see my essay.

[2] Even regression models may be used. Indeed, such models were introduced by Gauss (1809), to find Ceres. Astronomers first discovered this asteroid through the telescope, but lost it when it got too close to the sun. Finding Ceres again became one of the major scientific problems of the day. To solve it, Gauss derived the equations connecting the observational data to the parameters of the orbit, using Newtonian mechanics. He then linearized the equations and estimated the parameters by "the method of least squares." Finally, he used the parameters to predict the current position of Ceres: a prediction born out by astronomical observation. Regression models in the social sciences are the same—without Newtonian mechanics or Ceres.

For example, whatever his failings, Mendel did uncover the chance basis of heredity. Two aspects of Mendelian theory are worth noting. First, at the macroscopic level, the model deals with definite, measurable characteristics: the seeds of a pea-plant are either yellow or green, and it is possible to count them (without censoring the data). A relevant comparison is to defining or measuring such social-science constructs as "intelligence," "anxiety," or "partnership." Second, and perhaps even more important, at the microscopic level current theory offers a physical source for the assumed randomness: when a cell splits, the chromosome strands wind up in one fragment or the other.

By contrast, few if any social-science regression models have an explicit source for their disturbance terms. As a result, the assumptions made about these terms, as well as the equations themselves, are usually quite *ad hoc*. Typically, the equations are not derived from theory; nor are they tested against the data in any meaningful way, because the models are not required to make a track record of successful predictions.[3]

2. THE SOCIAL-SCIENCE EXAMPLES

Fienberg makes a generalized reference to *Behavioral and Social Science Research: A National Resource* by Adams *et al.* (1982). This work is a 700 page review of about 2,000 publications; the citations include such items as a paper by Aigner on optimal experimental design, a paper by Goldstein and Brown on lipoproteins, and Hofstadter's book *Godel, Escher, Bach*. It is not clear what Fienberg has in mind. Indeed, I found little discussion bearing on the present issues; and what there was tended to the Panglossian. The following seems a fair example. As background, in my opinion, econometric models have been relatively unsuccessful as forecasting devices, especially when used mechanically, i.e., without massive subjective adjustments to the equations: see Christ (1975), Freedman-Rothenberg-Sutch (1983) or Zarnowitz (1979). Here is what Adams *et al.* (1982, Vol. I, p. 71) has to say on the matter:

---

[3] Fitting equations to a data set is different from using those equations to predict something outside that data set. The latter is the more relevant concept.

Economies like that of the United States are highly complex and relatively volatile, fluctuating as a result of the interaction of specific events and policy manipulations. Given this, it used to be extremely difficult to predict short-run changes in the economy with accuracy. While it still is not possible to predict such changes with complete accuracy, the development of computer data bases and of large-scale models of the U.S. economy (and now of other economies as well) has substantially improved prediction, so much so that economic forecasting has become a substantial industry both in the United States and abroad, with a commercial market exceeding $100 million in the United States.

In short, since regression models sell, they must be legitimate: like chiropractic, krebiozen, or est.

Fienberg makes a much more specific reference to Prewitt (1980), citing, e.g., Freud's theory of the unconscious. Well, I agree. Freud is an ideal social-science investigator. He collected lots of interesting data by novel methods, and formulated some brilliant theories to explain his findings. Also, he never ran any regressions.

Fienberg repeatedly asserts that statistical models have been used to considerable effect in the social sciences, but little detail is given. The names of Quetelet, LaPlace, and Poisson are dropped. There is quite specific reference to modeling the jury decision-process: presumably, Poisson (1837). Now this model is both quantitative and stochastic, and it has inspired a large literature. But the work of Poisson and his followers has almost no empirical content, because it ignores all the social and institutional aspects of jury trials: the key assumption is that jurors act independently of one another. In this respect, Poisson exemplifies what I object to in quantitative social science. Freud is a better role model.

3. STATISTICAL MODELS IN THE SOCIAL SCIENCES

I think it is fair to say that Fienberg agrees with me on one major point: Most statistical work in the social sciences cannot be justified in any conventional way, because the underlying stochastic models have not been validated. Fienberg believes, however, that the statistical calculations are useful even without the stochastic models. As he says:

> Using maximum likelihood estimation based on a fictitious model and conventional test statistics as data analytic devices in such settings seems to me just as useful as hinges, froots, and flogs with median polish.

This is a critical issue, on which he and I disagree. For reasons given above, I question the data-analytic value of fitting large, complex, fictitious models to data. To review briefly: with one fictitious likelihood function you will get one set of fictitious parameters; with another fictitious likelihood function, you will get quite a different set; and therefore both sets seem meaningless to me. What is needed is a stochastic model for the data. Fienberg replies as follows:

> The key here is recognizing that the "parameter estimates" are simply the result of a form of curve-fitting, and that p-values associated with test statistics have no direct probability interpretation. Relating such quantities to the assumed but non-existent stochastics often provides a convenient frame of reference. Indeed, residual analysis in such a situation can often be used to provide empirical support for stochastic assumptions about discrepancies between observations and model predictions.

This passage is the centerpiece of Fienberg's argument, but there are many questions to ask. Do the p-values with "no direct probability interpretation" have some indirect interpretation? If so, what is it?[4] How can "assumed but non-existent stochastics" provide "a convenient frame of reference"? Convenient for what? With "non-existent stochastics," how can residual analysis "provide empirical support for stochastic assumptions?" Where are all these analyses anyway? They are conspicuously absent from the present volume.

My view is almost diametrically opposed to Fienberg's: I see investigators fitting big models as a substitute for doing data analysis. Indeed, looking at complicated, high-dimensional data sets is hard work, and statisticians are only beginning to be helpful. But some useful techniques are available: projection pursuit, kinematic displays, tree-structured regression. References are given below.

I also think the data-analytic issue is secondary. Investigators, and who can blame them, use the statistical results not just to describe the data, but to make inferences about the phenomena they are studying. For example, Markus (1983, reprinted in this volume) asserts:

---

[4] The scope of Freedman and Lane (1983), cited by Fienberg, is rather narrow: it does not cover logistic models, for example.

> One implication of [the statistical calculations] is that any difference between the mean partisan strength of a cohort entering adulthood and that of the remainder of the electorate will tend to persist for some time.

To make this sort of reasoning stick, investigators need some theory to connect behavior with equations.   In conventional terms, that sort of theory is a stochastic model.   Social-science investigators like Markus almost never have properly validated stochastic models, and that is why their inferences usually seem shaky to me (see Freedman, 1983).   I see no viable substitutes for stochastic models in the realm of data analysis.

To restate my view: If the assumptions of a statistical method do not hold water, neither do its conclusions.   Therefore, statistical methods should not be used without looking hard at their assumptions.   I have told some success stories in the natural sciences, and some failure stories in the social sciences; see Freedman (1981) and Freedman-Rothenberg-Sutch (1983).   What Fienberg has to do to make his case is to show some examples where the fictitious models really help.   His prose is wonderful, but I think the examples are irrelevent.

Where does that leave the argument?   The following seems to be a fair summary of the position:

1. Fienberg and I agree that there is not likely to be much payoff for social scientists in running large regression models, at least over the near term.   One reason is that the requisite underlying stochastic assumptions usually cannot be validated.   To make regression models viable, better theory is needed, and better data.

2. He believes that fictitious models are useful data-analytic devices, and I disagree.   He does not cite specific examples where such models have been useful.   I have given examples where reputable social-science investigators have made faulty inferences with statistical models, by ignoring the stochastic assumptions.   I have also discussed examples of successful models in the natural sciences, both stochastic and nonstochastic: "successful models" is not a vacuous concept.

3. We both like history of science.

REFERENCES

Adams, R. McC., Smelser, N.J., and Treiman, D.J. (eds.) (1982). *Behavioral and Social Science Research: A National Resource*, **I**, **II**.

Washington, D.C.: National Academy Press.

Breiman, L., Friedman, J., Olshen, R., and Stone, C. (1983). *Tree Structured Methods in Classification and Regression.* Belmont, Calif.: Wadsworth.

Donoho, D., Huber, P., and Thoma, M. (1981). The use of kinematic displays to represent high dimensional data, in W. Eddy (ed.), *Computer Science and Statistics, Proceedings of the 13th Annual Symposium on the Interface.* New York: Springer-Verlag, pp. 274–278.

Fisher, R.A. (1918). On the correlation between relatives on the assumption of Mendelian inheritance. *Trans. Roy. Soc. Edin.* **52**, 399–433.

Fisherkeller, M.A., Friedman, J.H., and Tukey, J.W.T. (1974). *PRIM-9* an interactive multidimensional data display system. Stanford Linear Accelerator Publication No. 1408.

Freedman, D.A. (1981). Some pitfalls in large econometric models: A case study. *Journal of Business* **54**, 479–500.

Freedman, D.A. (1983). Comments on a paper by Markus. Technical Report, Department of Statistics, University of California, Berkeley.

Freedman, D.A. and Lane, D. (1983). Significance testing in a nonstochastic setting, in P. Bickel, K. Doksum, J.L. Hodges, Jr. (eds.), *A Festschrift for Erich L. Lehmann.* Beimont, Calif.: Wadsworth, pp. 184–208.

Freedman, D.A., Rothenberg, T., and Sutch, R. (1983). On energy policy models. *Journal of Business and Economic Statistics* **1**, 24–36.

Friedman, J. and Tukey, J.W.T. (1974). A projection pursuit algorithm for exploratory data analysis. *IEEE Transactions and Computers* **9**, 881–890.

Gauss, C.F. (1809). *Theoria Motus Corporum Coelestium.* English translation published by Dover, New York, 1963: *Theory of Motion of the Heavenly Bodies Moving Around the Sun in Conic Sections.*

Huber, P. (1981). Projection pursuit. Technical Report PJH-4, Department of Statistics, Harvard University, Cambridge, Mass.

Markus, G. (1983). Dynamic modelling of cohort change: The case of political partisanship. *American Journal of Political Science* **27**, 717–739. Reprinted in this volume.

Poisson, S.D. (1837). *Recherches sur la probabilite des jugements en matiere criminelle et en matiere civile.* Paris: Bachelier.

Prewitt, K. (1980). Annual Report of the President 1979–1980: The council and the usefulness of the social sciences. *Annual Report 1979–1980.* New York: Social Science Research Council.

AUTHOR INDEX

SUBJECT INDEX